In Quest and Crisis:
Emperor Joseph I and the Habsburg Monarchy

In Quest and Crisis:

Emperor Joseph I and the Habsburg Monarchy

by Charles W. Ingrao

Purdue University Press
West Lafayette, Indiana
1979

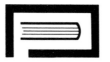

Library of Congress Catalog Card Number 77–88358
International Standard Book Number 0–911198–53–9
Printed in the United States of America

To my parents
Michael Anthony Ingrao
Lillian Frances Ingrao

Contents

Acknowledgments

It is truly a pleasure to acknowledge some of the many debts that I have incurred in the preparation of this book. A number of individuals facilitated my research, especially Dr. Anton Porhansl and the staff of the Austro-American Fulbright Commission, Dr. Anna Hedwig Benna at the *Haus- Hof- und Staatsarchiv,* Professor Abbott Gleason at the Harvard University Libraries, Prince Leopold von Salm-Salm and Dr. Adrian Vliegenhardt at the *Fürstlich Salm-Salm'sches Archiv,* the International Research and Exchanges Board and Dr. Oszkár Sashegyi at the *Magyar Országos Levéltár,* Prince and Princess Reuss at the *Sinzendorf Familien-archiv,* Professor José Amor y Vázquez at the *Archivo Histórico Nacional,* and Count Nostitz at the *Allgemeines Verwaltungsarchiv.* In addition, the assistance I received from Piroska Molnár Haywood in researching the Magyar language sources proved as thorough as it was indispensable to the preparation of the chapter on Joseph and Hungary.

I received much valuable advice from my dissertation advisor, Norman Rich; Burr Litchfield; and the late William Church of Brown University; John Hattendorf of the U.S. Naval War College; Ragnhild Hatton of the London School of Economics; and Anna Benna, all of whom read the entire manuscript, as well as from several of my colleagues at Purdue. Our departmental secretarial staff labored many hours in typing the final draft. Moreover, in preparing this volume, both Verna Emery, my editor, and Don Carter, graphic designer for the Purdue University Press, spared no effort in responding to my requests.

For years, my wife Kathleen sustained me with her patience, understanding, encouragement, and courageousness. Finally, as I look back I would be remiss in omitting the names of David Morgan and Willard Wallace, of Wesleyan University, whose contribution goes back the furthest and for whom this book represents the final paper in a twelve-year tutorial.

Note on Form

Editorial limitations have led me to delete all but the most essential background details, except where their retelling promises to shed light on issues of greater significance. In dealing with place and personal names, I have tried to use those forms which might be most readily recognized by the reader. Hence, except where accepted usage has dictated otherwise, I have translated into English the first names of all figures of princely rank and have used those place names that were employed most often during the period, inserting the modern spelling in parentheses, when different. As a guide I have followed the form used in Shepherd's *Historical Atlas*. To those who are offended by use of the German designation for many Hungarian towns, I submit that the modern names used in the succession states are generally beyond the recognition of the reader, while the Hungarian form is as obsolete today as the German. In addition, it might be pointed out that, during the eighteenth century, the population of all these towns was indisputably German. Unless stated otherwise the words *imperial* and *empire* refer explicitly to the Holy Roman Empire, *Erblande* to the Bohemian and Austrian crownlands, and *monarchy* to the Austrian Habsburg monarchy.

To enable the reader to weigh more easily the significance of various amounts of money, I have converted most sums into (Rhenish) florins. At the start of Joseph's reign the ratio between currencies was roughly 6 florins: 4 taler: 1 pound sterling: 1 dubloon: 1 pistola: 12 livres. After the great financial crisis of 1706 the British pound rose perhaps a third in value against the florin.

Finally, I have attempted to be exact in drawing up each of the accompanying maps and take full responsibility for any mistakes I have committed here or elsewhere in the text.

xi

I

Introduction

Not since the reign of Charles V has our state experienced such
a crisis.
—*Charles Theodore Otto Prince Salm*

The rise of the Austrian Habsburg monarchy to the first rank among European states represents a paradox to the early modern historian. In its wars against France and Turkey in the period 1683–1718 it won a string of victories unprecedented in Austrian history. By 1720 it was already the largest state in both population and area in central or western Europe. Yet, throughout this period, because of profound financial, and hence military, insufficiencies, it clearly did not rank with France in its ability to sustain an independent foreign policy. This became apparent during succeeding decades when it experienced a number of embarrassing and, at times, nearly calamitous defeats. After examining the path of the Habsburg monarchy's internal development and foreign policy during the last quarter of the seventeenth and first half of the eighteenth century, one is tempted to conclude that its fundamental strength and reason for success lay in its very weakness as a military power. While not posing a threat to the balance of power or even to its own neighbors, the Habsburg monarchy was between 1681 and 1720 the principal beneficiary of a series of coalitions aimed against France and Turkey. With the ultimate defeat of these two powers, however, it ceased to benefit from the dynamics of balance of power war and diplomacy and entered upon a period of diplomatic insecurity and isolation.

The brief reign of Emperor Joseph I marks the turning point in the monarchy's fortunes. Heretofore, historians have treated Joseph's reign as nothing more than a chapter in the complex chronology of the War of the Spanish Succession. Although the seven years between the battle of Blenheim and the emperor's death are unquestionably among the most dramatic and decisive in Austrian history, his reign has nonetheless been denied an autonomy or significance of its own. There

1

has been no biography of Joseph since 1798, when the last of five sterile chronologies was published. Although the great German and Austrian scholars of the nineteenth and twentieth centuries have paused briefly to reflect on his character, they have left us with little more than shallow and colorless vignettes. In fact, both his personality and his politics deserve more than casual treatment. Joseph's achievements had a long-range effect on the monarchy's future conduct of foreign and domestic policy. It was he who presided over the conquest of Italy in 1706–1707 and whose subsequent policies laid the foundations for 150 years of Austrian hegemony in the peninsula. Similarly, the position which he assumed—and stubbornly adhered to—in dealing with the great Rákóczi rebellion played the major role in recovering all of Hungary for the dynasty. Although he died barely two weeks before the final suppression of the revolt, the compromise that he had devised for the Magyar nation was destined to stand as a landmark in the evolution of Austro-Hungarian relations until the end of the monarchy.

Although the brevity of his reign and the financial considerations of the war effort cut short the emperor's program of administrative reforms within his hereditary Austrian and Bohemian lands, his policies nonetheless presaged further, more successful attempts at mid-century. Only in Germany, where the ever-fading loyalties of the armed estates continued to frustrate the pursuit of a dynamic imperial policy, was Joseph obliged to adopt policies initiated by his predecessors. Yet, here too he found considerable room to expand his father's practice of using those remaining imperial prerogatives to serve Austrian interests both within and beyond Germany's frontiers.

These were considerable accomplishments for any reign, let alone one of only six years' duration. In fact, there can be little question that the principal aims of Habsburg policy in Italy and Hungary had been accomplished by the time of Joseph's death. As a result, by 1709 Vienna's alliance diplomacy no longer dealt solely with Austrian interests but was beginning to focus instead upon purely dynastic concerns in Spain and the Low Countries. By then, however, the alliance system from which the monarchy had derived so many advantages and upon which it was forced to rely was beginning to fall apart.

Notwithstanding the significance of this period, very little has been written on it in the English language. For example, to read about Joseph's struggle with Clement XI—the last war fought between the emperors and Rome—one can turn only to the translation of von Pastor's *History of the Popes.* For Hungary's great Rákóczi rebellion, there is only Baron Hengelmüller's sixty-year-old study, and while this is a work of masterful clarity and perception, it covers only the first three years of the revolt. Although there are some excellent English-language monographs dealing with Charles XII's celebrated invasion of Germany and with the ill-fated peace talks at The Hague and

Gertruydenberg, all view these events almost exclusively from the side of Joseph's antagonists, leaving the reader uninformed about the role played by the government in Vienna. For these reasons, this study will at times depart from the narrower subject of Joseph I and dwell on some of the great issues and events of the reign.

On the other hand, this book does not pretend to provide an intimate portrait of the emperor's life and character. Indeed, it is no accident that historians have heretofore neglected Joseph as the subject of a full-length biography. Certain gaps within the documents render it exceedingly difficult to define Joseph's personality and identify his own contribution to the making of policy. Barely a few pages of Joseph's private correspondence have survived. There remain instead only the official instructions to his foreign representatives, in which the real motives behind his foreign policy often lie hidden under elaborate legal rationalizations and in which the emperor's own ideas are invariably hopelessly intertwined with those of his ministers. Moreover, in the reports of foreign diplomats and of Joseph's own ministers, the conventional use of the "imperial we" in describing council decisions often makes it impossible to separate the emperor's initiatives from those of his advisors. Even in the official protocols of the all-important Privy Conference, the historian is hampered by missing records— particularly in the first three years of the reign and in the deliberation of German and Hungarian affairs—as well as by the illegible scrawl of the Privy Conference secretary, Johann Georg von Buol. Despite these handicaps it is possible to paint a portrait of Joseph I, albeit one in which the sharpest contours and most vivid hues are carefully shaded to correspond to our imperfect perception of the man. The image that emerges is not altogether flattering. Over the past century the great Austrian and German historians Arneth, Noorden, and most recently, Braubach have all pointed out that Joseph was not only the energetic and decisive ruler of popular conception but an individual who suffered from considerable personal weaknesses as well. Any evaluation of the emperor must, however, determine to what extent character strengths and flaws actually affected the formulation and execution of policy.

Such an approach is helpful not only in analyzing Joseph's foreign and Hungarian policies, where his contribution was greatest, but also in evaluating his attempts at fiscal and administrative reform in his hereditary Austrian and Bohemian lands. This is so not only because the hereditary lands were the heart of the monarchy's fiscal base and therefore the key factor in its military effort, but also because the whole question of the dynasty's approach to internal reform is a major thread that ties together the entire course of Austrian history and pulls it inexorably toward the cataclysm of 1918. The history of the Habsburg monarchy's internal development is essentially the story of abortive initiatives and lost opportunities. More specifically it constitutes a narrative of the state's continuing failure to maximize military power by rationalizing its political institutions. Most historians would agree that the dynasty itself played a pivotal role in the monarchy's uneven growth, eventual decline, and ultimate collapse by failing to provide the necessary leadership to reform and strengthen its political infrastructure. In fact, the dozen men who presided over the monarchy's fortunes in its last three centuries generally shared traits that contributed directly to its dissolution. Though they were intensely pious, virtuous, and dedicated bureaucrats who indulged readily in the day-to-day problems of administration, they often lacked the imagination and courage to institute the sweeping political reforms that were necessary to bring the Habsburg monarchy into line with its neighbors. They were particularly reluctant to undermine the power of the church and nobility—and later on, of the so-called master nationalities—whose corporate privileges often weakened the financial strength and fundamental political unity of the monarchy. There were, of course, some notable exceptions to this stereotype. Maria Theresa grasped the essential needs of the state and her son Joseph II readily ignored all obstacles in seeking to extend her reforms. No ruler, however, strayed further from this stereotype than Joseph I, who shared neither his family's practical political shortcomings nor its high sense of dedication and moral rectitude. Though time and circumstances never afforded him the opportunity to undertake a comprehensive program of reform, what we do know of Joseph's policies and personality does enable us to view him in the context of the rest of the dynasty and the domestic challenges it faced.

Notwithstanding an initial and necessary investigation of administration and finance, the bulk of this study is devoted to an examination of the critical events unfolding outside the hereditary lands. Though German nationalist historians often misinterpreted Joseph's intense Francophobia and extensive use of imperial prerogatives as a commitment to rebuild a powerful *Reich*, recent historiography generally accepts the view that the emperor's policies responded principally to Austrian state and Habsburg dynastic interests. It is perhaps more profitable to examine how he himself defined these interests in establishing priorities between the several fighting fronts, especially since his decisions proved instrumental in determining the extent and limits of the monarchy's expansion during his reign. The book itself is organized topically, rather than chronologically, in order to dramatize the essentially *radial* nature of Joseph's policies and to assist the reader in identifying the emperor's objectives and priorities in Germany, Italy, and Hungary. Indeed, such a model could be employed beyond the limited parameters of Joseph's reign. From the acquisition of Hungary and Bohemia in 1526 to the end of the monarchy in 1918, Habsburg foreign policy was largely dictated by the monarchy's attempts to enhance its security by the maintenance of buffer zones in each of four distinctive geographical areas: Germany to the northwest, Italy to the southwest, Turkey and the Balkans to the southeast, and, to a somewhat lesser degree, Poland and later Russia to the northeast. To a certain extent, the monarchy's fall in 1918 can be traced to the gradual dissolution of these buffer zones.

During Joseph's youth his father, Leopold I (1657–1705), had achieved relative security in all four regions. In response to Louis XIV's aggression, the German princes had belatedly rallied behind Leopold in defense of the empire's western frontier. With the empire's assistance, Leopold had also expelled the Turks from most of the Hungarian plain and seemingly pacified the rebellious Magyar nobility. The Italian peninsula was, as it had been for two centuries, protected by the Spanish Habsburgs. Meanwhile, a weak but massive Poland ruled by the Saxon elector and former imperial general Augustus the Strong provided the monarchy with its most extensive *glacis*.

This favorable constellation disappeared following the death of the childless Charles II in November 1700 and the succession of Louis XIV's grandson, Philip of Anjou, as king of Spain. Leopold began the War of the Spanish Succession ostensibly to secure the entire Spanish inheritance for Joseph's younger brother, Archduke Charles, but primarily to prevent Italy from falling into Bourbon hands. Though England, the United Provinces, and virtually every German state allied with Leopold, the desertion of Bavaria and Cologne (1702) and the outbreak of the Rákóczi rebellion (1703) opened two more fronts perilously close to Vienna and, for a time, raised the possibility that enemy forces operating in northern Italy, Bavaria and Hungary would converge on the city. The simultaneous progress of the Northern War between Charles XII of Sweden and Denmark, Russia and Saxony-Poland further worsened an already ominous situation by bringing the armies of the emperor's old Swedish enemy into neighboring Poland (1704). Having entered the war in quest of Italy and—with his allies' aid—the rest of the Spanish inheritance, Leopold faced a military crisis and ultimate political settlement that could eliminate the monarchy as a major European power. Though the great allied victory at Blenheim (Höchstädt) soon removed the Bavarian threat to the empire—and to the dynasty's preeminent position in Germany—Leopold's prospects elsewhere remained bleak. With the death of Leopold nine months later, Joseph inherited the task of restoring the favorable constellation that had been upset by the death of Charles II and of exploiting the opportunity that the Grand Alliance offered his dynasty in its quest of the Spanish inheritance.

II

The Erblande:
Administration and Finance

One would have to be insane to want to assume the direction of state affairs in a government like ours.
—Johann Wenzel Count Wratislaw

At Joseph's succession an extensive program of internal reform was needed to finance the war effort and avert a military collapse. Two centuries after its creation, the Danubian monarchy remained essentially a Renaissance state. It was still primarily a dynastic combination with the monarch himself providing the single thread that wove together its patchwork political fabric. While Bohemia was no longer the hotbed of rebellion it had been a century earlier and was now commonly grouped with the Austrian lands as part of the *Erblande,* or hereditary lands, the dynasty's Hungarian subjects still did not identify with or feel any loyalty toward the monarchy as a whole. Each crownland continued to be ruled by separate laws and legislative bodies. Moreover, the monarchy's central administrative offices still reflected past and present political divisions. The Austrian, Bohemian and Hungarian lands were each represented by a chancery responsible for expediting all official correspondence with the provinces. In fact, the Austrian Chancery still comprised separate dispatch offices which reflected the former existence of Habsburg apanages in Inner Austria (Styria, Carinthia, Carniola, and Görz) and in the Tyrol and Hither Austrian lands of Vorarlberg and southern Germany.[1] Similarly, the authority of the monarchy's councils for war and finance—the *Hofkriegsrat* and *Hofkammer*—did not extend either to Inner Austria or to the Tyrol and Hither Austria because separate military and fiscal offices sitting in Graz and Innsbruck had survived the subsequent reunification of the Austrian dominions with their autonomy intact.

Though it is true that regional loyalties and bureaucratic anachronisms still remained in evidence throughout Europe, the Habsburg monarchy had made unusually slow progress in clearing them away. It

7

also lagged behind the other major European land powers, such as France, Spain, and Prussia, in eliminating the power of its estates to vote and collect taxes. The government in Vienna always got less than it asked for from the estates, which habitually underestimated their ability to pay and based tax assessments on obsolete censuses and land registers dating as far back as the fifteenth century.[2] Even the actual amounts promised by the estates always fell short partly because tax collection was almost never supervised by royal officials and because the estates generally made no attempt to pursue or punish tax delinquents.[3] Although the *Hofkammer* did control the collection of regalian revenues from state monopolies, tolls, royal domains and assorted indirect taxes, much of these funds was swallowed up by its labyrinthine bureaucracy, which was generally corrupt and thoroughly inefficient.

While Emperor Leopold was not responsible for the system over which he presided, he was wholly incapable of undertaking any meaningful reform. Like so many of his line, the aging monarch combined the greatest piety, integrity, and devotion to his responsibilities with a total lack of innovation and daring. In an age of growing political secularism, he remained a religious bigot and tool of Jesuit court intrigue; in an era when monarchs everywhere were attacking the prerogatives and privileges of the nobility and church, he persisted in viewing these very classes as pillars of the state not to be undermined, whatever the cost.[4] In administrative matters, he could create committees to investigate or compensate for existing defects but could not tear down faulty machinery and build anew. The Venetian ambassador had explained that because the emperor "was afraid of stumbling, he walked slowly."[5] In his last years, Leopold had, in fact, stood still. Even one of his court biographers conceded that "the general disorder of present affairs has as its principal source a certain indolence for which the emperor is felt to be responsible."[6]

The emperor's inability to make changes when and where they were needed extended into the ministry. Though Louis XIV had begun long ago to rely on hardworking professionals like Colbert, Louvois, and Vauban, Leopold's last ministry was composed primarily of courtiers who owed their positions to his personal favor or to the intrigues of his other ministers and Jesuit advisors. Moreover, since the emperor seldom found advancing age and incompetence sufficient grounds for dismissal, these men tended to remain at their posts until they died. While their indecisiveness and lethargy mirrored, rather than compensated for, Leopold's waxing years and waning energies, their inexperience and generally deficient intellect tended to compound the administrative and fiscal chaos afflicting the government.

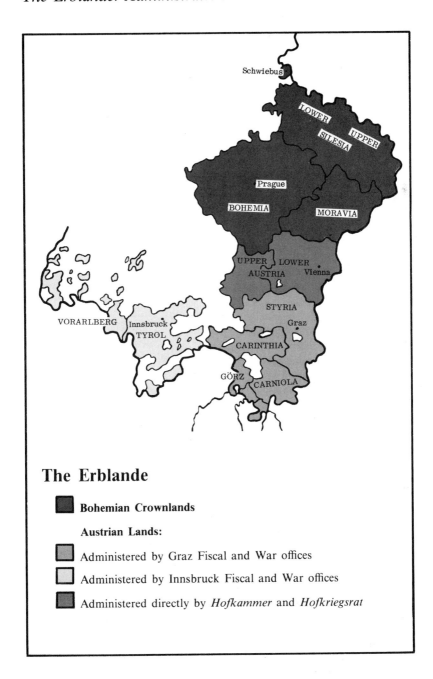

The Erblande

Bohemian Crownlands

Austrian Lands:

Administered by Graz Fiscal and War offices

Administered by Innsbruck Fiscal and War offices

Administered directly by *Hofkammer* and *Hofkriegsrat*

Joseph and the Young Court

The outbreak of the War of the Spanish Succession greatly intensified the need—and hence the pressure—for remedial fiscal and administrative reform. By the spring of 1703, the political alignment at court resembled two concentric rings. An inner circle composed of the emperor's chief ministers represented the ruling core of the government. Meanwhile, a second ring of younger and less influential ministers, supported by many of the monarchy's generals, diplomats, and allies, was pressing in around it agitating for change. While the emperor stood at the center and was in close contact with the first circle, the men in the outer ring were striving to break through the barrier of incompetence that separated them from the monarch.

Among their number and gradually emerging as their leader was Leopold's elder son, Joseph. The Habsburg heir was, by common admission, a young man of undoubted intelligence. As a child he had been an eager and excellent student and had soon proved himself his father's equal as an accomplished linguist, musician, and composer.[7] At twenty-four, he was handsome and well-proportioned with reddish-blond hair, blue eyes, and a fair complexion. Unlike virtually all of his Austrian and Spanish Habsburg forebears, he showed no trace whatsoever of the protruding Habsburg jaw and lower lip that were so prominent among his father's features. Significantly, the differences between father and son went more than skin deep. Joseph was by temperament totally unlike Leopold. In contrast to the stolid and slow-moving emperor, he was quick of mind and action and exhibited energies exceeding the norms of youth. Spirited and impatient by nature, he was wholly out of humor with the inertial air of sobriety and indecision generated by his father.[8]

To his father, Joseph's youthful energy and fiery temperament were a constant source of concern and friction. Given his own lifelong disinclination for the martial arts, Leopold was wholly out of sympathy with his son's longing for the rigors and excitement of military life. He was also clearly angered by the reckless disregard for safety which Joseph displayed during their hunting trips together.[9] What distressed the emperor most, however, were his son's numerous love affairs. Indeed, while Leopold had been scrupulously faithful in almost forty years of marriage—a remarkable record for any baroque monarch—stories of Joseph's "gallantry" with various noblewomen and even with Hofburg servant girls were already common gossip among the Viennese. Nevertheless, all attempts by Leopold and Empress Eleonore to impose their own moral standards only resulted in harsh words and strained relations with their son.[10]

At first the emperor's doubts about Joseph's maturity inclined him to delay his apprenticeship in state affairs. Eventually, however, Leopold adopted the advice of his son's governor, Prince Salm, who suggested that Joseph would mellow once ne had married and been entrusted with limited responsibilities.[11] To the imperial family's relief, Joseph's marriage in February 1699 to Wilhelmine Amalia of Hanover appeared to have the desired effect of making him "more mature and diligent."[12] Amalia readily won Joseph's undivided affection, bearing a daughter, Maria Josepha, less than ten months after their wedding and two more children, Leopold Joseph and Maria Amalia, within the next two years.[13] Soon afterward the emperor also permitted his son to participate in policy-making. Once he had entered the government, Joseph became a thorn in the side of his father's ministers. His partisanship reflected not only his youthful impetuosity but also the profound influence of his childhood tutor and governor, Prince Salm. Himself the ruler of two small Rhenish principalities, with a long record of service to the dynasty, Charles Theodore Otto Prince Salm had long been in the forefront of those who criticized the ineptitude and indecisiveness of Leopold's ministry. As a former Protestant and student of the *philosophes,* he was also disinclined to mix confessionalism with state policy. He was, in fact, a dedicated opponent of the court Jesuits, who accused him of having been tainted with the Jansenist heresies of friends at Port Royal.[14] By entrusting Joseph's religious education to another of the society's enemies, Franz Ferdinand von Rummel, Salm arranged for him to become the first Habsburg heir in over a century not to receive instruction from Jesuit tutors.[15] Even before his admission to the government, Joseph had raised more than a few eyebrows at court by naming a Protestant nobleman to his bedchamber. He had also taken up the gauntlet of Rummel's defense against numerous Jesuit intrigues, at one point directing the defenestration of one member of the society who had appeared nightly by his bedside disguised as a ghost, urging his tutor's dismissal.[16] As the youngest councillor of state, his views mirrored those of Salm, who became his closest advisor and ally. Following the death of Charles II, he opposed all suggestions of compromise and became a determined advocate of war against France.[17] A few months later, when war preparations began to falter, he was unable to hide his impatience with his father's ministers. "In all my life I have never seen such lethargy," he complained to John William, the elector palatine. "I will neither be still nor silent until I am satisfied that everything planned has been set in motion."[18] At the same time, Joseph began to press his father to allow him to go personally to the front.[19] Although these requests were turned down at first, Leopold eventually granted Joseph permission to spend the 1702 campaign with the imperial army besieging the French fortress of Landau. Upon his return to Vienna, Joseph found the atmosphere at court favorable for an expansion of his political responsibilities. Not only was he admitted to all policy deliberations, but he also began to preside over council meetings in his father's absence.[20]

Although Joseph had entertained the hope of returning to the front in 1703, the worsening military picture soon made it apparent that his participation in a further campaign was out of the question.[21] By April he had resolved instead to work for a solution to the chaos which was paralyzing the government's ability to continue the war. Joseph placed the blame squarely on the incompetent presidents of the *Hofkammer* and *Hofkriegsrat,* Counts Salaburg and Mansfeld, and saw a remedy to the present crisis only in their immediate dismissal.[22] For assistance he could not rely on Salm, who was in Westphalia convalescing from a bad attack of gout.[23] Nevertheless, by their consistent criticism of the Leopoldine regime, Joseph and Salm had served as catalysts for the formation of a *young court* of junior officials who were impatient for reform and who were now eager to lend a hand in the intrigue against Salaburg and Mansfeld. Joseph's most active allies were *Hofkammer* Vice President Gundaker Starhemberg and Prince Eugene, who had recently come to Vienna to plead for better support for his deteriorating army in northern Italy. Among Leopold's German vassals, Joseph was also in close contact with the imperial commander-in-chief, Margrave Louis William of Baden, and with the emperor's brother-in-law, Elector John William of the Palatinate. Although they were not presently in Vienna, both men had been writing Leopold since March, urging him to dismiss Mansfeld and Salaburg. In fact, Louis William had even dispatched a special representative to Vienna to cooperate with those who were plotting against the *Hofkammer* and *Hofkriegsrat* presidents. Even the ambassadors of the maritime powers, George Stepney and Jacob Hamel Bruynincx, were lending support, however discreetly, for a change in the ministry.[24]

The fate of Salaburg and Mansfeld was sealed following the bankruptcy of the estate of the great Jewish financier and military purveyor Samuel Oppenheimer, who had personally assumed over eleven million florins in unsecured government notes, but whose death in May 1703 exposed the *Hofkammer*'s inability to pay its debts.[25] As the monarchy entered what was perhaps the greatest fiscal crisis in its history, Leopold began to realize that only drastic measures could restore confidence in the *Hofkammer*'s finances. Characteristically, the emperor did not act until the end of June when, following the decisive intervention of his Jesuit confessor, he dismissed Salaburg and Mansfeld and replaced them with Gundaker Starhemberg and Prince Eugene.[26] The closed circle around the emperor had at last been broken.

For the next year, Joseph's reform party was clearly the dominant force at court. Nevertheless, the financial and military situation with which they had to contend seemed to indicate that the purge had come too late to save the monarchy. While the French, Bavarian, and Hungarian rebels continued to press their offensives in the south, west, and east, the funds needed to oppose them appeared to be beyond the reach of the *Hofkammer*. The annual *Contributio* voted by the estates represented only a small fraction of the revenue needed for the coming campaign. Meanwhile, regalian revenues had been pledged through 1704.[27] To avert the twin specters of bankruptcy and defeat, Leopold created a commission to find ways of meeting these anticipated demands. Chaired by Joseph and including Starhemberg, Eugene, and Salm among its members, the *Mittelsdeputation* represented yet another advance in the power and influence of the young court. Although the emperor was at first reluctant to implement many of the commission's suggestions, in the end he adopted almost all of its recommendations for tapping additional sources of regalian revenue.[28]

Joseph's *Mittelsdeputation* was also obliged to authorize a series of loans, including many of a compulsory nature. By the beginning of 1704, forced loans were being extracted from the *Erblande*'s Jews and wealthy nobility, and every officer at court had been compelled to advance a sum computed at twice his yearly salary.[29] Meanwhile, the emperor had finally yielded to his son's insistent demands that he remove the clergy's exemption from an August edict ordering the collection of all private silver.[30] Truly voluntary loans were more difficult to procure in view of the dismal state of the government's credit. Nevertheless, the Bohemian aristocrat Count Czernin still ventured the war's largest private loan of 1.2 million florins, while Margrave Louis and Elector John William secured 500,000 florins from the Dutch by pawning some of their own estates.[31] Since these funds still did not cover all expenditures, additional credit had to be secured by anticipating future revenue from the *Contributio* voted by the estates.[32]

To help raise more funds, the reform party initially supported Leopold's decision to establish a state-owned Giro Bank.[33] The emperor hoped that private investment would enable the bank to grant the government long-term loans far in excess of its own investment. Yet, with the fate of Samuel Oppenheimer still fresh in their minds, investors were not about to entrust their own funds to any state-run enterprise. Indeed, the *Hofkammer* soon reinforced their reluctance by withdrawing all of its own funds from the bank's endowment.[34] Reasoning that no state-run bank would ever be able to command the confidence of private investors, the young court now began to press for the creation of an entirely new, semi-independent institution that would not be directly subject to the financial demands and failings of the *Hofkammer*.[35] The path Leopold took conformed with his inclination for half measures rather than complete change. In June 1704 he announced plans for investing forty million florins in the state bank over the next twelve years, including an immediate payment of 5.5 million florins. Notwithstanding these intentions, the *Hofkammer* was barely able to deposit 500,000 florins in the state bank during the next twelve months. The great hope for large-scale private investment remained illusory and, by the end of the year, the Giro Bank was on the verge of bankruptcy.[36]

Despite this setback, the young court still seemed to be at the height of its power. Over the past year, it had added a number of new figures to its ranks. The recently departed Archduke Charles's representative in Vienna, the duke of Moles, and the returning Austrian ambassador to Paris, Philip Ludwig von Sinzendorf, had both joined the circle around Joseph. In January 1704 the elector palatine, John William, responded to the invitation of Prince Salm and journeyed to Vienna in the hope of boosting and benefiting personally from the rise of the reform party. The elector was quickly accommodated by the emperor, who admitted him to war deliberations, all of which were now being placed under Joseph's personal direction.[37] It was in these meetings, led by Joseph and composed of Salm, Eugene, Sinzendorf, and the elector, that military strategy for the 1704 campaign was formulated independently of Leopold and the other ministers. In early April when these men resolved to make Bavaria "the primary objective of all operations" and to seek Anglo-Dutch assistance in gaining a decision there, it was Joseph who decided that Prince Eugene would lead the imperial forces and who then prevailed upon the emperor to approve the project.[38] His influence with Leopold had grown so much during the last year that, in the eyes of one observer, he had assumed the power of a prime minister.[39] The emperor acknowledged his son's pleas, and when word arrived in Vienna a few days later that Marlborough had also agreed to march on the Danube, the road to Blenheim was open.

Notwithstanding these promising developments, events in the summer of 1704 reversed the rising political fortunes of the young court. Though momentarily stunned by the purge of June 1703, most of Leopold's ministers had remained in their posts. Even Mansfeld, while no longer *Hofkriegsrat* president, had remained at court, where he was soon able to renew the struggle for power in conjunction with the lord high steward, Count Harrach, and the emperor's Jesuit advisors.[40] Mansfeld found his work greatly simplified by the absence of most of the reform party from court. During the spring, Eugene had departed for the front in Germany. John William followed in August, disappointed at not having found a permanent berth for himself in Leopold's ministry. A few days later Joseph also left Vienna for a second siege of Landau, taking Salm and Sinzendorf with him. When he hastened his return to court during December, after receiving word that his father had fallen seriously ill, Joseph found that his party had lost its advantage.[41]

As long as Leopold remained ill, Joseph ruled in his father's stead.[42] Once he had regained his strength, however, the emperor systematically began to reorder the political relationships at court in favor of the Mansfeld-Harrach faction.[43] The first signs of a new purge surfaced in January when Leopold named Harrach to replace the late Count Kaunitz as the new director of Hungarian affairs.[44] A further hint of Leopold's intentions emerged a week later when he convened the

Lower Austrian Diet. Although Joseph and his adherents were well represented in the emperor's entourage, Leopold elected to rely exclusively on the counsel of Mansfeld and Harrach during the delicate negotiations with the estates.[45]

During the following month, the trend against the young court continued as Leopold filled two more high positions with men sponsored by his old guard. Although Joseph and Salm questioned his competence, they were helpless to prevent Leopold Count Herberstein from succeeding to the *Hofkriegsrat* vice-presidency.[46] A few days later Joseph's choice for governor of Bavaria was overlooked by the emperor, who appointed instead the Mansfeld faction's candidate, Count Löwenstein.[47] Clearly the boldest and most damaging stroke against the reform party came at the beginning of February when the emperor started excluding his son from council meetings and ceased altogether to confer with him on matters of policy.[48] Leopold offered no explanation for the purge. Yet, the implications of Joseph's exclusion from state affairs were all too clear to the anxious members of the reform party. Although he and his allies were still convening sessions of the *Mittelsdeputation,* Joseph was soon reporting to Salm that "Mansfeld and Harrach govern all matters more than ever"; and Salm himself was compelled to admit that, despite the great progress that had been made immediately following the 1703 purge, "everything has gone up in smoke."[49]

Faced with the hopeless situation at court, Joseph was more eager than ever to serve at the front during the 1705 campaign, and he again began making preparations to join the imperial army in Germany.[50] However, shortly before he was scheduled to leave Vienna, he was obliged to postpone his plans when his father suddenly fell ill. As in December, Joseph assumed full control of the government, pending his father's recovery.[51] But on this occasion, the young Habsburg was not destined to relinquish his power. On 5 May after having reigned nearly a half-century, Leopold I died.

First among Equals

Having only recently suffered the humiliation of being excluded from participation in state affairs, Joseph now had the power to reorder the government. His first opportunity arose appropriately enough during his father's burial. In his funeral oration, delivered in the presence of the Dutch and English envoys, the Jesuit Wiedemann praised Leopold's zeal in containing Protestantism, while warning ominously that only princes educated by Jesuits were likely to be prosperous and victorious. Terming the eulogy "impertinent and unreasonable," Joseph immediately expelled Wiedemann from his dominions and suppressed 2,000 copies of the sermon which had been prepared for distribution throughout the *Erblande.*[52] If Joseph's Protestant allies were satisfied by the punishment meted out to Wiedemann, they were elated to learn shortly thereafter that the remaining Jesuits at court had received notice that they would no longer be permitted to meddle in political affairs.[53]

During the rest of May, the young emperor concerned himself primarily with the selection of new ministers to replace the incompetents of the preceding regime.[54] There was never any doubt that Salm would supersede Harrach as lord high steward, or *Obersthofmeister,* a position equivalent to that of prime minister. Similarly, Prince Eugene and Starhemberg were quickly confirmed in their respective positions. Not until early June, however, did Joseph fill the important posts of Austrian and Bohemian court chancellor.

In selecting an Austrian chancellor, he had to choose between two men with totally different backgrounds and personalities. After three decades in the emperor's service, the 58-year-old legist Johann Friedrich Baron Seilern enjoyed a solid reputation as an exacting and energetic bureaucrat who found "his greatest pleasure in work and in the preparation of imperial legal matters."[55] Since 1702 he had been Leopold's chief legal council, drawing up not only the family succession patent in 1703 but also the dying emperor's testament. A commoner by birth, Seilern had never acquired the urbanity of an aristocrat. Indeed, his excessive pedantry and preoccupation with his work tended to preclude the cultivation of friendships, and his contact with the ladies at court was so minimal that any extended conversation with them was considered worthy of comment among his colleagues.[56] By contrast his rival, Philip Ludwig Count Sinzendorf, was the product of a wealthy Austrian family who owed his rise at court to his mother's connections and to his own talents as an able courtier. Though only thirty-three, he had already served as ambassador to France as well as in various diplomatic missions in Germany and the Netherlands. In creative ability, application, and knowledge, Sinzendorf was unexceptional.[57] Nevertheless, his charm and flexibility were definite assets to any diplomat. During the alliance negotiations with England, Sinzendorf made an excellent impression on the duke of Marlborough; and during the second siege of Landau two years later, he scored equally well with Joseph, who promised him the post of Austrian chancellor.[58] Although Joseph could not easily dismiss the arguments presented by Salm and Moles on Seilern's behalf, he was still unwilling to go back on his word.[59] Resorting to a compromise suggested by his lord high steward, Joseph announced on 3 June that he would appoint both men Austrian chancellor. In recognition of Seilern's greater experience and rank in the Privy Council, the emperor awarded him seniority over Sinzendorf. Meanwhile, by entrusting Seilern with legal and internal administrative matters and Sinzendorf with foreign policy and occasional diplomatic missions, Joseph divided the two men's responsibilities according to their own personal predilections and talents.[60]

Three days later the emperor announced his choice for Bohemian court chancellor. Though he retained the elderly, but energetic Count Kinsky in the largely ceremonial post of *Oberster Kanzler,* Joseph reserved the more important position of court chancellor formerly held by Kinsky for another Bohemian nobleman, Johann Wenzel Count Wratislaw. Wratislaw had begun his career in the Bohemian Chancery in 1695 and had returned to it in recent months.[61] However, it was the outstanding service he had performed as ambassador to England that most impressed Joseph. It had been Wratislaw who had negotiated the Grand Alliance in 1702 and engineered the duke of Marlborough's march to the Danube two years later.[62] As early as 1703, he had reacted to the growing impatience of the British government by actively encouraging the reform party in its efforts to establish itself at court. Arriving in Vienna after Blenheim, Wratislaw immediately entered its ranks, becoming the young court's unsuccessful candidate for the Bavarian governorship.[63] Although illness and obesity had robbed him of his youth and often compelled him to work from a sickbed, the 35-year-old chancellor was nevertheless exceptionally thorough and diligent. A knowledgeable and sharply perceptive thinker, he offered intellectual resources which made him outstanding among Joseph's ministers.

With the core of his cabinet set, Joseph now moved to establish a formal policy-making body. Theoretically this function was served by the Privy Conference (*Geheimkonferenz*) and its parent body, the Privy Council (*Geheimrat*). However, since Leopold had always found it easier to appoint new members than to remove old ones, both bodies had literally outgrown their usefulness. While the Privy Conference rarely met in full session, the larger Privy Council had totally ceased to function as a deliberative body and was now convened only on formal state occasions.[64] Although he had no intention of expanding its role beyond that of a ceremonial body, Joseph reduced the number of privy councillors from about 150 to 33. While all of the original membership was allowed to retain the title and privileges of a privy councillor, only the smaller group could attend future meetings of that body.[65] Those who had been disenfranchised did not accept the reform without protesting and pressing the emperor to reconsider his action. Notwithstanding these remonstrances and suggestions of a compromise solution brought forward by Harrach, Joseph stood firmly by his decision.[66]

The day after he reduced the size of the Privy Council, Joseph abolished his father's Privy Conference altogether. In its place he created a group of eight independent, smaller conferences to deal with all aspects of the monarchy's foreign and domestic policy. Seven of these divided Europe among them while the eighth was entrusted with the deliberation of financial and military problems.[67] To assure that policy-making remained properly coordinated between the different committees, Joseph placed Salm and at least one Austrian chancellor on each of them. The remaining membership consisted of men who were specialists in each field. For example, Wratislaw joined Salm and Sinzendorf in the Conference that dealt with Anglo-Dutch-French affairs, while the former ambassador to Portugal, Count Waldstein, and the duke of Moles were present in the Spanish Conference. Finally, in the event that a particular issue arose that transcended the jurisdiction of two or more committees, a joint meeting would be held.

The appointments and reforms which Joseph instituted in the opening weeks of his reign occasioned widespread expressions of hope, if not of outright relief, both within the monarchy and among its allies. In energy and ability, there was little comparison between the new and old regimes. In age alone the contrast could hardly have been greater. While Leopold's closest advisors had generally been in their mid-sixties, the young emperor and his ministers averaged barely forty years. However, notwithstanding its obvious strengths, the new regime was not without its own weaknesses. Indeed, within a short time, the personal flaws of Joseph and his ministers came to dominate the atmosphere at court. Despite its common purpose and apparent unity during the waning years of Leopold's reign, the circle of ministers around the new emperor soon fragmented into rival factions and personalities. Perhaps it was inevitable that personal conflicts and power struggles would emerge within a ministry composed of so many young and ambitious men. Nevertheless, the reappearance of dissension at court in the months after his succession came as an unwelcome surprise to Joseph.

Prince Salm was at once the cause and the target of the new intrigues. During the opening weeks of the reign, Joseph conferred closely with him and adopted many of his suggestions regarding new appointments and reforms within the government. Moreover, it became apparent from the reorganization of the Privy Conference that Salm was destined—or at least intended—to become, in the words of George Stepney, "the great director of the whole machine."[68] Yet, however firmly he had established himself as Joseph's prime minister, there were signs that the prince's steadily worsening health might eventually force him to step down. During each of the past three campaigns, Salm had been obliged to beg Joseph to excuse him from accompanying him into the field due to his weakening constitution.[69] Though the two men did in fact leave Vienna together the previous autumn, Salm had retired to his estates in Westphalia rather than participate in the siege of Landau. While there Salm even wrote Joseph and Leopold requesting permission to retire permanently from court.[70] Though this petition was not accepted, a bad attack of gout prevented him from returning to court until the end of April, despite Joseph's desperate pleas for assistance against Harrach and Mansfeld.[71]

With Joseph's succession, Salm temporarily put off any thought of resigning. Despite his continued application and ability, however, the

lord high steward's abrasive character soon encouraged certain ministers to begin working for his early retirement.[72] While Salm's hot
temper and arrogance had already begun to alienate many of his
former allies, it was his intention of establishing his personal authority
and supervision over the other ministers that brought about the revolt
against his leadership.

The lord high steward's attempts to intervene in military affairs
quickly won him the lasting enmity of Prince Eugene. In Salm's
opinion, Eugene had failed to bring needed reforms to the *Hofkriegsrat* during the two years since his elevation to the presidency. Its
administration was still plagued by confusion and the army itself was
ill-equipped, poorly led, and without adequate discipline. While not
hesitating to praise Eugene's outstanding qualities as a field commander, Salm reasoned that his prolonged absences from Vienna during
the campaigning season were preventing him from attending adequately to administrative problems. One week after Joseph's succession, Salm presented a lengthy memorial boldly suggesting that the
Hofkriegsrat administration be entrusted to someone else. As a former
field marshal, he even mentioned himself as a possible replacement. He
pointed out that on only one occasion in the past had a *Hofkriegsrat*
president served in the field, and even then had entrusted most of his
administrative duties to his vice-president. The lord high steward
concluded that Eugene's removal from inner court circles would certainly help reduce the intensity of the court intrigues in which the
young Savoyard had taken such an active part in recent years.[73]

If Salm had hoped to reduce friction within the ministry by removing or at least superseding the *Hofkriegsrat* president, he had badly
miscalculated. Joseph could not consider an act which would deprive
his best general of a great deal of his power and income. Instead, Salm
was only able to secure the naming of his protégé, Leopold Count
Schlick, as commissary general a few weeks later.[74] In the end Schlick's
appointment merely exacerbated the rift between the two princes.[75]

Serious friction also developed between the lord high steward and
Count Wratislaw. Although the two men had been closely allied during
the struggle against Leopold's ministers, they soon clashed over Wratislaw's role in the new government. During the months following his
return from England, the young Bohemian nobleman had established
himself so firmly in Joseph's favor that, by the time of Leopold's death,
he enjoyed the new emperor's confidence more than any other minister
except Salm.[76] Viewing the ambitious Wratislaw as a threat to his own
preeminent position at court, Salm sought to limit his role within the
new ministry. As early as January, the lord high steward had sought to
discourage him from seeking the Bavarian governorship; and with
Joseph's succession, he successfully used his influence to restrict the
new Bohemian chancellor to membership in only two committees of
the Privy Conference.[77]

Wratislaw did not hesitate to pick up the gauntlet thrown down by the wily lord high steward. He became Salm's sharpest critic at court and soon joined Prince Eugene in plotting against him. Aware of their designs, Salm appealed to Joseph to forbid them from secretly corresponding with each other during Eugene's absence at the front.[78] While the emperor apparently turned down this request, he hastened to reaffirm his complete confidence in the lord high steward at the beginning of 1706, when a triumvirate of Wratislaw, Eugene, and Moles made a concerted attempt to bring about Salm's dismissal.[79] A few months afterward Joseph went a step further in assuring Salm that "I will not permit the formation of court factions and cabals, which experience has shown are always harmful and invariably the cause of confusion."[80] Moles was promptly notified that he was being sent to Barcelona, where he would act as the emperor's permanent representative. The idea of dispatching an envoy to Spain to advise the inexperienced Habsburg pretender was itself not new.[81] However, the sending of Charles's own ambassador back to Barcelona was a clear reflection of Moles's fall from favor.[82] In fact, while the duke did manage to delay his departure for several months, Joseph had him excluded from further meetings of the Conference.[83]

Moles's dismissal was not a difficult decision for the young emperor to make. He was technically a foreign subject and was neither a particularly competent nor indispensable councillor.[84] Yet, for Joseph to go beyond Moles in purging his court of intrigues was infinitely more difficult. To resolve the power struggle himself meant choosing between Salm and Wratislaw, the two men whose advice he valued most highly. Both men shared responsibility for the present division within the ministry, and while it was clear that the aging lord high steward was a difficult man to deal with, the blunt and sarcastic Bohemian chancellor was certainly no more popular among his colleagues. Faced with what he considered an impossible decision, the emperor elected to tolerate the continuing court intrigues, content instead with holding the balance between the factions that began to form around Salm and Wratislaw.[85]

It is difficult to assess the extent to which the division within the ministry obstructed the conduct of state business. In his monumental scholarship on the subject, Max Braubach merely presents the testimony of contemporaries and assumes that the intrigues about which they wrote must have proved detrimental. Yet, like the sources he cites, Braubach does not venture to explain exactly how the personal animosities at court might have adversely affected the formulation or execution of state policy. Judging from the wealth of misinformation contained within their reports, it is clear that those foreign observers who described with alacrity the latest turns in court intrigue were not in a position to ascertain what effects it was actually having on the running of the government. Rather, their consciousness was limited to the status of personal relationships and did not extend into the intricacies of policy-making. In their private and official correspondence, the ministers themselves often referred to "disturbances" and division at court. Members of each faction would speak critically of their opponents' intrigues and somewhat self-righteously call for an end to them. Nevertheless, although they occasionally accused each other of incompetence, they were never able to specify how these personal conflicts were in fact interrupting the smooth flow of government business.

The hostilities between Joseph's ministers appear to have been more intense than those which existed at other courts during the period. Nevertheless, a close examination of the records of the Privy Conference indicates that, as far as the making of policy was concerned the two sides tended to bury their personal differences and concur with remarkable regularity. On the rare occasions when a deadlock did occur within the Conference, the emperor resolved it personally. The division within the ministry does not appear to have affected the dispatch of administrative matters either, since that was carried out by the rather able and industrious secretaries who staffed the various central offices and who kept the state machinery functioning despite the intrigues which raged among their superiors.

If his ministers had their flaws, so did Joseph.[86] Although the years immediately following his marriage to Amalia had occasioned great expectations for the future of the dynasty, it eventually became evident that the young heir had not yet mended the reckless ways of his youth. He continued to exhibit a blatant disregard for his own health. Early in 1702 he had fallen perilously ill following intemperate consumption during carnival celebrations at court. He persisted in going on long, exhausting hunting trips, travelling in small groups of two or three and, at times, venturing alone into the thicket.[87] The source of greatest consternation was Joseph's renewed liaisons within a short time after his marriage. So notorious was Joseph's behavior that even Prince Eugene advised one young officer on his way to Vienna to "avoid the parties of the king of the Romans [Joseph] and all those that smack of libertinism."[88] Only one year before his death, Leopold reacted angrily by banishing or imprisoning those members of his son's retinue who he felt had catered most to their master's vices.[89] With Joseph's succession, however, no one remained to hinder his pursuits. Foreign diplomats who had initially praised the vitality of the new emperor and spoken glowingly of the initiatives he had taken in reforming the administration soon began to fill their reports with news of his obsessions for hunting and women.[90]

During the opening years of the reign, the principal objects of Joseph's attention were the widowed Catarina di Balbiano, her daughter, and Marianne Pálffy, the daughter of the Croatian ban. He does not appear to have continued his liaison with the two Balbiano women following the mother's remarriage in 1707. Nevertheless, much to the distress of the widowed Empress Eleonore and the reigning Amalia,

Joseph's relationship with Pálffy lasted until the day of his death.[91] Although he still loved his wife and did not wholly forsake her, the rift between them widened progressively, until the depth of its personal tragedy came to be overshadowed by a crisis of much greater significance.[92] Joseph's only son had died within a year of his birth. Meanwhile, the nature of the emperor's life style and Amalia's own deteriorating health made the prospects of their having additional offspring remote.[93] Unless she could provide Joseph with a son, the only remaining male Habsburg would be the emperor's brother, Charles. Yet, the archduke was himself without heirs, and his succession in Vienna would jeopardize the dynasty's prospects of attaining both the imperial and Spanish thrones. Joseph, however, did not share his ministers' alarm over the succession, and instead of altering his strenuous and at times dangerous pursuits, he continued to place confidence in his own youth and the ultimate prospects of producing a male heir.[94]

If the emperor pursued his diversions with a passion, there are indications that he was less inspired by affairs of state. If we are to believe the testimony of one French agent, cited by Braubach, Joseph wrote love letters to his mistresses during sessions of the Conference.[95] Austrian historian Anna Benna also points to evidence of his doodling during its deliberations.[96] While the presence of sketches among the emperor's Conference notes is understandable in view of the extraordinary length of some meetings, the subjects of some of the drawings, which include numerous hunting and military scenes as well as some remarkable vignettes of men hanging from gallows and heads stuck on pikes, would seem to suggest that Joseph's temperament was not ideally suited to the performance of his responsibilities.[97]

Whether the emperor's preoccupations actually interfered with the dispatch of state business is, of course, a separate and more important matter. His frequent hunting trips never prevented his ministers from meeting regularly and preparing material for his consideration.[98] Moreover, upon his return, Joseph would quickly attend to the matter at hand, either alone or at the head of a Conference. The question arises whether he was adequately acquainted with the background of the issues he was acting upon. The historian Arnold Berney charges that often Joseph was not and that he was content instead to follow blindly the advice pressed upon him by his wife and ministers.[99] Upon close examination, however, the secretaries' minutes of Conference meetings as well as Joseph's own notes clearly indicate that he rarely failed to recognize the problems involved in each decision.[100] Berney's assertion that the emperor allowed himself to be led by others also fails to stand up under close scrutiny. Regarding Amalia, Berney is apparently unaware of her estrangement from Joseph and bases his claim principally upon the reports of the Prussian ambassador, Friedrich Heinrich von Bartholdi, who blamed the empress's Hanoverian family loyalties for Joseph's anti-Prussian policies.[101] Bartholdi himself would have been surprised to learn how few friends his master had within the Conference, where all Austrian policy toward Berlin was formulated and where Amalia's own views counted for naught.[102] When differences did arise among his ministers, the records of the Conference clearly demonstrate that the emperor chose freely between them in resolving upon a decision. No individual enjoyed mastery over his mind, and in fact, most of his advisors were moved at one point or another to complain indignantly that he was ignoring their solutions in favor of someone else's. On occasion Joseph also contradicted the advice of all his ministers in setting policy. Nevertheless, in a Conference which seldom suffered serious division, Karl Otmar von Aretin's description of Joseph as first among equals most accurately describes his role in policy-making.[103]

Braubach, who gives lip service to Berney's charges, limits himself to the more restrained criticism that, while Joseph's pursuits may not have caused chaos within the government, his actions demonstrated that he was surely not the man to bring about the radical reforms which the monarchy needed.[104] Before accepting this judgment, however, one must examine to what extent the new emperor's lack of application could have had a bearing on the fate of his administrative reforms. Admittedly certain rulers have been credited with working out the finest details themselves in making complicated changes in their state machinery. Nevertheless, the role of a monarch's ministers has been overlooked too often in apportioning the credit for reforms. In the case of Joseph, he was surrounded by men who recognized the administrative system's most pressing inadequacies and who were willing to do the needed footwork to see them reformed. Ministers such as Salm and Starhemberg had long been eager to initiate a thorough reform of the monarchy's finances, only to be frustrated by the indecisiveness of Joseph's predecessor.[105] Upon his succession, it became Joseph's primary responsibility to give these individuals the direction and firm support that they had been unable to secure from his father. Beyond performing this function his labors were unnecessary and could easily be duplicated by others.

Reform versus Necessity

Unfortunately, more than just an energetic ministry and a decisive ruler was required to carry out a comprehensive program of reform. Another prerequisite was peace. In the spring of 1705, Joseph's most immediate need was not to reshape the administration but to raise money for the war effort. Major constitutional and administrative reform was, of course, the most ideal solution to the present financial crisis. Yet, it would be very risky to launch such a program in time of war. The estates of the *Erblande,* and even the emperor's own bureaucracy, had a vested interest in the existing administrative system and would surely resist any attempt to deprive them of their patronage or control over sources of crown revenue. Although their opposition would never become an open revolt as it had in Hungary, any attempt by the estates or government bureaucracy to obstruct reform could easily throw the *Hofkammer*'s finances into confusion. Given the monarchy's already desperate military position, chaos within the administration could be catastrophic. Should he encounter their opposition, Joseph did have the option of continuing to work with the estates and bureaucracy in finding palatable expedients and expanding conventional sources of revenue. Although this was not as attractive financially, it offered at least a viable alternative to reform. The estates had already demonstrated a willingness to help finance the war effort, and as long as the military crisis lasted, they could be expected to continue their support. This still left unanswered what would happen once the military situation improved. Nevertheless, until peace had been achieved, Joseph had no alternative but to cultivate their cooperation.

Given the monarchy's desperate position at the end of Leopold's reign, the estates were initially quite responsive to Joseph's needs. Hence, the new emperor achieved immediate results in his efforts to increase the taxes voted by the estates. With the loss of Hungary, the *Contributio* collected in the *Erblande* was the crown's principal source of revenue. In 1701 Leopold had obtained a 50 percent increase to around 5.3 million florins.[106] By 1705, however, this sum represented barely a quarter of the year's estimated expenditures. One month before Leopold's death, Joseph had led the *Mittelsdeputation* in boldly proposing that the *Contributio* be increased by an additional 3.4 million florins.[107] As emperor he immediately began working with "all diligence possible" to gain the estates' consent, at one point even convening the Lower Austrian Diet three months early in order to allow sufficient time for negotiating a new agreement.[108] By the year's end, the estates had voted the increase. In Bohemia where the increase was funded by a comprehensive chimney and land tax, the 1706 *Contributio* represented the first time in its history that the nobility had submitted voluntarily to more than token taxation.[109] Yet, despite this initial success, the yield from the *Contributio* never again equalled the nine million florins collected in 1706 and gradually declined each year thereafter.[110] To some extent this falloff can be attributed to the depleting effects brought by the heavy burden of taxation, as well as to the continuing devastation of the easternmost *Erblande* by Hungarian rebel raids. However, while the estates' ability to pay the *Contributio* declined with each year, its willingness also ebbed considerably. Although they had agreed to make greater sacrifices during the critical years of 1705 and 1706, they saw no reason to bear as heavy a burden once the monarchy and its allies had gained an upper hand in the struggle against Louis XIV. Negotiations with the diets became increasingly more difficult and often protracted over months. In fact, terms governing the collection of the 1708 *Contributio* were not reached with certain diets until the second half of that year.[111] Moreover, at no point did the estates demonstrate a willingness to enact permanent administrative or constitutional changes that might deprive them of their sovereignty over taxation. Hence, Starhemberg's plan for updating the land and population registers in the Tyrol, Hither Austria, and Inner Austria was quickly killed by the estates.[112] They also frustrated the *Hofkammer* president's design for replacing the *Contributio* with a "universal excise" that would be applied at the same fixed rate throughout the *Erblande* because, as a regalian tax administered by royal officials, it could be increased and collected by the *Hofkammer* without their approval or participation.[113]

In their reluctance to relinquish control over the administration of taxes, the estates also defended the autonomous Fiscal and War offices in Graz and Innsbruck. All four bureaus had survived the reunification of the Austrian lands despite dismal records of corruption and inefficiency.[114] Nevertheless, when in March 1704 Sinzendorf actually urged their subordination to the *Hofkammer* and *Hofkriegsrat,* Leopold shelved the idea because he was unwilling to risk alienating the provincial estates which controlled them.[115] Immediately after Leopold's death, however, Prince Salm received Joseph's permission to carry through the change.[116] The Inner Austrian and Tyrolean-Hither Austrian estates reacted immediately by flooding Vienna with petitions and by ordering their employees in the Fiscal and War offices to ignore Salm's directive.[117] In their opposition, the estates were joined by the Austrian Chancery, which had formerly processed all correspondence between the Fiscal and War offices and their counterparts in Vienna and was now reluctant to relinquish this role. Under Seilern's direction it delayed as long as possible in relinquishing its correspondence with the Graz and Innsbruck offices, despite reminders and reprimands from Prince Eugene, Starhemberg, and Joseph himself.[118] Though he eventually overcame Seilern's resistance, the emperor found the estates' opposition insurmountable. Following an unsuccessful attempt to reach a compromise with them, Joseph reluctantly issued orders temporarily staying the transfers of jurisdiction.[119] For the rest of 1706 and 1707, Prince Eugene was compelled to deal with the Tyrolean estates in making dispositions for his army in Italy instead of being able to issue orders directly to the Innsbruck War Office in his capacity as *Hofkriegsrat* president.[120] Meanwhile, in Inner Austria the autonomous Fiscal and War offices continued to exercise their stranglehold over the administration of the Croatian military border. Only in 1709, four years after Salm's original directive, was each of the offices finally subordinated to the *Hofkammer* and *Hofkriegsrat.* Even then Joseph was not totally victorious, for the Inner Austrian estates preserved the right to staff most of the positions in the Graz War Office and were given special representation on the *Hofkriegsrat* as well.[121]

When he did not have to contend with the opposition of the estates,

Joseph generally achieved better results. He was particularly successful in his attempt to reform and expand the collection of the crown's regalian revenue. Before his succession, most regalian income was consumed at the regional level by embezzlement and by the salaries of large numbers of superfluous bureaucrats. In fact, many local offices were so overstaffed and inefficient that the taxes they collected were insufficient to cover their operating expenses. In his first year as emperor, Joseph worked closely with Starhemberg in streamlining the *Hofkammer* bureaucracy by purging scores of local officials and even by reducing its Vienna staff from seventy-four to thirty-two. He also attempted to reduce corruption by extending bookkeeping practices to the local level.[122] He supplemented the money saved by these reforms with large increases in existing taxes as well as with various expedients, including new levies on court officials and the extraction of a "free gift" from the Catholic clergy.[123] By 1708 regalian revenue had jumped from 3.5 to over eight million florins annually.[124] Because of this increase and the higher yield in the *Contributio,* the *Hofkammer* could now expect to raise between sixteen and seventeen million florins from the *Erblande* during most years, as opposed to less than nine million at the end of Leopold's reign.

Of course, Joseph did derive some additional income from outside the *Erblande.* In the opening years of his reign, however, only the empire provided any significant revenue. The largest single contribution came from Bavaria which was occupied by Austrian troops and provided a steady annual income of between 1.2 and 1.5 million florins.[125] The emperor also enjoyed certain "reserved rights" by which he was entitled to exact contributions from those lesser imperial princes and cities that owed their allegiance directly to him. During the second siege of Landau, Joseph had exercised these prerogatives by extracting 300,000 florins from the imperial knights of the Upper Rhine.[126] Shortly after his succession, he appointed the talented and energetic C. J. Schierendorff to be *Hofkammer* secretary and instructed him to launch a thorough investigation into possible imperial tax privileges. Within a short time, Schierendorff had uncovered a number of precedents to support the emperor in his resolve to extend taxation into the empire.[127] Despite these advances, however, imperial revenue never exceeded two million florins and, hence, never provided more than a modest supplement to income drawn from the hereditary lands.

With the *Hofkammer*'s annual expenditures ranging between twenty and twenty-eight million florins, Joseph still needed to borrow heavily. During the first year of the reign, however, the abysmal credit of the *Hofkammer* and the Giro Bank made even this alternative difficult. Immediately after his father's death, Joseph began the search for a sounder credit establishment.[128] Seven months later a commission headed by Starhemberg and the governor of Lower Austria, Count

Weltz, submitted its design for a new bank owned and operated by the city of Vienna. It reasoned that the city government's finances were strong enough to inspire confidence on the part of private investors and that its independence from the *Hofkammer* would preserve that trust. Joseph ratified the project on Christmas Eve and authorized the beginning of negotiations with the city government. Two months later an accord was reached, and on 1 April 1706 the Vienna City Bank began operation.[129]

By the terms of its charter, the city bank merged with and assumed the debts of its predecessor. *Hofkammer* revenues were turned over to it to help it discharge the Giro Bank's liabilities. Moreover, in order to guarantee that the bank would never suffer from the fate of its predecessor in having to overextend itself on behalf of the *Hofkammer,* the city was promised that it would retain control over all of the bank's financial transactions. In reality, the government secretly supervised the bank's operations through a *Ministerial-Bancodeputation* headed by Starhemberg and Weltz.[130] Nevertheless, despite severe fiscal pressures, Joseph made a conscious effort to make the bank more attractive to private investors by limiting the *Hofkammer*'s demands for credit. To encourage investment further, the emperor declared both the principal and 6 percent earnings of all investments immune from all forms of taxation, forced loans, or confiscations.[131] After slumping in its first year of operation, the new bank eventually won public confidence. Its earnings showed steady progress and the notes which it issued, after having fallen to 59 percent of their face value during 1706, quickly regained ready acceptance. Even old Giro Bank notes, which it had been authorized to redeem at a 20 percent discount, were soon being accepted among merchants at their full face value.[132]

Of course, the city bank was never able to liquidate all of the government's credit needs. Although it lent considerable support during its first year of operation, the *Hofkammer* still needed the celebrated Anglo-Dutch loans to finance Prince Eugene's victory in Italy.[133] In subsequent years, the bank's difficulties in meeting obligations to its own creditors periodically compelled Joseph to resort to forced loans and other private and foreign advances at interest rates averaging 12 percent. Nevertheless, between its inception and the end of the reign, the Vienna City Bank assumed twenty-four million florins or an average of roughly five million florins per year in government debts.[134]

The war's changing tide eventually brought the government new sources of revenue. With the conquest and occupation of Italy, between four and five million florins in annual military expenses were borne by the inhabitants of the peninsula. Beginning in 1708, the progress of Austrian arms in Hungary enabled the crown to raise between one and two million florins annually in taxes. Even the advancing front in Belgium allowed the Austrian forces there to transfer some of their operating expenses onto the local population.[135] Yet, while these conquests brought some relief to the emperor's finances, they also helped to extend his obligations to the point where, by 1711, he was the only belligerent committed to all five active fronts. Given the threat of French hegemony, the monarchy's immediate defensive needs, and the dynasty's broad claims to the entire Spanish inheritance, this commitment was wholly justified. Nevertheless, for a state that had entered the war with an army and annual budget barely one-tenth that of France, the burden was simply too great.[136] Until the end of Joseph's reign, the *Hofkammer* continued to struggle from one crisis to another, managing only with the greatest difficulty to supply the army, subsidize client princes, pay its own officials, and meet the demands of its creditors.[137] Of course, most of the belligerents experienced financial difficulties at one time or another. Yet, with the possible exception of Spain, the Habsburg monarchy surpassed all other states in the gravity and frequency of its fiscal crises.

Seen in this light, the remedial fiscal reforms initiated by Joseph and his ministers in the months following Leopold's death emerge as a pivotal factor in the fortunes of both the monarchy and the Grand Alliance as a whole. Without them the war's outcome could not have been the same. Given a period of peace, Joseph would have had the opportunity to carry out his ministers' fiscal designs more thoroughly. Nor is it likely that he would have stopped here. In his work on *Hofkammer* Secretary Schierendorff, Alfred Fischel has shown that Joseph foresaw the fiscal advantages to be gained in strengthening those sectors of the economy which traditionally bore the bulk of the *Erblande*'s taxes. The emperor showed an interest in plans put forward by Starhemberg and Schierendorff for the promotion of industry and commerce within the hereditary lands.[138] That only a handful of the designs were carried out stems principally from the scarcity of money, which made it impossible to obtain tax incentives, crown subsidies, or bank loans for business enterprises.[139] Joseph also demonstrated a willingness to pursue Schierendorff's revolutionary plans for improving the lot of the peasantry, realizing as he did that any measurable improvement in its lot would bring about higher agricultural production and ultimately an increased tax yield. When Schierendorff criticized the nobility's abuse of obligatory labor, or *Robot,* which each serf performed on the lands of his feudal lord, Joseph acted on his advice.[140] Though he realized that any attempt to issue a new *Robot* patent would encounter the strongest resistance from the estates, he readily agreed to experiment with Schierendorff's proposals on lands owned by the crown. Joseph's domains in the Silesian duchies of Liegnitz, Brieg, and Wohlau were selected for Schierendorff's project. All of the land on each estate was divided up among those peasants who had formerly cultivated them under feudal obligation. They paid only a fixed rent and were free to work as they wished on their own individual plot. Despite the vocal opposition of the Silesian Diet, the plan had been fully implemented by 1711 and, within a short while, was showing an increased yield over past years.[141] In all its essentials, Schierendorff's Silesian experiment was identical to the Raab System introduced by Maria Theresa in 1775. Yet, whatever prospects there were of applying further the principles involved in the project, were delayed by the war and ended abruptly with Joseph's death. Until late in the century, the initiatives which he had taken remained a forgotten, if prophetic, model for land reform within the Habsburg monarchy.

In addition to initiating Schierendorff's project, Joseph also appears to have taken a hand in eliminating *Robot* abuses on the Moravian estates of the powerful Liechtenstein family. When during the autumn of 1705 peasants in the Trübau and Türnau regions revolted and petitioned him to correct illegal extensions of *Robot* service, Joseph took the unprecedented step of meeting personally with the rebels' representatives on several occasions and establishing a commission to press the Liechtensteins to conform with existing laws. There can be little question that Joseph's concern for the peasants emanated in part from his fear of a full-scale insurrection on the borders of Bavaria and Hungary, where peasant discontent had already sparked revolts. Nevertheless, the emperor persisted in pressing the reluctant Liechtenstein family for a settlement favorable to the peasants long after the war had turned and the threat of Bavarian or Hungarian collusion had disappeared. In any event, Joseph's treatment of the initial outbreak seems to have prevented further violence and stands in sharp contrast with the government's brutal suppression of similar peasant movements in 1679–80 and 1775.[142]

Though the evidence is too fragmentary to venture more than a tentative impression, it would appear that Joseph was also prepared to ease his predecessors' regime of religious persecution whenever greater toleration promised to benefit the monarchy's economy and treasury. This was certainly the case in Hungary, though far more than economic considerations were at stake there. In addition, Norbert Conrad has pointed to Joseph's restoration of Lutheran churches and religious freedom in Lower Silesia in accordance with the demands made by Charles XII of Sweden as an example of the emperor's departure from the confessional absolutism of the past century. Joseph not only abided by the religious provisions of his treaty with Charles after the latter's disastrous defeat at Poltava but also commissioned the construction of additional Lutheran churches near the Saxon frontier in order to keep would-be emigrants and Sunday churchgoers in Silesia and to attract several large loans and "free gifts" from the Lutheran estates. Given the emperor's desperate fiscal needs, these actions may not appear that remarkable. Nevertheless, Joseph's pragmatism represented an advance from the religious policies of his father, who had rejected similar projects just a few years before.[143] Moreover, it is certainly true that Joseph was more secular in his overall outlook and far more inclined to challenge the church's privileged position within the monarchy. He had amply demonstrated this even before his succession by taking the unprecedented step of including a Protestant nobleman among his attendants, by leading the intrigues against his father's Jesuit advisors, and by successfully lobbying for the seizure of church silver to help finance the war effort. After Leopold's death, Joseph went a step further by depriving the church of its control over political censorship.[144] Hence, as do his attempts at urbarial reform, Joseph's religious policies distance him from the conventions of past emperors and place him in the mainstream of the more pragmatic physiocratic initiatives of the late eighteenth century.

Although the brevity of Joseph's reign and the demands of war preempted any chance of implementing a coherent or extensive economic policy, the young emperor's accomplishments in reforming the monarchy's administration and reviving its finances cannot be overlooked. In the first weeks of the reign, he had chosen a ministry admirably suited for the tasks which confronted it. Retaining only those incumbent ministers who had exhibited great talents in the past, he replaced the faceless mediocrities of his father's cabinet with a circle of experienced and forceful advisors. Working under his direction and enjoying his firm support, these men and their staffs drew up the plans for administrative reforms and fiscal initiatives. Joseph never attended personally to the groundwork that went into the preparation of each of these projects. It suited neither his temperament nor his sense of responsibility. If he was indispensable in the fight for reform, it was not as a foot soldier wading sword in hand through the thick of battle, where his energies would be consumed and his greater perspectives lost, but rather as the overall commander, piecing together information given him by subordinates, making judgments, and directing his lieutenants to press the attack. In this capacity, Joseph served well. During his reign, he proved that, unlike his father, he was willing to accept the casualties of a vigorous assault—the initial confusion which each move caused in the ranks of the bureaucracy and the intensifying resistance which the estates offered against his onslaughts. Admittedly the emperor was compelled on occasion to relent whenever confusion within the administration or growing opposition from the estates threatened to defeat the overall objectives behind his reforms. Chaos within the bureaucracy or the intense hostility of the estates were two specters that could not be faced in a time of international crisis. Therefore, when confronted with these threats, Joseph often chose the expediency of a strategic retreat over the risks of a pyrrhic victory. The extent and complexity of the challenge were perhaps too great to be discharged during a six-year period of recurrent fiscal and military crises. Nevertheless, the record of these few years offered a sharp rebuke for past slumbers and a good omen for future progress.

III

Germany:
Blenheim Aftermath

*The imperial constitution is little respected and everyone acts
according to his own wishes.*
—Friedrich Karl Count Schönborn

Joseph's association with Germany began long before his succession as
Holy Roman emperor. As a child he grew up in the shadow of the
recurrent military crises and humiliations which afflicted the empire. In
the summer of 1683, he and his family were forced to flee Vienna
before the onrushing Turks. He was only six when, in the following
year, Louis XIV compelled his father to conclude a "twenty years'
truce" that recognized France's occupation of Alsace and Lorraine,
and barely ten when Louis broke the peace by sending his armies
across the Rhine and ordering the systematic devastation of the Palatinate. Following his election in 1690 as king of the Romans and heir to
the imperial throne, Joseph was obliged to celebrate his coronation at
Augsburg because the traditional site of Frankfurt was exposed to
attack by the French.

While the young Joseph was often compelled to share in the empire's
humiliation, he also experienced at first hand its successful attempt to
unite against the Turkish and French invaders. Many German princes
who had previously opposed the emperor politically and eagerly
sought alliances with his French and Swedish enemies now joined in
providing him with badly needed troops and money. Troops from the
empire comprised the largest allied contingent in the relief of Vienna
and played a major role in the subsequent reconquest of Hungary.
Indeed, Joseph's coronation as king of Hungary in December 1687
marked the triumph of German as well as Austrian arms and was
celebrated as such throughout the empire. Although the struggle
against powerful France was not nearly as successful, Germany stood
united here as well. As in Hungary, Joseph's coronation at Augsburg
represented a victory for German solidarity, for it marked the final
defeat of Louis XIV's plans to secure the imperial crown for his own

31

son. Joseph's election coincided with a great wave of anti-French feeling and national self-awareness that was then sweeping through the empire. Everywhere there was a revulsion against all things French as German writers who had once eagerly affected French customs now warned against France's cultural, as well as military supremacy and endeavored to develop a national consciousness of their own. Meanwhile pamphleteers both in Germany and the *Erblande* continued to advocate a common front against France, generally linking the fates of the Habsburg dynasty and the empire and often showing little distinction in their loyalties to both.[1] For the first time since before the Reformation, Germany appeared united against a foreign enemy.

Emperor Leopold, who had already banned the use of French in his presence, was careful to entrust his son's education to men who could instill in him the growing sense of national awareness. Like Prince Salm, Father Rummel was a native German and ardent patriot.[2] Nor was Joseph's "instructor in historicis et politicis," the Austrian scholar H. J. Wagner von Wagenfels, the man to overlook the dynasty's mission in Germany. His celebrated *Ehrenruff Teutschlands* called upon the empire to unite behind the crown and appealed for a revival of German national identity. So inflammatory was the book's criticism of French cultural and political arrogance, that its publication was delayed for several years out of fear that it would provoke Louis's displeasure.[3] Aside from these men, Joseph met many of the German princes who commanded the imperial forces fighting in Hungary, including Charles of Lorraine, Max Emanuel of Bavaria, Augustus the Strong of Saxony, and the great Louis William of Baden, to whom he became especially close. He also became a good friend of the elector palatine, John William, a *Reichspatriot* who, like Salm and Baden, was accustomed to witnessing the occupation of his possessions by French armies.

Even the great master of Austrian baroque architecture, Johann Bernhard Fischer von Erlach, fit in well with the circle of Joseph's friends and tutors. Appointed in 1689 to give the young heir daily instruction in his craft, Fischer soon won Wagner's acclaim as the first architect to supplant the previously dominant French and Italian forms with a distinctly German style. When Fischer did employ the motifs of his French counterparts, he did so in order to project Joseph as a German Sun King. The plans for the Schönbrunn Palace, which he drafted shortly after Joseph's coronation at Augsburg, clearly reflected his desire not only to emulate but to surpass the grandeur of Versailles; envisioned by Fischer as the principal residence of the German emperors and kings of Hungary, Schönbrunn represented a grandiose attempt to contest Louis XIV's place as Europe's most illustrious monarch.[4]

If Schönbrunn represented the latest example of Germany's continuing effort to redeem its self-respect in the face of France's cultural achievements and military conquests, it also served as a reminder of the essential futility of that quest. Although work on the palace began in 1696, the lack of funds immediately prompted a drastic reduction in the building plans and eventually brought construction to a virtual halt.[5] When in the following year, peace was finally concluded with Louis XIV, the empire failed to win back Alsace or to secure Lorraine's frontier against future French occupations.

In the face of setbacks such as these, it was not unnatural that Joseph should emerge from his early years with an almost insatiable hatred of France and a desire to vindicate the humiliations which the empire had suffered from Louis's aggressions. When the time came to find a bride, Joseph made it clear that he would never accept "a French wife or any other Latin . . . foreigner."[6] Louis XIV's ambassador to Vienna, Marshal Villars, reported with regret that the young Roman king was a "strong enemy of France" and would gladly lead his armies against it at the first opportunity.[7] Villars's prediction proved highly accurate when Charles II died a short time afterward. Replying to Elector John William's entreaties that he place himself at the head of the imperial army, Joseph wrote: "I despise the devilish French so strongly that I want nothing more than to teach them a lesson and show them what Austrian and imperial troops [*kaiserlichen und Reichstruppen*] can accomplish together."[8] As we have seen, Joseph twice received his father's permission to participate in the two successful sieges of Landau. On both occasions, Louis William of Baden retained the real direction of operations, while the Roman king's responsibilities were limited to boosting morale and guaranteeing by his presence that the emperor would not become delinquent in furnishing men and supplies for the siege.[9] Nevertheless, the enthusiasm with which Joseph received his charge and the preference which he expressed for service in Germany reflected his continuing close association with the empire.

With Leopold's death, Joseph's participation in German affairs evolved beyond the holding of largely ceremonial honors as commander of the imperial army and king of the Romans to the actual leadership of the empire. In view of his earlier experiences and education, the young emperor appeared admirably suited to the formidable task of directing the empire in its continuing struggle with France. Upon his succession, however, Joseph confronted political realities which forced him to reassess his relationship with the empire. Though he liked to visualize a Germany united against its enemies, the new emperor was now obliged to recognize that it was in reality little more than a loose and generally unruly association of largely independent states, held together solely by the chance coincidence of each prince's individual interests. Though he still remembered how the German princes had rallied to the defense of the empire in recent decades, he also recognized that they had acted more out of a widespread fear of foreign aggression than out of any genuine sense of patriotism or loyalty to the crown. Now that the defeat of Turkey and the recent victory over the French at Blenheim had greatly decreased the threat to Germany's security, the princes could be expected to react even more readily to the pull of particular interests away from the common goal of defending Germany and toward the pursuit of their own ambitions.

Of course, Joseph was not the first emperor to face the task of leading a divided *Reich*. For 250 years, the Habsburgs had confronted the concurrent problems of growing princely egocentrism and the declining power of the crown. They adjusted to the situation in two ways. First, they gradually abandoned hope of dealing with the empire as an organic entity and instead attempted to secure the princes' political support by catering to their individual interests. Second, having recognized the futility of sustaining a sense of princely patriotism and loyalty to the crown, they began to give a higher priority to their own dynastic interests and to pay less attention to the needs of the empire. In effect, the Habsburgs now perceived Germany more as a diplomatic combination, in which they needed to satisfy the interests of their allies while discreetly pursuing their own ends, than as a functioning political body. In assuming this stance, they had no realistic alternative.

The new emperor was no stranger to the policies of his predecessors. In his last years as Roman king, he had witnessed, and at times participated in, his father's negotiations with individual German princes; hence, he recognized the importance of servicing their interests. Similarly, under Wagner's tutelage, he had learned not only of the monarchy's "mission" in Germany but also of the contemporary theory and practice of *raison d'état;*[10] notwithstanding the ideals and fantasies of his youth and his genuine concern for the empire's welfare and security, Joseph appreciated the logic of favoring tangible dynastic advantages over the common goals of the empire. Consequently, when he succeeded to the throne, he had no intention of altering either the tactics or direction of his father's German policy.

Imperial Institutions: Habsburg versus Schönborn

Joseph's determination to pursue this course immediately brought him into conflict with the archbishop-elector of Mainz, Lothair Francis von Schönborn. As archchancellors of the empire, the Mainz electors presided over a number of imperial institutions, including the Regensburg Diet, the Imperial Court Chancery, and the Imperial Chamber Court, and generally regarded themselves as the guardians of the empire's ancient institutions. Elector Lothair Francis was no exception to this rule. As the nephew of Elector John Philip von Schönborn, he was especially cognizant of his responsibility to lead the empire's smaller states in preserving its constitutional integrity. Yet, because he recognized the divergence between dynastic and imperial interests,

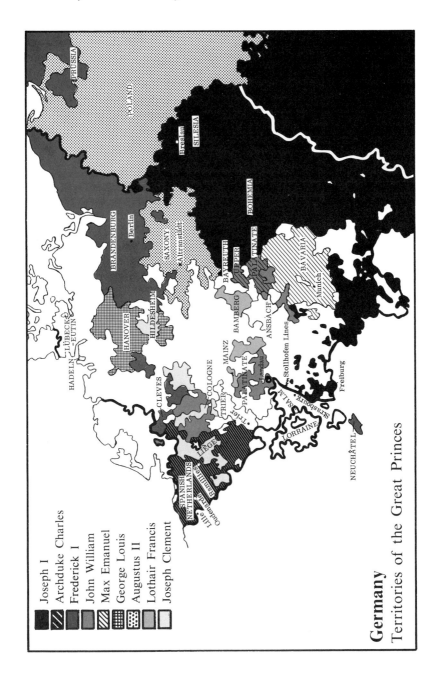

Germany
Territories of the Great Princes

Joseph I
Archduke Charles
Frederick I
John William
Max Emanuel
George Louis
Augustus II
Lothair Francis
Joseph Clement

Joseph was eager to usurp the archchancellor's prerogatives in order to facilitate the dispatch of Habsburg *Realpolitik.*

Joseph's first target was the Imperial Court Chancery, which had long been a source of friction between the crown and past archchancellors.[11] The chancery handled all imperial correspondence that passed to and from the monarch. Since the emperor directed all diplomacy in his capacity as ruler of Germany, this included not only communications with the institutions and princes of the empire but with foreign princes as well. At least technically, however, the chancery was not administered by the crown but was responsible to the archchancellor, who nominated an imperial vice-chancellor to represent him in Vienna and run the chancery in his absence.

In the waning months of his reign, Leopold had refused to confirm Lothair Francis's selection of his 21-year-old nephew, Friedrich Karl von Schönborn, as imperial vice-chancellor and had insisted on a candidate whose loyalty to the dynasty was unimpeachable.[12] Upon his succession, however, Joseph readily confirmed Friedrich Karl.[13] Moreover, in the formal notification that Joseph sent to Lothair Francis on 15 June, he promised that the new vice-chancellor would be entrusted with "the most important and secret affairs" of state.[14] Since past imperial vice-chancellors had been permanent members of the Privy and Aulic councils, this pledge could hardly have come as a surprise to the elector. Yet, since Schönborn was the representative and kinsman of the archchancellor, it was unreasonable to expect that he would inherit intact the power and influence enjoyed by his predecessors. Consequently, when he arrived in Vienna, Schönborn discovered that he had been excluded from membership in the new Privy Conference. He immediately protested his disenfranchisement and appealed to his uncle for assistance.[15] On 12 December the elector responded with a letter to Prince Salm, offering to provide the emperor with a regiment of dragoons for service in Hungary on condition that he elevate his nephew to the rank of privy councillor.[16] The persuasiveness of the elector's logic was irresistible. Although Joseph did not admit him to every Conference, he permitted the vice-chancellor to participate in any meetings relating in some way to the empire. In the following April, after definite commitments had been made for the dragoon regiment, Schönborn was formally raised to the rank of privy councillor.[17]

For the second time in less than a year, Joseph had bowed before Lothair Francis's wishes, albeit in exchange for certain concrete military advantages. Nevertheless, as he would so often do in the future, the emperor only permitted the archchancellor and his nephew the appearance of power, while denying them the substance. Friedrich Karl was still excluded from those Conferences that dealt with exclusively dynastic interests. Moreover, in those meetings which he was allowed to attend, he was virtually an outcast. Indeed, it is unlikely that even the vice-chancellor himself realized the full extent of his isolation within the ministry until he had gained admission to the Conference. His only advocates at court were the two German-born empresses. Vocal and often irrepressible, they remained until the end of the reign the only two figures who consistently backed him in his advocacy of imperial interests. On occasion they could count upon Prince Salm, to whom both women were related by marriage, to support their views within the Conference. However, Schönborn's hopes of cultivating the lord high steward as an ally were frustrated by the personal antipathy that arose between them.[18] In addition, the vice-chancellor soon discovered that long years of service to the emperor had inclined the prince to give Joseph's dynastic interests precedence over those of the empire. The same could also be said for the other two Germans on the Conference for imperial affairs, Baron Seilern and Aulic Council President Count Öttingen.

While he effectively curtailed Schönborn's participation and influence within the Privy Conference, Joseph also reduced drastically his administrative authority as imperial vice-chancellor. Even before Leopold's death, Count Sinzendorf had suggested that all diplomatic correspondence be transferred from the Imperial to the Austrian Chancery.[19] Joseph's appointment of Sinzendorf as Austrian chancellor for foreign affairs foreshadowed his intentions of seeing through this proposal. In October 1706 Sinzendorf submitted a more detailed outline of his ideas and the emperor ordered them carried out.[20] While the Imperial Chancery continued to handle communications with the German princes, its Austrian counterpart was now entrusted with the expedition of Joseph's foreign correspondence. On occasion when the empire's interests were clearly involved, a duplicate set of instructions or credentials was dispatched through the Imperial Chancery. In addition, because Joseph did not wish to lose the precedence that the imperial title gave him in his dealings with foreign princes, Schönborn was still instructed to sign and apply the seal of the Imperial Chancery to documents that were being presented to foreign diplomats or ministers. Yet, since he did not handle the correspondence with these princes and was not privy to the deliberations of the other Conferences, the vice-chancellor was often unaware of these policies, even though he was expediting them in the name of the empire.[21] Despite his protests, however, Friedrich Karl was unable to prevent Joseph from stripping the Imperial Chancery of much of its former power and responsibility.

Joseph also achieved success in his struggle with Lothair Francis for control of the imperial judiciary. The emperor's key weapon in this contest was the Imperial Aulic Council (*Reichshofrat*), another institution whose history reflected the long-standing constitutional rivalry between the crown and the German estates. Since the estates controlled the older Imperial Chamber Court (*Reichskammergericht*), the Habsburgs had long cultivated the growth of their own Aulic Council, especially because its judicial authority gave them the power to bribe or blackmail those princes who were involved in the empire's many territorial and constitutional disputes.[22] After reforming its organization during his first year as emperor, Joseph greatly expanded the Aulic Council's operations, making it his most effective instrument for negotiating with and intervening in the affairs of his German vassals.[23] Since the Chamber Court had not met since 1704, due to personal and religious conflicts among its judges, the Aulic Council was even able to examine cases which were rightfully the domain of the Chamber Court and which, in some instances, had already been deliberated by it. Moreover, in an effort to keep the Chamber Court inactive Joseph secretly encouraged its Protestant minority in their disruptive personal attacks on the Court's Catholic leadership.[24] Led by Lothair Francis, the Imperial Diet remonstrated in vain against the Aulic Council's usurpations. Meanwhile, in Vienna the vice-chancellor supported his uncle's position, even though he himself was extremely active in the council's work. Nevertheless, Schönborn's efforts were sabotaged by his two colleagues on both the German Conference and Aulic Council, Öttingen and Seilern, as well as by Consbruch, his own secretary. Only in January 1711, after a gap of nearly seven years and less than three months before the end of the reign, did the Chamber Court resume its operations and put an end to the judicial piracy of the Aulic Council.[25]

By permanently broadening the competency of the Austrian Chancery and at least temporarily expanding the operations of the Aulic Council, Joseph strengthened his political position within the empire. Control of its only functioning judicial authority afforded him considerable leverage with those German princes who either sought or feared the legal intervention of the crown. Meanwhile, the demotion of the Imperial Chancery greatly facilitated his efforts to exclude what he obviously regarded as the foreign presence of Lothair Francis and his nephew from the center of the government. In seeking to consolidate the slender reins of imperial power in his own hands and in distinguishing between German and Austrian interests, Joseph was following in the direction of his predecessors. In his six years as emperor, he would never stray from that path.

Joseph's *Volte Face*

Joseph's most pressing responsibility as Holy Roman emperor was to sustain Germany's military effort against France. As we have seen, he had already assumed an active role in his last years as Roman king, both as titular commander of the imperial forces before Landau and as the young court's spokesman for a joint Anglo-Austrian offensive against Bavaria. As Max Emanuel and the shattered remnants of the Franco-Bavarian army retreated across the Rhine in the weeks after Blenheim, Joseph could contemplate for the first time the launching of a major attack against France itself.

Though he was initially enthusiastic about the prospects of carrying the war into Alsace and Lorraine, where the empire could regain some of its lost territories and strengthen its western frontier, Joseph was destined never to achieve this objective. One major reason for this failure was the inadequate military support provided by the German princes, many of whom had higher priorities than the reconquest of Alsace. As a rule only the smaller principalities of the so-called Nördlingen Association regularly sent full contingents to the imperial army, principally because their greater exposure to French aggression impelled them to fight for the conquest of a strong *Reichsbarriere* on the empire's western frontier. By contrast most of the larger states of northern Germany never met the troop quotas stipulated by the Imperial Diet, often because they preferred to enlist their forces in the Anglo-Dutch army in Belgium in exchange for the payment of an annual subsidy. Moreover, Hanover's forces served in Anglo-Dutch pay not only because of the attractive financial terms but also because Elector George Louis was eager to strengthen his position in England as Queen Anne's heir. Meanwhile, Augustus the Strong of Saxony never provided a full *Reichskontingent* because, as king of Poland, he was already committed to the pursuit of more critical dynastic ambitions in the Northern War with Charles XII of Sweden. Although Brandenburg-Prussia did provide a corps of 12,000 troops during the war's early years, Joseph soon discovered that he could keep them committed only by acceding to a steady stream of financial and territorial demands.[26]

Equally important, however, was the emperor's own reassessment of the monarchy's military priorities in the aftermath of Blenheim. In the months prior to the battle, Max Emanuel's forces controlled most of southern Germany and threatened the *Erblande* themselves; hence, the survival of both the Habsburg monarchy and the empire as belligerents in the war against Louis XIV necessitated a concerted effort to halt the Franco-Bavarian offensive. Following the allied victory, however, the western approaches to the Erblande and Germany itself were secured. The German front lost the top priority it had enjoyed during the crisis year of 1704 and was obliged once again to compete with the Italian and Hungarian theaters for the limited resources at the monarchy's command. In this competition, it could fare only third best. Since the imperial army was already operating on French soil, its needs were clearly less crucial than those of the currently hard pressed Austrian forces in Italy and Hungary. Furthermore, as highly as he prized the empire's prospective conquests in Alsace, Joseph could not place them ahead of the monarchy's immediate national and dynastic objectives on these other fronts. Consequently, on each occasion that he balanced the merits of launching an offensive in Alsace or Lorraine against reinforcing his forces in Italy and Hungary—and later on in Spain and Belgium—Joseph found them insufficient to commit the major share of the monarchy's military might.

At first Joseph appeared willing to focus his attention on the German front. At the close of 1704, he helped lay the diplomatic groundwork for the invasion of Alsace in the following spring. While attending the second siege of Landau, he used his camp at nearby Ilbesheim to negotiate with Max Emanuel's representatives for the surrender and occupation of Bavaria. Early in the war, Joseph had violently objected to meeting the extravagant terms that Max Emanuel had demanded in exchange for his neutrality. Again, during the dark months before Blenheim, he had led the young court in steadfastly opposing any attempt to reach an accommodation with the then triumphant elector, preferring instead to "bring him to reason by force—and to be there in person."[27] Though his father had not permitted him to participate in the Blenheim campaign and though he entrusted the actual negotiations to the more experienced hands of Wratislaw, Sinzendorf, and his own chamberlain, Johann Leopold von Trautson, Joseph now had the satisfaction of presiding over the formal capitulation which was signed in his name on 7 November.[28] By providing for the surrender of the numerous Bavarian strongholds still in Max Emanuel's possession, the Ilbesheim convention permitted the emperor to dispense with the need for lengthy siege operations and to mass all available forces on the French frontier.

From his camp at Ilbesheim, Joseph also helped arrange for the continued military cooperation of Prussia, whose participation was crucial to the success of the coming campaign. The negotiations with the agents of King Frederick I proved difficult, however. Although Leopold had already bestowed on Frederick the royal title of *König in Preussen* and secured his admission as a sovereign and equal member of the Grand Alliance, he had been unable to discharge other financial commitments which Frederick had also demanded as his price for entering the war, including the emperor's promise to pay an annual subsidy of 150,000 florins and to provide winter quarters for Frederick's troops. In addition, though Leopold had agreed to entrust Frederick with Spanish Guelders (as security for outstanding Spanish Habsburg debts) and to support his claim to the German possessions of the childless William III of Orange, the emperor had failed to prevent the Dutch from occupying each of these territories.[29] At first the king had fulfilled most of his military obligations to the alliance, appreciating as he did the emperor's desperate financial position and the common interest in defeating the French. In fact, in 1703 he granted Leopold a two million florin loan and, at the beginning of the following year, offered the emperor 14,000 additional troops to help stem the Franco-Bavarian offensive in southern Germany.[30] Frederick's perspectives had changed, however, following the victory at Blenheim. With Bavaria's occupation imminent, the emperor now had access to a new source of income. Moreover, should the emperor still refuse to meet his treaty obligations, Frederick could now safely withdraw his 12,000 men from the imperial army and commit them to the Northern War, where he might win territorial advantages comparable to those being denied him in the west. Following Leopold's instructions, Joseph not only acceded to Frederick's demands for winter quarters for his troops but also joined Prince Eugene and Wratislaw in visiting the duke of Marlborough, whose army was covering the siege of Landau, to enlist his aid in keeping Prussia tied to the Grand Alliance.[31] The stratagem was well conceived. Marlborough shared not only Vienna's concern for Frederick's continued loyalty but also its hope that the king might send troops to Italy, where the duke of Savoy was in danger of capitulating to the French.[32] In the end, Joseph and his cohorts persuaded Marlborough to undertake his famous Berlin embassy, during which the English generalissimo secured Prussia's military commitment by pledging English support for Frederick's remaining fiscal and territorial demands and by providing for the dispatch of 8,000 Prussians to Italy with Anglo-Dutch, rather than *Hofkammer* subsidies.[33]

At the onset of the 1705 campaign Joseph cooperated closely with Marlborough in executing the duke's plan for joint allied operations against France. Marlborough's strategy called for Louis William to position the imperial army on the Rhine west bank near the Alsatian frontier while he proceeded up the Mosel River into Lorraine. The duke had chosen the Mosel Valley for his offensive because it was at this point in the frontier that there were the fewest fortresses protecting France and obstructing the road to Paris. More formidable than these were the political obstacles that blocked Marlborough's path. Since the massing of troops on the Mosel would dangerously weaken the residual Anglo-Dutch army guarding the United Provinces, it was essential that he quickly grab the initiative by stealing an early march on the French with an overwhelming force. Toward this end, he requested reinforcements from the margrave's army, including all 12,000 Prussians, which were to join Prussian mercenaries already serving in Marlborough's army to form a united corps of 20,000 men. Leopold frustrated these dispositions, however, because he feared that the formation of such a force would inspire Prussian pretensions to a special military position in the empire.[34] More ominous yet was the opposition of Louis William. Though he had rightly gained a reputation as one of Germany's most able generals, the fifty-year-old margrave was at least as difficult to deal with as an ally and colleague as he was as an opposing general. Stubborn and proud he was often driven by a concern for his own reputation and jealousy of his fellow commanders. In 1704 he had strongly opposed and resented the march of Eugene and Marlborough to the Danube, while he was being relegated to an insignificant defensive role on the Rhine frontier.[35] Now, in the spring of 1705, he was determined to prevent Marlborough from placing him in another supporting role. Hence, he resisted the duke's request for additional reinforcements and, instead, advocated retaining a closer balance between the size of the two armies that would permit the launching of a joint offensive into France.

Fearing that Louis William was planning to obstruct his Mosel strategy, the duke wrote twice to Wratislaw in Vienna asking him to secure Joseph's help in gaining the margrave's cooperation.[36] At the time of this appeal, Marlborough was unaware that Joseph had assumed control of the government. Instead, he was seeking the Roman king's intervention out of knowledge of his vocal support for the Mosel plan and his longstanding friendship with the irascible margrave. Nevertheless, when his letters finally reached Vienna, Joseph had already succeeded to the throne and was presumably in the position to reverse his father's policy and force Baden's compliance with Marlborough's wishes. In fact, Joseph was determined to do just that. He was eager to please the duke, whom he not only admired as a great military leader but whom he was already beginning to regard as a faithful guardian of the monarchy's interests. Moreover, he valued the presence of an Anglo-Dutch army on Germany's western frontier, where it could win territorial advantages for the empire at little cost to the *Hofkammer*. He had already approved Marlborough's project at the end of April, soon after replacing his dying father at the head of the government.[37] Now, on 9 May he responded to the duke's latest request by writing Louis William instructing him to cooperate fully with Marlborough's operations on the Mosel.[38] For some time, Joseph received no reply from his imperial commander. When word finally arrived, the margrave limited himself to prophesying the failure of the Mosel offensive and made no mention of his having transferred the prescribed forces to Marlborough's command.[39] Though the emperor dispatched fresh instructions to Louis William, repeating the order to reinforce the duke's army, the time for decisive action had already passed. Citing poor weather, supply problems, and increased French activity on his own front, Baden had passed over Marlborough's impatient pleas for troop transfers from the imperial army.[40] Meanwhile, the duke was also being frustrated by the late arrival of the Prussians, who had not known until recently that they would be forming on the Mosel, and the Dutch, who were holding back some troops in order to meet increasing French pressure on their own front.[41]

In mid-June with only 50,000 British and Dutch under his command instead of the 90,000 allied troops on which he had planned, the duke decided to scrap his Mosel project.[42] On the eighteenth he wrote Joseph informing him that he was breaking up the army. He sent most of the Prussian corps, which had just arrived the day before, to join the margrave, while marching with the rest of the army to the assistance of the hard-pressed Dutch.[43] Marlborough's vanity would not permit him to accept responsibility for the Mosel fiasco. Before breaking camp, he sent a trumpeter to the enemy lines with a remarkable message for the French commander on the Mosel, Marshal Villars: "I regret that the Prince of Baden has broken his word and that I can only hold him responsible for frustrating all our plans."[44] When word reached Vienna two weeks later of the breakup of Marlborough's army, the emperor made a belated effort to keep alive the possibility of a resumption of allied operations on the Mosel later on in the campaign. While appealing to the duke to consider reviving his plan, Joseph dispatched a circular letter and later an emissary to the Rhenish princes to drum up support for sending additional men and supplies there.[45] In fact, despite his exasperation and bitterness, the duke had still not given up on the idea of returning to the Mosel in August, once the Dutch had been sufficiently attended to.[46] A few weeks later, however, the incompetent palatine commander of Trier dealt these hopes a final blow by abandoning the city and putting to the torch the huge store of munitions that Marlborough had left there.[47]

If the English and Dutch were dismayed and angered by Louis William's behavior, all Germany was deeply mortified by it. In Berlin the Prussian king wrote his wife, "It is a disgrace that we must rely on foreigners to save Germany." In his frustration, he ordered his 12,000-man contingent not to rejoin the margrave's command in Alsace but to proceed instead to the Anglo-Dutch army in Belgium.[48] Although Frederick was eventually persuaded to rescind this order, Elector John William went ahead with plans to transfer his small imperial contingent to Marlborough's command. With his dominions now secure from French attack, he enlisted it in the English army in exchange for an annual subsidy.[49]

Realizing that its allies were holding it responsible for Baden's misconduct, Vienna fumbled to justify his inaction.[50] Privately, however, the attitude of Joseph and his ministers was one of anger and frustration. Louis William had not only discredited the empire as an ally of the maritime powers but had aborted an excellent opportunity to enlist their military support in regaining Alsace and the rest of Lorraine. Despite Marlborough's pleas that he be dismissed or transferred to another command "anywhere but the Rhine," Joseph could not afford to replace the margrave because of the reputation and considerable influence which he still enjoyed among the small princes of the Nördlingen Association.[51] He could, however, strip him of much of the military power he had wasted so disgracefully during the spring.

The emperor presently had ample reason to reconsider his commitment to the imperial war effort. In July he had begun receiving urgent pleas for help from Prince Eugene. Arguing that the collapse of operations on the Mosel had permitted the French to dispatch strong reinforcements to their army in Italy, Eugene urged the emperor to offset this threat by sending him Austrian troops currently serving with the imperial army.[52] Upon receiving the prince's pleas, Joseph wrote to the margrave repeating this argument and predicting that it might become necessary to transfer forces from his command to the Italian front.[53] For the moment, however, Joseph was reluctant to weaken his forces in Alsace. Since the beginning of the war, Vienna had been very sensitive to criticism from its allies that the Austrian contingent with the imperial army was understrength. Joseph had, in fact, endeavored to fill his quota and during June had proudly pointed out to his allies that the Austrian forces on the Rhine and Mosel totalled nearly 28,700, or only 1,300 short of the prescribed level.[54] To transfer Austrian troops south would once again make Vienna vulnerable to Anglo-Dutch criticism and would also invite the other German princes to remain or become delinquent in filling their own contingents. Nevertheless, the emperor recognized that the need to succor Prince Eugene clearly outweighed whatever claim the margrave could still make on the monarchy's resources. Consequently, beginning in the summer of 1705, Joseph redirected his attention and the flow of men and materiel southward from the Upper Rhine to the banks of the Adige.

Rather than weaken his imperial contingent, Joseph first attempted to strengthen Eugene's army by raising fresh troops and taxes in occupied Bavaria. The electorate was hardly in the position to bear these new burdens. Two years of heavy taxation under Max Emanuel and new levies recently introduced by Leopold and Joseph had destroyed the population's ability and willingness to pay, and had already given rise to widespread unrest.[55] Nevertheless, the emperor responded to Eugene's latest pleas by assessing new taxes and instituting compulsory recruiting throughout the electorate.[56] Under Prince Eugene's direction, the *Hofkriegsrat* also began funneling the proceeds from the various taxes already in existence to the army in Italy. Joseph's measures violated the mandate of the Regensburg Diet, which had awarded his father the administration of Bavaria with the understanding that its wealth would be used to maintain the electorate's quota to the imperial army. To preserve some semblance of legality, the *Hofkriegsrat*'s recruiting order specified that the 3,000 troops being raised would form part of the electorate's imperial contingent, even though they were intended for service in Italy.[57] Sensing the growing unrest that the recruiting order was causing throughout Bavaria, Count Löwenstein's civil administration appealed to the *Hofkriegsrat* to repeal the order. The *Hofkriegsrat* not only rejected the governor's petition but soon doubled the quota of recruits to 6,000 men.[58] At the same time, Eugene wrote Löwenstein from Italy instructing him to deliver these reinforcements as soon as possible.[59] The governor achieved no better success in his appeals to Joseph, who shared Eugene's opinion that the growing unrest in Bavaria was a price that would have to be paid if the needed succor was to be sent to Italy. In a 16 September letter to Löwenstein, he also refused a request that soldiers no longer be quartered on the population, asserting that the measure was a necessary one and that the only thing that could be done would be to enforce discipline more strictly among the troops.[60]

Meanwhile, news from Italy of Eugene's defeat at Cassano finally moved Joseph to divert some of his forces from the imperial army. Advising the margrave to halt further offensive action, he ordered the dispatch of several Austrian battalions from Alsace.[61] Since he was presently engaged in siege operations, Baden treated Joseph's command in the same fashion as those he had received during the Mosel offensive. Failing to get confirmation from him, the emperor angrily dashed off three more letters repeating his earlier instructions.[62] Only after the fall of Drusenheim on 24 September did the margrave acknowledge Joseph's orders—by pleading with him to rescind them.[63] Finally, on 5 October when the fall of the Alsatian town of Haguenau seemed imminent, the imperial commander notified Vienna that he was complying with its wishes.[64] To justify these withdrawals, Joseph instructed his ministers to petition the Imperial Diet for a resolution declaring the campaign in northern Italy a *Reichskrieg*. If the diet would be so accommodating as to expand this declaration to include Hungary as well, they were even empowered to promise Joseph's personal participation in the 1706 campaign.[65] This dramatic offer notwithstanding, the young emperor was now committed to new military priorities that placed the empire's interests clearly behind those of his own dynasty.

Joseph's *volte face* was equally evident from the stance that he now assumed toward the king of Prussia. Although he had worked hard during the previous autumn to keep Prussian troops committed to the imperial army, Joseph had always shared his father's reluctance to meet each of Frederick's financial and territorial demands, which threatened to place a heavy burden on the *Hofkammer* and further strengthen Prussia's position as the second largest and most powerful state in the empire. Joseph had already come to regret the bestowal of the royal title on Prussia and its subsequent admission to the Grand Alliance, realizing that they had inspired Frederick's pretensions to full equality with Europe's other crowned heads and destroyed what remained of the lord-vassal relationship between Vienna and Berlin.[66] Nevertheless, he had continued to bend before Frederick's demands lest Prussia follow Max Emanuel's lead in deserting the empire or, at the very least, join Augustus in the Northern War. Now, however, he had less reason to appease his most dangerous vassal. Although the Prussian troops in Italy formed a vital part of Prince Eugene's army, their presence was guaranteed by Anglo-Dutch subsidies rather than by Vienna's goodwill. Meanwhile, the front in Alsace hardly seemed worth the sacrifice of additional concessions. Consequently, since the failure of the Mosel offensive, Joseph had turned a deaf ear to Frederick's latest demands. By September these had grown to include not only the delivery of the unpaid subsidies and the renewal of the Prussian army's quartering privileges but also Joseph's formal recognition of Frederick's claims to the succession in the Franconian duchies of Ansbach and Bayreuth. In meetings with the emperor and his ministers, Count Bartholdi warned that his master would withdraw his Italian corps and sever relations unless these terms were met. Nevertheless, once he had received word that the maritime powers had agreed to continue support for Frederick's Italian corps, Joseph formally rejected Bartholdi's demands, secure in the knowledge that Frederick would never renounce a second year of huge Anglo-Dutch subsidies.[67] In fact, he had judged correctly. Upon receiving word of Vienna's refusal, Frederick made no move to withdraw his Italian corps; instead he ordered his 12,000 troops in Alsace to go into winter quarters.[68]

The recall of the Prussian imperial contingent coincided with the duke of Marlborough's arrival at court. The duke had come to Vienna, however, not to discuss Frederick's wavering commitment in Alsace but in response to Joseph's insistent pleas for additional Anglo-Dutch support in Italy.[69] Consequently, while the two men did dwell on the next campaign in Alsace and tentatively agreed to revive Marlborough's ill-fated Mosel strategy, the great bulk of his two-week stay was devoted to preparations for Prince Eugene's projected relief of Victor Amadeus's beleaguered forces.[70] Similarly, when Marlborough journeyed on to Berlin at the end of November to renew the November 1704 troop convention, it was the Prussian corps in Italy rather than the one in Alsace that was uppermost in his mind.[71] As expected Frederick was more than willing to extend the treaty for another year. Meanwhile the question of the king's commitment to the imperial army was never discussed. As the duke explained afterward in letters to Schönborn and Sinzendorf, he elected not to bring up the delicate subject in view of "the mood in which I found the king."[72]

For the while, Frederick's recall of the Prussian imperial contingent had only a minimal effect on the conduct of the war. It did force the margrave to halt operations against the Alsatian town of Homburg, which he had besieged despite the recent Austrian troop transfers to Italy, and compel him to withdraw his army into winter quarters. With the campaigning season coming to a close, however, Baden would have soon retired anyway. Meanwhile a far greater need for these forces had arisen in nearby Bavaria where the peasantry had at long last risen in revolt. The rebellion was a classic peasant uprising wholly without support from other social groups and without a well-articulated patriotic or political appeal.[73] Nevertheless, Joseph initially underestimated its following among the peasants and reacted to the first reports of disturbances merely by instructing Löwenstein to suppress them and press on with the recruiting.[74] Only after they had spread through most of eastern Bavaria and the Upper Palatinate did he adopt a different strategy. Joseph met with a delegation from the Bavarian estates to whom he expressed the wish to "adjust partially" the taxation and recruiting policies he had followed to date, and he instructed Löwenstein to hold further talks with them in an attempt to find a less abrasive method of dealing with the peasantry.[75] Meanwhile, he dispatched an emissary with the power to make "moderate and moving representations" to the rebels and extend an amnesty offer to all but the leaders of the insurrection and former army officers.[76] While Joseph hoped that these efforts at conciliation might help pacify the rebels, he was also willing to use force to end the insurrection. In an 18 November Conference, however, the emperor expressed the fear that the barely 7,000 troops presently stationed in Bavaria would not be able to accomplish the job by themselves, and thus concluded that it would be foolish to take action against the rebels until he could be sure that they could be totally suppressed by the military. Otherwise, public outrage would only intensify and the rebellion would spread to other parts of the electorate.[77] Consequently, while he was extending the olive branch to the rebels, Joseph also summoned reinforcements from the retiring imperial army as well as from neighboring Bohemia.[78] In the end the rebellion was indeed settled by the sword with the massacre on Christmas Day of an attacking force of 2,000-3,000 peasants just outside the Munich city walls.[79] Upon hearing news of the slaughter, many peasants took advantage of Joseph's offer of amnesty and returned to their homes. Moreover, as the rebel ranks started to diminish, the Austrian garrisons were being reinforced by approximately 12,000 men from the imperial army and the *Erblande,* as well as by several thousand additional troops passing through the electorate on their way to Italy.[80] In most cases their help was neither needed nor summoned. With the destruction of the last rebel army at Aidenbach on 8 January the rebellion came to an end.

No serious repression or recriminations followed in the aftermath of the revolt. After they had been captured, virtually none of the peasant leaders were executed but were instead given fines or short prison terms.[81] Moreover, in the ensuing months, Joseph made good his pledge to moderate his policies. He abolished compulsory recruiting, clearly the principal and immediate cause of the insurrection.[82] He also ordered severe punishment for soldiers who committed crimes against the local populace and even attempted to pay compensation for the past indulgences of the imperial troops quartered in the electorate.[83] Finally, the emperor began to consult with the Bavarian estates and acceded to their wishes that taxes be lowered to reflect the steadily diminishing resources of the country's peasantry.[84] Considering the harshness with which most peasant uprisings were put down during this period, Joseph's policy of appeasement was most remarkable. Yet, it should be kept in mind that he pursued this course solely out of fear that another revolt might someday break out in the electorate. He realized that the recent insurrection could have become considerably more difficult to suppress and might have even spread into his own hard-pressed dominions.[85] Indeed, had it received wider support or occurred at a different time of year, the revolt could have led to a reopening of the Bavarian front. Instead, it was put down by troops already stationed in Bavaria or routinely returning from the front for winter quarters and had no measurable effect on the past or future campaign.

With the suppression of the Bavarian peasants' revolt, operations in the empire came to a close. From a strictly military standpoint, the 1705 campaign in Germany was anticlimactic, especially when compared to the dramatic events of the previous year. It did, however, complete a catharsis in the political outlook of the new emperor that makes it crucial to an understanding of his German policy. By abusing his mandate over occupied Bavaria and his command over the imperial army in Alsace to reinforce his forces in Italy, and by risking the indispensable military support of his most powerful vassal, Joseph had in the space of six short months eschewed the fresh image of the fiercely patriotic Roman king and assumed the old face of past Habsburg emperors. It was only inevitable that he refocus his attention on purely dynastic concerns once he had succeeded his father as ruler of the sprawling Habsburg dominions. Moreover, the shift in priorities was not without its merits, given the desperate situation in Italy and the relative security of post-Blenheim Germany. To a large extent, however, Joseph was prompted in his actions by the exasperations of the past campaign. From his good friend and mentor Louis William of Baden, he had gained some compelling insights into the limitations of the imperial army and of his own authority as emperor. He would not serve another year in the margrave's apprenticeship.

Paying the Price

As yet Joseph had little reason to regret his new course. Though he had given the highest priority to the war effort in Italy, the impact on Germany had been minimal. The transfer of Austrian troops to the peninsula had not upset Louis William's offensive operations if only because the French, who were still recovering from their losses at Blenheim, had committed the bulk of their forces against Marlborough's army and had left Alsace weakly defended. Nor had the sudden withdrawal of the Prussian imperial contingent or the outbreak of the Bavarian peasants' revolt seriously jeopardized Louis William's position, coming as they did at the end of the campaigning season. It was only a matter of time, however, before the French would be able to take advantage of the weakening of the imperial army. In fact, the year 1706 marked an end to Germany's successes against Louis XIV and the resumption of the failures and frustrations through which it had suffered for half a century.

Ironically 1706 is perhaps best remembered in German history as the year of the imperial ban, when Joseph I triumphantly pronounced the empire's formal judgment against the renegade Wittelsbach Electors Max Emanuel and Joseph Clement of Cologne. On the surface, the emperor's action, which stripped the two electors of their princely rights and privileges, stands out as one of the last demonstrations of German unity and central imperial authority before the cataclysm of 1740. In fact, a closer examination of the process against Max Emanuel and Joseph Clement merely underscores the impotence of the crown in the face of the intense rivalries and ambitions of the more powerful imperial princes.

The moving force behind the proclamation of the ban was not Joseph but Elector John William, who hoped to regain possession of the Upper Palatinate, which had been transferred to Bavaria after the banning of the palatine elector, Frederick V, during the Thirty Years' War. Of course, Joseph had his own reasons for cooperating with John William. He welcomed the opportunity to punish the two electors for having broken the peace of the empire and openly allied with its enemies. He also recognized the need to reward his good friend John William for his valuable diplomatic support during the last years of peace, when he had actively assisted Emperor Leopold in securing the loyalty of the Nördlingen Association and several of Germany's armed estates. In addition, however, Joseph secretly hoped to profit from the judgment against Max Emanuel by annexing the rest of Bavaria to the *Erblande.*

Before Joseph could place Max Emanuel and Joseph Clement under the ban of the empire, he needed the consent of the Electoral College. Given the nature of imperial politics, however, this was not only a step that had to be taken but an obstacle that needed to be overcome. In fact, Prussia had decided to use the proceedings to advance its own interests. As early as 1703, Frederick had approached Max Emanuel with an offer to frustrate any judgment against him in exchange for French recognition of the Prussian royal crown. Soon afterward, Frederick let it be known in Vienna that he would vote for the ban, but only after he had received compensation for John William's impending acquisition of the Upper Palatinate either in Bavaria or from among the elector palatine's holdings on the Lower Rhine.[86] To strengthen his position in the Electoral College, he secured the support of Augustus the Strong, who was still hoping for Prussian support in the Northern War. John William duly opened negotiations with Frederick. Yet, when he refused to comply with the king's latest demand—freedom of worship for all of his Calvinist subjects—the talks reached an impasse.[87]

Since it was not legally necessary for him to convene a formal meeting of the Electoral College and since a majority of its membership had already given its consent, Joseph could have pronounced the verdict against the two Wittelsbachs without further delay. Nevertheless, he was convinced that if the judgment against Bavaria and Cologne were to be recognized throughout Germany, a unanimous declaration of the six remaining electors would be necessary.[88] Instead he attempted to persuade Prussia and Saxony to drop their insistence on freedom of worship for John William's Calvinist subjects. It was not difficult for Joseph to secure the defection of Augustus, who had since despaired of receiving Prussian assistance against Sweden. Frederick proved more obstinate, however; when the Electoral College assembled on 5 June, the Prussian delegate frustrated his colleagues by refusing to vote on the question.[89] Four months passed without any break in the deadlock. Only on 21 November, after John William had capitulated to Berlin's demand for freedom of worship for his Calvinist subjects, did Frederick finally agree to vote for the ban. When the Electoral College met six days later, the vote against Max Emanuel and Joseph Clement was unanimous.

Since the entire process had been conducted in secrecy, it still remained for the emperor to announce publicly their conviction. Although he delayed for five months until the Bavarian revolt had been completely suppressed, Joseph pronounced judgment on 29 April. The declaration stripped both electors of their rights and privileges. It made no mention of any permanent or territorial adjustments, however, since these dispositions were to be made later in consultation with the remaining electors. In placing Max Emanuel and Joseph Clement under the ban, Joseph intended to enhance his own prestige as emperor. The ceremony itself—during which he destroyed the electors' investiture patents and heralds and threw them out the window—was carried out with great pageantry and described by Swedish Ambassador Strahlenheim as "the most overwhelming I have ever seen." Meanwhile, the imperial declaration distributed throughout the empire carried Joseph's name only and made no mention of the participation and requisite approval of the "disinterested" electors.[90] Yet, if the last ban to be issued in the empire's history bore Joseph's seal, it did not bear his stamp. He had neither instigated nor concluded the diplomacy which had made these judgments possible. Instead, he had merely responded cautiously to the initiatives of one elector and paused helplessly before the obstructionism of another until a suitable political settlement could be negotiated.

While Joseph was trying, however unsuccessfully, to resolve John William's conflict with Frederick, his own dispute with the Prussian king over the payment of past subsidies and the provision of winter quarters continued to strain relations between Vienna and Berlin. Yet, whereas the question of Max Emanuel's fate and the disposition of the Bavarian patrimony could be postponed until another season, the matter of the empire's military preparedness was of immediate importance. During the winter, the Dutch had vetoed Marlborough's plan for another joint allied offensive on the Mosel, thereby frustrating any chance for an invasion of Lorraine and leaving Louis William's imperial army with the sole responsibility for protecting the newly won territories in Alsace.[91] Hence, if Joseph were to escape the consequences of his Italian policy, it was crucial that he compensate for his own slackening military commitment to the empire by securing the return of the Prussian imperial contingent. Nevertheless, although Frederick attempted to soften the emperor's position by announcing that he had been "secretly" negotiating with the French, Joseph continued to reject Berlin's demands.[92] Seeing no other way of forcing Joseph's hand, Frederick now played his last and highest trump, by announcing that the worsening situation in the east required that he recall his forces from the Rhine.[93] At first the emperor and his ministers refused to be intimidated. They were still confident that Berlin was merely bluffing and could be made to lower its demands. Only on 30 March, with the beginning of the 1706 campaign just weeks away, did the Conference agree to meet the king's most immediate demand for 200,000 florins "on condition that Frederick furnish his imperial contingent and send it to the Upper Rhine." On the following day, Joseph wrote a letter to Frederick in his own hand, announcing his decision to deliver the sum and appealing warmly to the king's loyalty to the empire to provide the Prussian *Reichskontingent*. At the same time, in a conversation with Bartholdi, Sinzendorf hinted at the possibility of a closer alliance between Berlin and Vienna and offered to discuss the idea with Frederick during the Prussian king's next visit to the Bohemian spa of Carlsbad.[94]

Joseph and his ministers were disappointed at having failed to reduce the price for Prussia's continued presence on the Upper Rhine. Having finally capitulated, however, they now expected no further difficulties in securing the return of the 12,000 Prussians for the 1706 campaign. To their dismay, Berlin still had further demands to make. On 15 April Bartholdi announced that his master would send his 12,000-man contingent to the front only if it were permitted to operate on the Mosel in conjunction with 5,000 Prussian mercenaries currently serving in Dutch pay. It would not be dispatched to Alsace unless Vienna agreed to make additional financial and territorial concessions. This announcement was followed several days later by a message from Berlin reporting that Frederick was marching his forces away from the margrave's army to the Prussian duchy of Cleves on the Lower Rhine. To justify this action, Frederick cited once again the growing menace from Sweden.[95] There was now little Joseph could do to retrieve the Prussian corps for service with the imperial army. Even if he were willing to concede to Frederick's latest demands, it would take over a month for the Prussian troops to cover the 400 miles between Cleves and Alsace. The only remaining solution was to work for a revival of the Mosel strategy, despite the certain opposition of the Dutch. Following a 27 April Conference, Joseph decided to deliver the 200,000 florins to Berlin despite Frederick's trickery, in the hope that he would fulfill his alliance obligations.[96] On the following day, Salm wrote to the duke of Marlborough acquainting him with the situation and appealing to him to reassemble an army on the Mosel.[97]

Before he could intervene, however, disaster struck the imperial army. In the first week of May, a strongly reinforced French army under Marshal Villars fell upon the unsuspecting and heavily outnumbered margrave. Within a few days, Baden was forced to retreat hurriedly across the Rhine, abandoning his Alsatian conquests of the previous year. Fortunately, Marlborough's great victory over Villeroi at Ramillies on 23 May prevented the French from pursuing the margrave into Germany. Instead, he was obliged to dispatch heavy reinforcements northward to help blunt the allies' rapid march through Belgium. Moreover, Frederick now realized that he no longer had any leverage to employ against the emperor and that further obstinacy on his part would only deprive him of a share of the military and political advantages being won in the west. The king therefore ordered his forces in Cleves to march to the front. In mid-June the 12,000 Prussians reached their destination, not the Upper Rhine or the Mosel, but the Anglo-Dutch army in Belgium. Although he had decided against entering the Northern War, Frederick had nonetheless deserted the empire. With the imperial army disintegrating before his own eyes, the margrave wrote Marlborough and the Dutch Estates, appealing desperately for reinforcements. Yet, their desire to exploit Ramillies to the fullest and, later on, the growing strength of the new French army in the Low Countries obliged them to turn down Baden's pleas.

Since half of his meager force of 26,000 was consigned to garrisons and most of his artillery had been abandoned in Alsace, the margrave was in no position to launch a counterattack against Villars's own depleted command.[98] Yet, Joseph and his ministers currently looked at the margrave's responsibilities in a different light. They realized that, unless he could make an offensive gesture toward Alsace, the French would continue to concentrate their forces in Belgium and frustrate the further progress of Marlborough's army. At the end of June, they decided to dispatch Count Schlick to the imperial army in an effort to determine at first hand whether it was capable of making an offensive thrust at Villars. The commissary general's mission was not, however, intended solely as a reconnaisance. After two years of frustration and fiasco on the Upper Rhine, many of the emperor's ministers were looking for the chance to dismiss the irascible margrave.[99] A report by Schlick showing that the imperial army was in adequate fighting condition would strip Baden of any excuse for his earlier defeat and present inactivity, and discredit him further in the eyes of the empire's princes and foreign allies. Moreover, soon after Schlick had departed Vienna, yet another reason appeared for having him submit a report that was damaging to the margrave. On 4 July Joseph ordered an additional 3,000 Austrian troops transferred from the Upper Rhine, this time to the Hungarian front.[100] The withdrawal brought the usual pleas from Louis William but, more important, it prompted renewed criticism from the British and Dutch. Joseph answered his allies' protests by arguing that these troops were only being wasted on the Rhine and could be more profitably employed elsewhere.[101] If Schlick's report indicated that it was Baden's lack of initiative, rather than the lack of troops or supplies that was preventing the imperial army from engaging the enemy, Vienna would be able to rebut its allies' protests.

There can be no question that Schlick appreciated the significance of his mission. Before his departure, the ministry reminded him that it was in the emperor's interest that the report he sent back to Vienna incriminate Louis William. At the same time he was told that should his findings exonerate Baden, he would have to share responsibility as commissary general for the *Hofkriegsrat*'s failure to maintain the emperor's quota of men and supplies on the Upper Rhine.[102] When Schlick's report reached Vienna at the end of August, it placed the margrave in the most unfavorable light. Armed with this verdict, the emperor's ministers again began to push for Baden's dismissal.[103] Although he refused to take this step, lest he alienate the princes of the Nördlingen Association, Joseph did order his imperial commander-in-chief either to recross the Rhine and resume offensive operations in Alsace or to send the bulk of his army to Belgium, leaving only enough men behind to garrison the frontier fortifications.[104] When Baden failed to respond to this command, the emperor instructed the ranking Austrian general on the Upper Rhine, Field Marshal Thüngen, to assume command of Baden's field force. In mid-September Thüngen crossed the Rhine with a body of 15,000 men.[105] Staying in Alsace for two months, he retreated back into Germany on 16 November upon the approach of Villars's army.[106]

Militarily, Thüngen's autumn "offensive" achieved nothing. It did not win territory nor did it relieve pressure from the Anglo-Dutch army to the north. Rather, Thüngen's only accomplishment was political in nature, for he completed the emperor's campaign to discredit and humiliate Louis William. What was so remarkable about this campaign was that it was conducted in part by Baden's former friends. Prince Salm, once a close associate of the margrave, was among those who greeted Schlick's report with a call for the field marshal's dismissal.[107] Emperor Joseph, only a few years earlier a student and unabashed admirer of the great *Türkenlouis,* now insisted to his allies that the imperial army stood at 40,000 strong and owed its immobility solely to the margrave's own incompetence.[108] It is remotely possible that neither Salm nor Joseph was aware of the fabrications in Schlick's report, that they believed the figures presented by the *Hofkriegsrat,* and were not privy to the conspiracy being fomented by men like

Wratislaw. This was definitely true of Schönborn, who sincerely believed that the imperial army was capable of launching an offensive
and who was the principal advocate of an attack across the Rhine.[109]
Yet, even if the emperor and his lord high steward were unaware of the
poor state of the margrave's army, they did not look far or hard to find
the truth. Louis William's own misconduct made it impossible to
justify saving him or his army when more vital Austrian interests were
at stake. It was now more important that the monarchy be spared from
further Anglo-Dutch criticism and that the armies in Italy and Hungary continue to receive all possible military and financial assistance.
Meanwhile, the imperial army could be allowed to become, in the
margrave's own words, "a small body between two great arms."[110]

In fact Joseph's abandonment of Louis William in the autumn of
1706 symbolized his gradual desertion of imperial for dynastic interests. With the empire seemingly secure from immediate danger, he had
begun over the last two campaigns to reorder priorities between the
Rhenish, Italian, and Hungarian theaters of war. In taking these
actions, he had proven himself no different from the majority of the
German princes. Moreover, he had demonstrated once again that, if
crisis—rather than patriotism—had been the genesis of Blenheim,
particularism had been its legacy.

Charles XII at Altranstädt

While he was awaiting word from Schlick, Joseph received the news of
Charles XII's invasion and occupation of Saxony. For the emperor,
who had witnessed threats to the *Erblande* from the west, south, and
east, the presence of a Swedish army along its northern frontier was
most unwelcome.

Of course, Charles had not invaded Saxony in order to attack the
emperor, but rather to compel Augustus to withdraw from the Northern War and abdicate the Polish crown in favor of his own candidate,
Stanislaus Leszczyński. Moreover, Joseph had every reason to believe
the repeated assurances of the Swedish ambassador, Count Strahlenheim, that his master's actions were aimed solely against Augustus.[111]
Since his succession, Charles had been on excellent terms with the
emperor and with the other members of the Grand Alliance. In fact,
though his determination to punish Augustus and Tsar Peter had
precluded his entering the war against Louis XIV, Charles had promised as late as 1704 to provide the imperial army with a full contingent
of troops to represent the Swedish possessions in Germany.[112] Nevertheless, the presence of Charles and his army in the heart of the
empire caused great uneasiness in Vienna. Joseph and his ministers
were well aware of the young king's "very particular humor" and
viewed his eccentric behavior as proof of his unpredictability. At the
same time, they were cognizant of the inflexible determination which

he had shown in his relentless pursuit of those who had attacked him several years earlier. Moreover, Charles's strict adherence to Lutheranism caused them the greatest concern. Shortly after arriving in Saxony, he had visited the battlefield of Lützen, where his predecessor Gustavus Adolphus had fought and died for German Protestantism.[113] During his negotiations with Augustus's ministers, Charles had insisted on including an article in the peace treaty prohibiting the building of Catholic churches anywhere in the electorate. Charles clearly felt an obligation to protect his coreligionists; Vienna feared that his concern extended to the Habsburg dominions.

In particular the status of the principally Protestant populations of Lower Silesia was considered as a possible target for the Swedish king. Under Emperor Leopold, Silesia's Protestants had been denied the free practice of their religion promised at the Peace of Westphalia. Their schools had been closed and their churches seized by the Catholic clergy; in many cases they were compelled to attend mass, marry, and baptize their children in the Catholic rite.[114] During his army's brief passage through Lower Silesia and, more recently, at his Saxon camp at Altranstädt, Charles had received numerous appeals for help from groups of Silesian Protestants.[115] Since Sweden had been a party to the Peace of Westphalia, Charles had the legal right to demand redress of their grievances. Joseph also feared that the Swedish king would champion the cause of the Hungarian rebels. Soon after arriving in Saxony with Charles's army, Stanislaus Leszczyński had received a congratulatory letter from Prince Rákóczi, offering him his friendship and recognition as king of Poland.[116] Upon learning of the letter, Joseph and his ministers correctly interpreted it as an attempt by Rákóczi to enlist Swedish support for the Hungarian rebels, many of whom had revolted against religious persecution under Leopold. Although Charles was not presently seeking an understanding with Rákóczi or pressing for an end to religious persecution in Silesia, the presence of these potential avenues of Swedish diplomacy made the court in Vienna increasingly anxious for Charles's prompt departure from Saxony.

Realizing that the *Erblande* were totally defenseless against Swedish attack, Joseph made every effort to avoid provoking Charles. Though the Swedish army had violated Silesian territory during its march into Saxony, he lodged no protest and even sent instructions to Regensburg to prevent the introduction of any resolution condemning Charles's invasion of the empire.[117] At the same time, he began to work for a speedy settlement between Charles and Augustus. Such an accommodation was clearly in his best interest. Aside from prompting Charles's departure from the empire, it would also free Augustus from the Northern War, thereby enabling him to participate more fully in the struggle against Louis XIV. For this reason, Joseph had been urging a separate Saxon-Swedish peace even before Charles's invasion.[118] Nor did he now regret Augustus's imminent loss of the Polish crown, having already suffered the pretensions of one sovereign prince among his German vassals. Hence, he was prepared to push for a settlement, whatever its cost to Augustus. During October he dispatched Wratislaw to Saxony with instructions to offer his good offices to the Swedish king.[119] Although Charles did not accept the emperor's good offices, peace was soon concluded between the two belligerents at Altranstädt. To Joseph's dismay, however, Augustus was in no rush to execute the terms of his capitulation. Although he had been permitted by the treaty to retain the royal dignity, Augustus had been obliged to renounce all claims to the Polish crown. Nevertheless, Augustus persisted in minting coins with the inscription *Augustus Rex Poloniarum* and continued to withhold formal recognition of Stanislaus Leszczyński as king of Poland. Though obligated to secure an Anglo-Dutch-imperial guarantee of the treaty, he made no effort to obtain it from any of the three powers. Most distressing to Charles was Augustus's refusal either to surrender 1,200 Russian troops serving in the Saxon army or to hand over Johann Patkul, the Swedish-Livonian nobleman who had authored the original Russo-Danish-Polish coalition against him. Instead, he had kept Patkul confined to a Saxon prison and had placed his Russian mercenaries on the Rhine in the pay of the Franconian and Swabian Circles.[120] Until Augustus fulfilled the terms of his capitulation, it was clear that Charles would remain in Saxony, replenishing his supplies, raising fresh recruits, quartering his troops on the elector's subjects—and posing a threat to the security of the *Erblande.*

With the beginning of the new year, the emperor learned from his ambassador at Altranstädt, Count Zinzendorf, that Charles's departure also hinged upon his own recognition of Stanislaus as king of Poland and his personal guarantee of the treaty of Altranstädt.[121] As early as the previous September, Joseph had made it clear to his ministers that he would be willing to recognize Stanislaus if asked to do so by Charles XII.[122] Yet, in a Conference held on 31 January, a majority of the emperor's ministers now urged that he withhold recognition until Charles could be obliged to make corresponding concessions to Vienna. It was not Joseph's nature to submit meekly to another prince's ultimatum. Nevertheless, he realized that the cards were not his to play. In replying to his ministers, he stated that while he would try to secure some concession from Charles, preferably a promise from Stanislaus not to meddle in Hungarian affairs, he would nonetheless eventually recognize the new Polish king. At the same time, the emperor and his ministers agreed that a guarantee of the Altranstädt treaty would also be given to Charles XII, though only after England and the United Provinces had announced their own willingness to do so.[123]

Over the next few days, Zinzendorf met with the king's chief minister, Count Piper, in an attempt to tie Joseph's recognition of Stanislaus to a number of possible Swedish concessions. It was hoped that Charles might be induced to recognize the archduke as king of Spain, pledge a Swedish contingent for the imperial army, or at the very least, promise to leave Germany once the emperor had given his recognition. Charles refused to make any reciprocal concessions, however, and warned ominously that he would not tolerate any further delay in securing compliance with his demands.[124] In a 10 February Conference, the emperor's ministers recommended that the king's terms be met immediately, without waiting for the English and Dutch to announce their willingness to follow suit. They dismissed the principal reason for their earlier reluctance to recognize Stanislaus—the hostility of Tsar Peter—by arguing that Charles XII and Stanislaus posed a far greater threat to Hungary and by adding that, in the event of an attack from the east, Sweden and Poland would make better allies than far-off Russia. In addition, the Conference pointed out that, while further delay only increased tension with Charles, Prussia's recent recognition of Stanislaus had seemingly won it the Swedish king's favor.[125] Ten days later the emperor directed Zinzendorf to capitulate, though only after making one more effort to extract some concession from Charles's ministers.[126] Faithfully carrying out his instructions, Zinzendorf met with Stanislaus and Piper on 26 February in a final attempt to secure a settlement satisfactory to his master. After several hours of fruitless negotiation, however, the Austrian envoy produced the desired document without having won anything in exchange.

It had been Joseph's intention and hope to appease Charles XII by meeting his demands. Yet, a series of unforeseen events now began to conspire against the achievement of a quick and easy settlement. Before the end of February, word reached Vienna that a group of Swedish recruits plying their trade in a Breslau tavern had been attacked by the local city guard. A Swedish corporal was killed in the assault, and the survivors were ignominiously paraded through the streets of the Silesian capital. In Vienna itself an incident of far greater seriousness occurred. At a dinner held on the evening of 6 March, one of Joseph's attendants, the Hungarian Count Czobor, made some disparaging remarks about Charles XII in the presence of the Swedish ambassador. Strahlenheim reacted by striking Czobor several times and, on the following day, demanded satisfaction from the emperor. Though Czobor was placed in chains and transferred to a prison in Graz, Joseph subsequently learned that Charles would be satisfied with nothing less than the nobleman's execution.[127] While the emperor could grant satisfaction for the Breslau and Czobor incidents, Charles soon raised the price of appeasement by making a further demand. Though he had finally recognized Stanislaus and handed over Patkul, Augustus had still not delivered the 1,200 Russians to Charles on the grounds that they were no longer under his command. Hence, on 11 April Piper handed Zinzendorf a sharply worded letter requiring that

Joseph hand over the 1,200 soldiers.[128] The latest Swedish demand placed Joseph in a grave dilemma. To surrender the troops would surely enrage the tsar, who had originally agreed to their transfer to the Rhine in the expectation that they would be beyond Charles's reach. To withhold them would be to invite Swedish retaliation. The emperor answered the king by claiming that, while he did not have the power to deliver these troops, he would be willing either to count them as Sweden's imperial contingent or to petition the tsar to free an equivalent number of Swedish prisoners of war. Rejecting Joseph's suggestions, Charles warned that he would not leave the empire until the troops had been surrendered and that, if necessary, his own army would seize them.[129]

Despite Charles's growing demands and threats, there was still little prospect of war between Sweden and Austria. Charles had only recently rebuffed an embassy from Louis XIV by treating the French plenipotentiary, Baron Besenval, rather rudely and by reiterating his determination to resume the struggle against Russia as soon as possible.[130] By contrast, when the duke of Marlborough arrived at his camp at the end of April, Charles afforded him a cordial reception. In fact, if Charles sought a closer understanding with anyone, it was with the maritime powers, whose combined fleets and pro-Swedish Baltic policy made them the best guarantors of Swedish security in the west.[131] In their meetings together, Charles made his pacific intentions clear to Marlborough, who had by now become conditioned by his own experiences and ego into interpreting the emperor's every sigh as a call for his personal intervention. He did indicate, however, that he would seek satisfaction for the Breslau and Czobor incidents and was determined to gain possession of the 1,200 Russian mercenaries. Charles also disclosed for the first time his determination to seek the restoration of religious liberty to Silesia's Protestants, but accepted Marlborough's request that he await the convening of a general peace conference before presenting this demand.[132] Following his meetings with Charles, the duke hastened back to the Low Countries. Like a famous specialist called in to diagnose some mysterious illness, he had come to Saxony and concluded that there was no serious threat to the life of the patient.

Upon leaving Altranstädt, Marlborough wrote to Salm and Sinzendorf. Although he did not acquaint them with Charles's ultimate intentions regarding the Silesian Protestants, he did urge them to remove those sources of friction which still existed between their master and Charles XII.[133] To the emperor and his ministers, however, Sweden's terms were still unacceptable. In a 13 May Conference, it was agreed that Czobor and the adjutant of the Breslau city guard could be handed over to Charles, but the ministers remained firm in urging Joseph to refuse to surrender the 1,200 Russian mercenaries. Aside from cautioning against provoking Russia and arguing that Sweden had no legal claim to these men, they reasoned that if Charles were in fact intent upon war, he could still use the grievances of the Silesian Protestants as a pretext for attacking the monarchy. It would be better to resist Sweden now, while the maritime powers and Russia could be counted upon as allies, than to risk war later over an issue which might not prompt the support of an angered tsar or the Protestant sea powers. The emperor himself was greatly irritated to find that his recognition of Stanislaus had not sufficiently appeased Charles XII. Nevertheless, he was willing to surrender Czobor and the Breslau adjutant if these concessions would satiate the Swedish king. For the moment Joseph fully accepted the reasoning behind the Conference's advice against turning over the 1,200 Russians as well.[134] What he still did not know was that the fate of these men was passing out of his hands.

As early as the previous September, Joseph had been considering removing the tsarist mercenaries from the empire before their fate became a subject of conflict between him and Charles.[135] On 14 April he had directed the *Hofkriegsrat* to "insinuate" to the commander of the Russian contingent that he march his men to the Netherlands, from where they could easily arrange to escape by sea to their homeland.[136] If the plan was carried out, Joseph realized that he could explain to Charles that the Russians had deserted the imperial army without his knowledge and had taken ship from a foreign port.[137] In the early part of May, the tsarist mercenaries did begin their march but, instead of proceeding north to the Lower Rhine, they hastened eastward through Franconia and the Bohemian crownlands in an attempt to join their countrymen in Poland. Though Joseph eventually learned of the surprise Russian march, there was nothing he could do to prevent it without forcing a confrontation either with Charles XII or the tsar.[138] The only course remaining to him was to inform Charles of the mercenaries' escape and to claim with some truth that he had neither known nor been able to prevent it.[139]

Upon learning of the Russians' escape, the Swedish king immediately recalled Strahlenheim from Vienna and let it be known that unless Joseph awarded him compensation for the mercenaries' flight, he would seek satisfaction by quartering his army in the *Erblande* and having it live off the countryside.[140] It was clear even to Charles's own ministers that the latest turn was threatening to jeopardize their carefully laid plans for a return to the east. Fearing a conflict on two fronts, one of the king's counsellors wrote, "God preserve us from war with the emperor."[141] Indeed, Charles's vindictiveness was threatening to involve Sweden in a struggle of far greater proportion and danger. However, fresh reports from the Upper Rhine indicated that it was the emperor who had the most to fear from the king's wrath.

The Empire under Siege

Although Joseph was still maintaining publicly that the imperial army stood at 40,000 men, its actual strength had fallen in past months to only half that figure.[142] Most recently the under-strength Saxon contingent had been withdrawn by Augustus.[143] Yet, the principal cause for the alarming decline in the strength of the imperial army had been the virtual disappearance of the Austrian contingent, which had fallen to only 2,200 men.[144] Moreover, in view of Prussia's behavior, the emperor had given up on further attempts to recruit Frederick's renewed participation on the Rhine frontier. During the previous June, he had halted delivery of the 200,000 florins to Berlin, declaring that Frederick would now have to look to England for payment of the owed subsidies.[145] No longer restrained by the need to humor the king, Joseph had also initiated a campaign against further Prussian territorial expansion in the empire which was to last until the end of the reign. Although an August 1706 Conference recommended that he invest Berlin with the title or expectancy to a number of small territories on the Lower Rhine, including the Orange counties of Moers and Lingen, the emperor decided to withhold formal recognition indefinitely.[146] In Franconia he supported Lothair Francis's efforts to frustrate Frederick's intentions of inheriting the Hohenzollern duchies of Ansbach and Bayreuth. Prussia's claims to these territories had been secured in 1703 by the so-called Kulmbach treaty, by which Frederick awarded generous subsidies to the Hohenzollern heir presumptive and his family in exchange for their renunciation of all claims to the succession.[147] Yet, when Bartholdi applied for an imperial patent recognizing Prussia's succession rights, his petition was rejected by the vice-chancellor on the flimsy pretext that an Aulic Council would first have to decide on the legality of the treaty.[148] Meanwhile, Mainz and Joseph tried to drum up opposition to Prussia among the Franconian states and offered bribes of their own to the Kulmbach heirs.[149] Frederick reacted angrily to the emperor's intrigues. Deciding that reconciliation with Vienna was unattainable, or perhaps undesirable, he entered into an agreement with England that expanded the number of Prussian mercenaries in Anglo-Dutch pay to include virtually all of the 12,000 troops recently removed from the imperial army.[150] Having judged the emperor an unreliable ally, Frederick had elected to place his trust in England. However, by divorcing the faithless Joseph and wedding himself to the sea powers, the king had made Germany the orphan of Prussian diplomacy.

While the imperial army continued to shrink in size, it suffered an even more serious blow with the loss of Louis William. The margrave had died on 4 January at the age of fifty-two. Though he had become almost impossible to deal with, he had remained to the end a competent field commander. The same could not be said for his successor, the old Margrave Christian Ernest of Bayreuth, who owed his selection as imperial commander-in-chief solely to intensive lobbying by the Protestant German princes.[151] Faced with an inadequate army and an incompetent commander on the Upper Rhine, the emperor and his allies considered taking additional action to forestall disaster. While Louis William was still alive, Marlborough had suggested attaching the accomplished Austrian general Guido Starhemberg to the imperial army in the hopes that "the reputation that he has justly acquired will, without doubt, encourage all Germany to use their utmost efforts to assist him."[152] With Baden's death, the urgency in having a general like Starhemberg on the Upper Rhine became even more apparent. Yet, after considering the move, Joseph decided that he would not alter his original plan to place the Austrian field marshal in command of the more crucial Hungarian front.[153]

In itself the failure to secure either Prussian assistance or a competent field commander on the Upper Rhine did not foreshadow disaster in the upcoming campaign. Thanks to the increased contributions of the Nördlingen Association, there were 26,000 imperial troops present on the front at the beginning of May. Although this number still left Christian Ernest considerably weaker than Villars, the difference in numbers was counterbalanced by the superior defensive position enjoyed by the German army. While the left bank of the Rhine was protected by Landau, the right bank was covered by the so-called Stollhofen lines, a formidable system of fortifications which closed the gap between the river and the Black Forest. Meanwhile, passage through the Black Forest was blocked by the Hither Austrian fortress of Freiburg. Appreciative of this impressive array of natural and man-made defenses, Wratislaw assured the archduke as late as 24 March that "there is nothing to fear along this front, even though it is our weakest."[154] Christian Ernest was also well aware of the strength of his positions. Yet, when on the rainy evening of 22 May, he learned that Marshal Villars and his staff were attending a ball in Strasbourg, the margrave permitted his commanders to suspend their patrols along the Stollhofen lines. The ball was a trick, and while Villars and his generals danced in Strasbourg, the French army quietly crossed the Rhine and overran the unguarded fortifications. Deprived of his defenses, Christian Ernest could only retreat before Villars's 40,000 men. Within a fortnight, the French army had turned the northern edge of the Black Forest, occupying much of Swabia and Franconia and reaching at one point within only twenty miles of the Bavarian frontier.[155]

By himself Villars could expect to go no further. He had extended his forces as far as possible in order to exact heavy contributions from the occupied territory but could not expect to hold them indefinitely. Yet, with a second army of 40,000 Swedes only 200 miles to the northeast, the possibility of delivering a knockout blow against the emperor was very real. Even before Villars's break-through, Joseph had appealed to the sea powers for assistance in calming the incensed Swedish king.[156] Now with the emergence of a dual threat to the *Erblande* and Bavaria, he agreed with his ministers that Anglo-Dutch mediation should be sought.[157] The emperor's allies were more than willing to serve in this capacity. However, the Swedish king announced that he would not treat further with Vienna until Czobor and the Breslau adjutant had been executed for their crimes.[158] To emphasize this point, Charles dispatched four regiments into northern Silesia at the end of June and declared that they would remain there until he had received satisfaction.[159] Though Joseph was too proud to submit to these demands, he was too realistic to reject them outright. In Conferences on 3 and 8 July, he decided to surrender Czobor and the adjutant to Charles along with a payment of 4,000 taler in reparations from the city of Breslau. In this way Joseph hoped to save both men from death or long prison terms by relying on the leniency which only Charles was permitted to exercise.[160] Meanwhile, the emperor agreed to award Sweden satisfaction for the escape of the Russian mercenaries and dispatched Wratislaw to Altranstädt with full powers to conclude an agreement.[161] On the thirteenth the two prisoners were dispatched toward Saxony with Wratislaw following them one day later.

Wratislaw arrived at Altranstädt equipped with a number of possible and relatively painless solutions to the present crisis. In his first meeting with Count Piper on 26 July, he expressed Joseph's willingness to compensate for the Russians' escape by providing Charles with the funds necessary to raise an equivalent number of Swedish soldiers and by provisioning his army during its return passage through Silesia. On the twenty-eighth the king's rejection of this offer was communicated to the Anglo-Dutch mediators Robinson and Haersolte and was followed two days later by a renewed threat to invade the *Erblande* unless satisfaction was given soon.[162] Wratislaw now proffered more substantial concessions to Charles, offering to secure patents from the emperor (1) investing him with the Elbian fief of Hadeln; (2) confirming the succession of his cousin, Christian August of Holstein-Gottorp, as bishop of Lübeck; and (3) exempting Sweden from providing its contingent to the imperial army.[163] Having shunned territorial gain in the past, Charles piously rejected the offer of Hadeln. He did, however, accept the other two offers advanced by Wratislaw and, in place of Hadeln, Piper now presented the mediators with a third and final condition for a settlement.[164] As Robinson and Haersolte reported to Wratislaw following the meeting:

> The king their master desires one thing more, namely that a formal declaration be proclaimed in Silesia before his majesty passes through there, by which assurance will be given the Protestant inhabitants of Silesia that the Protestant religion will be reestablished there without delay and guaranteed for the future, according to the treaties of Westphalia.
>
>   The Count [Piper] repeated to us two or three times that his majesty desires this [concession] more than all the others. [165]

Recognizing the gravity of Charles's new demand, the mediators protested vigorously, adding that their governments did not wish to guarantee any agreement that included such a clause.[166] Moreover, upon learning of the king's terms, Wratislaw also appealed to Piper, emphasizing that it would be very humiliating for his master to have to restore Protestant worship in Silesia while under the threat of Swedish reprisals.[167] These remonstrances notwithstanding, Charles remained steadfast in his determination to press this demand on the emperor. The only thing Wratislaw and the mediators could do was to contrive a recess in the negotiations in order to give the Bohemian chancellor time to secure Joseph's capitulation.[168]

Wratislaw knew exactly how reluctant Joseph would be to concede to Charles's latest demand. In the two years since his succession, the emperor had received a number of petitions from both the *corpus evangelicorum* of the Imperial Diet and the Protestant estates of Lower Silesia, urging him to restore religious freedom according to the terms of the Peace of Westphalia. While he had deemed it wise to answer his loyal Silesian vassals with a vague promise to redress their grievances, Joseph had seen no reason to discomfort the neighboring Catholic estates by rushing to act on this pledge.[169] More recently Salm had urged him to forestall possible Swedish intervention by quickly summoning a Silesian delegation and presenting it with a rescript restoring religious freedom in the duchy.[170] The emperor did in fact direct the Protestant estates to send a deputation to Vienna. However, when it arrived at court on 17 June, he elected to go against the advice of the Conference, which was calling for the immediate conferral of the rescript. Instead, Joseph announced that he would withhold it until its proclamation became absolutely necessary.[171] In standing firm against the plea of his ministers, Joseph was acting from pride in his sovereignty rather than from religious intolerance. In fact, it is clear from his own notes of the 17 June Conference that he was prepared to grant religious freedom in the duchy but was unwilling to do so as long as his actions would be interpreted as a response to Swedish pressure.[172] Instead, he preferred to remain silent in the hope that Charles XII and his ministers would continue to avoid the subject during the negotiations.

Now that the truth was known, the emperor realized that he must pay the price for his recalcitrance. He fully agreed with Wratislaw that to reject Charles's terms would result in war and a Swedish occupation of most of the *Erblande*.[173] Consequently, on 12 August he announced that he would meet all three conditions put forward by Charles, pending the king's promise to leave the empire immediately and to give him six months to complete the restoration of Protestantism in Silesia.[174] On the following day, the Bohemian Chancery prepared the necessary rescript for publication in Silesia. On the fourteenth, however, a second proclamation arrived from Altranstädt, this one composed by Charles's ministers at Wratislaw's request. There were two principal differences between the two documents. While Joseph's decree promised to build new Protestant churches and schools to replace those that had been closed or seized by the Catholic clergy, Charles's called for the full restoration of all formerly Protestant churches and schools. In addition, the Swedish proclamation allowed for the establishment of a commission, headed by Strahlenheim, to supervise the execution and continued observance of the treaty terms.[175] The emperor was not eager to confiscate Catholic churches, regardless of their previous origin. He also hoped to exclude the Swedish heretic from participating in religious reforms within his own dominions. Therefore, in a 14 August Conference, he and his ministers agreed to ignore the Swedish proclamation and coyly send their own version on to Altranstädt.[176]

When Wratislaw received Joseph's rescript three days later, he was not pleased. He had asked Charles's ministers to draw up a proclamation of their own in order to prompt a quick agreement with the king. If the emperor now rejected their terms, he feared that Charles might lose all patience and order his forces into the *Erblande*. Writing to Joseph immediately, Wratislaw criticized his plan for a religious settlement in Silesia as "long in length, short in content, disastrous in its consequences" and reminded him that "I am not dealing with a reasonable man but a lunatic."[177] On the following day, he dutifully submitted Joseph's rescript to an angry reception by Charles's ministers. Moreover, after it had been scornfully rejected, Wratislaw learned that the Swedish monarch had ordered his army to proceed eastward in the general direction of Silesia and Poland. Informing Joseph of these ominous developments, the Bohemian chancellor made it clear that only immediate submission to Charles's terms would save Silesia from occupation and ensure the Swedish army's direct passage into Poland. He pleaded with his master not to test the righteous will of the Swedish king, arguing that the cost of building new Catholic churches would be far less than the expense of hosting an occupying army in the monarchy's richest province.[178] For a full week, Wratislaw anxiously awaited a reply from Vienna. On 24 August Piper had given him three days in which to capitulate. Yet, by the afternoon of 27 August, still no word had come from Joseph. Anticipating catastrophe should Charles's terms go unmet, Wratislaw notified Piper of his master's ratification of the Swedish proclamation. Later that evening, Joseph's acceptance arrived.[179]

Although the crisis had now passed, there were still several points to be settled upon in the final agreement. Only on 1 September was the Second Treaty of Altranstädt signed and submitted for ratification. Aside from waiving Sweden's obligation to provide its imperial contingent and recognizing the Holstein-Gottorp succession in Lübeck, the emperor pledged to restore Protestant religious freedom in Silesia as outlined at the Peace of Westphalia. Specifically, the eight Protestant estates of Lower Silesia were to regain control over all schools and churches that had been closed or seized since 1648. In Upper Silesia where Protestantism had never been officially recognized, Lutherans could no longer be compelled to participate in Catholic religious rites and were restored the right to worship in private. Silesia's tiny Calvinist community, which had received no mention at the Peace of Westphalia, gained nothing by the new agreement. To ensure faithful execution of the treaty terms, a supervisory commission was established under Swedish direction. Meanwhile, to guarantee against future religious oppression, any Protestant prince or estate was given the right to protest publicly any infractions committed by the crown. In a supplementary agreement, Charles's pledge to leave the empire immediately was balanced by the confirmation of his right to reenter it should the terms of the treaty not be carried out or observed in the future.[180]

Armed with Wratislaw's signature and the mediators' pledge of an Anglo-Dutch guarantee, Charles soon headed eastward to join his army.[181] On 12 September Zinzendorf presented him with Joseph's ratification at the Silesian town of Reichenbach, and, one week later, he crossed into Poland. Within three days, the last Swedish soldiers followed him over the Silesian frontier, more than a full year since they had first crossed it.

While word of Charles's long-awaited departure was being greeted in Vienna, attempts to force Villars back across the Rhine were also meeting with some success. During recent weeks, the arrival of reinforcements for the imperial army had compelled the French to pull back from their forward positions in Franconia and Swabia into the pocket of land situated between the Rhine and the Black Forest. The emperor's contribution to this counteroffensive had proved minimal, if not inglorious. During the summer months, preparations for offensive operations in Italy and Hungary had left Joseph without troops of his own to send to the Upper Rhine. Instead, he had approached each of the larger German princes for help in repelling the French invasion. Once again he appealed to Frederick to dispatch part of the largely idle Prussian army. To help stir the king's patriotism, the emperor arranged on the following day for the Aulic Council to reserve its recent judgment against Berlin's purchase of the Lower Rhenish principality of Tecklenburg. Nevertheless, the king again rejected Joseph's plea by continuing to tie his cooperation to a long list of demands.[182]

Joseph also sought Augustus's assistance in the knowledge that his withdrawal from the Northern War had freed a sizeable body of Saxon troops for service elsewhere. In fact, during his recent trip to Altranstädt, the duke of Marlborough had enlisted 4,600 Saxons in the Anglo-Dutch army and had written Vienna encouraging it to sign up an additional 5,000 cavalry that Augustus was willing to send to the Upper Rhine.[183] Unfortunately, Augustus was eager to dispense with these forces principally because the Swedish occupation of Saxony had deprived him of the means of paying or quartering them. Consequently, he was unwilling to contribute them as part of his imperial contingent but was instead demanding a subsidy of 150,000 taler in return. Reluctant to bear this burden, the emperor turned the matter over to the diet, which soon entered into negotiations with Augustus. These talks dragged on for over two months without settlement. Eager to relieve himself of further responsibility for maintaining these troops, Augustus ordered them into neighboring Thuringia, where they proceeded to live off the land, despite the protests of the diet and the defenseless Saxon princes.[184]

If the emperor demonstrated leadership in meeting the crisis created by Villars's breakthrough, it was in engineering the dismissal of Christian Ernest, who was replaced at the beginning of September by George Louis of Hanover.[185] The elector arrived at the front shortly thereafter, accompanied by several thousand Hanoverian troops. He also benefited from Marlborough's dispatch of the 4,600 Saxon mercenaries currently serving in Anglo-Dutch pay, as well as from the addition of small contingents sent by the Lower Rhenish Circle and the emperor himself.[186] Over the next few weeks, he gradually forced Villars to retreat southward along the right bank of the Rhine. Finally, on the evening of 29 October, the French commander pulled his troops back over the river into Alsace.

With Villars's withdrawal, the longest year of Joseph's reign came to an end. Together with the uneventful campaign in Belgium, the failure of Prince Eugene's Toulon offensive, and the crushing defeat suffered by the Anglo-Dutch-Portuguese army at Almansa, the occupation of Saxony and southwest Germany had signalled a dismal setback for the Grand Alliance. Fortunately the empire had escaped relatively lightly from the threat of disaster. Its greatest losses had been financial. Swabia had been obliged to pay an estimated nine million florins to the French; Saxony had been drained of approximately twenty-three million by Charles XII.[187] Aside from these losses, the emperor had been forced to make a number of political concessions to the Swedish monarch. Yet, in recognizing Augustus's abdication, the Holstein-Gottorp succession in Lübeck and the absence of a Swedish contingent in the imperial army, Joseph merely confirmed the status quo. Only in restoring limited Protestant worship in Silesia had he been obliged to make any meaningful concessions; and as the Protestant Marlborough observed in a letter to Wratislaw, the emperor could always "await the time when more just measures can be undertaken" in the duchy.[188] Even the surrender of Czobor and the Breslau adjutant proved painless as both men were soon pardoned and released from Swedish prisons. As light as Charles's terms were, they could have been even less oppressive had Joseph tempered his stubborn pride with a bit more foresight. By taking the initiative in restoring Lutheran worship in the duchy, he would have probably prevented Swedish participation in the restitution and certainly spared himself the greater humiliation of submitting to Charles's threats.

While it is possible to criticize the emperor for his obstinacy, it would be unsound to assert that his tactics brought the monarchy to the edge of war with Sweden. Always a tenacious adversary at the bargaining table, Joseph would invariably concede in the end if he felt a satisfactory settlement could be reached. During the year-long negotiations with Charles XII, he capitulated only—but always—when he felt further resistance would result in an open break. Indeed, he is reputed to have rebutted papal criticism of his restoration of Lutheran worship in Silesia with the remark that he would have become a Protestant himself had Charles so required.[189] Though the anecdote may be apocryphal, it nonetheless underscores Joseph's willingness to sacrifice his religious loyalties and personal prestige in order to attain more tangible political objectives. In fact, Joseph was willing to concede to Charles's every wish, except the demand that he hand over the 1,200 Russian mercenaries, because he realized that a Swedish invasion of the *Erblande* would be impossible to prevent and would result in a total collapse of the monarchy's war effort. Throughout the period of Charles's stay in Saxony, he did endeavor to gather a coalition of princes to help fight Sweden should a break occur. One ally on whom Joseph could count was the tsar—hence his steadfast refusal to surrender the Russian mercenaries. Yet, while Russia was close enough to pose a threat to Hungary, it was too far removed from central Europe to prove a reliable ally. Consequently, while he maintained close contacts with Russia and toyed with Peter's offers to join the Grand Alliance and make Prince Eugene king of Poland, Joseph refused to commit himself to any binding agreement unless he was actually attacked by Sweden.[190]

The emperor could expect even less help from the German princes, especially from the king of Prussia. Since the outbreak of the Northern War, Frederick had cautiously courted both sides in an attempt to ensure Prussia's security and open the possibility of territorial expansion in the east. With the Swedish king's occupation of Saxony, however, Frederick clearly perceived where his interests lay. Ignoring pleas for diplomatic assistance from both Augustus and the emperor, the king immediately began to seek closer ties with Charles XII. Aside from quickly recognizing Stanislaus and guaranteeing the treaty with Saxony, he sought a more intimate alliance with Sweden, this time aimed against his present German allies.[191] As early as September 1706, he suggested a partition of Poland to the Swedish monarch. Soon afterward he urged a "confessional alliance" of England, Hanover, Sweden, and Prussia aimed at backing Protestant aspirations in Silesia and Hungary and electing a Protestant Holy Roman emperor. Frederick's grandiose plans came to naught as Charles rejected the possibility of dividing up Poland, while England and Hanover refused to join in any treaty directed against their Habsburg ally.[192] Nevertheless, on 16 August 1707 while Charles XII was angrily threatening to invade the *Erblande,* the two kings concluded a "perpetual alliance" with the avowed purpose of championing the political independence of the German princes and the rights of Protestant populations in the empire, Hungary, and Poland. Six days later a second accord was reached by which Prussia gave its guarantee of the impending treaty between Sweden and the emperor in exchange for Charles XII's promise to extend to Calvinists the rights granted to Silesian Lutherans under the treaties of Westphalia and Altranstädt.[193]

Intercepted messages had kept Joseph fully aware of the progress and content of Frederick's intrigues.[194] He does not appear, however, to have been alarmed by the steady deterioration of his relations with Berlin. Indeed, during June he had taken the step of recalling his envoy from the Prussian capital, following Frederick's refusal to send reinforcements to the imperial army. By now he realized that the indecisive Frederick would never translate his own interests and hostilities into an attack against the monarchy. Such an action would have to await a different time and a bolder leader. Nevertheless, when Frederick withdrew Bartholdi from Vienna early in September 1707, the last tie was severed between the emperor and his Prussian vassal. Formerly united by a common interest and antipathy toward France, the two princes were now bound principally by political inertia and the persuasive rhetoric of Anglo-Dutch subsidies.

Indeed, it had been the maritime powers, with their close ties to both Sweden and Prussia, which had given Joseph a large measure of security against each of these powers. During the crisis created by Charles XII's invasion of the empire, they had remained faithful to their Habsburg ally and continued to provide an invaluable check against a possible Swedish attack or Prussian desertion of the Grand Alliance. Unfortunately the circumstances surrounding the maritime powers' defense of Austrian interests and security encouraged a certain degree of friction between London and The Hague on the one hand and Vienna on the other. From the very start of negotiations with Charles XII in the early months of 1707, the English and Dutch had made it quite clear to Joseph that "we must suffer what he pleases" in order to secure a prompt, peaceful Swedish withdrawal from Germany.[195] While the emperor did not disagree with the logic of this argument, it soon became apparent that it was he alone who was expected to bow before the blows of Charles's iron will. Meanwhile the maritime powers, whom the Swedish monarch had asked to recognize Stanislaus and guarantee the terms of Augustus's capitulation, proved reluctant to make any sacrifices of their own because the Dutch refused to risk Russian retaliation against their lucrative Baltic trade.[196] Joseph and his ministers were also somewhat irritated by the conduct of their allies during the final mediation. Notwithstanding their expressions of sympathy and outrage at the Swedish demands, the English and Dutch were unable to remove the impression in Vienna that they were less than distressed by the restoration of Protestant worship in Silesia.[197]

Of course, the maritime powers had also found cause for complaint against the emperor. They had grown contemptuous of his inability to weather diplomatic and military crises without having to make desperate, eleventh-hour appeals to his allies.[198] Moreover, they had come to resent the emperor's inability—or unwillingness—to field an adequate army on those fronts for which he held primary responsibility. Looking back at the disastrous course of the 1707 campaign in Germany, Marlborough had written to the Dutch grand pensionary, Anthonie Heinsius, pointing bitterly to the large sums raised by Villars during his short stay in Swabia as proof of the German princes' ability to contribute manfully to the war against France.[199] In the duke's judgment, neither the body of the empire nor its head was fulfilling its obligations as allies. In fact, in reviewing the state of the empire at the end of 1707, such an assessment is unavoidable. Only the Franconian and Swabian circles had discharged their responsibilities fully, for only they had to face the threat of occupation by the French. For the other German princes, including the emperor, the Rhine frontier like the empire itself was at best of only secondary importance.

The Electors' Pound of Flesh

Fortunately for the empire, the front that had been Joseph's primary consideration during the first three years of his reign ceased to be of great military importance after 1707. With the conquest of the Italian peninsula, the emperor was now prepared to help retrieve the damaged pride and reputation of the empire and its army. To reinforce the already adequate force put together under George Louis, Joseph withdrew several thousand troops from both Italy and Hungary, bringing the Austrian imperial contingent up to nearly 20,000 men. In addition he secured a pledge from Elector John William to send 10,000 palatine troops to the front in exchange for his promise to complete the transfer of the Upper Palatinate. Although Augustus remained impervious to Joseph's continuing pleas for troops, the duke of Marlborough did permit the 4,600 Saxon mercenaries whom he had enlisted the previous year to remain with the imperial army. In addition, the English and Dutch governments also agreed to assign to the empire 10,000 Hessian troops that had recently returned from Italy, as well as a force of 4,000 Württemberg infantry. Even the Imperial Diet was able to help provide for Germany's defense. While all attempts to enforce the existing military quotas on its membership continued to fail, and while a recent levy of one million florins went largely uncollected, enough money was raised to provide a supplementary force of 4,500 for service on the Upper Rhine.[200]

With this considerable build-up of the imperial army, Joseph was for the first time spared the humiliation and frustration of having to play for Prussian cooperation. Ironically Frederick was more eager than ever to make a deal. In November the ruling tribunal of the Swiss territory of Neuchâtel had formally recognized Frederick's succession as its prince. Within a matter of weeks, however, Marshal Villars had occupied the principality despite Berlin's pledge to honor its neutrality. To regain Neuchâtel, the Prussian king immediately approached Vienna with plans for an invasion of Burgundy from the Upper Rhine.[201] Though Joseph had always supported the king's pretensions to Neuchâtel, he now rejected Frederick's offer and soon adopted the duke of Savoy's plan for an allied effort against Provence rather than an attack into Burgundy.[202] As in past years, the king reacted to Joseph's recalcitrance by threatening to withdraw his Italian corps from the war unless various financial and territorial demands were met.[203] Nevertheless, the emperor once again called Frederick's bluff by rejecting most of them.[204] In the ensuing weeks, Joseph was to have the satisfaction of securing a resolution from the Imperial Diet threatening sanctions against Prussia for its delinquency in providing its *Reichskontingent* and of seeing the Kulmbach heirs formally repudiate the terms of the 1703 succession treaty.[205]

Despite the continued absence of a Prussian contingent, the considerable reinforcements brought together by the emperor and his allies had raised the imperial army to 80,000 men. Yet, while George Louis was to command the main body on the Upper Rhine, the arrival of Prince Eugene from the Italian front necessitated the establishment of a second, independent force. Joseph hoped that Eugene would be able to command on the Mosel, but realized that the high percentage of Anglo-Dutch mercenaries in the imperial army made the reopening of this front dependent upon the cooperation of his allies. Therefore, when Eugene left Vienna for talks with Marlborough and Heinsius, the emperor instructed him not to insist upon a Mosel strategy and empowered him to shift his army to Belgium, as long as the allies were willing to help supply and quarter it.[206]

When the three men met at The Hague on 12 April, they did indeed agree to assemble a sizeable force on the Mosel. Aside from commanding the 10,000 palatine and 12,500 Austrian troops, Eugene was to be reinforced with the 4,600 Saxon and 10,000 Hessian mercenaries.[207] However, Eugene's presence on the Mosel was only intended to serve as a decoy. At a given moment, he was to join Marlborough's army in an attempt to surprise and overwhelm the French forces operating in Belgium. Although they looked forward to joining their commands and sanguinely anticipated a second Blenheim, both Marlborough and Eugene foresaw the same difficulty that had arisen some years earlier. Like Baden before him, George Louis would surely resent being relegated to a secondary role in the upcoming campaign and might refuse to go along with it. Consequently, the two commanders agreed that their real intentions were to be kept from the elector until the last possible moment. When they visited him at Hanover at the end of April, no mention was made of Eugene's planned descent. Indeed, in order to secure George Louis's consent for a second imperial army on the Mosel, Marlborough was obliged to detach an additional 5,000 German mercenaries from his command, thereby raising to 47,000 the size of the main imperial army.[208]

Having secured the elector's cooperation, the two generals departed from Hanover, each intent upon concluding arrangements for the coming campaign. Nevertheless, as in past years, Vienna's hopes for a successful campaign hinged as much upon the completion of delicate political preparations as upon the execution of strictly military arrangements. In the spring of 1708, two highly explosive constitutional issues had yet to be settled before the offensive against France could resume: the formal admission of Hanover to the Electoral College and the punishment of Max Emanuel under the imperial ban.

Since 1692 when Emperor Leopold had first raised the Guelphs of Brunswick-Lüneburg to the empire's ninth electorate, George Louis's formal entry into the Electoral College had been blocked by the Catholic electors and by many of Hanover's neighbors in the Diet of Princes who were both jealous and resentful of not having been called upon to ratify the new electorate. The Catholic electors eventually agreed to admit Protestant Hanover in exchange for the full admission of Bohemia, which as a sovereign kingdom had heretofore been excluded from collegial deliberations and voted only in imperial elections.[209] Moreover, by 1706 Joseph had removed the opposition of the Diet of Princes by announcing that the Hanoverian, and all subsequent electoral nominations, would be submitted to it for approval.[210] At this point, however, the proclamation of the imperial ban against Max Emanuel and Joseph Clement revived the opposition of the Catholic electors, who feared once again for their majority in the Electoral College. While Cologne would eventually resume its place in the college, it was possible that Bavaria would be permanently excluded from it. Furthermore, since John William's Palatinate-Neuburg dynasty was almost extinct, it was entirely possible that he would be succeeded someday by the ruling duke of Palatinate-Zweibrücken— Charles XII of Sweden—thereby evening the confessional balance in the Electoral College at four apiece.[211] The Catholic electors reacted to this threat by demanding that the admission of Hanover be made subject to the stipulation that, should either the Bavarian or Palatinate-Neuburg electorates be lost, an additional Catholic elector would automatically succeed in its place.[212] Joseph consented to the electors' terms, albeit only after having extracted some concessions of his own, including the right to nominate the Catholic substitute. Yet, his adoption of the plan for a future Catholic substitution brought intense opposition from the Protestant princes. Led by Sweden, they demanded that they also be given the right to replace any Protestant electoral dynasty that either converted or died out. When in the spring of 1707 the emperor refused to allow a Protestant counter-substitution, further negotiations broke down.[213]

While the personal jealousies and religious paranoia of the German princes were primarily to blame for the long delay in seating Hanover in the Electoral College, the emperor himself was responsible for postponing punitive action against Max Emanuel. By the end of 1706, the emperor had abandoned all hope of annexing Bavaria to the *Erblande,* feeling with considerable justification that princely opposition to the monarchy's aggrandisement, coupled with the inevitable Prussian and Saxon demands for compensation, would prove insurmountable. He intended instead to offer Max Emanuel restitution of the rest of the electorate, minus the Upper Palatinate and minor territorial adjustments, in exchange for French countercessions in Alsace and Lorraine.[214] Having decided to forego his original plans for annexation, Joseph now favored delaying Max Emanuel's formal punishment as long as possible in order to continue his own exploitation of the Upper Palatinate as a source of revenue and a quartering ground.[215] As early as May 1706, Joseph had given in to John William's threat to withhold reinforcements from the Italian front by promising to cede the coveted territory. Yet, he was able to postpone the transfer by insisting that it first meet with the requisite approval of the Electoral College.[216] Of course, both men realized that such a procedure would consume time and invite renewed attempts at political blackmail by Prussia and Saxony. In fact, for a full year, the emperor's hold on the Upper Palatinate was protected by the ambitions and demands of Frederick and Augustus. Only on 2 May 1707, after John William had made various concessions to them, did the Electoral College meet at last, voting unanimously to transfer the Upper Palatinate and take away the Bavarian electoral franchise. Even then, however, Joseph delayed ceding the Upper Palatinate by summoning a series of increasingly feeble excuses.[217]

While Joseph and his ministers were busily making preparations for the 1708 campaign, they began to become aware of the dangers involved in leaving the fates of the ninth electorate and the Upper Palatinate unresolved. The first clear indication came from John William, who declared in December that he would withhold his 10,000-man corps from the front unless the 2 May 1707 resolution was carried out. To dramatize his threat, he immediately removed his financial backing from a crucial one-million-taler loan currently being negotiated by the Nördlingen Association.[218] Learning of John William's intentions, George Louis promptly announced that he would not assume command of the imperial army in the spring unless the promised palatine units were provided.[219] If the emperor did not break under the electors' pressure, he at least bent before it. On 3 February he declared that he would execute the 2 May resolution, but only after John William had met certain conditions. His principal counterde-mand called upon the elector palatine to relinquish control of the city of Kaiserswerth, a dependency of Cologne that had been seized from Joseph Clement in 1702 and formally annexed to the Palatinate. Joseph's terms were in keeping with his policy of defending the em-pire's *Kleinstaaterei* against the ambitions of the larger German princes. Moreover, his consciousness had recently been reinforced by the Cologne cathedral chapter's offer to pay him 30,000 taler for the city's restitution.[220] Yet, his actions also reflected a strong reluctance to concede anything to another prince, whether he be an ally or an enemy, without first achieving corresponding advantages. With the campaign still some months away, Joseph felt that there was yet time for such a diplomatic maneuver.

For nearly three months, John William held out against the emper-or's terms, while Eleonore and the arch-and vice-chancellors applied heavy pressure on Joseph to withdraw his demand for Kaiserswerth.[221] Finally, at the beginning of May, the elector capitulated. Joseph now announced that John William's investiture would follow within three weeks' time.[222] Yet, only five days later, the emperor modified his promise. In the expectation of attaining one more advantage, he declared that he would reconvene the Electoral College in order to cast his own vote for the 2 May resolution in his capacity as king of Bohemia. By exercising this long-dormant franchise, Joseph intended to demonstrate that the incumbency and voting privilege of Bohemia in the Electoral College predated and were legally independent of any future compromise involving Hanover's admission into that body.[223] However, the process of reconvening and polling the college would consume more than the three weeks in which he had promised to ratify the 2 May resolution. Therefore, on 29 May John William ordered his already overdue imperial contingent to halt its march to the Mosel.

Having attempted to squeeze the most out of his loyal vassal, Joseph had now pressed too hard. He realized that the 10,000 palatine troops would resume their march only after he had formally ratified the document. Yet, rather than lose face by foregoing the upcoming electoral conclave, Joseph merely rushed to convene it. Instead of sending his own representative to Regensburg, he commissioned the delegate from Trier, Franz Wilhelm von Wetzel, to cast the Bohemian vote. Wetzel's instructions arrived on the evening of 9 June and, although the following day was a Sunday, a meeting was promptly scheduled for the morrow. On the next morning, the six electoral delegates convened at the house of the Saxon representative and cast their votes. As soon as the meeting was over, word was rushed to Prince Eugene in Frankfurt. The prince had written to John William on the day of the conclave appealing to him to permit his troops to resume their march to the front.[224] Although he was not moved by this plea, the elector reacted more positively to a second letter which he received from Eugene on the eighteenth, notifying him of the collegial vote and assuring him that the emperor would ratify it immediately.[225] Though John William could have been excused for a show of skepticism, he accepted the prince's assurances and directed his forces to resume their march.[226] Four days later, the contingent reached the Mosel at Coblenz. True to Eugene's word, Joseph ratified the collegial resolution on 23 June.[227] Although the emperor managed to contrive further technical delays in transferring the Upper Palatinate, John William was finally invested with the territory at the beginning of August.[228]

Only one week after he had capitulated to John William, Joseph was able to reach an agreement with the Imperial Diet concerning Hanover's admission to the Electoral College. As in his negotiations with John William, the emperor was motivated in his dealings with the diet principally by concern for the success of the upcoming campaign. Unlike the elector palatine, George Louis had exhibited extraordinary patience in waiting over fifteen years for his family's elevation to the Electoral College. Yet, now that his admission appeared imminent, he had grown increasingly irritated with the latest obstacle presented by the Catholic electors and was less than pleased with the firm support Joseph had given their substitution project.[229] Following his 29 April meeting at Hanover, Prince Eugene had sensed George Louis's indignation and urged Joseph to resolve the crisis lest it have ill effects on the campaign on the Upper Rhine.[230]

While the emperor could appreciate George Louis's impatience, he saw no reason to capitulate to the terms presently being demanded by the Protestant princes. He was especially unwilling to permit them to usurp the crown's traditional right to nominate electors by allowing the establishment of a Protestant substitution. Moreover, in the absence of any direct threats from George Louis and with the Upper Rhine front assuming only secondary importance in the upcoming campaign, Joseph felt no compulsion to reach a costly settlement in the diet. Therefore, as campaigning weather approached, he pushed for an accord with the Protestant princes, but only one that safeguarded his own interests as emperor and king of Bohemia.[231] In the compromise that he presented to the diet, the emperor did waive his right to nominate a Catholic substitute to the Electoral College. Instead, the archchancellor was to exercise two votes in that body until a more permanent arrangement could be worked out. Otherwise, he stood firmly by his interests. There was to be no Protestant countersubstitution. While Hanover was to enter the college, Bohemia's incumbency was explicitly recognized beforehand. In addition, the kingdom's full admission to the Electoral College was to be accompanied by its seating in the Diet of Princes and the Imperial Chamber Court. Finally, though Joseph's compromise promised Bohemia's future par-

ticipation in the system of military circles (from which it had heretofore been exempted), the pledge was worded in such a way as to enable
him to postpone indefinitely the assumption of this increased defense
burden.[232] After weeks of negotiation, the Protestant princes agreed to
accept this settlement, principally on the argument of Prussia and
Saxony that further delay in admitting Hanover was against their own
interests.[233]

With the conclusion of both issues, Vienna was able to turn its full
attention to military operations. The settlement with John William had
come not a moment too soon. Since mid-June, Marlborough had
begun appealing to Prince Eugene to execute the planned descent into
Belgium, but the late arrival of the palatine contingent had prevented
his departure.[234] Finally, on 29 June he broke camp on the Mosel and
headed west. In order to convince George Louis of the necessity and
spontaneity of his action, Eugene presented the imperial commander-
in-chief with a letter from Marlborough describing the supposedly
desperate state of the Belgian front. Marlborough had given Eugene
the letter some time before solely for the purpose of deceiving George
Louis.[235] When the prince reached the Belgian front, he found that the
position had indeed become desperate. In the first week of July, the
northern Belgian towns of Ghent and Bruges had opened their gates to
the French, thereby threatening Marlborough's rear. Nevertheless,
with the arrival of Eugene's army, the two generals were able to save
the situation. On 11 July two-thirds of Marshal Vendôme's French
army was surrounded and nearly destroyed by the combined allied
force at Oudenarde. Though darkness saved the enemy from annihilation, Vendôme was obliged to withdraw his defeated force northward
to Bruges and Ghent. Over the next few months, Eugene and Marlborough were virtually free to pursue objectives along the Belgian-French
frontier. After a particularly difficult siege, they captured Lille,
France's second largest city; and once Vendôme had returned home for
winter quarters, Ghent and Bruges were retaken as well.

Although the French withdrew large numbers of troops from Alsace
after Oudenarde, George Louis was unable to profit from his heavy
numerical superiority over the enemy. In fact, during early autumn, he
began claiming that the French were massing on his front and demanded that reinforcements be sent from Belgium. Yet, no sooner had
Marlborough complied with these appeals than the elector began
sending the imperial army into winter quarters.[236]

With the close of the 1708 campaign, the Upper Rhine ceased to
command a significant role in the strategy of the Grand Alliance.
Indeed, as a factor in the continuing struggle against Louis XIV,
Germany was destined to serve as little more than a recruiting ground
for its allies. To some extent, the emperor himself was responsible for
the gradual decline in Germany's contribution to the war effort. The
young prince whose political consciousness had been weaned in a

period of resurgent German patriotism and whose royal apprenticeship
had been so closely tied to the empire's fortunes had inevitably ma-
tured to the realities of his dual role as emperor and Habsburg monarch. Though retaining the intense Francophobia of his youth, he had
diverted his energies from the pursuit of imperial interests to the
achievement of purely dynastic goals. With the security brought by the
victory at Blenheim and the fall of Landau, he was able to react to the
frustrations of commanding the imperial army by redirecting his
resources to the south and east. In the process he largely ignored the
Rhine frontier and broke openly with his former tutor and friend,
Louis William of Baden. Though victory in Italy did eventually draw
his armies back north, Joseph willingly deferred to the military genius
of Eugene and Marlborough, as well as to the political considerations
of alliance diplomacy, by scrapping the long-favored Mosel strategy in
favor of a campaign in Belgium. Such was the cost of his dynastic
interests that there was no sequel to Blenheim during his reign, only a
disappointing aftermath.

Of course, if Blenheim permitted the emperor to concentrate on
purely dynastic matters, it also encouraged the German princes to
focus their attention on less patriotic pursuits, to the severe detriment
of the military effort against France. Consequently, while the Age of
Louis XIV had brought an Indian summer of princely loyalty to *Kaiser*
and *Reich,* it had already begun to dissipate before Joseph assumed the
throne. To enlist his vassals' political and military cooperation, the
young emperor was obliged to treat with them in much the same
manner as had his predecessors. This implied the conduct of a diplomatic rather than paternalistic policy and the use of the crown's legal
authority to arrange deals with or level threats against his vassals. To
some extent, Joseph's politicization of imperial policy debased the
image and sanctity of his legitimacy and helped suppress the last
vestiges of loyalty among the larger German princes. Nevertheless, in a
political system characterized by intense personal jealousies and religious paranoia, this was a most effective way of enlisting the temporary
assistance, if not the permanent allegiance, of the individual German
states.

Taken in this light, Joseph's policy toward the Palatinate appears
reckless and self-defeating. Yet, the intimate relations between Joseph
and John William were the product of a past marriage alliance and the
present coincidence of interests vis à vis France and Bavaria. As long
as the emperor continued to service John William's interests, as he did
in the summer of 1708, the bond between the two men would remain.
At some point in the future, however, the dynastic ambitions of John
William or his successors were liable to preclude further cooperation,
regardless of past allegiances. Clearly this had been the lesson of the
past few years. Despite a long and close alliance, Max Emanuel had
broken with Vienna following Leopold's refusal to concede to his

extravagant demands. Shortly afterward Frederick had forsaken his entente with Joseph once he realized that the emperor was unwilling to sanction further Prussian expansion within the empire. Though he had not yet clashed with Vienna, Augustus II's grandiose designs had led him into the catastrophic Northern War and left him useless as an ally in the struggle against France. Even in the relatively recent emergence of Hanover, the seeds of future conflict with the crown could be seen. No prince had been more favored by Joseph than George Louis. After years of stalemate, the young emperor had been instrumental in securing Hanover's entry into the Electoral College. Unlike Prussia or Saxony, Hanover had never been cited or threatened by Vienna for its delinquency in supplying a full imperial contingent; and following Christian Ernest's dismissal from the imperial army, it was George Louis whom Joseph appointed commander-in-chief. Nevertheless, within a short while, the new elector had begun to imitate the tactics of the other great princes. At the end of 1707, he began pressuring the emperor to permit him to use the income of the neighboring bishopric of Hildesheim to help finance his imperial contingent.[237] Since the cathedral chapter of Hildesheim—whose ruler was the banned Joseph Clement—was presently fulfilling its financial obligations to the empire, Joseph refused the request. Nevertheless, George Louis subsequently seized Hildesheim in open defiance of the appeals and threats coming from Vienna.[238]

Such were the dynamics of princely dynasticism that only the smaller states and ecclesiastic electors could be expected to uphold the empire's laws and interests. To these princes, it was the best hope for survival; to the lay electors, it was more often an obstacle that had to be overcome, either by force or with the emperor's collaboration. In this respect only did Joseph I still rule Germany.

IV

Italy:
The Struggle
for Hegemony

In Italy it is necessary to combine legality with pragmatism.
—Johann Friedrich Baron Seilern

While Joseph considered Germany the least crucial front in the war, he prized Italy as his most important objective. It is not difficult to see why. For two centuries his Spanish Habsburg cousins had dominated the peninsula and, hence, protected the monarchy's southwest flank from any encroachment by the French. Charles II's will had not only deprived it of this valuable bulwark but placed two hostile powers on its Alpine frontier. The value Joseph put on the peninsula was hardly a departure from the priorities that Leopold had established in his last years. Prior to Charles II's death, the old emperor would probably have accepted a partition, had his share of the succession included the whole of Spanish Italy. Moreover, during the subsequent alliance negotiations with England and the United Provinces, he instructed Count Wratislaw to secure Italy for the dynasty, even at the cost of renouncing all claims to Spain and the Indies.[1]

With his succession, Joseph merely intensified this commitment. Until Italy had been conquered, he authorized a greater expenditure for the Italian front than for the campaigns in Germany and Hungary combined.[2] The young emperor excused his virtual abandonment of Alsace and Lorraine by citing the need to reassert the empire's claims to jurisdiction over much of northern Italy.[3] It was true that, with the exception of Venice and parts of Genoa, Tuscany, and Parma, all of the territory north of the Papal States was still theoretically within the Holy Roman Empire. Yet, if imperial prerogatives had faded in Germany, they were even less visible here; the ultimate victory of the medieval popes followed by two centuries of Spanish Habsburg hegemony had largely eroded the effectiveness of imperial authority in the peninsula. Joseph's real objectives were, first, to replace Spanish with Austrian—not imperial—rule, thereby reconstituting Italy as a buffer on the monarchy's southwest flank and, second, to exploit it for the duration of the war as a valuable source of additional revenue. Whenever he did revive and utilize his imperial prerogatives, he invariably had these more tangible and immediate ends in mind.

The Winning of Italy

Although both father and son regarded the peninsula as their primary objective in the war against Louis XIV, it is unlikely that victory in Italy could have been achieved under Leopold's leadership. Since the outbreak of the struggle, Joseph and the young court had been fighting in vain to obtain adequate support from the emperor for the Italian front.[4] By the beginning of 1705, however, the situation in the peninsula appeared hopeless. Philip V still controlled all of Spain's Italian possessions—the duchy of Milan, the Presidii ports of Tuscany, the tiny enclave of Finale, and the kingdoms of Naples, Sicily, and Sardinia. Meanwhile, Marshal Vendôme's Franco-Spanish army had succeeded in bottling up Prince Eugene's much smaller force inside neutral Venetian territory with its back to the Tyrolean Alps. Although Duke Victor Amadeus of Savoy was now a member of the Grand Alliance, his lands were virtually surrounded and under intense pressure from the Bourbon armies. As Prince Eugene prepared to return to Italy at the beginning of 1705, it had become clear that Victor Amadeus could not hold out much longer. Before leaving Vienna, Eugene pressed the emperor for more money and troops to march to his cousin's relief. In making these remonstrances, he received strong support from Joseph.[5] At first, Leopold refused these requests. Nevertheless, when on 14 March Eugene handed in his resignation as *Hofkriegsrat* president, Leopold capitulated and promised to meet his needs by providing a war chest of 800,000 florins and a 300,000 florin monthly subsidy.[6] In Leopold's behalf, it can be argued that he recognized the impossibility of providing such sums. Only with the greatest difficulty was Joseph able to prevent him from reneging on his pledge a few days later, and when Prince Eugene finally left for Italy on 17 April "to work yet another miracle" like Blenheim, he departed without the promised funds.[7] Immediately after arriving at the front the prince wrote Joseph pleading with him to use his influence to secure the needed aid from the emperor.[8]

It was only with Leopold's death that Joseph was able to work effectively on Eugene's behalf. As we have seen, he attempted to subordinate the Bavarian, Tyrolean, and Inner Austrian military administration to the prince's personal direction. He also concluded a subsidy treaty on 25 May with Elector John William that called for the dispatch of 4,000 palatine mercenaries to the peninsula. By summer the Austrian army had more than doubled in size to approximately 30,000 men, including not only these 4,000 palatines but the 8,000 Prussians

Imperial Italy

Acquired by Victor Amadeus

Acquired by Archduke Charles

Acquired by Joseph I

Habsburg Monarchy in 1700

Savoy-Piedmont in 1700

enlisted by Marlborough.[9] Yet, when on 16 August Eugene attempted
to cross the Adda River at Cassano in hopes of breaking through the
French lines, he was met and turned back by Vendôme. Upon receiving
news of the prince's defeat, Joseph promptly redoubled his efforts.
New plans were made at once to accelerate and increase the raising of
taxes and recruits from the *Erblande*.[10] Austrian contingents were
recalled from the Rhine, and the possibility of transferring troops from
Hungary was discussed as well.[11] Negotiations were opened with the
rulers of Saxony, Württemberg, Wolfenbüttel, and Würzburg in an
effort to secure their assistance.[12] Even the tsar was approached with a
project for sending 6,000 Russian mercenaries to the peninsula.[13] Most
of these initiatives fell through, however, and although 3,000 troops
were transferred from the Upper Rhine during October, it proved
impossible to weaken the army in Hungary by withdrawing some of its
forces for service in Italy. Meanwhile, despite some success in increasing crown revenue, the government was still unable to furnish more
than a third of the sums originally promised by Leopold.[14]

Fortunately Joseph received a better response from his allies. On 25
August he had instructed his representatives in London and The
Hague to seek a loan of 400,000 taler from the maritime powers. At
first the chances of securing Anglo-Dutch financial assistance appeared
slight. The Estates General had turned down a similar request earlier in
the year, and on 28 September the British government announced its
unwillingness to extend further credit without Dutch participation.[15]
Nevertheless, from their talks together during the siege of Landau,
Joseph was aware that the influential duke of Marlborough was
extremely concerned about Savoy's fate.[16] In fact, the duke now
pressed both governments to conclude financial arrangements with the
emperor, arguing that a collapse of the Italian front would permit the
French to reinforce strongly their armies in Belgium and Alsace.[17]
When in early October the Dutch finally agreed to negotiate a loan for
Prince Eugene's army, Marlborough quickly made arrangements for
his journey to Vienna.

As plenipotentiary of both England and the United Provinces, the
duke arrived in Vienna on 12 November fully empowered to grant the
emperor succor for the next campaign in Italy. His hosts realized,
however, that the extensive financial assistance would be forthcoming
only if they could demonstrate that they had been endeavoring to carry
their full share of the burdens of war. During past years, the duke had
not held this view and had often been severely critical of the slowness
and lethargy that had characterized military preparations under Leopold. Consequently, Joseph and his ministers made a concerted effort
to impress upon Marlborough not only their inability to prosecute
further the war in the peninsula but also to convince him of the
exhaustiveness of their own efforts to sustain and strengthen Prince
Eugene's army.[18] Judging from the duke's correspondence, there is

little doubt that the emperor and his ministers conveyed their message clearly.[19] Within a week of his arrival in Vienna, Marlborough concluded negotiations for a loan of 300,000 taler. In view of the urgency of Prince Eugene's needs, he asked his government to rush the first 100,000 taler directly to Venice from its offices in Frankfurt. The remaining sums were to be divided equally between England and the United Provinces and sent on immediately following the treaty's ratification.[20] In a series of interviews with the emperor and his ministers, the duke made a number of additional commitments. Besides promising to help raise a further 250,000 pounds upon his return to England, he agreed to enlist in Anglo-Dutch pay the 4,000 palatine mercenaries that had been engaged by Joseph in the previous May. The emperor was experiencing difficulty in providing the sums required by John William, especially since the elector was now demanding that a larger number of palatine mercenaries be taken into allied pay for the 1706 campaign. Marlborough obliged by writing John William from Vienna offering to finance an Italian corps of 10,000 mercenaries under palatine command comprising the 4,000 men originally engaged by the emperor, 3,000 additional palatine recruits, and a contingent of 3,000 troops from Saxe-Gotha.[21]

Although the duke left Vienna on 22 November, his diplomatic efforts for the Habsburg cause in Italy continued during the winter months. After having passed through Berlin in order to renew the Prussian subsidy treaty, Marlborough returned to The Hague from where he continued to supervise the subsidy negotiations with John William until their successful conclusion in the opening week of January.[22] Within a few days, he was back in London where the Austrian ambassador, Count Gallas, began reporting his energetic lobbying for further financial aid for the army in Italy.[23] By February arrangements were completed for the 250,000 pound loan he had promised during his stay in Vienna. Like the earlier "Marlborough loan" negotiated in November, the latest advance was to be sent directly to Venice rather than through the *Hofkammer* in Vienna in order to save time and insure that the entire sum arrived intact. This loan was, however, being advanced by private sources rather than by the English or Dutch governments. On 18 March the public was invited to subscribe to the loan by advancing its own personal credit against an annual payment of 8 percent interest. Within six days the entire sum had been pledged. Among the 300 individuals who signed their names were the prince consort (20,000 pounds), Marlborough (10,000 pounds), the duke's son-in-law, the earl of Sunderland, and the lord of the Exchequer, Godolphin (5000 pounds each).[24] Queen Anne refrained momentarily from pledging her own fortune to the Habsburg cause in the peninsula. Nevertheless, within a few months, she extended 50,000 pounds of the crown's wealth in the form of a loan calculated at a more modest 6 percent interest.[25]

While Marlborough was laboring mightily to increase allied support for the upcoming Italian campaign, the government in Vienna was also straining to bolster its own commitment. So extensive were the emperor's own expenditures in Italy during the opening months of 1706 that the absence of specie in the capital itself brought a precipitous drop in food prices despite severe grain shortages.[26] After returning from the front on 23 January, Prince Eugene remained at court for nearly three months busily making preparations for the campaign.[27] His prolonged stay in Vienna was partly responsible for the crushing defeat suffered by his army at Calcinato on 19 April. Returning to the front hours after the battle, Eugene gathered together the shattered remnants of his army and withdrew them deeper into Venetian territory. Nevertheless, once entrenched behind the Adige River, the prince was able to receive and maintain the reinforcements that now began to join him. By mid-May his command had grown to 50,000 men, a third of which consisted of Anglo-Dutch mercenaries.[28] In addition, he soon learned that the duke of Marlborough was transferring a further 10,000 Hessian mercenaries from his army in Belgium.[29] While this latest reinforcement would not be arriving for some weeks, Eugene's force was already sufficiently strong to begin the march to Turin. Opposite it was Marshal Vendôme with 44,000 troops. One hundred fifty miles to the west was a second French army of 48,000 under La Feuillade, which was besieging the Savoyard capital. With a total force of only 16,000, Victor Amadeus could not be expected to delay for long Turin's capture. On the evening of 17 July, barely one week after Vendôme had assured Versailles that Prince Eugene would never be able to relieve the beleaguered city, the forward units of the Austrian army crossed the Adige, slipped around the French lines, and began the long march to Turin. At this point, the prince benefited once more from the helping hand of his English colleague. Following Marlborough's crushing victory at Ramillies on 23 May, Louis XIV had ordered Vendôme to return homeward in order to replace the disgraced Villeroi. Considering the recent turn of events on the Adige, the marshal was only too glad to comply. Vendôme was succeeded by the young and militarily inexperienced duke of Orléans and by Marshal Marsin, whom Marlborough and Eugene had defeated two years before at Blenheim. Choosing not to intercept Eugene, who was proceeding quickly along the south bank of the Po, Orléans and Marsin fell back on Turin with most of their forces and prepared for the battle. On 7 September the combined French armies were outmaneuvered and defeated by the much smaller Austro-Savoyard forces. With Marsin mortally wounded, Orléans hastily withdrew his beaten army, at first in a southerly direction, then westward through the Alpine passes into France.

Unlike Blenheim and Ramillies, Turin was not a victory of annihilation. Indeed, during the entire day, not even half of the French army was deployed on the battlefield by its incompetent commanders. Nevertheless, Eugene's triumph was as dramatic and decisive as its forerunners. Like Blenheim and Ramillies, the victory at Turin forced—or at least encouraged—the French to abandon an entire theater of the war; like Blenheim, it left thousands of enemy soldiers cut off from France. In fact, the 23,000 French troops whom Marsin and Orléans had left at the Adige had fought a battle of their own two days later at Castiglione, soundly defeating a corps of Eugene's army and the recently arrived Hessian mercenaries. Upon receiving word of Turin's relief and Orléans's westward retreat, the French commander Medavi prudently disbanded his victorious force and distributed it among the numerous northern Italian fortresses still under Bourbon control. Moreover, there was also a small Spanish army of perhaps 8,000 men in southern Italy that was prepared to defend the kingdom of Naples against Austrian attack.

Once again, the emperor was faced with the prospect of conducting a long siege campaign behind his own front lines. With most of northern and all of southern Italy still in Bourbon hands, he could anticipate spending the rest of the 1706 campaign and all of 1707 reducing these strongpoints. Yet, whereas Blenheim had destroyed the French field army and temporarily removed the threat of Louis's sending a relief force from France, Eugene's victory had merely repelled but not annihilated Orléans's large army. The threat of a renewed French invasion from the west was, therefore, very real and carried with it the danger of being caught in a vise between Orléans's and Medavi's larger forces. Even if Versailles elected not to risk sending Orléans back across the Alps, Eugene still faced the dual problem of protecting his communications with the *Erblande* and at the same time preventing Medavi from retreating into Naples where he could make southern Italy virtually impregnable to Austrian attack.[30]

While Joseph and Eugene were contemplating these difficulties, a solution appeared from a most unexpected quarter. At Versailles, Louis XIV had indeed elected against sending a relief army to Medavi's aid. Yet, in order to save his forces in northern Italy, he decided to offer his Habsburg enemy a settlement that would serve admirably each sovereign's interests. On the night of 14 December, two Bourbon officers named Javallière and Saint Pater entered Prince Eugene's headquarters in Milan. Although they had come with the announced intention of arranging a prisoner exchange, they divulged instead Louis's offer to surrender all of northern Italy to Joseph in exchange for the safe passage to France of Medavi's entire army. Upon receiving this startling proposal, Eugene correctly informed the agents that he was not empowered to deal with them and seriously doubted whether his master would agree to negotiate the matter without conferring first with his allies. However, while the prince was aware of the formalities and contractual obligations of alliance diplomacy, he was also atune to the realities of the military and political situation in the peninsula. With the stroke of a pen, the strategic difficulties facing his army would be removed; more important, the emperor would be assured full possession of northern Italy and the prospect of an easy conquest of the south. Therefore, while awaiting instructions from Vienna, he prudently kept secret the true nature of the agents' mission and quietly ushered them out of Milan after a stay of only eight days.[31]

Joseph did, in fact, notify his allies about the French initiative.[32] Nevertheless, when they reacted negatively to the prospects of allowing Medavi's troops to return to France, he continued to consider the project. He realized that the prospective negotiations did not involve the making of peace but merely the conclusion of a military convention similar to those between a besieging general and a fortress commander.[33] Hence, despite their tremendous strategic importance and the disapproval of the maritime powers, Joseph knew that the decision whether or not to conclude an agreement was ultimately his.

Ironically it was the English and Dutch themselves who inadvertently influenced the emperor's decision to treat with Louis XIV. During January, the court learned that the English, Dutch, and Savoyards were determined to launch the 1707 campaign with a surprise thrust against the French naval base at Toulon.[34] The project was the brainchild of the English government. Toulon's capture would not only force the destruction of the French fleet bottled up in its harbor but would also provide the British navy with a port where its Mediterranean fleet could spend the winter without having to return home at the end of each campaign. The idea of a descent on Toulon was not a new one. The English had first brought up the plan during the secret alliance talks with Savoy in 1703. At that time, however, both the Austrian and Savoyard negotiators had made it clear that northern Italy would have to be conquered first before any concerted offensive could be launched against southern France. Moreover, at Austrian insistence, the final treaty specified that all of the peninsula as well as Sicily be secured before undertaking any venture in the west. In recent weeks, however, the English general Peterborough had visited Victor Amadeus and won him over to the plan by offering him added financial and territorial advantages as well as the overall military command of the expedition.[35] Only after they had gained the duke's approval and begun making preparations for the invasion did the English finally notify the emperor of their intentions. Joseph was unwilling to obstruct his ally's Toulon strategy. In view of its recent endeavors to assist the Austrian war effort in the peninsula, such an act would surely be treated in London as an expression of the grossest ingratitude. Nevertheless, with the present project calling for him to provide the full Austrian troop commitment of 20,000 men established by the 1703 treaty, it would be impossible for his remaining forces to reduce the French-held fortresses in northern Italy or to invade Naples.[36] While the duke of Marlborough was promising to support an attack against southern Italy following the capture of Toulon, there were several reasons for the emperor to believe that such an expedition might never be undertaken.[37] If Toulon were seized by the allies, it might become impossible for the Austrian army to return to Italy without dangerously weakening the new front established in southern France. Moreover, the English and Dutch would be able to argue with some justification that Naples represented an unnecessary expenditure of men and money since its small Spanish army was cut off from the main theaters of the war and thus virtually useless to the Bourbon powers. Finally there was always the possibility that England and the United Provinces might conclude peace with France without securing southern Italy for the archduke. In the months following Ramillies and Turin, Louis XIV had approached the maritime powers with a plan for peace. While the allies had notified Joseph of these feelers and had ultimately rejected Louis's proposals, it was generally feared in Vienna that they would not hesitate to accept a settlement that reserved southern Italy as compensation for the duke of Anjou. If in the end the Spanish empire was to be partitioned, Joseph was determined to secure all of the peninsula for his dynasty rather than accept far-off Spain and the Indies.[38]

With these considerations in mind, Joseph grabbed at Louis XIV's recent offer as the solution to his dilemma. The disclosure of the English government's own secret Toulon diplomacy and intended violation of the 1703 treaty removed whatever reservations he had against dealing with the French. Moreover, by conceding the evacuation of Medavi's army, Joseph hoped to appease his allies by providing the required 20,000 men against Toulon, while still retaining enough troops to garrison northern Italy and seize the kingdom of Naples. When Javallière and Saint Pater reappeared at Eugene's headquarters early in February, the prince was fully prepared to treat with them. After a week of secret negotiations, tentative agreement was reached. While Javallière left for Versailles in order to gain Louis's final approval, Eugene notified Victor Amadeus of the impending settlement and invited him to become a party to it.[39] In view of his own eagerness to secure his eastern flank and occupy those territories promised him in the Treaty of Turin, the duke did not hesitate to join in the projected settlement.[40] With Javallière's return from Versailles, the final text was composed and signed at Milan on 13 March. Concluded by the emperor, Savoy, France, and Spain, the convention provided for the prompt evacuation of Medavi's army to France. Despite Louis's attempts to neutralize southern Italy, it received no mention in the final treaty and was therefore surrendered to ultimate conquest.[41]

In a letter to the emperor, Prince Eugene predicted that the maritime powers would recognize the wisdom of the Treaty of Milan.[42] It had, after all, freed a large number of allied troops for an expedition against

Naples without detracting from the current allied preparations for a thrust into France.[43] Notwithstanding this optimistic appraisal, Joseph's allies were as displeased as they were surprised by the treaty's disclosure. They realized that, while the convention enabled the emperor to pursue his own interests in southern Italy, it simultaneously freed over 20,000 enemy soldiers for operations against English and Dutch armies fighting along France's frontiers.[44] Indeed, once the treaty had guaranteed the recovery of Medavi's army, Louis XIV dispatched 8,000 troops from Orléans's army to Spain, where they played a decisive role in the annihilation of the Anglo-Dutch-Portuguese army at Almansa. Once they had received word of the battle, the English renewed their appeal that the Naples expedition be postponed by arguing that all available troops were now needed in southern France where they could help relieve some of the pressure on the beleaguered allied forces in Spain.[45] Once again, the emperor ignored their pleas. Since February, he had resolved to go ahead with preparations for the invasion, regardless of his allies' wishes.[46] On 17 April he had given the order to march, and, one month later, 10,000 troops under Marshal Daun proceeded south from their camp near Turin.[47]

Coupled with the subsequent success of Daun's expedition, the failure of Prince Eugene's march on Toulon greatly exacerbated Anglo-Dutch resentment at Joseph's "ingratitude." The Dutch grand pensionary, Anthonie Heinius, found the emperor's actions "so unaccountable" as to believe rumors that he had secretly concluded a separate peace with Louis XIV.[48] Joseph had, in fact, been motivated merely by a single-minded determination to secure his interests in Italy. Moreover, during the next few years this same determination would justify other actions—and find other victims.

Apples of Discord

Despite the failure of the offensive against Toulon, the 1707 campaign had ended with the allies in firm control of Italy and the central Mediterranean. With the exception of the Tuscan Presidii ports, the Bourbon enemy had been expelled from the length of the peninsula. Meanwhile, in the surrounding waters, the Anglo-Dutch navy was in complete command. In fact, although the French had succeeded in the end in denying Toulon's port facilities to their enemies, they had been obliged to scuttle their own Mediterranean fleet in order to prevent its capture. Consequently, while Sicily, Sardinia, and the Balearic Islands remained in Spanish hands, their fall appeared to be close at hand.

Hence, the situation confronting Joseph in the summer of 1707 was drastically different from the one which he had faced immediately following his succession. Totally excluded from the peninsula barely two years earlier, he was now, it seemed, master of its fate. Moreover, his experiences here would not repeat the frustrating example of Germany following its liberation after Blenheim. There his freedom had been inhibited by the conflicting ambitions of powerful princes and the competing interests of the other European powers; bound by these considerations, he had been obliged to pursue the policies of his father, albeit with greater energy and facility. In Italy these restraints were mere shadows of the great obstacles that had confronted him to the north. Nevertheless, Joseph was soon to learn that, as in Germany, military victory was rarely the harbinger of political tranquility— especially among allies. Potential problems which could be safely forgotten in time of military crisis and defeat would invariably come to the fore once victory had been achieved.

Even before the conquest of Italy had been completed, Joseph could see this transformation taking place in the policies and attitudes of Victor Amadeus of Savoy. An able and cooperative ally in time of crisis, the duke had become increasingly difficult to deal with following the victory at Turin. During the Toulon offensive, he had proven to be more of a liability than an asset and his relations with Eugene had become so strained that the prince flatly refused to serve alongside his royal cousin in any subsequent campaign.[49] Within a short time after the duke's return from Toulon, greater difficulties arose between him and the emperor regarding the settlement of the terms of their 1703 alliance treaty. Savoy had been won over to the Grand Alliance by a combination of huge subsidies and extensive territorial concessions. While the maritime powers provided the financial support, the emperor agreed to confer parts of the Milanese as well as the imperial fief of Montferrat upon his new ally. Yet, while Leopold had been willing to concede Montferrat, which was the property of the pro-French duke of Mantua, he had shown the greatest reluctance to share Lombardy with Victor Amadeus. Not until November 1703, after months of negotiations, had the emperor agreed to concede the Milanese districts of Lomellina, Sessia, Alessandria, Valenza, and Novara to the duke along with the adjacent territory of Montferrat. Even then, the fate of the strategic Vigevanese had remained unsettled with Victor Amadeus demanding its cession and Leopold promising merely to grant an "equivalent" territory at a later date. Only in the following July, with the fear growing in Vienna that hard-pressed Savoy might come to terms with France, did the emperor finally agree to give up the Vigeva- nese as well. In addition, Leopold soon assured Victor Amadeus that he would become the first Habsburg governor of Milan following its capture from the Bourbons.[50]

At the time, the emperor made these commitments more out of desperation than sincerity. It was considered more imperative to secure Savoy as an ally than to resist the duke's demands for territories which might remain in Bourbon hands until the end of the war. Only follow- ing the battle of Turin did these concessions assume more relevance and receive closer consideration in the councils of the emperor. Even before Lombardy had been fully conquered, both Salm and Wratislaw began urging Joseph not to appoint Victor Amadeus governor of the strategic territory.[51] Accepting this counsel, the emperor disregarded his father's promise and instead awarded Prince Eugene the post. In addition, Joseph and his ministers reevaluated the monarchy's obligations regarding the cession of the Milanese districts and Montferrat to Savoy. The Treaty of Turin had left unclear whether these lands were to be turned over to Victor Amadeus immediately or only following the conclusion of peace. The emperor had several reasons for wishing to postpone the transfers until the end of the war. Not the least of these was his proverbial reluctance to yield revenue-bearing territories to a foreign prince. In addition, Joseph feared that, if Savoy were given its promised share of Lombardy prior to the end of the war, the archduke would lose considerable support among the Spanish people for having agreed to a partition of their empire. Moreover, the emperor realized that, if Victor Amadeus were allowed to gain immediate possession of the territories specified in the 1703 treaty, there would be little to guarantee that the duke would continue to wage war against Louis XIV as a member of the Grand Alliance. In the previous conflict, Victor Amadeus had in fact deserted the anti-French coalition, signing a separate peace with Louis in exchange for considerable territorial advantages. Only by withholding part of the spoils promised the duke in 1703 could Joseph be certain of retaining his continued fidelity.

At first, it appeared as if Victor Amadeus would not press for the immediate transfer of either Montferrat or the Milanese towns that had been secretly promised him. As late as November 1706, he was asking only that he be given the revenue from these lands and was not even opposing the administration of public oaths of allegiance to Archduke Charles.[52] By the beginning of February, however, the duke was demanding possession of Montferrat on the grounds that its cession would not constitute a partition of the Spanish empire and was also threatening to protest openly the administration of any further oaths in the Milanese districts secretly pledged to him.[53] Responding to intensive Anglo-Dutch pressure, Joseph moved to appease Victor Amadeus by secretly handing over Lomellina, Valenza, Sessia, and Alessandria at the end of the month.[54] Nevertheless, on the day following the Austrian evacuation of these territories, Prince Eugene reported the duke's renewed demand for Montferrat as well as for the immediate transfer of the Vigevanese.[55]

Victor Amadeus was not the only Italian ally with whom Joseph clashed during the course of 1707. Within a few months, the entire Spanish inheritance in the peninsula had become a bone of contention between him and his brother, Archduke Charles. Unlike the dispute with the duke of Savoy, the division between the two Habsburgs represented as much a conflict of personalities as it did a disagreement over the legacy of Charles II. Since their youth, Joseph and Charles had shown themselves to be of two totally different natures. Reserved, slow-moving, humble, and conscientious, the Jesuit-trained Charles shared few of the traits of his versatile but volatile older brother. Favorably impressed by what he interpreted as the younger Charles's superior maturity, the then French ambassador, Marshal Villars, commented that "the archduke has the goodness and gentility of the house of Austria."[56] In fact, as he was to demonstrate so clearly in his later life, Joseph's brother was a colorless figure of unquestioned mediocrity. Yet, it was young Charles's mellowness and outward humility that appealed most readily to his father's conception of the qualities of a ruler. By exhibiting openly his partiality to the younger son and betraying his innermost feelings against the older Joseph's birthright, Leopold planted the seeds of resentment and jealousy which were to trouble future relations between the two Habsburg princes.

The first open conflict occurred in 1703 immediately prior to the archduke's departure for Spain. Hoping to forestall a future succession struggle between Joseph and Charles or their heirs, the old emperor resolved to establish firmly each son's rights and secure their mutual recognition of them. However, if it was Leopold's intention to prevent a future Habsburg *Brüderzwist,* his actions inadvertently prompted a sharp conflict between the two heirs. Although he was willing to renounce the bulk of his claims to the Spanish inheritance in favor of his younger brother, Joseph was determined to make some innovations in the succession compact proposed by Leopold. At the instigation of Salm, Archchancellor Lothair Francis, and Elector John William, Joseph urged his father to escheat the imperial fiefs of Milan and Finale and to award them to him rather than to Charles. The archduke opposed this suggestion vigorously. Nevertheless, the emperor and his ministers soon came to appreciate the advantages of attaching these territories to the Austrian lands, thereby keeping them from ever again falling into the hands of the monarchy's enemies. After a number of meetings of the Privy Conference, Leopold agreed to bestow the two fiefs upon his elder son.[57]

Joseph also obliged his brother to consent to a modification in the order of succession in the Spanish lands claimed by the dynasty. Leopold intended to establish a law of succession by which no female could succeed either in Spain or in the Austrian lands until all the males of both Joseph's and Charles's line had died out. Although this arrangement ignored the Castilian practice of permitting daughters to succeed ahead of male cousins and portended the possibility of one man becoming ruler of both the Spanish and Austrian Habsburg dominions, it was strictly in accordance with the dynasty's adherence to the Salic Law forbidding the succession of female members of the family. Should the male issue of both Habsburg lines die out, however, Leopold was then prepared to permit surviving daughters to rule, with

Joseph's female descendants reigning in Vienna and Charles's in Madrid. Yet, Joseph insisted on making one innovation in his father's plan for a female succession. While he was ready to permit Charles's male line precedence in the Spanish succession, he steadfastly refused to allow his brother's female descendants to succeed ahead of his own daughters in either Spain or the *Erblande*. The young archduke objected strongly to the relegation of his own daughters behind Joseph's. Nevertheless, since Joseph's claims were in full accordance with Habsburg succession practices, Charles was again forced to submit to his brother's will.[58]

On 5 September 1703, the emperor and his two sons met together in the Favorita Palace to swear formally to each of these agreements. Since it was imperative that Joseph's acquisition of Milan and Finale not become known in Spain, the documents pertaining to this matter were sworn to in the highest secrecy. Moreover, it was agreed that, should these territories ever be conquered, they would be secretly administered by Joseph while remaining ostensibly part of the archduke's Spanish patrimony.[59] Soon afterward, the two brothers pledged to uphold the succession law adopted by Leopold, with its emphasis on the precedence of collateral male over direct female issue and with its placement of Joseph's females ahead of Charles's in Spain as well as in the *Erblande*. Because of its disregard for Castilian custom and because of Anglo-Dutch sensitivity to any future unification of the Spanish and Austrian lands, the *Pactum Mutuae Successionis* was also kept secret. In fact, although an edited version of the document was presented before a gathering of dignitaries and foreign diplomats one week later, its complete text was not fully disclosed for two decades.[60] Within a few days, Charles departed in quest of the Spanish crown. Yet, although he was never to see his brother again, the seeds of distrust and jealousy that had been sown between them survived his absence. While Charles left Vienna greatly angered by the concessions forced upon him by his brother, Joseph continued to harbor resentment against his father's favorite. As one observer remarked, the Roman king's "hatred of his . . . brother grows daily [and] will, it is feared, never be extinguished."[61] Moreover, Leopold did not help to relieve these feelings. As he entered his last illness, the old emperor became preoccupied with concern for the fate of his younger son.[62] Ten days before his death he ordered Seilern to draw up a testament willing the Tyrol and Hither Austria to Charles in the event that no part of the Spanish inheritance could be won. He then obliged Joseph, whom he had only recently excluded from state affairs, to swear to uphold this bequest.[63]

With the conquest of Italy and Charles's belated landing in Catalonia, any chance that Joseph would have to cede the Tyrol to his younger brother disappeared. Only the memory of his father's last act remained to trouble him. With the fall of Italy, however, new sources of friction arose to disturb his relations with Charles. The first difficulties occurred over the government of Milan. True to his compact with Charles, Joseph was determined to guard closely the secret of his acquisition of the duchy. Only a small circle of ministers was told of the transfer, and at first not even Prince Eugene was informed of it, despite his appointment as governor of the territory. Furthermore, in an effort to preserve the appearance of Charles's sovereignty in Lombardy, all major appointments and administrative decrees were first sent to Barcelona for the archduke's signature before being forwarded to Milan. Yet, if he was willing to risk the considerable delays and confusion which these precautions entailed, Joseph was reluctant to bestow upon his brother the customary imperial patent of investiture that would have formalized his installation as duke of Milan. Since the conferral of such a patent would constitute an official transfer of jurisdiction from emperor to vassal, Joseph feared this step would encourage his brother to establish permanent control over the duchy. In fact, his suspicions were not wholly without foundation, for the archduke had not yet fully reconciled himself to the loss of Milan and still hoped to regain it at a future peace conference.[64]

The emperor's hesitancy to issue the patent excited both the curiosity and impatience of his allies. The maritime powers had been disturbed to learn that the first official proclamations in Lombardy had made no mention of Charles but had been published only in the name of his imperial overlord.[65] Yet, as they pressed Joseph to carry out and Charles to seek the formal transfer of the duchy, they were puzzled to find that even the archduke appeared "content [that] the Emperor should remain possessed of it."[66] More dangerous for Charles than the meddling of the English and Dutch were the growing suspicions of his own Spanish ministers. It was the archduke's constant fear that his supporters would discover the truth and hold him responsible for dismembering the patrimony of Charles II.[67] Consequently, he was reluctant to dismiss the counsel of his Spanish advisors regarding the disposition of affairs in Lombardy, lest they ascertain the actual status of the duchy's sovereignty. Upon the urging of these ministers, he frequently granted pensions and benefices to his supporters out of the annual revenue of Milan and also sought to appropriate part of the duchy's wealth for military expenditures in Spain.[68] Irritated by Charles's apparent disregard for his authority in Lombardy, Joseph reminded his brother that he was not sovereign in the duchy and that no future appropriations were to be made from its revenue.[69] In fact, by the end of 1707, the archduke seemed to have accepted the loss of Milan, even though pressures from his ministers continually obliged him to act otherwise.[70] Nevertheless, despite the archduke's belated resignation, his relations with Joseph remained troubled by the bitterness that he felt over his forced cession of the duchy and the constant need to conceal its loss from his allies and ministers.

Before affairs had been settled in Lombardy, a second struggle erupted between the two brothers over the administration of Naples. Unlike Milan, Naples had not been ceded to Joseph by the secret family compact of September 1703. Therefore, within a short time after the victory at Turin, Charles had begun to consider the choice of a viceroy to administer the kingdom in his name. The man whom he selected was Cardinal Vicenzo Grimani. The most active advocate of the Habsburg cause in the Vatican, the aggressive and ambitious Grimani appeared the obvious choice for the post. Valued as an expert on Italian affairs, he had been appointed by Joseph to the Italian Conference in 1705, despite his frequent absences from Vienna. Moreover, the cardinal was particularly well versed in Neapolitan affairs. Since the beginning of the war, he had maintained close ties with the pro-Habsburg elements within the kingdom and in 1701 had plotted and directed an abortive rebellion against Bourbon rule. In recent months, he had been a driving force behind plans for an invasion of the kingdom and had succeeded in obtaining the Vatican's permission for the passage of Daun's army through the Papal States.[71]

Having made his decision, Charles duly notified Vienna of his intention to appoint Grimani viceroy.[72] What he did not know was that his brother was determined to fill the position himself. Although they realized that they had no jurisdiction in Naples, Joseph and his ministers considered the archduke too young and inexperienced to be permitted to select his own viceroy.[73] Indeed, they regarded his choice of Grimani as totally unacceptable. To them it was essential that the new viceroy prove himself capable of governing wisely and gaining the loyalty of the Neapolitan population.[74] Should he fail in this, the Spanish forces in neighboring Sicily could easily cross into the kingdom and lead a successful revolt against Habsburg rule. Yet, during his tenure at the Vatican, the cardinal had demonstrated a remarkable talent for alienating his colleagues and becoming the most hated diplomat in the city. In addition, both Salm and Wratislaw expressed the opinion that only the elevation of an imperial subject would guarantee the unswerving loyalty of the new viceroy to the Austrian as well as the Spanish branch of the dynasty.[75] Though presently serving in Rome as the imperial *Conprotector Germaniae,* Grimani was himself a Venetian and had spent several years in the Savoyard service. When on 26 April Joseph met with his ministers to select a viceroy, no thought was given to Charles's candidate. Instead, the name of Georg Adam Count Martinitz was unanimously agreed upon.[76] Himself a member of the Italian Conference, Martinitz had proven an able and diligent statesman during his years as imperial ambassador to the Vatican. Moreover, he was a popular figure among his fellow Bohemian aristocrats and was strongly favored by those Neapolitan noblemen who had been residing at court since the abortive 1701 revolt.[77]

On 2 May Count Wratislaw wrote to the archduke informing him that Joseph had appointed Martinitz viceroy in his name and urging him to avoid further friction by accepting his brother's choice.[78] Yet, while Charles could reconcile himself to the loss of Milan, with its countless humiliations and political risks, he could not bring himself to retreat further before Joseph's aggressions. He stood firm not only because he had to avoid the impression that he had ceded all Italy to his brother but also because his angered pride and sense of justice required it. Replying to Wratislaw's letter, Charles announced that he would not confirm Martinitz's appointment under any circumstances. Furthermore, he pointed out that only his reluctance to worsen relations with his brother was preventing him from going through with his original intention of naming Grimani and presenting Joseph with an ultimatum demanding Martinitz's immediate withdrawal. Instead of openly challenging the emperor, Charles suggested ways in which the Martinitz nomination could be gracefully put aside and even offered to select as viceroy a third, mutually acceptable candidate if the Bohemian count's appointment was rescinded.[79]

Although he was hesitant to force Martinitz's recall, the archduke immediately began working to undermine the new viceroy's authority. On 31 July he named Field Marshal Daun to be commander-in-chief of all Spanish military forces and installations in the kingdom. Since the Habsburg claimant had no army of his own in Naples, the appointment seemingly added little to Daun's power and responsibilities as commander of the occupying Austrian army. However, by having made him a representative of the Spanish crown, Charles hoped to use Daun as the sole instrument of his rule in Naples, thereby circumventing the presence of Martinitz. The archduke could not have chosen a better figure to pit against his Bohemian viceroy. Even before they had entered Naples, Daun and Martinitz had begun to clash over the proper division of their authority. Once the field marshal learned of his appointment, the struggle intensified, with Martinitz gradually losing ground to his rival. Over the next few weeks, Charles totally ignored his viceroy by conducting all administrative matters, including the crucial handling of patronage, through his commander-in-chief. Meanwhile, at the instigation of Cardinal Grimani, the Neapolitan nobility began to press for the replacement of the politically impotent Martinitz.[80]

Although greatly irritated by his brother's opposition, Joseph had come to regret his earlier appointment of Martinitz and was presently eager to extricate himself from further embarrassment. When on 15 September he received the viceroy's request to retire, ostensibly on grounds of poor health, Joseph quickly accepted his resignation. Over the next few months, Daun served as interim viceroy while the two brothers consulted with each other before deciding on a permanent successor.[81] In the following June, with Daun preparing to return to the front, the emperor reluctantly agreed to the appointment of Grimani. Since it was "felt that it would not be good to have two Italians in one government together," Joseph asked only that the German prince of Hesse-Darmstadt be named to replace Daun as commander-in-chief.[82] The archduke agreed to this request, and on 28 June Hesse-Darmstadt arrived in Naples, followed five days later by Cardinal Grimani.[83]

Unfortunately this compromise did not wholly solve the administrative problems of the last year. Within a short time, Hesse and Grimani were fighting over the proper division of their administrative responsibilities, just as Daun and Martinitz had clashed before them.[84]Nevertheless, the subsequent conflict within the Neapolitan government was destined to remain a purely local confrontation, brought about by the awkward dichotomy existing within the royal bureaucracy and not by the rivalry of the two Habsburg courts. Indeed, both Joseph and Charles intervened in the dispute with the firm intention of restraining rather than encouraging the pretensions of their deputies.[85] The Habsburg brothers had become allies at last.

Imperial Renaissance

By seeking the cession of Milan and Finale, as well as control over the Neapolitan viceroyalty, Joseph demonstrated his ability to distinguish between his purely "Austrian" objectives and the broader concerns of his dynasty. In Italy, however, the monarchy's and dynasty's interests also competed with those of the Holy Roman Empire. Since the beginning of the reign, Joseph had proclaimed to the German princes his intentions of reviving imperial authority south of the Alps. His subsequent use of imperial prerogatives was, in fact, so extensive that modern German historians have portrayed him as a devoted champion of the empire's pretensions in northern Italy.[86] Yet, as in the escheatment of Milan and Finale in 1703, Joseph usually used his imperial prerogative to further Austrian objectives and always placed the empire's interests behind those of both monarchy and dynasty. Throughout the war, his greatest concerns remained the provision of immediate military needs and the establishment of Austrian, rather than the restoration of imperial (or Spanish Habsburg), hegemony in the peninsula.

At no time was Joseph or anyone else in Germany ever aware of the exact extent of imperial jurisdiction in northern Italy. Indeed, the absence of firm and closely defined constitutional prerogatives or institutions was unquestionably Joseph's greatest weapon in denying the Italian states any legal protection against his actions. None of the north Italian princes sat in the Imperial Diet. Except for Savoy, they were neither represented in nor under the jurisdiction of the Imperial Chamber Court. Instead, the sole imperial judicial authority in northern Italy was the Aulic Council, and from its rulings in Vienna, there was no appeal.[87] Consequently, whereas in Germany the emperor's legal prerogatives and the judgments of the Aulic Council were but tools of princely diplomacy through which he could offer or withhold concessions, in Italy they were powerful instruments of policy and arbitrary force. Moreover, as Joseph prepared to revive and expand the scope of imperial authority within the peninsula as a ruling device of the dynasty, he realized that there would be no organized opposition to frustrate his intentions. In Germany he was constantly held in check by the larger armed estates as well as by the *corpus evangelicorum*. In imperial Italy, there was only Savoy, a state with minimal interest in the fate of its neighbors. Meanwhile, Joseph could hope to rely upon the latent patriotism of Germany's more powerful princes to help support the renewal of the empire's authority beyond the Alps.

Within the Italian Conference itself, Joseph found his ministers both inclined and equipped to push his claims in the peninsula. As a member of the Aulic Council and a proven champion of imperial prerogatives in Germany, Count Schönborn had earned a berth in the Italian Conference as early as 1706. In admitting him to its deliberations, Joseph realized that Schönborn was essentially indifferent to the pursuit of purely Habsburg interests. Yet, he viewed the possibility of a conflict between imperial and Austrian policy to be even more remote in Italy than it was in Germany. In addition, Joseph considered Schönborn's admission as a necessary step in gaining support for his Italian policy from the archchancellor and the rest of the empire. Count Martinitz was also a fervent advocate of the emperor's pretensions to jurisdiction in northern Italy. Indeed, so strongly had he disputed rival papal claims during his embassy to Rome that he was eventually recalled from his post at the request of Innocent XII. Finally, as the foremost legal mind at court, Baron Seilern held an important place in the Italian Conference. Although the high esteem in which he held his own pedantry inclined him to be rather long-winded and stubborn during deliberations, the Austrian chancellor's ability to apply his extensive legal knowledge to justify even the most tenuous imperial claims made him indispensable to the formulation of Joseph's Italian *Reichspolitik*.

As long as the war lasted, Joseph's principal objective in the peninsula was to find new sources from which to maintain his Italian army. Consequently, while the government in Vienna was anxious to establish its own political mastery over the northern end of the peninsula, its policies invariably translated into financial terms. In this sense, the method by which Joseph sought to punish those princes who had allied or cooperated with the Bourbon powers is particularly instructive. In the closing days of his reign, Emperor Leopold had ordered the preparation of a list of disloyal Italian vassals. In most instances, disloyalty constituted nothing more than the involuntary compliance of the smallest princes to Philip V's demand that they recognize

Spanish rather than imperial vassalage. Nevertheless, this was regarded in Vienna as sufficient grounds for placing the offending princes
under military execution and confiscating their territories.[88]

Most of the larger states, such as Tuscany, Genoa, and Parma
proved able to evade these demands by the payment of a tribute.
Among their number, only Savoy and Mantua became active protégés
of the Bourbon powers. In the case of Savoy, all plans to place it under
the imperial ban were dropped following its desertion of the French
alliance in 1703. Meanwhile, with Prince Eugene's victory at Turin,
Joseph immediately made preparations for punishing the Gonzaga
duke, Charles Ferdinand of Mantua. On 20 November 1706, he formally asked the Aulic Council to pass judgment on the duke, and in the
following May, his conviction was ratified by the Electoral College.[89]

Although Joseph intended to cede Montferrat to Victor Amadeus as
agreed to in the Treaty of Turin, he secretly hoped to join Mantua itself
with his own Milanese lands. Nevertheless, with Savoy's recent demands for the immediate surrender of Montferrat, financial considerations intervened to frustrate the proclamation of the ban. Realizing
that he could more easily retain possession of Montferrat as long as no
formal pronouncement was made against Charles Ferdinand, Joseph
elected to suspend the final judgment. For a full year, he continued to
administer both Mantua and Montferrat in the face of intense Anglo-
Dutch pressure to complete the process against Charles Ferdinand and
transfer Montferrat to Savoy.[90]

While those princes who had committed crimes against the empire
were liable to execution under the ban, all of the imperial vassals in
northern Italy were subject to the payment of a war levy. During 1705
Joseph had ordered Schierendorff to research these obligations and by
the end of the year had even sought the assistance of the Anglo-Dutch
navy in collecting them from Tuscany and Genoa.[91] Although the
maritime powers turned down the request, the emperor was able to tax
his Italian vassals immediately following the victory at Turin. The
imperial war levy was divided into two distinct categories. The coastal
states of Genoa, Tuscany, Lucca, and Massa were subject to the
payment of a *Contributio*. Meanwhile landlocked Modena, Mantua,
Mirandola, Parma, and Guastalla were obligated to quarter imperial
troops on their soil or to pay an equivalent sum in money.[92]

Though the Austrian army was quartered throughout much of
northern Italy during the winter of 1706-1707, the *Contributio* was not
levied until the following spring. At that time, the General War
Commissary negotiated agreements with each of the coastal states,
albeit with the help of ultimata and execution threats delivered to each
prince by Prince Eugene.[93] After 1707 the sums collected under the
Contributio fell off considerably, partly because the first year's levy
had been intended as back payment for the previous campaigns but
also because of the growing inability of each of the vassal states to

sustain the heavy financial burden. Similarly the territory eligible for winter quartering was soon exhausted, forcing the emperor to search for new sources of revenue within the peninsula.[94] Yet, while his ministers busied themselves in the preparation of expanded tax and quartering prerogatives, Joseph encountered in the pope a new and formidable obstacle to the establishment of imperial taxation and Austrian hegemony in northern Italy.

During the last European conflict, considerable friction had arisen between Vienna and Rome regarding the extent of imperial jurisdiction north of the Papal States. With Martinitz's recall and the end of the war, the dispute had subsided. Yet, with the commencement of the struggle for the Spanish succession, relations between the two courts had taken a disastrous turn. At the request of Charles II, Innocent XII commissioned a council of cardinals in the summer of 1700 to judge the merits of the rival Bourbon and Austrian Habsburg claims. The council decided in favor of the French candidacy. Although Innocent died shortly thereafter, the election of Gian Francesco Albani as Clement XI did nothing to prevent a steady worsening of relations with Vienna. Elected only two weeks after the death of Charles II, the new pope was more a scholar and poet than a statesman and was not partial to the pretensions of either the Habsburg or Bourbon pretenders. Nevertheless, owing to the pro-French leanings of most of his cardinals, the initial Bourbon domination of the peninsula, and his own inexperience as a statesman, Clement was unable to maintain a neutral course during the early years of the war.

Indeed, it was not too long before the government in Vienna became convinced that the new pope was a strong supporter of the Bourbon cause. While holding firm in his recognition of Philip as king of Spain, Clement refused to allow any public displays of loyalty to the Habsburg pretender by papal or foreign subjects. Following the collapse of the revolt in Naples, he arrested those Neapolitan noblemen who had sought refuge in Rome. Meanwhile, though placing an embargo on all trade with Prince Eugene's army, Clement freely permitted the French to purchase supplies and refused to protest their frequent incursions into papal territory.[95] Indeed, in one notorious incident near the papal town of Ficarolo, Clement's officials failed to honor their guarantee of a truce between opposing Austrian and French forces and permitted the French to fall upon their unsuspecting enemy.

In reality, the pope was sincerely interested in maintaining complete neutrality during the present struggle. In many instances such as in the Ficarolo affair, the independent actions of local officials and the influence of French bribes had compromised his intentions. More often fear of French retaliation motivated him to grant concessions to the emperor's enemies. Yet, regardless of the reasons behind his actions, Clement's course had aroused considerable resentment and distrust in Vienna.

Joseph's succession did nothing to ease relations between the two courts. Indeed, it only had the effect of shortening the fuse prior to the explosion. Within weeks after his father's death, Joseph had already begun to challenge the Holy See. Since the Middle Ages, it had been customary for each new emperor to commission an embassy to appear before the pope notifying him of his succession and seeking in return a bull of confirmation. Although the procedure had long since become a formality and no longer implied any act of submission to papal authority, most new emperors had continued to follow it in order to receive from the pope a second document granting them the *preces primariae,* or right to fill the first imperial benefice vacated during their reign.[96] After consulting with his ministers, Joseph decided not to commission the traditional embassy. Instead, he merely wrote to Clement informing him "in no very obliging style" of the change in regime.[97] Moreover, in a further Conference on 19 June, the emperor adopted the position that exercise of the *preces primariae* was not dependent upon papal sanction but was rather an inalienable prerogative of each new emperor. Later in the day, he appointed a canon to a vacant benefice in the bishopric of Hildesheim.[98]

While Joseph was preparing to challenge Clement's authority to dispense the *preces primariae,* he received word from Rome that papal magistrates had jailed the son of an imperial diplomat for a period of three weeks after he had refused them permission to search his home. The emperor now judged that the time had come to seek redress for the series of insults and injustices to which his family had been subjected. While exiling the Vienna nuncio to Wiener Neustadt, he instructed his Roman ambassador to leave the Papal States immediately. Clement reacted to the sudden break in relations by writing Joseph and professing in very conciliatory language his total impartiality in the present conflict. Of somewhat more importance were the letters which he dispatched simultaneously to the four Roman Catholic electors as well as to all of the influential churchmen in Vienna offering to submit to mediation each of the sources of conflict between the two courts.[99] Although the emperor rejected these overtures, he saw in the pope's letters a willingness to normalize relations. Hence, Joseph soon replied to Clement by inviting him to dispatch a papal emissary to Vienna with full powers to grant a redress of grievances.[100]

The next year brought a lull in diplomatic activity between the two courts as Vienna concerned itself with preparations for the decisive 1706 campaign while Rome looked on in curious anticipation. New sources of friction arose over Prince Eugene's incursions into Bologna and Ferrara, first during the march to Turin, and later in the year, when both Austrian and French troops established winter quarters in the two provinces. Eugene defended his actions by citing the need to prevent Medavi's escape to Naples.[101] Nevertheless, as Clement's threats of retaliation became more strident, Joseph ordered his commander to provide suitable compensation for the army's requisitions as well as for the excesses committed by his troops. In a convention concluded in February 1707 between representatives of the pope and the Austrian military, Eugene agreed to evacuate the Papal States in exchange for the delivery of supplies from Ferrara and Bologna. In addition, Clement took the first step toward granting satisfaction to Joseph by agreeing to pay 240,000 florins in compensation for the Austrian losses suffered at Ficarolo.[102]

Within a few months, the occasion of Daun's march to Naples gave Joseph an excellent opportunity to press the pope for a further redress of grievances. In giving Daun's army permission to pass through the Papal States, Clement had specified that it should pursue an easterly route leading through the Abruzzi. Yet, on orders from Joseph, the Austrian force was directed to proceed down the west coast of the peninsula passing within one to two days' march of Rome itself.[103] In mid-June Daun camped his army for five days at the town of Tivoli only sixteen miles from the papal capital. Meanwhile, he and Martinitz rode into Rome with the intention of seeing the pope.

In view of the high priority given to the Naples invasion, the interview with Clement was not intended to be a serious negotiation leading to an immediate settlement of the difficulties existing between Vienna and Rome. Rather the embassy's purpose was merely to present to the pope "without ceremony" a list of gravamina. Most of the points dealt with the fate of those Neapolitan exiles who had been condemned by papal courts.[104] At Joseph's suggestion, however, an article was inserted requesting formal recognition of the archduke in the lands presently held by the allies.[105] Once again Clement expressed a willingness to compromise by promising to look into the injustices committed against the Neapolitan noblemen. Moreover, he expressed the hope that the emperor would soon reestablish formal diplomatic relations. Regarding recognition of the archduke, the pope proved somewhat less pliable. While offering to convene a cardinals' commission to deliberate the matter, he emphasized that its decision would have to be free from outside pressure and be accepted without reservations by the emperor.[106] Although Martinitz expressed his own disappointment with the "insufficient satisfaction" granted by the pope, Joseph was almost certainly pleased by Clement's evident, if cautious, policy of conciliation.[107] As a sign of his own satisfaction, he ordered that the pope be paid compensation for the excesses committed by Austrian forces during the march to Turin. At the same time, he wrote to the irascible Grimani instructing him to avoid further friction with the papal court.[108]

If Joseph anticipated a thaw in relations with Rome, his expectations proved short-lived. As soon as Daun's army had crossed into Naples, Clement prepared to reopen the controversy over the limits of imperial authority in northern Italy. His principal target was the duchy of Parma, which the papacy had long claimed to be a fief of the Holy See. During the early years of the war, its duke had sought to prevent incursions by the French and Austrians by recognizing Rome's pretensions, hoisting the papal flag over his capital and admitting a papal garrison to the frontier city of Piacenza. With the Austrian victory, however, Parma found itself grouped together with its neighbors for the purposes of imperial taxation. By an agreement signed with the General War Commissary at the end of 1706, the duke pledged to discharge 540,000 florins in quartering obligations to Prince Eugene's army. Moreover, since the church possessed a full third of the duchy's landed wealth, it was agreed that a quarter of these taxes would be levied against the clergy.[109] On 27 July Clement issued a papal *breve* nullifying the validity of this treaty and forbidding the quartering of troops or collection of taxes in the duchy of Parma. In addition, the declaration commanded the clergy of both Parma and Milan to resist all forms of imperial taxation and excommunicated automatically anyone who sought to enforce these obligations on the church.[110]

While he was unaware of the exact nature of Parma's vassalage, Joseph was unwilling to surrender the duchy along with its revenue to papal suzerainty. Moreover, he was incensed by the inclusion of the Milanese clergy in Clement's declaration. He was aware that the Spanish had been permitted to tax the church in Lombardy in the early years of the war and felt that this privilege could not now be justifiably revoked. Rather than allow himself to be intimidated by Clement, Joseph ordered a continuation of his tax policies in both Milan and Parma. During October, Prince Eugene demanded a 300,000 florin subsidy from the Milanese clergy. A few months later, while most of the north Italian princes were negotiating reductions in their imperial taxes for 1708, Parma's obligations were again assessed at over a half million florins.[111]

Although he intended to remain firm in the face of Clement's defiance, Joseph realized that further action would have to be taken before the Vatican would consent to a full redress of grievances. It was now apparent that the pope's earlier effort at conciliation had been prompted in part by the victory at Turin and the menacing presence of Daun's army rather than by any sincere willingness to grant satisfaction. Clearly any further concessions would have to be won by the employment of similar means. As a youth, Joseph had been trained to distinguish between the pope's spiritual and temporal authority and to be prepared to oppose the latter to the point of war.[112] Hence, he did not now shrink from using force against Clement. Once the pope had chosen to reopen the controversy between imperial and papal suzerainty in northern Italy, Joseph promptly resolved to extend the struggle into the states of the church. Since most of the Papal States had formerly been fiefs of the empire, there were many territories to which the emperor could assert his rights. It was in the Ferrarese town of Comacchio, however, that Joseph had his best and possibly his only defensible legal claim. Unlike the rest of Ferrara, Comacchio had long been recognized as an imperial fief when in 1598 Clement VIII seized the entire duchy from the Este dynasty of Modena. Although the rulers of Modena subsequently acknowledged the loss of Ferrara, they had never accepted the legality of the papal seizure of Comacchio.

Aside from the legal justifications there were other reasons for contesting the fate of Comacchio. Throughout the early years of the war, Duke Rinaldo of Modena had been the only Italian prince to remain loyal to the Habsburg cause, principally because of the influence of his wife, Charlotte Felicitas, an elder sister of Amalia. For his allegiance, he had paid dearly at the hands of the French, and since the victory at Turin, Joseph had been seeking to compensate him for his losses. At first, Amalia and her kinsman Prince Salm had suggested the post of governor of Milan. However, his appointment had been frustrated by the opposition of Wratislaw and Seilern to the choice of any foreign ruler.[113] With the French evacuation of northern Italy, the possibility of compensating Rinaldo with the small duchy of Mirandola had also been discussed but not acted upon.[114] Urged on by Salm and Amalia, however, the emperor now accepted the plan to seize Comacchio as the perfect blend of Austrian interest and dynastic politics, held together by imperial right.

At the time Joseph decided to lay claim to Comacchio, neither he nor his ministers had at their disposal any firm proof of the justness of their intended claim. Therefore, during December he commissioned Seilern and the Aulic Council to search for legal records supporting the empire's rights to the town.[115] Under the direction of Schönborn, the Aulic Council also began preparing a rebuttal to Clement's 27 July declaration. By late January, the outlines of the imperial position against the papal *breve* began to take shape. While Joseph would reassert the empire's claims to Parma, he would also justify his opposition to the pope by arguing that no emperor could legally permit the surrender of imperial territory without the express approval of the diet. Furthermore, Clement's interdict against church taxation in Parma and Milan would be declared without legal foundation and, therefore, null and void.[116] By the end of March, the emperor had ratified this Aulic Council position as well as an additional argument formulated earlier in the month disputing the tax immunity of the clergy in the two duchies.[117]

Notwithstanding the legal arguments being prepared by his aulic councilors, Joseph still viewed the presentation of the imperial claims solely as a means of justifying his intended challenge to papal authority. While he was determined to assert his jurisdiction in Parma, he remained principally interested only in its value as a quartering ground and a source of tax revenue. As far as Comacchio was concerned, he was bent on using it only as a means of obtaining leverage against the pope and forcing him to concede on other, more important points. Indeed, on the eve of his celebrated seizure of Comacchio, he had no intention of presenting any formal claims to the former imperial fief.

Despite the single-mindedness of Joseph's intentions, however, his decision to challenge Clement in Comacchio did not meet with the approval of the strongest advocate of Austrian interests at court, Count Wratislaw. In fact, it was the Bohemian chancellor's determination to upset the preparations against the pope which now gave rise to the one major struggle over policy during the reign of Joseph I. Historians have often spoken of the opposing factions that centered around Salm and Wratislaw and have assumed that the personal animosity between the two men bore a relationship to the formulation of state policy. Citing the Bohemian chancellor's close adherence to the pursuit of purely Austrian interests and Prince Salm's imperial origins, historians have tended to divide the court into distinct Austrian and German parties. In reality, because of the frequent coincidence of imperial and dynastic interests as well as the precedence that Salm himself gave to the achievement of "Austrian" objectives, the two factions never clashed over German affairs. When there was division within the German Conference, it was Schönborn who was in opposition—and he invariably stood alone. The marriage of imperial claims and dynastic interests had been even more intimate during the opening year of Austrian rule in the peninsula. However, in Wratislaw's judgment, the present venture against the pope, whether launched in the interests of the dynasty or of the empire, threatened to reap a disastrous harvest within the Mediterranean world. He feared that any attempt to humiliate the papacy would further alienate what he recognized as a growing disaffection among both the peoples and princes of northern Italy to the presence of German troops and tax officials.[118] Moreover, he was convinced that an attack on the pope would badly sabotage Charles's efforts to win over the loyalty of his new subjects in Spain as well as in Naples.[119]

Regarding Salm as the mainstay behind the Comacchio project, Wratislaw began working to frustrate its execution by openly calling for his retirement from court. As in the 1706 conspiracy against the lord high steward, Wratislaw was readily seconded by Prince Eugene.[120] Indeed the *Hofkriegsrat* president had a strong personal motivation in seeking Salm's dismissal. Arguing that Eugene's imminent dispatch to Belgium would deprive Milan of effective leadership, Salm and Amalia had recently convinced Joseph to withhold his formal investiture as governor and to reconsider the candidacy of the duke of Modena.[121] Only by depriving Amalia of her faithful voice in the Conference could Eugene be sure of holding on to the lucrative post.

Although they had failed in their previous attempt to force Salm's fall, in the early months of 1708 Eugene and Wratislaw had good reason to hope for success. Since the beginning of the past year, the lord high steward had begun speaking of leaving court due to his steadily declining health.[122] In the previous November, he had asked Joseph for permission to retire. Refusing to accept his resignation, Joseph had persuaded Salm to stay at his post until the end of the war. At the same time, the emperor announced that his longtime friend and chamberlain, Count Trautson, would eventually replace the aging prince as lord high steward. Joseph had chosen the discreet and widely respected Trautson on the presumption that his complete innocence from court intrigue would serve to disarm the two hostile ministerial cliques in the period before as well as after his elevation. Yet, the prospects of Trautson's succession could not dampen the expectations and apprehensions brought about by the imminence of Salm's departure.[123]

The emperor himself was principally to blame for the orgy of factionalism and character assassination into which the court now fell. With the passing of time, he had surrendered himself more and more to the pursuit of his pleasures. Assisted by his favorite, Leopold Count Lamberg, who served both as his principal procurer and hunting companion, Joseph abandoned himself to his mistresses without regard for his wife's feelings and to his hunting trips with little concern for his own health and safety.[124] As a sign of affection for his *Oberstjägermeister*, the emperor had announced in November that Lamberg would soon be elevated to the rank of prince, thereby leading one observer to comment that it was indeed "a dignity so considerable to give a man whose merit consists only in the qualities of good hunting and excellent pimping for his master."[125]

Fortunately Joseph showered his friends with gifts and titles rather than the political power to which Lamberg also aspired.[126] Instead, it was to his ministers that the emperor was surrendering the reins of government. With increasing regularity, he absented himself from meetings of the Conference, often presiding over only those sessions that completed the discussion of a particular issue. Of course it is impossible to ascertain the extent to which Joseph concerned himself with state affairs outside of the Conference. It is certainly true that he consulted frequently with his ministers privately in his own chambers and even during hunting expeditions. Moreover, it still cannot be said that his absence from the Conference hindered the dispatch of policy. Nevertheless, by delegating to his ministers the preparation of state business, Joseph was putting considerable power in their hands. With Salm's resignation, the man who held the most power would be leaving the scene. A struggle was inevitable.

Throughout the winter months, the battle raged at court.[127] By March, however, Wratislaw and Eugene had failed once again to force Salm's resignation. It was at this point that they struck upon a new strategy to establish their own ascendancy at court and help divert the emperor from the Comacchio venture. During March they began pressing for the creation of a single policy-making body to replace the system of eight conferences created at the beginning of the reign.[128] In fact, in the spring of 1708, there appeared to be some valid arguments for undertaking such a reform. It had been found that the present division of the Privy Conference into several bodies had deprived the ministers of an overall view of state policy. Besides the emperor himself, only Salm could attend all meetings and exercise a unifying influence over the monarchy's affairs. However, with Joseph's frequent absence from the Conference and Salm's promised retirement, this advantage seemed lost. Of course, in urging this reform, Wratislaw and Eugene were principally motivated by the expectation that they would be included in the membership of their proposed "Great Conference" and thereby gain a voice in the formulation of Italian policy. So far, they had been totally excluded from the planning of the Comacchio project. Although he had been able to speak with the emperor in private and submit written counsel, Wratislaw's personal influence was considerably handicapped by his ignorance of the facts and arguments presented in the Italian Conference.[129] Meanwhile, those ministers who were making policy were of a totally different mind than he. Since the departure of Grimani and his friend Moles, Italian affairs had been left in the hands of Salm, Martinitz, Seilern, and the upstart Schönborn. Although he was close to both Martinitz and Seilern, Wratislaw realized that Martinitz's own inclinations and Seilern's obsession with the legal perversions of imperial law made both men intractible to his own influence. For most of the spring, he pressed Joseph to scrap the present conference system. However, the emperor expressed his reluctance to experiment with reform on the eve of his offensive against the pope. Wratislaw had lost another battle. Salm was still in command.

The Papal War

On 10 May a detachment of 2,000 Austrian troops under General Bonneval marched into the papal legation of Ferrara. Although the local governor had at his command 3,000 regular infantry plus an additional 5,000 militia, Bonneval succeeded two weeks later in besieging and occupying the town of Comacchio.[130] Upon receiving word of the Austrian incursion, Clement immediately protested to Joseph and appealed to the Catholic electors for support. The emperor replied on 26 June with a formal, strongly worded rebuttal of the 27 July 1707 *breve.* By defending Joseph's obligation to protect the empire's borders and by refuting the validity of the pope's Parma claims and excommunication threats, the document essentially reiterated the arguments drawn up earlier in the year by the Aulic Council. It did not, however, dwell upon the imperial pretensions to Comacchio.

To help drum up support for his own position, the emperor dispatched copies of the 26 June manifesto to the major German princes as well as to the Regensburg Diet. The most positive response came from the recently confirmed elector of Hanover, whose family was closely tied to the Estes of Modena both by ancient lineage and the more recent marriage of Charlotte Felicitas. Under the direction of George Louis's court librarian, the philosopher Gottfried Wilhelm Leibniz, a legal defense was prepared to support the imperial and Este claims to Comacchio. In Modena itself, Rinaldo commissioned his own librarian, Lodovico Antonio Muratori, to ready a similar presentation of his family's pretensions, thereby launching Muratori's career as a pioneer of modern Italian historiography. Within a short while, the efforts of these men had been supplemented by those of numerous German and papal legists and historians in a blossoming pamphlet war between the empire and Rome.[131]

Whether or not the present conflict was to remain solely a *Federkrieg* soon became the concern of the emperor's ministers. In a series of meetings between mid-July and early August, the Italian Conference debated the choice between further military action and the immediate opening of negotiations with the papacy.[132] Bowing at last to Wratislaw's wishes, Joseph introduced his Bohemian chancellor as well as Trautson, Sinzendorf, and *Hofkriegsrat* Vice President Herberstein into its deliberations. Remarkably, Wratislaw's entry did not bring any dramatic conflicts or shifts of position within the Conference. Although he had steadfastly opposed the seizure of Comacchio, Wratislaw readily joined with his colleagues in agreeing that it could not now be evacuated. Meanwhile, all of the ministers agreed to push for the opening of negotiations as soon as possible. Although Schönborn and Herberstein did advocate the use of further force if Clement refused to negotiate, they soon modified their position with the arrival on 2 August of a papal threat to excommunicate Joseph and go to war if additional Austrian troop advances occurred.[133] Indeed, the Conference had no intention of waiting for the pope to announce his willingness to open talks. The emperor had already chosen the war commissar for Italy, the Marquis Prié, to open negotiations with Clement at the Vatican, and the Conference was itself most anxious to send him on his way. His dispatch was delayed until the end of August, however, because of the court's inability to unearth sufficient archival evidence supporting its claims to Parma or to tax privileges over the Milanese clergy.[134]

While the emperor's ministers were anticipating the opening of negotiations with Rome, Clement was busily preparing to meet the invasion of Ferrara with armed force. Throughout the summer months, he worked feverishly to build up the papal army. He authorized the transfer of 10,000 troops from Avignon and the enlistment of 3,000 Swiss mercenaries. Recruiters were sent into both Parma and Tuscany, and large numbers of deserters from the Austrian army in

Naples were readily enlisted into the higher-paying, better-fed papal forces. Meanwhile, within the states of the church, Clement announced a 1 percent conscription of all males between the ages of twenty and forty. By the beginning of September, he had built his forces to a strength of 25,000 men.[135] Of course, though rich in numbers, the papal army was hardly of a professional caliber. Many of the men recruited within the Papal States had been drawn from the local jails on the promise of full amnesty. A large number of officers lacked military experience. Indeed, the army's commanding general, Luigi Fernando Marsigli, was hardly capable of inspiring confidence in his men. Formerly a general in the Austrian service, Marsigli had been arrested and later dismissed by Emperor Leopold following his surrender in 1703 of the formidable fortress town of Breisach after a siege of only two weeks, despite orders to hold his position at all costs. Called out of retirement by the pope, the unfortunate Marsigli at one point actually injured Clement while drawing his sword at a ceremonial review of papal troops.[136]

While the pope continued to strengthen his forces, the legate of Ferrara finally opened hostilities at the beginning of September. Under his direction, bands of armed peasants and papal militia encircled Comacchio and began ambushing foraging parties sent out by its 900-man garrison. Upon receiving word of these events, Joseph and his ministers became greatly alarmed. With the exception of Wratislaw, they had considered a papal counterattack unlikely and had continued to view the occupation as an effective means of forcing Clement to grant concessions. Now they were faced with the prospect of the town's capture and of a possible military confrontation with the pope. To meet the present crisis, Joseph reconvened the Conference, this time under his own direction. There was a general concern for Bonneval's ability to hold out. Aside from the small garrisons in nearby Mirandola and Mantua and 1,600 reinforcements transferred from southern France during August, there were virtually no Austrian forces within 100 miles of the besieged town. Upon the request of the governor of Mantua, Rinaldo had recently placed 5,000 men along his common frontier with Ferrara, but it was uncertain whether the duke would be willing to risk committing his forces to a fray with the papal army.[137] On 25 September the Conference decided to recall a large part of the 20,000 Austrian troops currently serving under Daun in southern France. In agreeing to this step, however, Joseph and his ministers were no longer concerned merely with relieving Bonneval. During the meeting, Wratislaw had urged that Daun's troops be used to overwhelm Ferrara and its papal garrisons in order to force Clement to accept a truce and disarm the rest of his army. Otherwise, he argued, the pope would refuse to come to terms with Prié and use the approaching winter to prepare the opening of a new front in central Italy.[138] Joseph readily accepted Wratislaw's proposal and immediately ordered Daun to proceed to Ferrara with all available Austrian and auxiliary forces.[139] To minimize the risk of a total break with Clement, he instructed his field commanders not only to maintain strict discipline but also to coordinate their advance closely with the progress of Prié's negotiations. Yet, despite these precautions and Prié's letters from Italy prophesying that peace could still be preserved, Joseph expressed to his ministers the fear that war was indeed inevitable.[140]

Within a few days new word from the peninsula seemed to confirm the emperor's pessimism. A ship convoy heading down the Po with supplies for Bonneval had been ambushed by regular papal infantry. Thirty Austrian soldiers had been killed in the assault and four of the vessels seized. Together with a report of the arrival of 5,000 papal infantry from Avignon, news of the attack convinced the court of the pope's determination to commit himself fully to war against the emperor. At the same time, it was learned that the French Marshal Tessé had appeared in Genoa on the first leg of an embassy that was to take him through each of the principal Italian courts and conclude in Rome itself. With rumors already circulating of an impending Venetian naval blockade of Comacchio, Joseph and his ministers were now obliged to consider for the first time the threat of an alliance between Clement and Louis XIV, and of an Italian league held together by papal subsidies.[141]

In a 12 October Conference, the prospects of such a coalition occasioned expressions of great concern principally because everyone realized that the Austrian army would have to fight virtually without the benefit of financial or military assistance from its allies.[142] In a bitter turn of fate, Joseph found that, while the heretofore unreliable Frederick had recently expressed approval of his policy and agreed to permit the dispatch of the Prussian Italian corps to Ferrara, none of the other electors to whom he had appealed in June and again in September had replied in support of his position.[143] In fact, Archchancellor Lothair Francis was firmly opposed to the emperor's papal policy. Early in June, he had turned down Joseph's request for the preparation of a list of the empire's grievances to be sent to Rome.[144] Moreover, throughout the summer, he had remained unimpressed by his nephew's assurances that Joseph's policy was aimed primarily at restoring imperial power and had joined the other Catholic electors in warning that a papal-imperial conflict would do great harm to the cause of European Catholicism.[145]

In Italy the emperor also found himself deserted by his Modenese and Savoyard allies. During the summer, he had moved to secure support from Victor Amadeus by belatedly placing Charles Ferdinand under the imperial ban and handing over Montferrat.[146] Since he was also involved in a bitter dispute with Clement, the duke responded in June with a memorial seeking imperial protection against papal pretensions in Savoy and suggesting mutual cooperation in opposing the

Vatican.[147] Encouraged by this response, Joseph had decided at the
end of September to ask Victor Amadeus as well as Rinaldo for at least
token military assistance in Ferrara.[148] With the recent turn of events,
however, the emperor presently found both princes unwilling to risk
their own fortunes in a war with the pope. Therefore, while they
continued to press Vienna to present their own claims during Prié's
visit to Rome, Victor Amadeus and Rinaldo prudently turned down
Joseph's request for troops.[149]

Perhaps the most predictable reaction to the Comacchio venture
came from England and the United Provinces. The maritime powers
were essentially sympathetic to Joseph's position against Rome.[150]
Indeed, the English had just dispatched a squadron of ships to the
Tuscan coast after having learned of Clement's offer to help finance the
Stuart pretender's recent descent on Scotland. Nevertheless, as the
threat of a full-scale war in central Italy mounted, both powers began
pressing Vienna to end all hostilities before the next campaign.[151]

With this intention firmly in mind, the court eagerly awaited Daun's
arrival in Ferrara. As in the suppression of the Bavarian revolt, the
emperor's strategy was greatly facilitated by the timely approach of
winter. With the Alpine passes filling with snow, Daun was able to
leave the front in Dauphiné and reach the northern border of the Papal
States by the end of October. Even before his arrival, however, the
situation in Ferrara had improved markedly. Having received some
reinforcements early in October, Bonneval had already broken out of
Comacchio and begun raiding nearby papal garrisons. On 16 October
he led a force of 500 men against neighboring Ostellato, killing 200 of
its 2,000 defenders. The town itself was plundered and razed, though
not before two priests had been hanged and five others jailed for
carrying firearms.[152] By the end of the month, Bonneval had seized or
burned several towns and reestablished contact with Modena and
Lombardy.

With Daun's arrival, the systematic occupation of the Papal States
began. Since the field marshal was eager to avoid further bloodshed,
especially at the hands of his Protestant Prussian and Saxon auxilia-
ries, no attempt was made to force a battle with Marsigli's army or take
by storm any of the more heavily fortified papal cities. Instead, the city
of Ferrara and fortress of Urbano were merely blockaded by Daun's
forces and the garrison of Bologna was neutralized by a convention
signed with the city government. Meanwhile, recognizing that his army
was no match for the smaller invading force, Marsigli also sought to
avoid battle. Perhaps styling himself a latter day Fabius Maximus, the
papal commander steadily retreated before the approach of the Austrian Hannibal. Within a few weeks, Clement's subjects had ceased to
identify his army as the *Papalini,* referring to it instead as the *Papagal-
lini,* or "pope's chickens." By the end of November, Marsigli had
abandoned Bologna, Ferrara, and Romagna to the enemy. While one
corps of his army had retreated southwest to Urbino, where it was

denied entry into the city by the frightened papal legate, Marsigli withdrew the rest of his forces southeast to Ancona, thereby leaving Rome exposed to attack.[153]

Of course, Joseph had no intention of taking Rome itself, realizing as he did the terrible effect its seizure would have on public opinion in Spain and Italy. Rather, with Marsigli's army effectively neutralized and a large part of the Papal States under Austrian occupation, he was now solely interested in prompting Clement to talk peace. To further incline the pope in this direction, he asked the British to keep their fleet in Italian waters and empowered Daun to resume his advance toward Rome if the Marquis Prié interpreted such a step as necessary to bring further concessions. At the same time, however, the emperor sought to preserve an atmosphere conducive to negotiation by appealing to the English to refrain from bombarding the papal littoral and by ordering Daun neither to assault Ferrara and Urbino nor to levy more taxes in the occupied territory than was necessary to sustain his army.[154]

While Joseph was working to bring him to the conference table, Clement was gradually, if reluctantly, moving in the same direction. Throughout September and October, the pope had remained steadfastly opposed to any negotiations with Vienna. In large part this determination had been reinforced by the tough talk of his francophile advisors as well as by the expectation of assistance from France. Indeed, when Marshal Tessé arrived in Rome on 13 October, he brought with him an offer of 15,000 French troops and grandiose plans for an Italian-French league directed against the emperor.[155] Within a short while, however, Clement began to question Louis XIV's ability to provide a sizeable contingent in the face of his recent setbacks in Belgium and southern France. Furthermore, although the Italian princes were obviously attracted to Tessé's generous offers of territorial gains in Lombardy and liberation from the Habsburg yoke, it was doubtful whether they would be willing to risk their very existence in a war against the emperor.[156] To ensure that he would not eventually be deserted by France, Clement informed the marshal that he would join in an alliance only after Louis had dispatched 8,000 to 10,000 troops to Rome.[157] Yet, with the English fleet in control of the Mediterranean and its own armies hard pressed following the defeat at Oudenarde, Versailles realized that such a commitment was beyond its reach. Moreover, it recognized that any Italian league would be ineffective without the active participation of Savoy or Venice. At the moment, however, neither of these states seemed inclined to make war on the emperor.[158]

When on 30 November Tessé informed him that France could provide only one battalion along with some officers and arms, Clement realized at last that he was at Joseph's mercy. Until now he had avoided undertaking any serious negotiations with the Marquis Prié, who had arrived in Rome only ten days after Tessé. On 4 December, however, the pope made his first positive offer of a settlement. Promising to disarm his forces in exchange for an Austrian withdrawal and Joseph's pledge to restrain Modena and the British fleet, Clement agreed to recognize Charles as "king."[159] Although this offer left many issues unsettled, it was clearly a signal for the start of serious negotiations.

Shortly before learning of Clement's initial proposal, Joseph and his ministers had begun drawing up their own list of peace terms. In the aftermath of the allied victory at Oudenarde, Joseph was more preoccupied than ever with his as yet unrealized dynastic objectives in Spain and America. Hence, as early as October, he had resolved to demand his brother's full recognition as king of Spain, including his right as Spanish monarch to fill vacant benefices and levy the lucrative papal *cruzada* on all his subjects.[160] By securing full recognition from the pope, he hoped to be able to counter the appeal of Philip V's propagandists, who had made issue of the archduke's reliance on the support of the Anglo-Dutch heretics as well as of the Protestant origins of both Charles's wife, Elizabeth, and the Empress Amalia.[161] In exchange Joseph was willing to concede the loss of Comacchio by submitting the dispute to a commission composed principally of Roman cardinals.[162] When on 1 December he convened the Conference to draw up peace terms, the emperor reconfirmed these priorities, adding only that Comacchio was to remain occupied until the cardinals' commission had judged against the imperial claims. At this point, he also tacitly conceded the loss of Parma—no documents had ever been found to support his position—stipulating only that those Austrian officials who had taxed Parma's clergy need not seek absolution from Clement.[163]

If there had ever been any question as to Joseph's ultimate intentions, there could no longer be any doubt. Had Schönborn or even Martinitz been present, remonstrance would have been made in favor of the empire's claims. Yet, while illness and pressing family matters had obliged Martinitz to leave court during autumn, Schönborn had not even been invited to attend the latest deliberations. Indeed, the man who had largely formulated the imperial position several months earlier had recently left Vienna for a tour of the *Reich* and was destined not to resume his place in the Italian Conference until peace had been concluded with Rome. Meanwhile, the admission of the Aulic Councilor Windischgrätz to the meetings of the next few weeks suggests that Joseph had chosen to replace the imperial vice-chancellor temporarily with one of his own subjects.[164]

Although Schönborn's absence dampened considerably the discussion of imperial interests, there was still much room to debate the final details of the emperor's demands. During two Conferences on 17 and 18 December, Seilern and Windischgrätz argued that further concessions should be extracted from the pope. While Seilern pushed for an advantageous settlement of the *preces primariae* issue and the presentation of Savoy's gravamina by Prié, Windischgrätz pressed for two months' free winter quarters for the invading Austrian army. In addition, both men called for the participation of the Imperial Diet or Aulic Council in the final settlement of the Comacchio question. Meanwhile, the other ministers present expressed a growing eagerness to achieve peace with Clement by seeking to limit the demands to be presented to Prié. Indeed, of all the ministers, only Seilern and Windischgrätz remained firm in calling for Charles's full recognition as king of Spain.[165]

Since both Salm and Wratislaw were unable to attend these two meetings, the emperor postponed making a final decision until each had submitted written counsel. In the *votum* that he presented to Joseph, Wratislaw once again betrayed his eagerness for peace with Rome. Pleading for an immediate end to the war, he passed over the demands advocated by Seilern and Windischgrätz, while calling for the total surrender of the imperial claims through the convocation of a cardinals' commission. Finally, although he admitted that the pope might be induced to address Charles by the title *rex hispaniarum*, Wratislaw termed as "almost an impossibility" the chances of securing full recognition for the archduke.[166] In his *votum*, Salm essentially echoed the points raised by Seilern and Windischgrätz. Regarding the recognition of Charles, however, he joined Wratislaw and the majority in urging Joseph to accept only a nominal concession from the pope.[167]

Notwithstanding the counsel of his two most intimate advisors, Joseph announced soon afterward that he would continue to demand full recognition for the archduke. Similarly he reiterated his earlier decision to submit the Comacchio dispute to a cardinals' commission.[168] Although this decision was immediately forwarded to Prié, the pope's continuing resistance to these terms encouraged another attempt by the Conference majority to modify Joseph's demands for Charles's recognition. Yet, in two further meetings held on 2 and 3 January, the emperor held firm, electing instead to await word from Rome.[169] He was confident that it would not be long before the deadlock was broken. Following a 12 December Conference, he had instructed Prié to give Clement until 15 January to comply with his terms. After that date, Daun's army was to continue its march toward Rome.[170] In fact, Joseph was not destined to wait in vain. Toward the end of January, the court received word from Prié. The pope had capitulated.

Austrian Hegemony

Signed only one hour before midnight on 15 January by Prié and the papal secretary Paolucci, the proposed settlement consisted of both public and secret articles. By the terms of the published treaty, Clement agreed to reduce his army to the prewar level in return for Joseph's promise to remove his army from the Papal States and to guarantee Clement against attack from his allies. The dispute over Parma and Comacchio was to be submitted to a commission presided over by the

Marquis Prié and consisting of three Roman cardinals and the Milanese Senator Caroelli. Should the commission uphold the pope's
claims to Comacchio (a foregone conclusion), the last Austrian forces
would be promptly evacuated from the town.

The fruits of Joseph's victory were to be found in the unpublished
treaty. Clement pledged to recognize Archduke Charles as king of
Spain in all his titles and privileges. To protect himself against the
recriminations of the Bourbon powers, the pope was to announce his
judgment only after a sham cardinals' commission had ostensibly
reevaluated the rival Habsburg and Bourbon claims and decided in
favor of the archduke. Until this judgment was announced, however,
an additional six Austrian regiments were to remain quartered in
Ferrara. The remaining secret articles consisted mainly of a number of
vaguely worded compromises hammered out between Prié and Paolucci. Clement yielded on two additional points by agreeing to grant a
full pardon to each of the Neapolitan exiles and by pledging to seek a
settlement in his dispute with Victor Amadeus over the nature of papal
prerogatives in Savoy. Meanwhile, the emperor also made a number of
concessions. Most important he was to repeal his 26 June manifesto, in
exchange for Clement's promise to remove the interdict from those
imperial officials who had defied the 27 July *breve*. Joseph was also to
pay compensation for excesses committed by Austrian troops passing
through the Papal States and to indemnify the Holy See for any losses
incurred due to Franco-Spanish retaliation for the recognition of
Archduke Charles. Finally the emperor was to send an embassy to
Rome to seek the *preces primariae*.[171]

The full text of the treaty did not arrive in Vienna until 14 February.
At that time, Joseph called his ministers together to examine the
settlement. With the papal war over and with peace talks expected to
begin soon with France, the emperor now decided to carry through the
long-awaited reform of the Conference. A single policy-making body
was established to replace the former system of eight Conferences. It
comprised both Salm and his designated successor, Trautson; the three
chancellors Wratislaw, Seilern, and Sinzendorf; and—as a concession
to the two empresses—Windischgrätz and the aging Mansfeld. When
present in Vienna, Prince Eugene and the Favorite's uncle, Cardinal
Lamberg, who was the imperial commissioner to the Regensburg Diet,
were also to be admitted. As in the past, Schönborn was to be permitted to attend only those meetings which had a direct bearing on
imperial affairs.[172] As the new great Conference assembled for the first
time, the imperial vice-chancellor was admitted to its deliberations. He
had not attended a Conference in ten weeks.

After a series of meetings, Joseph elected to accept the settlement
worked out by Prié.[173] Yet, in sending the treaty ratification to Rome,
he instructed Prié to refrain from handing over the document until the
pope had complied with the terms of the treaty.[174] In fact, although the

papal disarmament and Austrian withdrawal proceeded rather smoothly, difficulties soon arose in the further implementation of the settlement. One cause for delay was the ambiguous wording of some of the secret articles. For example, it was unclear whether the clause obligating Joseph to pay compensation for excesses committed by Austrian troops passing through the Papal States was meant to include the reprisals ordered by Bonneval and Daun during the recent invasion. Clement's negotiators claimed that it did; Vienna maintained that the article pertained only to excesses committed by Austrian troops marching to and from the kingdom of Naples.[175] Similarly the treaty did not specify whether imperial officials would have to seek absolution before being exempted from the 27 July interdict. Clement insisted that absolution would have to be sought; meanwhile, Joseph and his ministers remained adamant in refusing to allow any official to seek it, since that would constitute an admission of guilt and of the illegality of the 26 June manifesto.[176] Moreover, the dispute was complicated by the fact that the imperial vice-chancellor was among those individuals whom the pope had placed under the interdict, because he had signed the manifesto. Schönborn himself was strongly opposed to seeking absolution. However, Clement was able to exert considerable pressure on him by refusing to confirm his recent election as coadjutor of Bamberg until he had sought papal forgiveness.[177]

Aside from these disputed clauses, it soon became apparent that both parties were determined to postpone as long as possible the execution of certain treaty terms. Joseph was reluctant to rescind the 26 June declaration without securing the simultaneous retraction of the pope's 27 July *breve*.[178] In addition, he was still unwilling to seek the papal indult granting him exercise of the *preces primariae*. Insisting that "I have no need for it," Joseph flatly refused to commission an embassy and demanded instead that Clement issue a single indult awarding the *preces primariae* in perpetuity to all future emperors.[179]

Meanwhile, the pope was proving extremely reluctant to announce his formal recognition of the archduke. He had, in fact, convened the sham commission during March despite strong opposition from many of the pro-French cardinals and had received its "judgment" shortly thereafter.[180] Nevertheless, a combination of pride and fear of Bourbon retaliation against the church in France and Spain inclined Clement to hesitate before taking the final step. In response to pressure from the maritime powers, Joseph had already withdrawn the last six regiments from the Papal States during April.[181] Yet other means of leverage remained for use against the pope. During the summer, the emperor informed Clement that he would not permit the cardinals' commission to consider the fate of Comacchio and Parma until Charles had been granted recognition.[182] Meanwhile, with the campaigning season in the Alps coming to a close, Prié reminded the pope that Daun was capable of marching his army into the Papal States once again.[183] Finally, on

10 October Clement handed Prié a *breve* formally recognizing the archduke as Charles III of Spain. Four days later he publicly announced his decision before a consistory.

Having carried out his major and most burdensome obligation under the peace treaty, the pope now expected the emperor to discharge his responsibilities. He had recently dispatched his nephew Cardinal Annibale Albani to Vienna with this purpose in mind. In an interview with the emperor in mid-October, Albani presented a letter from his uncle announcing Charles's recognition and seeking in exchange the convocation of the cardinals' commission and the payment of compensation for Austrian troop excesses. In addition, Albani presented a second note in which Clement asked Joseph for a formal guarantee that he would compensate the church for all losses sustained from the anticipated Spanish and French reprisals.[184] The pope was essentially asking for Vienna to fulfill its last major treaty commitments. Perhaps he realized that, having at last recognized the archduke, he no longer had any other means of applying pressure on the emperor. Even the old recourse to French aid was now lost with the desertion of the duke of Anjou.

Following a 12 November Conference, Joseph replied to Clement's plea. He reiterated his intention of paying compensation for Austrian troop excesses, albeit only after a general European peace had been achieved, but once again excused all damages and quartering obligations incurred during the recent invasion as acts necessitated by the pope's own hostile acts. Clement's request for a formal guarantee was turned aside on the grounds that the two courts were not formally allied; instead the emperor pledged to seek his allies' cooperation in including a clause in the final treaty with France restoring all confiscated church property. Meanwhile, Joseph made no mention of a future convocation of the cardinals' commission but merely gave his assurance that he would discharge all of his obligations.[185] As an indication of his good faith, he now instructed Prié to hand over formal ratification of the *public* articles of the 15 January treaty.[186]

In fact, Joseph had every intention of permitting the cardinals' commission to do its work. Yet, with his ministers continuing to report a dearth of documentary evidence to support his claims to Parma and Comacchio, the emperor was determined to postpone the final, unfavorable judgment as long as possible.[187] By procrastinating, he had already reaped another year's revenue in both Comacchio and Parma, and had put off the inevitable disillusionment that his capitulation would have on the German princes.[188] Nevertheless, with Clement's continued compliance with the peace terms, Joseph was slowly moving toward the surrender of the two fiefs. By the end of 1709, the pope had yielded to Schönborn's obstinate refusal to seek absolution by accepting a compromise solution worked out by the Conference. The vice-chancellor was merely to write to Clement professing his utmost devotion and swearing that he had signed the 26 June manifesto only in his capacity as a minister and not out of personal conviction.[189] After Schönborn had written the letter, Clement issued a *revers* annulling the existence of his signature on the manifesto and absolving him of any wrongdoing. Immediately thereafter, the pope issued a bull confirming the vice-chancellor's election as coadjutor of Bamberg.

Upon reading the papal *revers,* Joseph broke into laughter.[190] It was apparent to him that Clement knew nothing of Schönborn's coauthorship of the 26 June manifesto and intense commitment to the imperial claims against Rome. Yet, the emperor was clearly impressed by this most recent papal concession, as well as by Albani's promise a few days earlier to speed the restitution of property confiscated from the Neapolitan exiles. Expressing his satisfaction with the pope's actions, Joseph announced on 11 March that he would direct Prié to deliver formal ratification of the secret articles of the treaty and to convene the cardinals' commission at once.[191] The commission met for the first time on 17 March. With Prié calling only one session each week, its deliberations lasted for nearly seven months. Finally, on 9 October the commission issued a statement settling the disputes over both Comacchio and Parma totally in favor of the papacy.[192]

Clement appeared to have won at last. Yet, Vienna was still not ready to yield. Within weeks after the cardinals' commission had begun its deliberations, the Aulic Council had been instructed to renew its investigation into the two disputes.[193] Although it failed once again to unearth any useful evidence, the Conference appealed to Joseph on the very day that the cardinals' commission was announcing its verdict, asking him to permit Austrian troops to quarter in Parma and Comacchio during the coming winter.[194] Moreover, when news of the commission's unfavorable decision reached Vienna, the emperor's ministers further urged that Prié be instructed to withhold his signature from the commission's declaration until the last possible moment.[195] On 31 October Joseph approved these recommendations.[196] At the same time, he sent orders to Modena to frustrate any attempts by papal agents to secure Rinaldo's renunciation of Comacchio.[197] It was not until January 1711, after he had been assured of yet another winter's quartering revenue, that Joseph indicated to his ministers that he was prepared to surrender Comacchio.[198] Before spring had arrived, Clement gave decisive impetus to these intentions by making an extraordinary secret offer to Vienna. On 5 March Albani disclosed the project to Trautson, the new lord high steward: if Joseph handed over Comacchio without further delay, Clement would support the emperor's seizure of Tuscany, following the expected extinction of the Medici dynasty. The pope would then cede directly to the emperor the papal legations of Bologna and Ferrara (including Comacchio) as well as suzerainty over Parma in exchange for the countercession of Tuscany. If Comacchio were not evacuated in the near future, however, Clement threatened to desert the Habsburg cause.[199]

Three days later, Trautson met secretly with Seilern, Wratislaw, and

Prince Eugene to discuss the offer. Since they expected other claimants to the Tuscan succession, the four men were delighted with the promise of papal support for the escheatment of the duchy. Furthermore, they were enchanted by the prospects of acquiring not only Bologna and Ferrara but also Parma, whose own dynasty was on the verge of extinction as well. Once merged with Milan and Mantua, these territories would form a considerable Habsburg state in northern Italy.[200] Since the project promised to be of great benefit to Austrian interests in the peninsula and since Joseph had already decided to release Comacchio, the ministers strongly urged its immediate acceptance.[201]

Yet, while the emperor duly accepted the plan a few days later, it remained for him to devise a way of surrendering Comacchio and Parma without arousing the suspicions or protests of the German princes. During their 8 March meeting, the four ministers had anticipated and offered a solution to this problem. They suggested that the emperor could avoid criticism by securing Electoral College approval for the capitulation. In view of their eagerness to avoid conflict with the Holy See, the Catholic electors could be counted on to endorse the move. Indeed, in order to deny George Louis a forum for pleading the case of his Este cousin, the ministers recommended that only the Catholic electors be summoned for a decision. Meanwhile, Prussia could be approached separately and asked for its approval. Finally, in order to prevent the princes from ever discovering the existence of the Tuscan exchange project, the four urged Joseph to keep Clement's offer secret not only from the electors but also from the other ministers.[202]

Endorsing this stratagem, the emperor convened a full Conference on 8 April to finalize his decision to surrender Comacchio. During the course of the meeting, no mention was made of the pope's secret offer. Instead, the four ministers who were privy to the scheme pleaded the need to preserve Clement's friendship and Catholic unity. At one point, Wratislaw even suggested the threat of papal rearmament and a renewal of hostilities.[203] As expected Schönborn led the opposition to capitulation, arguing heatedly that Comacchio's evacuation could be delayed indefinitely by entrusting its fate to the Aulic Council. Nevertheless, after four hours of spirited debate, the emperor closed discussion by reiterating the decision secretly agreed upon nearly a month earlier.[204]

The whole meeting had been splendidly staged. Of the five men who knew, only Joseph had failed to feign interest in the proceedings, choosing instead to express his boredom and impatience on the note sheet that usually accompanied him into Conference sessions.[205] Yet, for the emperor, the staged Conference of 8 April 1711 was significant not because it was irrelevant but because it was necessary. Indeed, it symbolized Joseph's constant need to deceive the empire while using its institutions and pretensions to advance his own interests in the peninsula. In examining the course of his papal policy, there can be no question that the stratagem—and the deception—had worked well. He had seized Comacchio three years earlier under the protective cloak of imperial law, but with the intention of using it merely as a bargaining counter in the pursuit of Austrian and Habsburg interests. When he stumbled soon afterward into an unwanted war, he readily sacrificed his disguise in order to protect what he alone interpreted as his most vital concerns. If, after the war had ended, he refused to concede the empire's claims, it was not because he valued them too highly; rather it was because their fate was too intimately tied with the political and financial considerations of the moment. Consequently, while Schönborn continued to regard Joseph's refusal to surrender Comacchio and Parma as a desperate attempt to protect the empire's interests, the emperor himself took satisfaction in the revenue which he continued to derive from the two fiefs.[206] Even in the final decision to capitulate, Joseph could take solace in the latest dynastic advantages offered by Clement as well as in his ministers' ingenious plan to protect him from the wrath of a disillusioned *Reich*.

If Joseph deserted the empire for good in the spring of 1711, his decision to strike a deal with the papacy also represented the final sacrifice of his "dynastic alliance" with Rinaldo of Este. For the past three years the emperor had maintained that Comacchio was the rightful territory of the dukes of Modena. Yet, in concluding the secret agreement with Albani, he not only abandoned these claims but also made arrangements for the future cession of all Ferrara to the Habsburgs. As in the case of the empire, Rinaldo's fall from grace started with the January 1709 treaty and proceeded gradually, if inevitably, toward the secret accord of March 1711. During the spring of 1708 Joseph had held out the Milanese governorship to Rinaldo as added compensation for his losses earlier in the war. Yet, while he instructed his brother to prepare the duke's investiture patent and eventually received Eugene's own resignation as governor, Joseph never made the appointment.[207] Instead, he delayed making a decision, while looking for adequate compensation for Eugene and weighing the arguments of his Austrian and Bohemian chancellors against the appointment of a foreign prince.[208] In the meantime the strategic duchy was governed by a junta of Austrian, Spanish, and Italian officials.[209] Then at the beginning of 1710, Charlotte Felicitas died suddenly, thereby breaking the close dynastic ties between Rinaldo and Joseph. By 1711 the indefatigable Wratislaw was able to report triumphantly to Charles that the emperor had decided at last against Rinaldo's appointment and in favor of Prince Eugene.[210]

In the end, the duke was to receive Mirandola as compensation— and then only on Joseph's terms. The emperor's original intention was to sell the tiny duchy to his brother-in-law partly as a reward for his loyalty but principally as a means of raising needed cash for the

Austrian war effort in southern France.[211] Consequently, on 4 December 1709 he secured a judgment from the Aulic Council placing the duke of Mirandola under the imperial ban and then stripped him of his territories.[212] However, when Rinaldo refused to pay the 600,000 florins set as the price for the duchy, the emperor decided not to go through with the transfer.[213] Instead, the banned duke of Mirandola was approached in March and offered full restoration of his lands in return for the payment of a 600,000 florin fine. Only when he too refused to meet this stipulation did Joseph agree to reopen negotiations with Rinaldo.[214] After three months of negotiations a final agreement was reached. Rinaldo was to be compensated at last with the duchy of Mirandola—at the cost of slightly over one million florins.[215]

The ultimate fate of the duke and duchy of Mirandola poses as yet another example of Joseph's utilization of imperial prerogatives in the pursuit of more immediate Austrian interests. As we have seen, however, the ban had been employed in Italy on a previous occasion with a similar objective in mind. Alluded to by some historians as an expression of Joseph's imperial mission in the peninsula, the proclamation of the ban against Charles Ferdinand of Mantua on 30 May 1708 had in fact been forced on him by the current need to appease the duke of Savoy. Moreover, the punishment meted out to Charles Ferdinand was itself of dubious constitutional legality. In the past, when an imperial prince was placed under the ban, only he and his immediate family lost their rights and privileges. Meanwhile, other lines of the same dynasty and more distant relatives were not affected by the judgment. Consequently, when a prince was convicted of a crime and stripped of some or all of his possessions, the sequestered territory would be awarded to a legitimate heir, just as if he had died without male issue. Yet, in the proclamation against Charles Ferdinand, all agnates were declared forfeit of their rights to succeed to the Gonzaga patrimony.[216] Joseph took this step in order to nullify the otherwise legitimate claims of the duke of Lorraine to Montferrat and of the duke of Guastalle to Mantua. Since the Treaty of Turin had required that he cede Montferrat to Savoy, the emperor was compelled to disregard the rights of the house of Lorraine. Nevertheless, since he intended to annex Mantua himself, Joseph welcomed the opportunity to disinherit the duke of Guastalla as well. That Joseph subsequently attempted to find compensation for Lorraine elsewhere in Europe demonstrates that he considered the sequestration of Montferrat—and therefore of Mantua—to be legally unjustified.[217] Indeed, in the months after issuing the ban against Charles Ferdinand, Joseph was also prepared to compensate Guastalla with a small piece of Mantuan territory.[218] At first, Joseph found Duke Vincent of Guastalla unwilling to give up his claim to all of the Mantuan succession.[219] In the end, however, the emperor was to have his way. Although most of the electors confirmed the validity of the duke's arguments, they agreed to permit Austrian annexation of Mantua in exchange for compensation for the duke. Meanwhile, with the help of Mainz and Trier, Vincent's attempts to lay the controversy before the Imperial Diet were successfully frustrated.[220]

With the formal annexation of the duchy of Mantua, Vienna added the last piece to its north Italian patrimony. Within a period of only six years, it had successfully swept away the past Spanish and promised Bourbon hegemony in the peninsula and established its own authority in their place. Following Prince Eugene's victory over the French, Joseph had maintained and strengthened his position in Italy largely through the bold and imaginative use of his imperial office. Yet, if the outpost he created bore the crest of the empire on its battlements, it was manned and commanded solely by Austrians and was destined to last, with one interruption, for 150 years. The relationship between Joseph's imperial and Austrian statecraft is most clearly illuminated by a close examination of the papal war. Like the medieval emperors before him, he had fought the pope in order to secure the financial benefits of imperial suzerainty over northern Italy and in order to legitimize his dynastic aspirations. Yet, Joseph was fighting not for the imperial but for the Spanish crown and valued his fiscal prerogatives in Comacchio and Parma only so long as the war lasted. Moreover, if he eventually compelled Joseph to discard the myth of his imperial pretensions to these two territories, Clement was obliged in turn to recognize and pay homage to the realities of Austrian hegemony in the peninsula. Forced into a humiliating and incriminating collaboration with the emperor, the pope had little reason to rejoice in his triumph in the struggle for Comacchio and Parma. Yet, in electing peace with Joseph, Clement had clearly made the best choice. The continuation of the war as an ally of France would hardly have saved him from disaster. Meanwhile, though he had been forced to wait for two years to secure the fruits of his compromise with Joseph, it appeared in the spring of 1711 that he had not waited in vain. Indeed, as he received word from his nephew of the emperor's promise to leave Comacchio, Clement could at that very moment take comfort from the dismal fate of another prince, as noble and sincere as he, who had refused to come to terms with Vienna and had instead put his faith in far off France . . .

V

Hungary:
The Rákóczi Rebellion

We have allowed ourselves to fall into a terrible labyrinth.
—Johann Wenzel Count Wratislaw

While Joseph was waging war in the west, he was also obliged to divert considerable financial and military resources to the suppression of the Rákóczi rebellion in Hungary, which had broken out in the spring of 1703 and would last until the very end of his reign. In many respects, the revolt was not unlike the numerous insurrections that had flared up throughout Europe during the seventeenth century in reaction to the progressive pace of royal absolutism. Moreover, Joseph's subsequent search for a lasting peace was hardly a unique odyssey in the history of Habsburg rule in Hungary. Nevertheless, his handling of the rebellion had a profound effect not only on the outcome of the war with France but also on the future course of Austro-Hungarian history.

The political and military situation Joseph inherited from his father could have scarcely been more difficult. The Leopoldine regime had alienated virtually every segment of Hungarian society. It had lost the support of much of the nobility, principally by circumventing their constitutional prerogative to vote and collect extraordinary taxes. It had sacrificed the loyalty of the town and peasant populations by greatly expanding the tax base and increasing already existing levies.[1] Leopold's pursuit of religious uniformity had antagonized Hungary's Protestants—who comprised roughly half of all commoners and the great majority of the gentry—as well as Transylvania's Greek Orthodox Rumanian peasantry. Finally, as in other countries ruled by "foreign" dynasties, there emerged among all classes and confessions a xenophobic reaction against the crown's failure to honor the nation's separate identity, a reaction that Leopold had fostered in numerous ways, whether by merging the kingdom's fiscal offices with the *Hofkammer,* by appointing foreigners to influential posts in the royal government, by employing German troops to collect the country's

123

taxes and garrison its fortresses, by creating the notorious *Commissio Neo Acquistica* to award lands recovered from the Turks to his court favorites and German settlers rather than to their original owners, or by exempting these and other recent immigrants from the full burden of taxation.[2]

During the first two years of the insurrection, the *kuruc,* or "crusader", leader, Prince Francis II Rákóczi, had been able to exploit these grievances. As a descendant of the last two independent princes of Transylvania and of several other past rebel leaders, Rákóczi was the logical choice to lead any Hungarian revolt. Indeed, when the insurrection first began, he and his close associate Count Miklós Bercsényi were in exile in Poland where they were trying to enlist French support for an uprising in Hungary. Yet, Rákóczi's following and early successes were principally due to his willingness to fashion a truly national coalition against the Habsburgs. Though he was an aristocrat and one of northeast Hungary's biggest landowners, he responded readily when his own serfs rose in revolt and appealed to him for leadership.[3] In fact, when he reentered Hungary some months later at the head of an army of peasants and Polish mercenaries, the prince appealed for support from the peasantry by promising to improve their lot and to exempt those who fought under his banner from all seignorial and royal taxes.[4] Though he was, like most aristocrats, a devout Roman Catholic, Rákóczi also placed national unity ahead of his own confessional loyalties by embracing the cause of Hungary's religious minorities. His advocacy of toleration was, in fact, instrumental in broadening his following among those non-Magyar nationalities whose resentment against Habsburg fiscal and administrative policies was not as strong. Hence, the Rumanians, Slovaks, and even the largely Lutheran German town populations joined the *kuruc* cause.[5] In fact, of all the non-Magyar nationalities, only the Catholic Croats and Greek Orthodox Serbs in the south and southwest remained loyal to the crown, principally because both groups enjoyed limited autonomy and social and economic privileges and because the Serbs were the only confessional minority whose religious freedom Leopold had respected.[6] Ironically Rákóczi encountered the most difficulty in winning over the Magyar nobility which feared that a *kuruc* victory might result in social revolution, while their involvement in an abortive uprising would lead to their proscription by the Habsburg regime. He did manage to assuage their fears, however, and once they realized that the insurrection would not be suppressed and that their estates were at the mercy of Rákóczi's peasant bands, the nobility took their place at the head of *kuruc* movement.[7]

Faced with a national insurrection, the scattered Austrian garrisons stationed in Hungary had been unable to confine the rebellion to the northeast part of the kingdom. By the end of 1704, virtually all of central Hungary lay in Rákóczi's hands. Only a thin strip of western

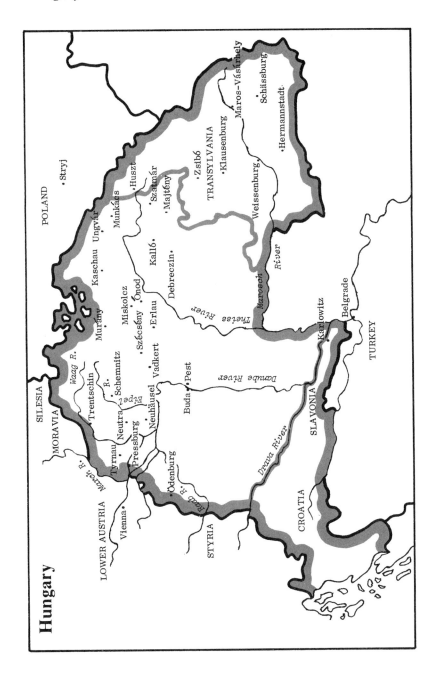

towns, the Serb areas in the south, and a half dozen or so scattered fortresses were still in royalist hands. In Transylvania the somewhat larger Austrian forces under General Rabutin still held all of the major towns. Yet, here too the countryside was mostly in the hands of the insurgents. Of the kingdom's three crownlands, Croatia alone remained untouched by the rebellion. Meanwhile, Rákóczi and his lieutenants had begun to carry the war into the eastern marches of the *Erblande,* where roving bands of *kuruc* cavalry burned and pillaged to within a few miles of Vienna itself. Though Leopold had recently assembled a small field army under General Siegbert Heister and had succeeded in retaking all of the Hungarian territory southwest of the Danube, the modest forces at his disposal were simply unable to accomplish the awesome task of conquering—and occupying—the kingdom's vast expanses. Despite several battlefield victories and a series of exhausting marches and countermarches, Heister was unable to continue offensive operations without leaving both the newly regained territories and the *Erblande* defenseless. Meanwhile, though he issued amnesty declarations wherever he went, the excesses of his Serb and Croat irregulars and his own personal cruelty frustrated any chance of winning back the loyalty of the emperor's Hungarian subjects. By the spring of 1705, Heister had little to show for his string of victories. At the same time, his own army was unfit for further operations, having been exhausted and seriously depleted by the extraordinary labors of the past campaign.

Though they described themselves only as "malcontents" and were not contemplating a complete overthrow of Habsburg rule, the *kuruc* leaders intended to correct more than just the immediate abuses of Leopold's regime. In addition, they were determined to revive those constitutional safeguards which had helped guarantee their political liberties in the past but which had been suppressed by Leopold at the Pressburg Diet of 1687. At informal discussions held during 1704 under the auspices of the English and Dutch ambassadors, the rebel leadership had already demanded the restoration of both the elective monarchy and the *jus resistendi,* the Magyar nobility's former right to oppose with armed force any alleged royal violation of the kingdom's laws and constitution. In order to ensure further the inviolability of their constitutional privileges, the Hungarians also demanded a foreign-power guarantee of the peace and even hinted at the reestablishment of an independent Transylvania with Rákóczi as its prince.[8] In order to strengthen their claim to the principality, which had long served as the sentinel of Hungary's political and religious liberties prior to its annexation in 1694, a rump Transylvanian Diet met at Weissenburg (Alba Iulia), dethroned Leopold, and elected Rákóczi as his successor.

As difficult as future negotiations might be, prospects for an early settlement were further complicated by Rákóczi's contacts with other European powers. Since 1704, Louis XIV had been sending him subsidies, munitions, and even some French soldiers and had also recognized Rákóczi as the sovereign prince of Transylvania.[9] Rákóczi had also taken advantage of the Habsburg monarchy's exposed position in central Europe by seeking military assistance from Protestant Sweden and Brandenburg-Prussia, as well as from the Turks.[10] He had also successfully cultivated the friendship of the maritime powers, who soon began pressing Vienna to accommodate the *kuruc* demands. In making these remonstrances, the English and Dutch were motivated both by the desire to refocus the monarchy's undivided attention on the western front and by their own inclination to support the *kuruc* struggle against absolutism and Protestant religious persecution. Nevertheless, while the maritime powers' meddling did not bring Hungary closer to peace, it did mark the beginning of six years of bitter recriminations between Vienna and its allies over how the revolt should be handled. In fact, in the months prior to Joseph's succession, the indiscreet and provocative remarks of the English ambassador, George Stepney, had drawn considerable criticism from Leopold's ministers who charged that his remarks encouraged the rebel leadership to be more obstinate and ambitious in making demands "to which no monarch in the world could agree."[11]

Joseph's Search for Peace

As long as Leopold reigned, it had been impossible to create an atmosphere of trust and reconciliation between king and country, for though he had recently pledged to obey the constitution and restore religious freedom, his word rang hollow against an historical landscape cluttered with the wreckage of his broken promises. Hence, as the rebellion entered its third year, Joseph's succession revived hopes for a prompt and peaceful settlement. Though he had also reigned as king since his coronation in 1687 at the Pressburg Diet, Joseph had played only a minimal role in Hungarian affairs and had therefore not become implicated in his father's tyranny. In fact, it was widely known that Joseph sympathized with the nation's grievances and was impatient with Leopold's failure to regain its loyalty.[12] In an attempt to profit from his son's innocence, Leopold had offered the *kuruc* Joseph's personal guarantee that he would abide by the constitution and had even volunteered to leave Hungarian affairs exclusively to his son's direction.[13] Yet, since these proposals failed to provide tangible security against a future tyranny by Joseph or his descendants, they also failed to satisfy the insurgents. On his own initiative, Joseph had also corresponded with the rebel leaders and, at one point, had secretly dispatched the loyalist Hungarian magnate Count Forgách to them, suggesting that they press for Leopold's abdication and his own immediate succession. Instead of communicating this message, however, Forgách chose the opportunity to defect to the *kuruc* cause.[14]

As king, Joseph intended to take full advantage of his own untarnished image to restore the faith and loyalty of his Magyar subjects. On 14 May he issued a circular letter for distribution throughout Hungary in which he dissociated himself from his father's policies and solemnly pledged to uphold his coronation oath to abide by the laws and sacred constitution of the kingdom. At the same time, he announced to his royal ministers that he would "examine into and redress" the grievances of the past reign.[15] Unfortunately, Joseph's freedom from any association with his father's policies also had its drawbacks. Since he had never violated Hungary's laws and did not contemplate doing so, Joseph did not now feel constrained to offer the rebels any tangible guarantees against a future tyranny. He did not intend to restore the *jus resistendi* and elective monarchy or recognize Rákóczi's claim to Transylvania since such concessions might prompt a return to the domestic anarchy that had plagued the kingdom in the past. Furthermore, while his father had only recently agreed to accept an Anglo-Dutch guarantee, Joseph renounced this concession, claiming that his own innocence made foreign intervention unnecessary.[16] Whether or not he could resist for long the temptation to ignore the kingdom's rights and privileges was, however, still subject to question. In the first month of his reign, Joseph adopted his father's practice of excluding his royal ministers from policy deliberations by appointing only Germans to the new Hungarian Conference.[17] Moreover, when the new Conference met for the first time on 8 June, the protocol of the meeting was drawn up by the secretaries of the *Hofkriegsrat* and Imperial Chancery, thereby suggesting that Joseph intended to follow his father's policy of formally treating Hungary as a conquered outpost of the empire.[18]

In a 2 June letter to Joseph, Rákóczi made it clear that he and the nation regarded "the beginning of this reign as a favorable light that diverts the clouds and tempests which have burst upon the nation."[19] Notwithstanding his expression of these sentiments, however, the *kuruc* chieftain was now less eager than ever to arrive at a settlement with the crown. The cause for the sudden hardening in his position was not to be found in any inherent distrust of Joseph, but rather in Prince Rákóczi's renewed faith in Louis XIV. During March, the new French envoy, Pierre Puchot Count Desalleurs, had arrived at the prince's camp with promises of higher subsidies and additional officers, engineers, and artillerists for his army. Rákóczi was greatly pleased by Versailles's increased commitment, not only because it promised to help him militarily, but also because he envisioned in Louis's support the prospects of entering into a formal alliance with France. The prince fully realized that he could secure far better peace terms as Louis's ally and as a participant at a future peace conference than he could possibly hope to get by negotiating directly with Vienna. Consequently, although Bercsényi urged him not to place all his faith in Desalleurs's promises, Rákóczi elected to stand firm in his peace demands in the hope that he could rely on a future understanding with France.

Furthermore, when word arrived of Leopold's death, the rebel leadership quickly realized that its bargaining position was now significantly stronger. During the previous year's negotiations, it had intimated that Joseph's succession as king in 1687 was invalid because, unlike his predecessors, he had not been freely elected by the diet.[20] Consequently, with Leopold's passing, Hungary was no longer obligated to recognize the legitimacy of Habsburg rule. Rákóczi acted accordingly. When the palatine's secretary arrived at his headquarters seeking permission to distribute Joseph's circular letter, the prince refused his request. At the same time, Bercsényi informed the secretary that there could still be no peace without a foreign-power guarantee and that a diet would soon be convoked to declare the throne vacant and elect a governor for the interregnum.[21]

Upon receiving the secretary's report, Joseph realized that a compromise with the rebels was still out of the question, a situation which he readily attributed to the French presence at Rákóczi's camp and the continued military successes of the *kuruc* armies.[22] Nevertheless, in response to continued Anglo-Dutch pressure, he reluctantly agreed to reopen negotiations with the insurgents.[23] Meanwhile, in order to improve his own bargaining position and increase the chances of reaching a satisfactory settlement, Joseph turned his attention to his Hungarian field army. In recent months, Field Marshal Heister had begun to draw considerable criticism for his conduct of the past campaign. Led by Prince Eugene and the Croatian Ban Count Pálffy, certain of Leopold's ministers had expressed outrage over his ruthless treatment of the Magyar civilian population. At the same time, Salm and Wratislaw had joined the *Hofkriegsrat* president in questioning the wisdom of Heister's tactics in the field. In their eyes, he had clearly failed to take advantage of his initial victories and had systematically "run one army after another into the ground."[24] As early as mid-January, Salm had begun urging Leopold to replace the field marshal by recalling either Prince Eugene or Guido Starhemberg from Italy.[25] Yet, although the old emperor initially agreed to make the change, he later reversed his decision and retained Heister. With Leopold's death, Salm and Eugene quickly renewed the call for Heister's dismissal and, barely one week into the new reign, the field marshal was notified of his transfer to Germany.[26] Joseph intended ultimately to replace Heister with Guido Starhemberg. However, since Starhemberg could presently not be spared from the Italian front, the emperor named the aged but able Count Herbeville to command during the coming campaign.[27]

Herbeville's was no easy charge. Since the outbreak of the revolt, most of the Austrian-held fortresses in eastern and central Hungary had capitulated one by one. Of late the situation had become particularly critical in Transylvania, where Rabutin held only a handful of isolated outposts while the insurgents enjoyed complete control over the surrounding countryside. Cut off from Vienna, his troops had gone for months without pay and, in some cases, had already mutinied.

Meanwhile, Rabutin himself was presently under siege in his capital at Hermannstadt (Sibiu).

Joseph and his ministers realized that the loss of Transylvania would have the gravest implications for the monarchy. Their worst fear was that a rebel seizure of the principality would encourage the sultan to reassert his past claims to suzerainty and intervene in the struggle on Rákóczi's behalf.[28] The French were constantly pressing the Turks to declare war on the emperor, and Rákóczi had already asked them to commit an auxiliary force of 12,000 men.[29] Paralyzed by seraglio intrigue and a lack of confidence in their army, the sultan's ministers had turned a deaf ear to these entreaties. Nevertheless, there remained the constant danger that Rákóczi's continued success might prompt the Porte to renew the centuries-old struggle for Hungary. Even if Turkey stayed neutral, Joseph still had to contend with Rákóczi's own designs on Transylvania. It had already become clear that his demand for the principality would be one of the main rebel conditions for peace. Only if Transylvania were fully regained could Vienna hope to persuade the prince to abandon his claim.[30]

In the beginning of June, Joseph began making preparations for Rabutin's relief. Although he had inherited a plan drawn up under Leopold calling for the dispatch of 7,000 Serb irregulars from southern Hungary, he chose instead to follow Prince Eugene's recommendation for a much stronger relief force.[31] According to the new design, Herbeville was to proceed with the main Austrian army to Buda, join the Serbians, and continue on to Transylvania. Along the way he was to revictual a number of isolated or besieged Austrian outposts. It was a bold strategy calling for a sustained march across 500 miles of hostile and largely barren countryside. Nevertheless, the objective appeared to be worth the risk.

The emperor's plan soon ran into difficulties. In seeking to strengthen Herbeville's army, Joseph had ordered a body of 6,000 Danish mercenaries to proceed to the Hungarian front from its quarters in the Upper Palatinate.[32] Since these troops had been originally intended for service in Italy, Prince Eugene probably never intended employing them in Herbeville's army. Protests came not from Eugene's headquarters, however, but from the British and Dutch, who were irritated by Joseph's reordering of priorities against the common interests of the alliance.[33] At the same time, the emperor's own ministers began to question the wisdom of transferring almost all available forces to Transylvania, where they would be unable to protect the *Erblande* from rebel raids. Their point was borne out dramatically during July and August when thousands of Magyar cavalry plundered and burned scores of towns in nearby Moravia.[34] Yet, having made his decision to relieve Rabutin, the emperor now refused to divert troops from his main objective.[35] Given the widespread devastation of the rebel raids, Joseph's was indeed a difficult decision. Nevertheless, he regarded

Rákóczi's pretensions to Transylvania a greater threat than the momentary peril to the *Erblande*. On 22 August, after months of painstaking preparation, in which large stockpiles had been gathered from both the *Erblande* and the surrounding Hungarian countryside, Herbeville set out for Transylvania.[36]

While Joseph was trying to improve his bargaining position, so was Prince Rákóczi. During July he summoned the nobility to meet together in a diet at the town of Szécsény. Rákóczi had a number of reasons for convening a diet. Since the outbreak of the revolt, he had led the rebel cause by the unanimous, but nonetheless largely tacit consent of his countrymen. If he was to have a free hand in dealing with Joseph, he would need a formal mandate from the Magyar nobility. In addition, the prince was aware of the pressing need to compose the growing differences between the groups actively supporting the rebellion. There was dissatisfaction among the kingdom's Protestants, who composed the great majority of the *kuruc* forces but who were still being denied freedom of worship and the restitution of churches that had been illegally seized during Leopold's reign. There was also growing unrest among Rákóczi's peasant soldiers, who had interpreted his earlier promises as the harbinger of permanent emancipation from serfdom but who, in many cases, had still not even received temporary remission of seignorial dues from their landlords.[37] Not so immediately apparent among the prince's motives were his continued plans for the conclusion of an alliance with France. Only one week after issuing the call for a diet, he had written to Louis XIV thanking him for the latest increase in subsidies and promising that the money would be used to serve French interests at the coming meeting.[38] In fact, what Rákóczi had in mind was the Magyar nobility's declaration of an interregnum and endorsement of a formal alliance with France. Three weeks later, he wrote to his agent at Versailles, Baron Vetes, assuring him that he would try to frustrate Joseph's peace overtures but that, in the meantime, Louis was to be induced to enter into an alliance with the insurgents. In the expectation that such a compact could be concluded, Rákóczi told Vetes that he would delay adjourning the diet until Louis's reply had reached him.[39]

In fact, the Szécsény meeting failed to fulfill all of Rákóczi's expectations. The assembled nobility did elect him to direct the Hungarian "confederacy" and commissioned him to appoint a 24-member advisory council. It also attempted to ameliorate the grievances of the country's Protestants by affirming their religious freedom and directing the partial restitution of former Protestant churches and property.[40] The nobility refused, however, to release Rákóczi's peasant soldiers from their seignorial dues for the rest of the war.[41] Furthermore at the last minute, Rákóczi decided not to move against Joseph because only twenty-five of the kingdom's forty-seven counties and only a handful of its great magnate families were in attendance, and because those who were present were confident of reaching a settlement with Joseph and would have never declared an interregnum.[42] In fact, when the convention adjourned on 3 October, Rákóczi had still not received news from Vetes. When word finally arrived, it promised a French alliance solely with Transylvania, and then only after Rákóczi had been formally inaugurated.[43] Undeterred by Louis's conditions, the prince immediately summoned an inaugural diet to meet at Weissenburg on 11 November. Meanwhile, having received the desired mandate from the Hungarian nobility, he was now ready to negotiate with Joseph.

On 20 October word reached Vienna that Rákóczi had appointed Bercsényi to head a commission to begin armistice talks. One week later the negotiators assembled. While Bercsényi and his colleagues took up quarters at Tyrnau (Trnava), the king's commissioners, led by Wratislaw and Cardinal Széchenyi of Kalocsa, established themselves at Pressburg (Bratislava), thirty miles to the west. To the mediators—Stepney for England, Counts Rechteren and Hamel Bruynincx for the United Provinces—was left the task of transmitting messages between the two sides and, hopefully, of bridging the political differences that separated them. Unfortunately, these remained substantial. Although the continuing military stalemate and the slow progress of Herbeville's relief force had inclined Joseph to moderate his terms, there were still a number of crucial issues over which he flatly refused to compromise.[44] Among these points were the enactments of the Pressburg Diet. Since he felt that there could be no peace as long as the rebels insisted on restoring the *jus resistendi* and the elective monarchy, the emperor considered himself justified in demanding a preliminary declaration from them recognizing the repeal of both provisions from the kingdom's constitution.[45] Moreover, he also hoped that the successful conclusion of Herbeville's march would induce Rákóczi to abandon his demand for Transylvania. Meanwhile, Bercsényi, whom *Hofkriegsrat* Secretary Thiel had dubbed "the Hungarian Cromwell," was even less inclined to compromise. He too demanded a preliminary declaration in which he insisted upon Joseph's restoration of the *jus resistendi* and recognition of the existence of constitutional limits on the exercise of royal authority.[46] Moreover, he proved so inflexible in his demands that even the Austrophobe Stepney was moved to blame him and his colleagues for the current stalemate in negotiations.[47]

Buckling under intense pressure from the mediators, Joseph acted to break the deadlock in the beginning of December by dropping his demand for a preliminary declaration. At the same time, he made a further concession to the insurgents by reissuing his negotiators' credentials through the Hungarian Chancery. Since the powers originally issued to Wratislaw and his colleagues had come from the *Hofkriegsrat,* Joseph's latest move represented both a tacit acknowledgement of the kingdom's autonomy and a fresh assertion of his own claim to the

Hungarian crown.[48] On the fourteenth Joseph made yet another concession to the insurgents by issuing a statement affirming their contention that the concept of heredity did not permit a king to violate Hungary's laws and constitution.[49]

Having demonstrated his willingness to compromise, the emperor now waited for Bercsényi to reciprocate, either by presenting a formal list of grievances or, at the very least, by consenting to an armistice.[50] Instead, the rebel chieftain notified the mediators that he was not empowered to proceed further on either issue.[51] Joseph was disappointed by Bercsényi's rebuff, but could hardly have been surprised. On the eighth he had received word that Herbeville had finally reached Transylvania. The insurgents were now clearly in a less favorable bargaining position and could not be expected to favor the immediate opening of peace talks. However, Joseph and the court still had no idea of how much progress the army was making in Transylvania. It was only on the twenty-third with the arrival of an officer from Herbeville's army that Vienna learned what Bercsényi had known for weeks.

Hampered by the harassment and scorched earth tactics of the rebels, as well as by difficulties in crossing the Theiss (Tisza), Herbeville had not reached the mountains leading into Transylvania until the beginning of November. Moreover, upon his arrival at the strategic Zsibó Pass, the field marshal found his path blocked by Rákóczi. The rebel prince commanded 24,000 men, compared to Herbeville's 20,000, and enjoyed as usual a clear superiority in cavalry. Fortunately for the Austrians, however, he overruled his subordinates and positioned his army within the pass, thereby largely sacrificing what advantage he had in numbers and mobility. On 11 November—the day originally scheduled for Rákóczi's inauguration as prince of Transylvania— Herbeville attacked the rebels and put them to flight. The victory was complete. The rebels left between four and six thousand dead, perhaps ten times Herbeville's losses. Moreover, the Austrian commander continued his pursuit of Rákóczi until the prince had withdrawn his army back into Hungary. Heartened by news of Herbeville's arrival, the Austrian garrisons at Hermannstadt and other outposts launched a series of successful counterattacks against the besieging rebel forces. By the end of the month, virtually all of Transylvania had been regained, as thousands of rebel soldiers and sympathizers streamed headlong into Hungary and neighboring Turkish Moldavia.[52]

With the encouraging news from Herbeville, Joseph now pressed even harder for the start of peace talks. Yet, Bercsényi was not to be moved. He persisted in his demands for a preliminary declaration from Joseph and also added a number of trivial procedural points aimed at upsetting further the progress of the truce negotiations.[53] However, these latest contrivances were not designed to destroy the prospects of peace talks; rather, they were merely intended to delay them until the rebel army could win advantages of its own on the battlefield. Indeed, with the main Austrian forces operating in Transylvania, the insurgents had already launched a new invasion of the Transdanubian counties, which were defended by only a few thousand Croat border-troops and Styrian militia. By mid-December these forces had been pushed back beyond the Raab and Drava Rivers. Two weeks later Bercsényi himself left Tyrnau in order to supervise operations west of the Raab and direct the siege of Ödenburg (Sopron).

In Vienna the euphoria that had accompanied word of Herbeville's triumphs quickly dissipated into a sense of frustration and pessimism. For the second consecutive year, the main Austrian army had prevailed in battle and achieved its primary objective only to find that it had deserted its past conquests to the enemy. Indeed, to many of Joseph's subjects, the relief of far-off Transylvania had been easily outweighed by the loss of the southwest, if only because its fall exposed the *Erblande* once again to the horrors of renewed rebel raids. Yet, as the emperor and his ministers looked ahead to the coming year, they had reason to be satisfied with the present situation. By tightening his hold on Transylvania, Joseph had postponed—if only temporarily—the threat of Turkish intervention.[54] Moreover, as he anticipated the opening of peace talks with the rebels, the young Habsburg could now hope to reassert his claim to the principality without prejudicing his chances of reaching a settlement.

The Tyrnau Peace Talks

Once he had received confirmation of Herbeville's occupation of Transylvania, Joseph was ready to begin formulating the position he would take in negotiating with the insurgents.[55] As the Conference started its deliberations on 19 January, there was little question that the emperor and his ministers considered themselves to be in a much improved bargaining position. Although it was still willing to abide by the concessions of the previous month, including Joseph's recognition of the existence of legal limitations on royal authority, the Conference was less inclined than ever to make any major constitutional or territorial concessions. At no point did it entertain the thought of renouncing the work of the Pressburg Diet; moreover, it confirmed that the past rebel demands for the cession of Transylvania to Rákóczi and for a foreign power guarantee of the final settlement were still totally unacceptable. In fact, the emperor announced that, since Transylvania had been restored to his possession he would not treat with anyone claiming to represent the principality, but only with the Hungarian confederacy.[56]

While Joseph was preparing his negotiating position, Rákóczi was also meeting with his advisory council at Miskolcz to compose the confederacy's peace conditions. Despite Herbeville's timely disruption of his inauguration and the subsequent loss of Transylvania, the prince still hoped for an alliance with Louis XIV.[57] He was, therefore, more determined than ever not to surrender those guarantees which he regarded as essential for the future preservation of Hungary's constitutional liberties. When the council convened on 25 January, in the presence of Swedish and Prussian agents as well as the ubiquitous Desalleurs, it adopted Rákóczi's call for a Prusso-Swedish guarantee, the restoration of the *jus resistendi,* and the cession of Transylvania. Meanwhile, the earlier *kuruc* demand for restoration of the elective monarchy was dropped, largely due to Joseph's recent admission that a hereditary succession did not free the monarch from constitutional limitations on his authority.[58]

By the beginning of March, meetings had begun at Tyrnau and Pressburg for the drawing up of an armistice. While the talks lasted, each side pr pared for the coming truce by seeking to make good the losses of the preceding campaign. For Joseph the reconquest of the Transdanubian counties became the main objective. During March, Count Pálffy led a three-pronged invasion of the southwest. The offensive failed, however, as Pálffy was able to retake only the territories west of the Raab. Meanwhile, farther east, Rákóczi sought to strengthen his bargaining position with the rescheduling of a diet to reaffirm his sovereignty in Transylvania. During January Rabutin had convened the loyalist nobility at Schässburg (Sighisoara) in order to repudiate the earlier work of the Weissenburg Diet. Since the principality was almost completely controlled by the Austrians, Rákóczi was obliged to call his own rump congress together in the northern edge of the principality, at the Partium town of Huszt (Khust). Yet, since he recognized the impropriety of holding an inaugural ceremony in the Partium, the meeting at Huszt limited itself to denouncing its Schässburg counterpart, concluding an alliance with the Hungarian confederacy and dispatching a delegation to the coming peace talks.[59]

By the beginning of May, both sides had agreed to a truce that was to be in effect throughout Hungary and Transylvania until 12 July.[60] Meanwhile, the peace congress was scheduled to convene at Tyrnau on 25 May. After three years of civil war and over two years of futile attempts at negotiation, the first formal peace talks were about to begin between the king and his Hungarian subjects. For the Anglo-Dutch mediators, the coming congress occasioned great expectations of a final settlement. To Joseph, however, the realities of the situation were much more painfully apparent. Notwithstanding the objectives of the peace talks, the two sides remained far apart on a number of individual issues. Most notable of these was the future status of Transylvania. Realizing that the success of the talks would hinge upon Rákóczi's willingness to surrender the principality, Joseph had already sent the wife of the rebel leader on a mission to her husband's camp with an offer of the imperial margravate of Burgau as compensation for his renunciation of Transylvania.[61] Nevertheless, Joseph's hopes that the offer would sway Rákóczi were soon disappointed.[62]

As the peace congress convened, it became immediately apparent that the question of Transylvania would remain a major obstacle to the success of the talks. During the opening week of meetings, the confederate negotiators, headed once again by Bercsényi, delayed presenting a formal list of grievances, arguing that their *postulata* could not be drawn up until the peace delegation of their Transylvanian allies had arrived at Tyrnau.[63] This three-man commission appeared within a few days. Yet, having declared in January that he no longer considered the principality to be in revolt against the crown, Joseph now refused to allow their formal admission to the peace talks. As a concession to the frantic mediators, the emperor announced only that he would permit them to mingle with the confederate delegates, but without the independent status which they claimed.[64] This arrangement was, however, unacceptable to the rebel leadership. In an interview with the mediators in his wife's apartments at the fortress of Neuhäusel (Nové Zámky), Rákóczi announced that the Transylvanian delegates would have to receive equal recognition with their confederate allies and added confidently that both rebel groups were already committed to the complete restoration of the principality's independence.[65]

While the arrival of the Transylvanians posed a threat to the continuation of the peace talks, it also enabled the rebels to compose a formal list of joint gravamina. On 13 June the mediators were at last presented with a copy of the *postulata*.[66] Consisting of twenty-three separate articles, the document included a large number of demands over which negotiation was clearly possible. Several implied merely the restoration of laws that had been blatantly violated by Leopold, but which Joseph was already pledged to uphold. Among these were the rebels' demands for a restoration of freedom of worship, the replacement of the *Hofkriegsrat* and *Hofkammer* with their Hungarian counterparts, and the restitution of the diet's exclusive sovereignty over taxation. Other articles, such as those calling for the suppression of the *Commissio Neo Acquistica,* the exclusion of foreign troops and tax officials from the kingdom, and the admission of Hungarian ministers to future peace conferences, were clearly negotiable, though not legally compelling. Moreover, Joseph had already indicated his acceptance of the conditions expressed in Article 20 of the *postulata,* which called for a general amnesty and full compensation for Rákóczi and Bercsényi. Only the first three articles listed in the *postulata* threatened to block an eventual settlement: the insurgent demands for (1) a foreign guarantee, now expanded to comprise not only Prussia and Sweden but Poland, England, the United Provinces, and Venice as well; (2) Transylvania's independence; and (3) modification of the enactments of the Pressburg Diet, including the full restitution of the *jus resistendi* and a new definition of the principle of heredity by the next national diet. To the rebels, it was these three points which offered them security against a repetition of the tyranny of the past. They might dispense with one or possibly even two of them. Yet, they would surely never agree to drop all three. In their quest for security, it was clearly the demand for Transylvania which was the most indispensable to the insurgents. While other foreign powers were liable to show indifference to Hungary's internal affairs, the Magyar princes of Transylvania had proven themselves the sentinels of the kingdom's constitution. Moreover, although the *jus resistendi* provided the Magyar nobility with a valuable legal justification for defending the country's laws against the threat of tyranny, the initial success of the present revolt and the crown's willingness to grant a general amnesty offered ready proof that it was not indispensable to the nation's survival.

It was to be the tragedy of the Tyrnau talks that, of all twenty-three articles contained in the *postulata,* the demand for Transylvania was the one condition that Joseph would never meet. Even before he had returned to Vienna to help compose the crown's reply to the rebel terms, Wratislaw had written Princess Rákóczi confidently assuring her that the king would never consent to the loss of the principality.[67] In fact, the crown's formal reply to the insurgents rejected the demands for modification of the Pressburg laws as well as for Transylvania, while postponing the question of a foreign guarantee until the end of the peace conference.[68] Yet, regarding Transylvania there was no room for compromise. Whereas the *jus resistendi* would promote internal chaos, and a European guarantee encourage foreign intervention, the creation of an independent Transylvania promised to combine both of these hazards, while also depriving Joseph of the richest of his Hungarian crownlands.

In view of the unavoidable deadlock over Transylvania, it was of little consequence that the king agreed to virtually all of the remaining terms presented in the *postulata.* In the official reply handed to the mediators on 28 June, Joseph restated his earlier promises to abide by Hungary's laws and constitution. He would restore freedom of worship and reinstate all organs of government, including the national diet, with all their traditional rights and privileges. In the future, he would consult with the estates before choosing negotiators for a peace conference. Although he expressed the fear that his action might set a "dangerous precedent," Joseph agreed to compensate Rákóczi and Bercsényi for their sacrifices. Similarly he consented to undo the work of the *Commissio Neo Acquistica,* though only after explicitly reserving the right of conquest in future instances. The king was somewhat less compliant in replying to the *postulata*'s demand for the expulsion of all foreign troops and tax officials. Although he promised to alleviate the abuses of foreign garrisons, Joseph pointed out that these troops were essential for the maintenance of internal order as well as for the protection of Hungary and the empire from Turkish invasion. Similarly, he contended that foreign-born tax officials holding the Hungarian *incolat* could not legally be considered apart from natives of the country. Nevertheless, he did promise to convene a gravamina diet in the near future to consider both problems, as well as an additional *kuruc* demand for the expulsion of the Jesuit order. Only regarding the relatively trivial call for the transfer of the Hungarian crown from Pressburg to the northern town of Murány (Muráň) did Joseph refuse either to concede or compromise.

These were considerable concessions by any standards. Yet, by rejecting the confederate demand for Transylvania, the court's 28 June reply to the *postulata* doomed all prospects of a settlement. Nevertheless, it soon became clear that, if the hopes for peace were to come crashing to the ground, the final impetus would come not from an impasse over the rebel gravamina but from the continuing dispute over the admission of the Transylvanian delegation. When the mediators presented Joseph's reply to the confederate negotiators, they flatly refused to receive it and declared that the talks could proceed no further without the official recognition of the Transylvanian commissioners.[69] Once again direct appeal was made to Rákóczi, this time by Wratislaw who journeyed to the prince's quarters at Neuhäusel. The Bohemian chancellor brought with him increased offers of imperial territory in exchange for Rákóczi's renunciation of Transylvania. When these tactics failed, he reminded the prince of the recent fate of Max Emanuel, as well as of the earlier example of his stepfather, Imre Thököly, and cautioned him against the dangers of continued resistance to the crown. Nevertheless, whether out of a sense of loyalty to his country or out of confidence in his own resources, the *kuruc* chieftain refused to be swayed from his demand for the principality.[70]

Sensing that disaster was at hand, the mediators continued to work frantically for a solution to the more immediate problem of the Transylvanian delegation. Finally, they persuaded the confederate negotiators to accept a compromise by which their Transylvanian counterparts would be admitted to the talks as the *Deputati Confoederationis Transylvanicae*.[71] Since this title implied only that the commissioners represented a confederation of malcontents—such as their Hungarian allies—rather than an independent principality, their admission to the peace talks would not prejudice Joseph's claim to sovereignty in Transylvania.

The mediators quickly presented the compromise to the court in the hope that it would now agree to the admission of the Transylvanians. In Vienna, however, the time for compromise had passed. With Wratislaw's return from Neuhäusel, Joseph and his ministers realized that a peace settlement was no longer possible. To prolong the negotiations, with or without the Transylvanians, would serve only to delay their inevitable collapse. In the meantime, military considerations were beginning to work against a continuation of the talks. For some months, the Austrian field army had been preparing to return from Transylvania. Yet, it had not been able to begin its march before the armistice went into effect. In recent weeks, however, the court started to receive urgent messages from Rabutin, who had since replaced

Herbeville, warning that he had exhausted his supplies and would soon have to leave the principality in order to find fresh sustenance for the army. At first, Joseph had overlooked Rabutin's pleas and had agreed to a two-week extension of the truce to 24 July. As he had then explained to Charles of Lorraine, the chief Austrian negotiator at Tyrnau, he was willing "to do anything that may contribute to peace."[72] Yet, with the failure of Wratislaw's mission and the realization that a peace settlement was no longer possible, Joseph now saw no further reason to restrain Rabutin. Indeed, with the rebel armies disbanding to attend to the summer harvest, now seemed the time to resume the offensive. Consequently, the emperor immediately began preparations for a resumption of hostilities, withdrawing an additional 4,000 troops from the Upper Rhine and ordering the Croatian border regiments readied for service.[73] In a Conference held on 11 July, he and his ministers agreed to reject both the mediators' compromise for admitting the Transylvanian delegation and the insurgents' recent call for an indefinite extension of the present cease fire.[74]

For the emperor, the decisions of 11 July were made with the greatest reluctance. Like his English and Dutch allies, he had long considered negotiation to offer the best, if not the only, hope of peace. Indeed, since the failure of his open letter of May 1705, his entire military strategy had centered around the need to prepare for the opening of talks with the rebel leadership. In Herbeville's success in Transylvania, Joseph had imagined the removal of the main obstacle to a settlement. Yet, as the last days of the armistice now spent themselves in a frustrating deadlock over the fate of the principality, he was obliged to face for the first time the prospects of a much longer and more taxing struggle. Still, in the closing moments, he worked to forestall the inevitable by sending Rákóczi's sister Juliana, on an eleventh-hour mission to her brother, and then by repeating to the mediators that he would extend the truce if the rebels renounced their claim to Transylvania.[75] In neither case, however, did Joseph expect a positive response. In neither did he receive one. He now looked to the future more with a mixture of hope and anxiety than with a sanguinary confidence in total victory.

With the expiration of the armistice on 24 July, the rebel peace commissioners departed from Tyrnau, leaving the Austrians to face the unrestrained wrath of the Anglo-Dutch mediators. In their impatience to mediate a settlement, Joseph's allies had failed to perceive that a peaceful solution to the conflict was still impossible. Instead they interpreted the court's refusal to admit the Transylvanian delegation or to extend the armistice as evidence of its insincerity and indifference to a negotiated peace. Moreover, the allies' anger at Vienna's intransigence was heightened—or, perhaps, unduly influenced—by the realization that they would have to fight on in the west without the aid of the thousands of Austrian troops presently tied down in Hungary.[76]

To a large extent, Rákóczi's diplomacy at Tyrnau was also responsible for placing the blame on Joseph and his ministers. He entered the peace talks fully aware that he could better afford to spend time on fruitless negotiations than could his Habsburg adversary. He had no second front to fight and his soldiers could use the cease fire to attend to the needs of the summer harvest. Consequently, it was less difficult for him to compromise on the admission of the Transylvanian delegation or to suggest an extension of the armistice, even though he too was aware that the peace negotiations would fail. Moreover, by appearing eager to compromise and anxious to reach a settlement, he and his lieutenants were able to shift pressure from the mediators and, ultimately, blame for the deadlock onto the hapless Austrians.

In fact, once it had become clear that the truce would expire, the confederate negotiators were able to concentrate on discrediting Vienna in the eyes of its allies. On 12 July following Joseph's refusal to accept the mediators' compromise proposal, the rebel commissioners belatedly agreed to receive the court's response to the *postulata,* thereby giving the impression of a desperate attempt to save the talks.[77] On the last day of the armistice, Rákóczi notified the mediators that he was fully prepared to dispatch letters to the confederation asking it to reconvene at Szécsény and withdraw from the recently concluded alliance with Transylvania. In this way, the Hungarian confederacy would be able to enter into negotiations with the crown without deserting its ally. Alas, added Rákóczi, this was now impossible because Joseph had permitted the truce to expire.[78] Rather than question the prince's sincerity, the mediators hastened to Vienna and, in an interview on 1 August, pleaded with the emperor to prolong the armistice. Unimpressed by Rákóczi's latest ploy, Joseph again refused.[79]

The confederate leadership supplemented these more subtle maneuvers with direct appeals for support, both abroad and among its own countrymen. Just before the expiration of the truce, the Hungarian commissioners issued a statement defending their own conduct and attributing the failure of the peace talks to the Habsburgs's "boundless lust for power." Meanwhile, Rákóczi issued a similar declaration for distribution throughout the kingdom and sent separate appeals to the Dutch Estates, Queen Anne, and the duke of Marlborough. The rebels fired their final salvo in a lengthy rejoinder to Joseph's 28 June reply, published for distribution throughout the courts of Europe.[80]

Not unexpectedly, however, the best propaganda for the rebel cause came from the irrepressible George Stepney. During the mediators' 1 August interview with Joseph, Stepney had joined with his colleagues in expressing the opinion that Rákóczi had been ready to conclude peace and that it was the Austrian ministers and generals who had been responsible for the rupture. By the end of the month, the ambassador's remarks were published in the English and Dutch press and were eventually reprinted in gazettes throughout central Europe.[81]

By their conduct, the Anglo-Dutch mediators and their home governments had done a great disservice to their Habsburg ally. In permitting the rebels to exploit their own impatience for a settlement, they had become the unwitting advocates of continued resistance to the crown. They had failed to recognize that the early deadlock over Transylvania had doomed any chance of peace and that the rebels had used the last three weeks of the armistice to put the pressure and blame on Vienna. What was perhaps most pathetic about the failure of the Anglo-Dutch mediators was their willingness to be flattered, if not seduced, by the generous compliments and courtesies paid them by the confederate leaders. Not once did they imagine that it was France in whose bed Rákóczi had chosen to sleep. The presence of Desalleurs at virtually all of the secret deliberations between the prince and his lieutenants bore witness to his intentions, although its significance was beyond the mediators' grasp. Of course, faith in French promises was all that sustained Rákóczi in his persistent hopes of a formal alliance against the emperor. Nevertheless, having already acted on faith in rejecting Joseph's first efforts at conciliation and in subsequently attempting to succeed to the Transylvanian throne, Rákóczi did not find it difficult to pursue the same course at Tyrnau. He realized fully the risks he was taking. Bercsényi had often advised him not to place too much trust in the promises of Louis and Desalleurs. Only recently Vetes had warned him that Versailles was interested solely in prolonging the revolt in Hungary rather than in making any firm commitments, and had urged him to come to terms with Joseph before Louis himself concluded peace with the allies.[82] Indeed, even Count Wratislaw, who knew little of Rákóczi's present designs but much about the nature of European diplomacy, had parted from their 30 June meeting at Neuhäusel with the prophetic advice: "Well, my prince, you are putting your faith in France, which is the hospital of princes who have come to grief through her broken pledges and promises. You will increase their number and die there."[83]

The Turning Point

Notwithstanding the advice of his lieutenants and his enemies, Rákóczi continued to look to Versailles rather than to Vienna for an ultimate settlement. During the spring, he had remained undeterred and unshaken by Louis's latest conditions for an alliance, which now included not only his belated inauguration as prince of Transylvania but also the formal renunciation of Habsburg sovereignty in all of Hungary. Realizing that his countrymen were as yet unwilling to dethrone Joseph, Rákóczi had agreed only to assume the Transylvanian crown.[84] Nevertheless, at the same time, he began preparing the way for a complete overthrow of Habsburg rule, should that step become necessary to assure continued foreign support for the rebel cause. As early as April, he had proffered the Hungarian crown to Augustus the Strong in return for an alliance against Joseph.[85] Following the failure of these overtures and the collapse of the Tyrnau talks, the prince turned to Charles XII, offering him the throne in exchange for a force of 6,000 Swedes.[86] Here too, however, Rákóczi's hopes went unfulfilled. Although he had not yet found a foreign prince who was willing to challenge Habsburg sovereignty in Hungary, Rákóczi soon felt himself compelled to go ahead with plans to dethrone Joseph. He reached this decision at the end of 1706 after having received word from Vetes that Louis XIV had begun secret peace talks with the allies.[87] Although Louis's overtures had proved fruitless, the prince feared more than ever that France would reach a settlement with its enemies and leave the rebels to carry on their struggle alone. Disregarding Vetes's warning that the French would "not prolong the war by one hour for the welfare of . . . the fatherland," he now moved to meet Louis's conditions for the conclusion of a formal alliance.[88] While proceeding with plans for his inauguration in Transylvania, Rákóczi issued a proclamation to the Magyar nobility summoning it to the northern town of Ónod at the beginning of May.[89]

In his declaration, the prince made no mention of his plan to use the coming diet to dethrone Joseph and renounce Habsburg sovereignty in Hungary. Nevertheless, the emperor and his ministers were well aware of his ultimate intentions. Through the imperial resident in Warsaw, as well as the intelligence of its British ally, the court had kept well abreast of Rákóczi's negotiations with Augustus and Charles XII.[90] Joseph still had several months in which to counteract Rákóczi's intended treason by offering more generous peace terms to the country. Since the collapse of the Tyrnau talks, he had remained steadfast in his refusal to accede to the principal rebel demands. During the previous August, he had rejected the petition of the aged palatine, Prince Paul Esterházy, and Counts Pálffy and Erdödy for a reopening of negotiations based on the creation of an independent Transylvania under Habsburg suzerainty. Instead, the emperor had sanguinely awaited Rabutin's return to western Hungary where he was expected to join with a second force of Serb and Croat irregulars forming under the newly arrived Guido Starhemberg.[91] In the intervening months, however, Rabutin's army had suffered a dismal setback. After wasting several weeks in a vain attempt to seize the important fortress of Kaschau (Košice), Rabutin had marched to Buda, his command suffering terribly from disease and winter cold. He did not reach his destination until January, too late to join Starhemberg, whose forces had accomplished little in the interim. Meanwhile, the rebels had continued to raid and plunder the *Erblande* almost at will.

As in past years, the Austrian setbacks served to heighten the rebel leadership's conditions for the reopening of peace talks. By December it was demanding Joseph's agreement to a foreign guarantee, the loss of Transylvania, and the immediate expulsion of all German troops from Hungary before negotiations could resume.[92] No monarch could have accepted such terms, which undoubtedly reflected the insurgents' confidence in a continuing military stalemate. Indeed, despite the failures of the last campaign and the imminent threat of a total renunciation of Habsburg rule by the rebels, Joseph still refused to agree to terms that would paralyze royal authority in the kingdom. He demonstrated this determination once more at the end of March when a group of loyalist magnates presented him with an alternative peace plan that reaffirmed the *kuruc* demand for the creation of an independent Transylvania under a freely-elected tributary prince and vigorously defended the need for a foreign guarantee to protect and reassure the country against a repetition of the tyranny of the past.[93]

With Joseph's refusal to make further concessions, the initiative passed once again to Rákóczi. By the beginning of April, he had already met with the insurgent Transylvanian nobility at Maros-Vásárhely (Târgu-Mureş), formally assuming the princely throne. Over the next few weeks, he began preparing for the upcoming diet at Ónod and the final blow to Habsburg rule in Hungary. The prince realized that there would be considerable opposition to his plans for a complete overthrow of the dynasty. Large numbers of the *kuruc* nobility shared the yearning for peace and compromise expressed so recently by their loyalist countrymen. All classes throughout the kingdom had suffered from the war, not only from the reprisals of the enemy but also the devastation wrought by the poorly paid and disciplined confederate forces. Moreover, the country's already fragile economy had been dealt a severe blow by heavy taxation and the massive issue of debased copper currency. Considerable dissatisfaction continued among the country's Protestants. All of the restorations promised by Rákóczi at Szécsény had not been carried out, prompting at least one synod in the northeastern counties to appeal to Prussia and Sweden for assistance.[94] Meanwhile, those areas of the confederacy which had suffered most from the fighting began calling for an end to the war. During the winter, a group of sixteen counties, including all of the southwestern districts, presented Rákóczi with a petition protesting its inability to make further sacrifices and threatening to come to terms with Vienna unless he moderated his demands.[95] At the same time, representatives of seven northwestern counties, led by the Thurocz noblemen Pál Okolicsanyi and Melchior Rakovsky, circulated a list of grievances against the confederate leadership and called for the conclusion of peace.[96]

The Magyar estates did not actually convene at Ónod until 27 May, almost a full month later than anticipated. Nevertheless, many magnate families still did not send representatives. The latter were immediately fined and two among them, Cardinal Széchenyi and Baron Szirmay, were deprived of their estates for having served as royal commissioners during the Tyrnau talks. Yet, if Rákóczi had hoped to intimidate his opponents by these actions, he was soon disappointed. On 3 June strong opposition developed to his program for a tax on the nobility and the minting of additional copper currency. After three days of spirited debate, the diet reached a stalemate, with a majority of the delegates holding fast against Rákóczi's proposals. On the fourth day the prince and his lieutenants took matters into their own hands. While a representative for the northwestern counties was speaking against the proposed copper issue, Rákóczi rose to his feet to accuse the opposition of personally insulting his integrity. Quickly shifting his ground, he alluded to the "seditious" petition circulated by the seven northwestern counties during the previous winter and then pointed angrily at the Thurocz delegation. Rakovsky and the son of the absent Pál Okolicsanyi rose to justify their opposition to a continuation of the war, prompting in turn a sharp rebuke from Bercsényi, who called upon the diet to punish them for their insolence. Rákóczi readily seconded Bercsényi, admonishing the delegates to grant him satisfaction. Yet, the assembly met both appeals with a tense silence. Reproaching the diet for its ingratitude and laxity in administering justice, Bercsényi drew his sword and personally struck down Rakovsky. He was quickly followed by Count Károlyi, who administered the fatal blow, and finally by a number of other nobles. After several blows had been delivered against Okolicsanyi and the body of the dead Rakovsky, Bercsényi called for the arrest and punishment of the remaining Thurocz deputies. On this occasion, his appeal did not go unanswered. Okolicsanyi and his colleagues were promptly seized and removed from the assembly. Okolicsanyi was condemned to death on the following day and, on 9 June, he was beheaded in a nearby field. In the same ceremony, performed before the assembled estates, the county of Thurocz was formally dissolved and divided among its neighbors, its shield shattered over the corpse of Melchior Rakovsky. Meanwhile orders went out for the arrest of Pál Okolicsanyi as well as other Thurocz noblemen who had failed to attend the diet. With the demise of the Thurocz delegation, all opposition to Rákóczi disappeared. On the day before Okolicsanyi's execution, the prince's tax and currency proposals were ratified by the diet. Six days later, on 14 June 1707, a declaration was passed formally renouncing the sovereignty of Joseph and his dynasty and declaring the throne vacant. On the recommendation of Desalleurs, the estates voted to offer Max Emanuel the crown. Until his acceptance, Rákóczi was to continue in power with Bercsényi as his deputy. In the meantime, each county or noble family that had not sent representatives to Ónod was given two months in which to accede to the actions of the diet or forfeit its rights and privileges.[97]

When he learned of the events at Ónod, Joseph had reason for both regret and satisfaction. He was, no doubt, gravely troubled by the rebels' renunication of Habsburg rule. Indeed, at the eleventh hour, he had sent the loyalist nobleman Gabriel Tolvay to Rákóczi with the offer of a truce. Yet, this half-hearted attempt to forestall a final break had failed when the prince arrested Tolvay upon his arrival at Ónod.[98] At the same time, the emperor could derive a certain sense of vindication from Rákóczi's most recent actions, interpreting them as proof that a reasonable compromise with the rebel leader had never been possible. Indeed, in dethroning Joseph, the rebel diet only served to reinforce the prevalent view at court that force was the only means by which peace could be achieved within the kingdom.

At that moment, however, there was some question as to how Habsburg arms should be deployed during the coming campaign. With Rabutin's departure from Transylvania, the principality had again largely fallen into the hands of the insurgents. All of the territory north of the Marosch (Maros, Mureş) River had been lost and the capital of Hermannstadt was once more under siege. To re-secure Transylvania, a second march similar to Herbeville's would have to be undertaken. Yet, as in 1705, there were simply not enough troops to recover the principality and, at the same time, secure the *Erblande* against further rebel raids. In a Conference held on 2 August, Joseph's ministers as well as field marshals Starhemberg and Rabutin debated what course to take. Nine of the ten men present opposed a second expedition; in fact, several advocated a further withdrawal of all remaining forces from the principality. Only Rabutin, whose task it would be to undertake such a venture, argued for Transylvania's recovery. Following the Conference, Prince Salm presented its judgment to Joseph. Yet, when the emperor convened a second meeting on the next day, he announced that he had decided to dispatch Rabutin "in order to secure Transylvania . . . lest its loss produce grievous consequences of which everyone is aware, and result in irreparable harm."[99] The field marshal received his orders on the following day and began his march within a fortnight. While they could not forestall or prevent Rabutin from reaching his destination, the insurgents made Joseph pay the predictable price for his decision. Throughout September *kuruc* cavalry spread destruction across the lightly guarded Styrian frontier.[100]

North of the Danube, however, the situation was different. At the start of the campaign, Rákóczi had planned to invade Silesia, hoping to profit from the religious unrest caused by Charles XII's presence in neighboring Saxony. Yet, once Rabutin had set out for Transylvania, the prince was obliged to transfer many of his troops to the east. Consequently, by skillfully deploying the modest forces under his command, Guido Starhemberg was able not only to protect Lower Austria and the Bohemian crownlands from rebel incursions but also to occupy the Hungarian counties lying between the March (Morava) and Waag (Váh) Rivers.[101] While Austrian arms were meeting with some success in the northwest, word reached Vienna during December that Transylvania had been completely recovered.[102] Rabutin had duplicated Herbeville's feat of two years past. A third campaign would never be needed.

The success of the 1707 campaign served to restore the court's confidence in force as a feasible means of achieving peace. Nevertheless, as the year drew to a close, Joseph also began to reevaluate the prospects of appealing for popular support. Indeed, if the Ónod and Maros-Vásárhely diets had virtually eliminated the possibility of future negotiations with the rebel leadership, they had also given him the opportunity to appeal directly to the Hungarian people. Over the past four years, most of Rákóczi's supporters and the overwhelming majority of his soldiers had been motivated by the prince's promise to alleviate the suffering of the country's serfs and religious minorities. Like previous meetings of the nobility, however, the Ónod and Maros-Vásárhely diets had largely ignored these promises and, hence, suggested to the rest of the nation that a *kuruc* victory would bring no change in their status.[103] Similarly, most of the nation had never favored a complete overthrow of Habsburg rule and was presently interested primarily in restoring peace and order to the largely devastated countryside. Following the events at Ónod, many former rebel partisans and sympathizers had also begun to despair of obtaining this objective through Rákóczi's leadership and were now prepared to return to their previous allegiance to the crown. In fact, in the waning months of 1707, encouraging signs of increased popular support began to appear in both Hungary proper and Transylvania, leading Bercsényi to confess: "The present situation is the same on the Marosch as on the Waag. There fight the Rumanians, here the Slavs. Alas, we have lost the support of the people."[104]

Joseph had first appealed for popular support during July and August by issuing a series of declarations condemning the actions of the Ónod Diet, to which over one hundred of the kingdom's magnates, bishops, and county, church, and municipal heads appended their names.[105] During September, he had received valuable assistance from Clement XI, who reacted to the Ónod Diet's expulsion of the Jesuit order by prohibiting the Hungarian clergy from participating further in the rebellion.[106] Then, following the end of the campaign, Prince Esterházy urged Joseph to convene his own diet in the coming months, arguing that such an assembly could be used both to demonstrate and appeal for popular support, and to provide a favorable contrast between the crown's honorable intentions and the violence recently employed by the rebel leadership. Joseph readily agreed to the plan and soon instructed Esterházy to issue a declaration summoning the Magyar nobility to assemble at Pressburg at the end of February. Soon afterward he announced to his ministers that he would preside personally over the opening and closing of the diet.[107]

The meeting at Pressburg promised to be the first diet convened by the crown in over two decades and, while Joseph's German ministers did not expect the estates to take any positive action toward a settlement, it remained nonetheless a means of persuading the Hungarian nation to invest its confidence in the sincerity of its young king. Of course, despite his pledge to abide by the constitution and laws of the kingdom, Joseph's promises did not necessarily presage a complete departure from the policies of his predecessors. Most notably he would remain a foreign prince both by habit and inclination. This became painfully apparent to Esterházy and his Hungarian colleagues during December, when Joseph continued to consult almost exclusively with his German ministers in making plans for the upcoming diet. Their sense of frustration increased further with the disclosure that the diet was to be presided over by the German cardinal, Sachsen-Zeitz, rather than Esterházy. Joseph had chosen to relieve the palatine of his traditional role primarily because of his advanced age and also, perhaps, because he was hated passionately by much of the insurgent nobility. Moreover, the youthful and able Sachsen-Zeitz had only recently succeeded as primate of Hungary. Nevertheless, the proud palatine felt gravely insulted and refused to accept the cardinal's invitation to participate in the preliminary negotiations for the opening of the diet.[108]

Notwithstanding the injured pique of Esterházy and the other royal ministers, plans for the coming diet continued to proceed smoothly. Following the 23 December Conference, Sachsen-Zeitz left for Pressburg to begin several weeks of consultations with the loyalist nobility. If the coming assembly were to fail, it would be Rákóczi rather than Joseph who was to be principally responsible. Toward the end of February, rebel raids in the area around Pressburg became so intense that the emperor was finally convinced by Sachsen-Zeitz and Prince Eugene not to attend the diet's opening session.[109] As the incursions intensified, however, the court was obliged to postpone the meeting itself until adequate protection could be afforded by troops returning from winter quarters.[110] When the diet finally convened at the beginning of April 1708, its membership proved no more representative than that of the two confederate assemblies at Szécsény and Ónod. Although a total of seventy-seven magnates, nineteen bishops, fifteen counties and eighteen towns were represented at Pressburg, virtually all of them came from those areas of the kingdom that were presently under Habsburg control. Meanwhile, fear of retaliation by Rákóczi's government kept the balance of the Magyar nobility from attending or sending any deputies to the diet.[111]

Despite the absence of any delegates from the rebel counties, deliberations were hardly characterized by unanimity either between the king and his subjects or among the estates themselves. Indeed, like most of its predecessors, the Pressburg Diet of 1708–1709 was to prove as free and chaotic in its debate as it was indecisive in its resolution. For most of its initial session, held during the spring of 1708, the diet was paralyzed by religious dissension. The Catholic and Protestant estates clashed immediately over the presentation of their gravamina. Although the Catholic majority was willing to call for the restitution of freedom of worship, the Protestant minority—like its counterpart at Szécsény and Ónod—formulated a much more comprehensive list of demands, including the full restoration of all property confiscated under Leopold I.[112] Meanwhile, a second conflict arose between the diet's ecclesiastical and lay delegates following the latter's attempt to exclude churchmen from the post of Hungarian court chancellor. The proposal was eventually dropped, though only after Sachsen-Zeitz and the nineteen bishops at the diet threatened to boycott the assembly.[113]

While the estates were preoccupied with these disputes, Joseph endeavored to use the diet as a platform for the presentation of his own program for reform. Aside from reiterating his intention to abide by the constitution and restore religious freedom, he now agreed for the first time to fill administrative positions solely with native Magyars, and also promised to withdraw foreign troops from Hungary after peace had been restored and to end compulsory quartering on the civilian population.[114] When the estates belatedly replied with their own list of gravamina, most of their demands merely repeated or amplified on what Joseph had already promised to concede. Aside from calling for the exclusion of the *Hofkriegsrat* and *Hofkammer* from Hungary and for the renewal of Joseph's Tyrnau pledge to restore all lands confiscated by the *Commissio Neo Acquistica,* the diet strayed from the king's reform proposals only in its rather ominous declaration that his personal guarantee was insufficient to safeguard the kingdom's laws.[115] Rather than continue negotiations at this time, however, Joseph heeded the advice of his German ministers and adjourned the estates, pending the composition of a formal reply to their grievances. Over the past four months the diet had accomplished very little in creating a consensus on what form a future settlement might take. In fact, it did not—and had never been expected to— exercise a sudden or dramatic influence on the continuing course of the war. Most, if not all, of Joseph's ministers were still inclined to agree with Sinzendorf, who wrote to the archduke on 31 July that "peace must be accomplished by force, not by negotiation."[116] Four days later, as the loyalist nobility began to depart from Pressburg, his prediction was thoroughly vindicated.

Victory and Compromise

For Prince Rákóczi, the climactic events of the Ónod Diet had been followed by a denouement of disillusionment and frustration. He had carefully engineered Joseph's dethronement in Hungary and Transylvania in the expectation that Versailles would at last commit itself to an alliance against the common enemy. Yet, in the months that followed, both Louis and Desalleurs found various means of putting off his repeated requests for such a treaty.[117] The prince was equally unsuccessful in his overtures to Max Emanuel. In July, Vetes transmitted to the exiled elector the Ónod Diet's offer of the Hungarian crown. Included in the communication was Rákóczi's request that he lead a force of 15,000 cavalry across Germany into Bohemia where he would be met by a confederate army invading from the east.[118] Max was, however, understandably hesitant to commit himself to so dangerous a venture. In the following January, after Rákóczi had instructed Vetes to renew the offer, Louis XIV rejected the entire project as impossible.[119]

While Rákóczi's dream of a foreign alliance faded, the realities of the worsening military situation became increasingly apparent. The new fiscal measures voted by the diet had done little to mobilize the country's diminishing resources. Designed to help pay and supply the *kuruc* army, the latest copper issue had instead rendered the existing confederate currency worthless, while dealing a devastating blow to the Hungarian economy.[120] Even the French subsidies upon which Rákóczi had relied in the past had ceased to arrive.[121] Assessing the miserable condition of the rebel army, Desalleurs predicted that, barring foreign intervention, "the next [1708] campaign will decide the war in Hungary."[122] Despite these setbacks, Rákóczi failed to awaken from his grandiose dreams of imminent diplomatic and military success. He refused to heed further communications from Vetes confirming that Louis would never permit Max Emanuel's dispatch to Hungary.[123] Instead, during the first half of 1708, he began making preparations for an invasion of Bohemia in the hope that he might yet prompt Louis to change his mind. Although he continued to authorize raids against the *Erblande,* Rákóczi devoted all his remaining resources to the Bohemian venture. Even Transylvania was sacrificed as most of the forces which Rabutin had expelled from the principality were now summoned to join him at his camp near Erlau (Eger).[124] In July preparations were finally completed, and Rákóczi began the march toward Bohemia.

Although the prince had divulged his intentions only to his closest lieutenants, Vienna was well aware of both the poor state of his army and the exact nature of his plans.[125] There was some question, however, whether the Austrian army would be able to meet the challenge. The late arrival of the 6,000 Danish mercenaries from their winter quarters in Germany had cut the size of the army in western Hungary to less than 10,000 men.[126] Meanwhile, Joseph had also lost his two most able field commanders. Reacting to appeals from the archduke and the maritime powers, he had recently dispatched Guido Starhemberg to Catalonia, while poor health had forced the sudden retirement of his intended replacement, Count Rabutin. To fill Starhemberg's post, Joseph was now obliged to recall Field Marshal Heister. To some extent the events of the last two campaigns had served to exonerate

Heister of the charges that had been levelled against him in 1705. As the rebellion entered its sixth year, the court had come to appreciate the difficulties involved in subduing and retaining possession of large tracts of rebel territory. Similarly the continuing atrocities committed by both sides had amply demonstrated that acts of mercy and tolerance had little place in a civil war. Nevertheless, in view of the present need to encourage defections from the rebel cause, Joseph was reluctant to appoint a commander with Heister's notorious reputation and did so only because no other general possessed sufficient ability and experience.[127]

On 4 August Heister intercepted the rebel army at the town of Trentschin (Trenčin), barely ten miles from the Moravian frontier. Although he commanded a force of only 7,400 men compared to Rákóczi's 22,000, the field marshal was completely victorious. After he had dispersed the insurgents, Heister proceeded to occupy the remaining northwestern counties almost without opposition. By the end of the campaign, he stood on the Eipel (Ipoly, Ipel') River; in his rear only the formidable Neuhäusel continued to hold out. The rebels still controlled roughly half of Hungary, including much of the south and southwest and all of the northern and northeastern counties. Nevertheless, the confederate disaster at Trentschin had completed a fateful turn of events initiated by Rákóczi himself during the previous year. At Ónod the Hungarian people had been told that there would be no peace— and no end to their sacrifices—without victory. After Trentschin, they realized that victory was impossible and, hence, that further sacrifice would be useless. As Heister made his way through the northwest, he found his army and his offers of amnesty well received by the local population. Within a short time, congregations from each of the surrounding counties began to appear at his camp to pledge their allegiance to the king.[128]

Nowhere was the inevitability of a Habsburg victory more evident than among the rebels themselves. Demoralized by the bleak military outlook and disenchanted with months of unpaid wages and years of unfulfilled promises, the men in the ranks became increasingly restive and reluctant to fight.[129] At the same time, several of Rákóczi's most trusted lieutenants began meeting secretly with Count Pálffy in an effort to secure a full pardon from Joseph. Although they were eventually betrayed by one of their number, their wavering loyalty conveyed an unmistakeable message.[130] In fact, Rákóczi himself had at last come to grips with reality. Shortly after the disaster at Trentschin, he had received Vetes's report of a 3 July interview with the French king and his foreign minister, the marquis de Torcy. During the meeting, Vetes had pressed once again for the formal alliance promised by Louis, threatening that Rákóczi would make an accommodation with Vienna unless it were concluded soon. To this Torcy replied brusquely that the prince was no longer in a position to reach a settlement with Joseph, having lost much of his popular appeal as a result of the recent diets at Ónod and Pressburg.[131]

Rákóczi appreciated at last the wisdom of Vetes's continuing pleas against putting further trust in France. As an alternative to the chimerical French alliance, he once again sought an understanding with either Sweden or Russia.[132] In addition, during October he also turned to Joseph's allies, imploring Queen Anne and the duke of Marlborough to revive the Anglo-Dutch mediation.[133] In the following month, he released Gabriel Tolvay and sent him back to Joseph with an offer to reopen negotiations. The prince timed his moves well. When Tolvay arrived at court, his return was greeted by a concerted peace offensive by the emperor's English, Dutch, and Prussian allies.[134] Yet, Rákóczi's conditions for a settlement were still too high. Despite the recent military setbacks, he continued to hold out for an independent Transylvania, albeit under Habsburg suzerainty, as well as for Joseph's acceptance of an Anglo-Dutch guarantee.[135] In fact, Joseph was not even willing to permit a resumption of mediation by the maritime powers lest it encourage rebel obstinacy and promote renewed friction within the alliance.[136] Consequently, while the court remained in contact with Rákóczi until the end of January, all negotiations were eventually broken off.[137]

In the ensuing months, Joseph continued to put his faith in force as the most effective means for achieving peace. As in the previous year, he showed deference to the wavering loyalties of his Hungarian subjects by convening the estates at Pressburg. Yet, in his belated reply to the diet's formal list of grievances, Joseph betrayed his confidence in the improved military situation by offering no additional concessions. He refused not only to submit to a foreign guarantee but also to free the Hungarian treasury from the control of the *Hofkammer,* arguing instead that its continued subjugation was necessary for the proper coordination of state finances. Moreover, he passed over a separate list of gravamina presented by the Protestant estates by merely reiterating his intention to restore religious freedom.[138] Perhaps the best sign of Joseph's waxing optimism was a measure which he now submitted to the estates, confiscating the property of any Hungarian subject who did not reaffirm his allegiance to the crown. Prince Salm had first suggested the presentation of this proposal during the previous year as a means of raising war revenue. At that time, however, the emperor had rejected it on the grounds that it would make the conclusion of peace more difficult.[139] Notwithstanding his earlier misgivings, Joseph now brought the measure before the diet, which soon approved it with minor modifications.[140]

With the diet's adjournment at the end of July, the emperor turned his attention once more to the slow but systematic recovery of central Hungary. Heister's preparations for the 1709 campaign had been hampered considerably by the devastating effects of the previous winter, as well as by the outbreak and rapid spread of pestilence throughout the kingdom.[141] Nevertheless, once the Austrian army had taken the field, it found an enemy incapable of offering serious resistance. An unhappy combination of sickness and desertion had badly depleted the ranks of the insurgents. Those who continued to serve the confederate cause did so without benefit of pay or the promise of victory.[142] Heister opened the campaign by retaking the Transdanubian counties and thereby removing the last base for rebel raids into the *Erblande*. By September he had joined Count Pálffy's forces north of the river and, in the next few months, succeeded in extending his conquests almost to the banks of the Theiss. So impressive was the field marshal's progress that even the previously skeptical Prince Eugene cheerfully saluted his "well known military ability, vigilence, and ceaseless toil."[143]

After the spectacular accomplishments of the past two campaigns, there was good reason to believe that 1710 would be the last year of the war in Hungary. Indeed, as his armies fanned out over the breadth of the kingdom, Joseph continued to make conciliatory gestures aimed at smoothing the way for a general pacification. His most immediate concern was to spare the civilian population from the excesses and heavy taxes with which it had come to associate the presence of the emperor's foreign troops. During the course of 1709, he had established a commission to investigate charges of outrages committed by the Austrian military.[144] With the approach of winter, he now appointed a number of Hungarian magnates to the General War Commissary and issued strict orders to his field commanders in an attempt both to forestall further acts of violence and ensure an equitable distribution of the *Quartierlast*.[145] At the same time, Joseph attempted to assuage the fears of his Protestant subjects by forbidding further religious persecution by the military and by taking the extraordinary step of ordering royal officials to begin making restitution of property confiscated from the Protestant minority during Leopold's reign.[146]

If Joseph continued to play for popular support from the mass of the country, it was because the travesties of Tyrnau and Ónod had convinced him that such a strategy offered the most direct—and possibly the only—path to a mutually acceptable and durable settlement. Moreover, with the victories of the past two years, the emperor no longer saw any need to treat with Rákóczi and the rebel regime. During the previous summer, he had rejected the prince's call for the opening of direct peace negotiations.[147] Three months later he had also declined Tsar Peter's offer of Russian mediation.[148] Instead, Joseph indicated that he would never again recognize or negotiate with the confederate leadership. In the future, he would permit them to approach him solely as individuals seeking pardon.[149] Following the emperor's rejection of Russian mediation, Rákóczi left Hungary for Poland, where Bercsényi had been for some months seeking the tsar's diplomatic assistance. With the total destruction of the last confederate field army at Vadkert on 22 January, the two men prolonged their stay there knowing that only outside intervention could save their cause.

It was partly in response to Rákóczi's diplomacy that Joseph and his ministers soon initiated their own attempts to cultivate the tsar's friendship. Yet, while the rebel chieftain was hoping to enlist Peter's aid in bringing peace to Hungary, Joseph was primarily interested in using Russia to counter the growing threat of war with Turkey. Notwithstanding the relentless intrigues of the French ambassador and the more militant Turkish ministers, the Porte had endeavored to remain neutral during the latest Hungarian rebellion. Yet, following Charles XII's disastrous defeat at Poltava (28 June 1709) and subsequent retreat across the Turkish frontier, the sultan's future course suddenly became as unpredictable as the mind of his Swedish guest. To ensure himself against a war with Turkey, Tsar Peter hastily concluded a thirty-year truce with the sultan that also allowed for Charles XII's safe return to Sweden.[150] The disclosure of this agreement sent shock waves through Vienna, for it not only suggested secret Turkish designs against the monarchy but also implied Russian neutrality in the event of an attack from the south. In two Conferences held on 15-16 February 1710, Prince Eugene urged as a countermove the immediate conclusion of a defensive alliance with the tsar, directed against Turkey.[151] Joseph readily agreed to the project since it presented him with a means both of providing a visible deterrent to Turkish attack and of frustrating further rebel overtures to either the tsar or the sultan.[152] An agent was immediately dispatched to Moscow to propose the alliance to Peter. The tsar, however, declined the offer.

Within a matter of months, Peter came to regret his decision. Despite the sultan's efforts to induce Charles XII to return homeward, the Swedish king refused to leave his camp at Bender, choosing instead to plot with the French for a Turkish attack against Russia. In November these intrigues culminated in a Turkish declaration of war against the tsar. When word reached Vienna, the emperor had ample reason to bless the fates. Had Peter responded affirmatively to his recent alliance proposal, he would now find himself involved in yet another major conflict. Instead, as the imperial resident reported from Constantinople, there was presently very little chance indeed that the Porte would soon choose to complicate its affairs by attacking the monarchy as well.[153] Following a series of Conferences during the winter of 1710-1711, Joseph and his ministers took the precaution of consulting Venice and Rome about the prospects of a renewal of the Holy League, as well as of urging the maritime powers to come to their aid in the event of a Turkish attack.[154] They remained confident, however, that the war clouds presently forming to the south would not drift over Hungary.

Not so with the maritime powers. Despite the assurances of their own ambassador in Constantinople that the sultan had no intention of attacking the emperor, the British were virtually in a state of panic.[155] Together with the Dutch, they now began to press harder than ever for an immediate settlement with the Hungarian insurgents, lest a continuation of the struggle encourage Turkish intervention. Joseph did not share his allies' anxieties and was only annoyed by their continuing attempts to pressure him into making an accommodation with Rákóczi. The successes of the past campaign had removed the need for further negotiations or concessions. Austrian forces marching out of Transylvania had completed the recovery of the region lying between the Danube and the Theiss. Neuhäusel had capitulated during September and, although Heister's deteriorating health soon compelled Joseph to replace him with Count Pálffy, the loyalist magnate had succeeded in forcing the rebels into the extreme northeast of the kingdom. At present they held only Kaschau, which was already under siege, Ungvár (Uzhgorod), Huszt, and Munkács.[156] Although further operations had been halted by the onset of winter, Joseph was fully prepared to wait until spring before delivering the *coup de grâce*.[157]

While he was unwilling to reopen negotiations with Rákóczi, the emperor was nonetheless prepared to amnesty the remaining insurgent forces in exchange for their oath of allegiance. Indeed, with the surrender of numerous rebel garrisons during the fall and early winter, he had empowered Count Pálffy to pardon and release all captured soldiers once a loyalty oath had been administered.[158] Since both Rákóczi and Bercsényi were still in Poland seeking foreign assistance, Joseph and his ministers now saw the opportunity to induce the remaining confederate forces to lay down their arms months before the arrival of spring. The key to the court's hopes was Count Sándor Károlyi, whom Rákóczi had left in command and whose defection it now hoped to obtain. During November, Pálffy had written Károlyi urging him to consider both his country's as well as his family's welfare in helping to bring an end to the hopeless struggle. The rebel commander replied by affirming his desire to reach an accommodation, but expressed fear for the fate of his family should his duplicity become known.[159] Joseph countered first by giving Pálffy full authority to restore all of Károlyi's lands and titles, then by promising to compensate the *kuruc* general for any damages and by assuring him that Rákóczi's two sons would be held as security for his own family's safety.[160]

Following these guarantees, Károlyi journeyed to Pálffy's camp on 21 January ostensibly to act as Rákóczi's emissary, but secretly to negotiate his own defection. Initially he did try to secure Rákóczi's acceptance of Joseph's demand that he declare his submission and ask for pardon.[161] Károlyi did in fact succeed in persuading the rebel leader to meet with Pálffy and when the three men gathered near Kalló on 31 January, Rákóczi was induced to compose a letter of submission. In return Pálffy agreed to a three-week truce to compose the final arrangements for peace. Yet, even now the fallen prince would not assume the humble garb of a penitent. The letter that he penned to the king was written more in the manner of an apology than of an act of submission. Moreover, although he addressed Joseph as king of Hungary, Rákóczi refused to abandon his own pretensions as a sovereign prince and signed the letter *servitor* rather than *subditos*.[162]

When the letter reached Vienna a few days later, it occasioned expressions of displeasure not only against the recalcitrant Rákóczi but also against Pálffy for having accepted and forwarded it in the first place. The Conference was also highly critical of Pálffy's decision to declare a truce since there was as yet no concrete evidence of the prince's willingness to capitulate.[163] Consequently, Joseph rejected the letter and promptly returned it to his commanding general.[164] In the meantime, the court continued to receive further indications both of Rákóczi's insincerity and Pálffy's naiveté. In a letter to Prince Eugene, the general expressed the belief that Rákóczi would not agree to surrender his remaining forts and garrisons in the northeast.[165] Yet, at the same time, he informed the court that he had agreed to the partial restitution of all estates confiscated from the insurgent nobility.[166] Joseph and his ministers had realized for some time that they would probably have to restore most of these lands before pacification could be achieved.[167] Nevertheless, they were dismayed once again to find that Pálffy had conceded a major point to Rákóczi without having gained any corresponding advantages.[168] In a 14 February Conference, they agreed to continue the talks, if only to preempt their allies' latest attempts to meddle in the negotiations and to refute the recent charge that certain ministers were holding up a settlement in order to retain ownership of confiscated rebel lands.[169] Pálffy was duly, if gently, reproached for his excessive leniency towards Rákóczi.[170] Yet he was not replaced. Instead, the *Hofkriegsrat* Councillor Karl Locher von Lindenheim was sent to assist him in the negotiations and prevent him from making any further unwarranted concessions to his countrymen. At the same time, Joseph issued lengthy instructions to Pálffy reminding him that Rákóczi must seek pardon as an individual subject rather than as a sovereign prince or representative of the Hungarian confederacy, and that he must agree to the surrender of all of the remaining rebel garrisons. Only then could the prince and his partisans reap the benefits of peace and a full amnesty. Should Rákóczi continue to prove obstinate, Pálffy should seek a settlement without him by using Károlyi to drive a wedge between the prince and his followers.[171]

When Locher arrived at Pálffy's camp on the evening of 24 February, he found that the prospects for dividing the rebels had improved dramatically. Rákóczi had left for Poland only three days earlier, intent upon resuming his appeals for foreign assistance. Pálffy and Locher now promptly agreed to deal with Károlyi separately in the hope of securing peace through his defection.[172] Negotiations with the rebel commander resumed on 11 March at Debreczin (Debrecen); agreement was soon reached on the outline of a peace settlement and, on 14 March, Károlyi swore his allegiance to Joseph. "The rebel Beelzebub is exorcised; the noble spirit returns", exclaimed Locher in a letter to Prince Eugene.[173] Károlyi now journeyed to the Polish town of Stryj (Stryy) in a final attempt to gain Rákóczi's submission and acceptance of Joseph's terms. His overtures were greeted with the utmost indignation by Bercsényi and the other rebel leaders, who quickly called upon Rákóczi to punish him for his betrayal. The prince refused to discipline Károlyi, but added nevertheless that he would neither submit nor agree to the surrender of the remaining rebel forces without the prior approval of the confederation. He suggested, therefore, that the current truce be extended until a diet could assemble at Huszt.[174]

When he received Rákóczi's reply, Pálffy viewed it merely as yet another ploy to delay the crown's efforts to achieve peace. Indeed, considering the difficulties involved in summoning the estates at that time of year, with the country suffering from pestilence and with almost all of the counties under Joseph's control, his suspicions were well founded. In any event, since his instructions did not permit him to recognize or treat with the confederacy, Pálffy was unable to agree to the convocation of a rebel diet. Instead, he countered by having Károlyi call upon the nobility from those northeastern districts still in *kuruc* hands to assemble at the nearby town of Szatmár. Meanwhile, Pálffy gave Rákóczi and his followers until 27 April to submit to the crown. After that, he would resume military operations and the insurgents' last chance for amnesty would presumably be lost.[175] Since many noblemen from other parts of Hungary had sought refuge in the northeast or were presently serving with the insurgent forces there, the diet that convened at Szatmár at the beginning of April 1711 was hardly a rump assembly. Nevertheless, regardless of their geographical diversity, the delegates were of one mind. When on 6 April Count Pálffy promised them full amnesty in exchange for only an oath of allegiance to the crown, they tumultuously accepted the offer.[176] Although they immediately sent a delegation to Stryj to plead with Rákóczi to submit to Pálffy's terms, it was clear that the estates no longer regarded their leader's approval as necessary for the final conclusion of a settlement.

When the prince and his lieutenants refused to submit, the Szatmár estates proceeded without them. On 27 April the final peace articles were drawn up by Pálffy, Locher, and Károlyi. By the terms of the agreement, the crown pledged once again to observe the kingdom's constitutional and religious liberties. As a concession to the nobility, all estates confiscated by the *Commissio Neo Acquistica* were to be restored to their former owners. Similarly, all lands were to be returned to those who swore allegiance to the crown within a period of three weeks, as well as to the widows and orphans of those who had died during the rebellion. Any insurgents living in exile were given the same amount of time to return home and pledge their loyalty. Prince Rákóczi, however, was to be allowed to retain all his estates while residing abroad, provided that he too swore his allegiance.[177] On 29 April Károlyi presented the peace articles to the diet, which solemnly ratified them. On the following day, he assembled a body of over 10,000 cavalry in parade formation on a field near the small town of Majtény. As Count Pálffy approached the rebel host, 149 flag-carrying horsemen formed a circle around him, Károlyi, and a group of *kuruc* officers and stuck their pennants into the earth. After Károlyi and the officers had sworn their allegiance and been answered in turn by Pálffy, the flags were removed by a formation of Austrian dragoons. Following this act, the rebel army withdrew from the field. The war in Hungary was over.

After eight years of bitter struggle, the forces of the crown had triumphed. Nowhere in the final peace instrument could there be found any reference to those rebel demands that had caused the collapse of all previous negotiations and against which Joseph had stubbornly fought for the entire length of his reign. There was no internal or external guarantee to promote either domestic anarchy or foreign intervention in the future; the word of the king remained the sole bulwark against a repetition of the tyranny of Leopold I and his predecessors. Only with regard to the restoration of lands confiscated by the *Commissio Neo Acquistica* did Joseph make a concession beyond the intent of his initial pledge of 14 May 1705.

Given the state of the rebels in early 1711, there can be little doubt that the emperor could have been considerably less generous or could have entrusted Hungary's fate to another month or two of campaigning. Indeed, in the instructions he sent to Pálffy on 18 February, Joseph made it clear that he intended to renew hostilities if his minimum peace conditions were not met.[178] Yet, though he had always remained firm both in refusing to concede to certain demands and in holding out for the satisfaction of others, Joseph also recognized from the beginning that the final peace would have to be acceptable to the Hungarian nobility. Hence, he never considered reneging on his promise to respect the kingdom's constitution and autonomy within the greater Habsburg state. To have done so would have been to violate the fragile faith of the Hungarian people which he had so painstakingly acquired after the tyranny of Leopold's reign. The legacy of Leopold I had shown that a harsh peace or a compromise later violated by the crown would never survive the sullen loyalty of the Magyar nation. In his long and difficult quest, Joseph had sought not only peace but a just, and thus secure, settlement: one that would be compatible with the proper functioning of royal authority and yet remain within limits acceptable to his own subjects.

The emperor's perceptiveness and sense of realism compare favorably with Prince Rákóczi's relentless pursuit of the chimerical alliance with France. Rákóczi had resolved from the start to hold out for some form of guarantee against a future Habsburg tyranny. Realizing at an early date that few such concessions would be forthcoming from Vienna, he had determined to enlist French support in pursuit of his goals. In the process, however, he lost all perspective of his own people's growing desire for peace and, indeed, of the unwillingness of many of his countrymen to overthrow Habsburg rule. Worse yet, though he refused to put any faith in Joseph's promises, Rákóczi blindly placed his trust in the word of Louis XIV. Under the prince's leadership, the rebel cause was soon lured into forsaking its integrity and abandoning itself to Louis's seductions only to discover too late that its suitor was unwilling to utter the vows of a permanent alliance.

Although he eventually emerged victorious, Joseph had also incurred considerable risks in waging the war. With each year that the revolt continued, there persisted the danger that Turkey would intervene on behalf of the insurgents and renew the centuries-old struggle for Hungary. This threat remained everpresent in the mind of the emperor until the final months of the reign. Only in December 1710, with the news of the Russo-Turkish war, and then in the following February, with the announcement of a special Ottoman peace embassy, could the court be reasonably sure of a continuation of friendly relations with the Porte.[179] In fact, when Seifullah Aga entered Vienna on 7 April 1711, he assured Prince Eugene of his master's peaceful intentions and asked for an extension of the 25-year truce agreed upon at the Peace of Karlowitz.[180] The Aga's arrival provided a fitting sequel to the negotiations then proceeding at Szatmár.

Even though the sultan maintained his neutrality throughout the struggle, the Rákóczi rebellion in many respects marked the close of the era of devastating Turkish wars. As in the conflicts of the past century, the civilian population both in Hungary and the eastern marches of the *Erblande* was subjected to wanton acts of cruelty and destruction. Like the Turks before them, the insurgents fought best in the countryside, in loosely organized bands of marauding cavalry, and worst on the battlefield, where their superior numbers could never compensate for the lack of discipline, training, or competent military leadership. As long as the emperor pursued fixed military objectives, as he did in 1705 and again after 1706, the enemy was unable to stop him.

In its destructiveness, the rebellion also resembled the wars of the last century. According to the estimates of historian Ignácz Acsády, 85,000 Hungarians alone fell in battle, while another 410,000 died from disease; by 1711 the population had been reduced to roughly half of the 1500 figure of five million.[181] So devastating were the effects of the plague that broke out in 1709 that Joseph was compelled to prohibit all commerce between Hungary and the *Erblande*.[182] Yet, while this measure apparently saved the hereditary lands from further devastation, they already bore the scars of seven years of human destruction.

Finally, as in the past conflicts with the Turks, the emperor was obliged to divert considerable resources from the continuing struggle against France. During the course of the rebellion, an average of twenty to thirty thousand troops were deployed in the kingdom. By the beginning of 1711, the number may have reached as high as 52,000, or nearly half of the entire Austrian army.[183] Of course, most of the forces fighting in Hungary were neither as well equipped nor as well trained as those engaged in the west. In addition, the cost of maintaining these troops was borne in part by the local population. Nevertheless, the prosecution of the war in Hungary represented a tremendous drain on the fragile finances of the Habsburg state. For each year that the war lasted, the *Hofkammer* lost up to four million florins annually in uncollected revenue. Meanwhile, an average of seven million florins was needed to equip and maintain the forces engaged against the insurgents, as opposed to four million for the army in Germany and ten million for the forces in Italy.[184] Finally, the devastation wrought by rebel marauders both in Hungary and the hereditary lands cannot be overlooked. Although there is no way of calculating precisely how great an effect these raids had on the ability of the *Erblande* to meet its fiscal responsibilities, they certainly provided the Styrian, Lower Austrian, and Moravian estates with ample justification for holding down the level of taxation.

Joseph was willing to make this awesome sacrifice in order to preserve intact his authority in Hungary. Yet, beyond the material losses which he suffered, he was also compelled to pay a political price of incalculable significance. The war in Hungary had always been a delicate subject between the emperor and his allies. Ever since the outbreak of the revolt eight years earlier, they had been unrelenting in the advice and criticism which they pressed upon his ministers. With George Stepney's transfer from Vienna shortly after the collapse of the Tyrnau talks and with the violence at Ónod in the following year, the ambassadors of the maritime powers assumed a lower profile in their discussion of his Hungarian policies. Nevertheless, as the war entered its final stages, they had once again begun to agitate for an immediate settlement. The British and Dutch had always irritated the emperor by their obvious show of sympathy for the rebels' religious and political demands. His resentment had only been heightened by the realization that London would have never tolerated the granting of similar concessions to its own Irish subjects.[185] Yet, what Joseph objected to most about the incessant meddling of his allies was that it never brought peace any closer but rather encouraged the insurgents to persist in their demands. In one unguarded moment in March 1711, he remarked to the British envoy Palmes that the conclusion of a settlement had been delayed six months by the meddling of foreign powers.[186]

However, it was the resentment of the maritime powers, and especially of England, that held the greatest significance for the immediate future. Though they were generally sympathetic to the plight of Hungary's Protestants and, in fact, often tended to exaggerate both their numbers and actual influence within the rebel movement, the British and Dutch were most upset by Joseph's seeming disdain for the common welfare of the alliance. They remembered well their own past sacrifices on behalf of Habsburg interests in Germany and Italy and expected the emperor to demonstrate his good faith by meeting the insurgents' demands and devoting his undivided attention to the joint effort against Louis XIV. The fact that they considered most of Rákóczi's conditions eminently just only reinforced their conviction that it was Vienna's responsibility to come to terms. Joseph, however, was determined to attend to what he rightly regarded as crucial interests in Hungary ahead of his less pressing dynastic concerns in Spain and the Low Countries. Meanwhile, the maritime powers were obliged to restrain their growing impatience and outrage as Joseph repeatedly refused to accept their mediation and conclude an immediate settlement with the rebels. When peace finally came to Hungary in April 1711, it was already too late for the frustrated and self-righteous British. As their new secretary of state, Henry St. John, exclaimed soon after learning of the peace of Szatmár: "Hungary has been the Gulph wherin the Plunder of Bavaria, and of Mantua, the revenues of Millan and Naples and the Contributions of the Italian Princes, all gain'd by the Assistence of the Queen and the States have been swallow'd up."[187] As we shall see, however, the bitterness with which St. John received the news was tempered by the knowledge that retribution was at hand.

VI

The Spanish Inheritance:
Alliance Diplomacy

*I fear that, if the war lasts much longer, our allies will do us
more harm than our enemies.*
—Leopold Prince Trautson

By the beginning of 1709, Joseph had largely reattained the secure
geopolitical position that the monarchy had enjoyed prior to the death
of Charles II. To the south, Italy was once again under the dynasty's
control. Following the occupation of Sardinia during the preceding
campaign, only Sicily and the Presidii ports of Porto Ercole and Porto
Longone remained in Bourbon hands. To the north and east, Charles
XII's invasion of Russia and Rabutin's reoccupation of Transylvania
had greatly reduced the threat of Swedish or Turkish intervention.
Meanwhile, Rákóczi's recent defeat at Trentschin foreshadowed the
restoration of Habsburg rule in Hungary. In the west, the recovery of
most of Belgium and the continued possession of Bavaria and Cologne
safeguarded the security of both *Erblande* and empire against invasion
from France. Except for Sicily, whose acquisition he perceived as
indispensable to the security of Naples and ultimately of the monarchy
itself, Joseph's most critical war aims had already been satisfied.
Hence, for the first time since his succession, he was afforded the
luxury of pursuing the less critical, though worthwhile, dynastic objective of Spain itself.

Until now the government in Vienna had consistently attached the
lowest priority to the Iberian peninsula. During the initial alliance
negotiations in 1701, Leopold had not even insisted on Anglo-Dutch
recognition of the dynasty's claim to Spain. Instead, it was Portugal's
King Peter II who first obliged the allies to recognize the archduke by
refusing to join the Grand Alliance unless Charles were brought to the
peninsula and eventually placed on the Spanish throne. Even then it
was only with the greatest difficulty that the English were able to
convince Leopold to permit his younger son to abandon the safety of
Vienna for the shores of far-off Spain—and then only after they had

promised the emperor that they and the Dutch would bear the full cost for the war in the peninsula. During the first two years of his reign, Joseph appeared equally diffident toward the war in Spain. As we have seen, his preoccupation with Italy helped compromise his brother's military position by enabling the French to reinforce Philip of Anjou's army on the eve of Almansa.

Fortunately for Charles, the occupation of Italy enabled Joseph to take a keener interest in his plight. As early as July of 1707, Joseph decided to send troops to Spain and by year's end announced to his ministers that the allied commitment there should be sufficient to permit the resumption of offensive operations.[1] Yet, despite his willingness to assist his brother, Joseph was still restrained by the limited resources at his disposal, as well as by the low priority which he continued to assign the war in Spain. For example, in arranging for the transfer of Austrian troops to the peninsula, he steadfastly refused to release the maritime powers from their earlier promise to bear alone the burden of maintaining the archduke's army.[2] In the final agreement negotiated between Prince Eugene and the duke of Marlborough in April 1708, Joseph obligated the British and Dutch not only to transport the initial 5,000-man Austrian contingent and to maintain it for the rest of the war, but also to reimburse him 120,000 florins in recruiting and training costs.[3]

Joseph was equally noncommittal in his appointment of a commanding general for the archduke's army. Toward the end of 1707, the British began pressing for the dispatch of Prince Eugene to Spain in the expectation that his presence there would commit the emperor more fully to his brother's cause. For several weeks, Joseph seriously considered adopting the British proposal and abandoning his original intention of appointing Prince Eugene to command in the empire during the 1708 campaign. Prince Salm strongly supported the idea, not only out of consideration for the dynasty's stake in Spain but also because he envisioned in Eugene's dispatch a ready solution both to the intensifying intrigues at court and to what he regarded as the *Hofkriegsrat* president's administrative incompetence.[4] In the end, however, Joseph could not sanction the dispatch of his best general to the peninsula, where he could neither direct overall military affairs nor be easily recalled in the event of an attack from Turkey or Sweden. Despite an eleventh-hour appeal by Salm, he eventually resolved that Eugene would command in the empire as originally planned and that Guido Starhemberg would be entrusted with operations in Spain.[5]

For the British, who had contributed so heavily to Eugene's victorious Italian campaign, the emperor's parsimony caused more than a little irritation. Of course, to a certain extent, financial and military considerations did not allow him the options open to the British. As he explained in a subsequent letter to Eugene: "They [the maritime powers] know far better than I how divided my military power is, scattered about in every corner of Europe, . . . how I stand in Hungary and Transylvania, how difficult it would be for me to raise a force to protect myself should a threat suddenly emerge from Sweden, which still must be reckoned with, how weak I am . . . in the empire where as head I should certainly be the strongest."[6] In addition, Joseph might have pointed out that he had over 10,000 men in Naples who could not be removed due to the threat of an attack from Sicily and another 20,000 serving with Victor Amadeus who could not be recalled without violating the terms of the Treaty of Turin. Nevertheless, to a large extent, Joseph was unable to assist his brother not merely because the funds were lacking but also because Spain was the last entry on a long list of priorities. This fact became apparent once again barely a week after the conclusion of the April 1708 convention, when Joseph learned that the British would no longer provide for Charles's court expenses. As long as it appeared that his allies would bear the costs of the Spanish front, Joseph had protested his own inability to supplement their funds. Following this announcement, however, he immediately revived a proposal made by Salm two years earlier calling for the *Hofkammer* to give the archduke 300,000 florins annually to help cover his court and military expenses.[7] On 31 August—four weeks after Trentschin and seven weeks after Oudenarde—Gundaker Starhemberg was able to write Charles informing him that the subsidy had been approved.[8] Moreover, as the campaign drew to a close, Joseph began pressing the British to increase their own commitment in the peninsula, emphasizing in one letter to Queen Anne that "Spain must be won on the soil of Spain itself." At the same time, however, he concluded a second treaty with the maritime powers for the dispatch of an additional 2,500 troops only after he had extracted terms similar to those of the April 1708 convention.[9]

Notwithstanding his recent advice to Queen Anne, Joseph realized that Spain could also be conquered in France by compelling Louis XIV to relinquish his claim to the peninsula. In fact, just as his enemies had once stood poised along the borders of the *Erblande,* far more formidable allied armies were now in position along France's frontiers. Yet, the task of conquering the remainder of the Spanish succession, whether it be on the battlefields of Castile or Artois, did not promise to be easy. Though Louis XIV had been shorn of his German and Italian allies and had been expelled from his forward bases within the empire, he now found himself in a considerably stronger defensive position. Instead of having to maintain armies beyond the Rhine and the Alps, he now benefited from interior lines and could shift or supply his forces much more easily than the allies. Moreover, France was still well protected from invasion by the most formidable natural and man-made defenses. The Alps rendered the southern frontier with Savoy secure. In the north, most of the former Dutch barrier fortresses remained in French hands and behind them lay the extensive system of fortifications constructed by Vauban in the second half of the last century, of which only Landau, Menin, and Lille had fallen. Furthermore, the defeats of the 1706 and 1708 campaigns had led to an improvement in the caliber of Louis's commanding generals. The Villerois, La Feuillades, and Marsins had at last been replaced by much more capable and daring men. Finally, with the war shifting to French territory, the king could appeal to his subjects to rise to the defense of their homeland. Destitute and discontented as they were, they could nevertheless be relied upon to answer their sovereign's call.

Unfortunately for the allies, many of the factors that presently promised to make offensive operations against France so difficult already obtained in Spain. With the exception of the Aragonese crownlands, all Spain had risen in support of the Bourbon pretender. Although the native forces which Philip was able to raise were of little value in themselves, he could rely upon his Castilian subjects to deny supplies and useful reconnaissance to the hated Catalans and Portuguese, and their Protestant allies. Meanwhile, Philip could always appeal to his grandfather for military assistance. Because of the great difficulties involved in shipping large bodies of men by sea, it was impossible for the allies to counter any sudden transfer of troops from France. Indeed, because of the hostility of the Castilian countryside, the allies were usually unaware of the size and location of their enemies until the very last moment. Further adding to these handicaps was the incompetence of the allied military leadership, which comprised a battery of English, Dutch, Portuguese, German, and Catalan generals who invariably fought among themselves as well as with the pretender's Austrian and Spanish ministers. Except for Starhemberg none was particularly able and all were prone to disregard the orders of their superiors or the unsteady advice of the young archduke.[10]

Spain and the Dutch Barrier

In addition to purely military obstacles, the dynasty's quest for Spain was further complicated by diplomatic considerations. The Grand Alliance had formed largely in response to the growing specter of French hegemony. Galvanized by this threat, the monarchy's allies had enabled it to avert certain defeat and, at the same time, to acquire a large part of the Spanish inheritance. Yet, each victory reduced the menace posed by Louis XIV and with it the commonly perceived need to continue the war. If Joseph was to retain his allies' support for his far-flung dynastic pretensions, he could not afford to rely solely on the fading French threat but rather on his allies' conviction that a continuation of the war would also serve their own selfish interests.

Unfortunately, during the opening years of his reign, Joseph had been less than generous in catering to his allies' *desiderata*. Relations with Prussia and Savoy had already deteriorated due to his reluctance to satisfy their territorial and financial demands. Both were now held to the Grand Alliance primarily by Anglo-Dutch subsidies and by the hope that the maritime powers would eventually attend to their territorial aims. Nor were the sea powers themselves pleased with Joseph's preoccupation with Italy and Hungary, or with his refusal to lend them more military assistance by devoting his full attention to the Upper Rhine, Spain, or the expedition against Toulon. Notwithstanding his apparent diffidence, however, the British were not likely to renege on their earlier pledge to press for the conquest of the entire Spanish empire, for they realized that Habsburg control over Spanish America would best serve their commercial interests. Even the Tory opposition in Parliament, though not as strongly motivated by mercantile considerations as the Whigs, remained united behind the call for "no peace without Spain." Indeed, despite recurrent setbacks in the field, Parliament continued to bear primary responsibility for the war in Spain, at times allotting nearly as much money for it as for the British army in Belgium.[11]

The Dutch, however, were not so committed. Sharing neither England's resources nor its enthusiasm for the war in Spain, they had gradually allowed their own subsidy and troop commitments to lapse. By the end of 1708, the last Dutch contingents had disappeared from Catalonia, while the naval units remaining behind were both understrength and ill-equipped.[12] By 1709 the United Provinces had, in fact, been at war for all but eleven of the past thirty-seven years and, due to their more modest resources, had suffered a far greater strain on their commercial economy than either France or England. To prolong the war now for the sake of Spain or Spanish America, whose markets were falling increasingly under British domination, was clearly not in their best interest. Since the victory at Ramillies and the conquest of Belgium in 1706, many Dutch politicians had begun to argue that France no longer posed a threat to the balance of power and had already "been reduced to what it ought to be."[13] Their conviction stemmed at least in part from the realization that, with the recovery of the Spanish Netherlands, the United Provinces had already attained their principal war aim: the creation of an extensive fortress barrier in Belgium to defend themselves from future French aggression. The Grand Alliance treaty had promised the Dutch a stronger barrier in the Spanish Netherlands, and although it did not specify how extensive the new system was to be, it entrusted them with custody over all conquered Belgian territory until a formal agreement could be arranged with Archduke Charles. In fact, since the conquest of Belgium five years later, the Dutch had established virtually complete control over the territory's civil and military administration, albeit in the name of Charles III and under the guise of a joint Anglo-Dutch condominium.

Under such circumstances, there was little Joseph could do to persuade the United Provinces to press on with the war for Spain. Yet, by attempting to limit their aspirations in Belgium, as well as in the neighboring imperial principalities, he further inclined the Dutch to disregard their treaty obligations to the dynasty. Joseph did agree in principle to his ally's right to erect an adequate fortress barrier on the Belgian-French frontier. By the time he became emperor, however, it had become evident that their conception of an adequate barrier extended far beyond his own interpretation of the Grand Alliance treaty. During the months following Ramillies, the Dutch had occupied not only the Spanish Netherlands but also the neighboring bishopric of Liège, whose ruler was the ill-fated Joseph Clement. Electing not to follow the example set by the emperor in Cologne and Hildesheim, the Dutch had denied Liège its claim to administrative autonomy and had even refused to permit its cathedral chapter to send representatives to the Westphalian Circle or imperial diets.[14] Meanwhile, the Dutch had also erected a strong protective cordon along their eastern frontier, where they had always enjoyed a certain degree of political influence with the Calvinist princes of northwestern Germany, as well as with those rulers whose dynasties were closely linked to the house of Orange. In addition, several of these states were tied to the United Provinces, as in past wars, by troop subsidy conventions (see map). Yet, the Dutch were now seeking to establish themselves more firmly in the northwest corner of the empire. In the opening months of the war, they had occupied a number of strategic points along the Ems, Mosel, and Lower Rhine. Immediately following the death of William III in March 1702, they had seized the Orange counties of Moers and Lingen, ostensibly on behalf of the prince of Nassau-Dietz, but in fact in order to prevent powerful Prussia from increasing its holdings on the Lower Rhine. Frederick and the Westphalian Circle had protested vigorously, and the *Reichskammergericht* had reacted with uncommon dispatch in judging against the Nassau-Dietz claims.[15] Nevertheless, the Dutch refused to withdraw. At the same time, they concluded a subsidy treaty with Elector John Hugo von Orsbeck of Trier that gave them the right to garrison the strategic fortresses of Ehrenbreitstein, Coblenz, and Trier. A subsequent accord with Orsbeck guaranteed them control of Coblenz and perhaps Ehrenbreitstein in any future war.[16] The Dutch completed their eastern fortress barrier with the occupation of Bonn, in the electorate of Cologne, in May 1703.

Although the emperor was willing to grant the United Provinces the right to defend themselves against future French aggression, he and his ministers were well aware that the Dutch could use the projected barrier to serve more than just a military function. Above all they feared the increased political influence which the Dutch would have in the northwest corner of the empire, not only among the Protestant princes and Calvinist minorities, but with the heretofore generally

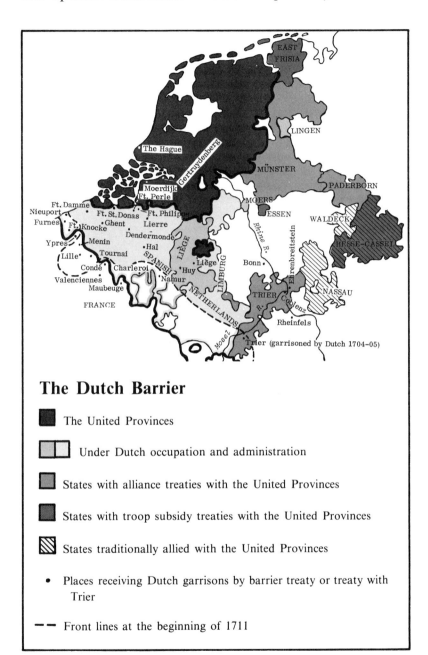

The Dutch Barrier

The United Provinces

Under Dutch occupation and administration

States with alliance treaties with the United Provinces

States with troop subsidy treaties with the United Provinces

States traditionally allied with the United Provinces

• Places receiving Dutch garrisons by barrier treaty or treaty with Trier

– – Front lines at the beginning of 1711

kaisertreu ecclesiastical princes as well. Moreover, it had become evident that the Dutch intended to exploit these territories for their own fiscal and commercial advantage. The Westphalian Circle had already charged them with pursuing a ruthless taxation policy in Liège, while the Cologne cathedral chapter had protested that they were using their garrison in Bonn to exploit the electorate commercially.[17] Meanwhile, they had greatly irritated the Prussians by diverting virtually the entire tax yield of Moers and Lingen into their own coffers and by refusing Frederick the right to administer Guelders, as promised by Emperor Leopold in 1702.[18] Yet, the most flagrant example of Dutch imperialism occurred in Belgium, which the United Provinces exploited both for its tax yield and as a market for exports.

Two attempts by the emperor to limit Dutch expansion during the second half of 1706 had already caused considerable ill feeling between the two allies. The first involved a struggle over the succession in the important bishopric of Münster following the death of its pro-Dutch prince, Frederick Christian von Plettenberg. Upon the payment of 250,000 florins, the Dutch secretly persuaded the friendly bishop of neighboring Paderborn to oppose Joseph's candidate, Charles of Lorraine. Prior to the election, imperial agents worked hard to win support for Lorraine, and at the eleventh hour, Joseph threatened to exercise his right to disqualify Paderborn. In the end, however, the Dutch managed to purchase enough votes to secure the election of their candidate. The emperor then refused to install Paderborn and soon persuaded the pope to deny ecclesiastical investiture as well. Only in March of the following year did both Joseph and Clement capitulate, though not before relations between Vienna and The Hague had been badly strained.[19] Within the next four years, the triumphant bishop confirmed the emperor's fears by entering into an intimate, long-term defensive alliance with the Dutch, first as prince of Münster, later as the ruler of Paderborn.[20]

The second conflict between the two allies arose over the status of the recently conquered Spanish Low Countries. At the time, Joseph expected that his brother would be entrusted with the territory's civil administration, as he had been following the occupation of the northeastern county of Limburg during the 1703 campaign.[21] Instead, the Dutch denied the archduke any voice in the government, promising only to rule in his name and devote all taxes to the common war effort.[22] At this point, the emperor and his ministers realized that they could not prevail against the Dutch without the decisive support of the English government. Upon the insistent urging of Wratislaw, Joseph moved to win them over by appointing the duke of Marlborough provisional governor of Belgium.[23] It was hoped in Vienna that the duke's prestige would enable him to secure a greater share of the government than might otherwise be obtained. Moreover, it was also expected that Marlborough, if not the London ministry in general, would become more favorably disposed to Vienna's position in the current dispute. Since the archduke had already left him with responsibility for forming the government in Belgium and had actually given him some blank patents for that very purpose, Joseph did not fear any indignant outbursts from Barcelona. Rather, it was from The Hague that the explosion came. Correctly interpreting the intent behind Joseph's move—as well as its likely effect—the Estates General immediately demanded that Marlborough decline the nomination lest his appointment give rise to "umbrage and jealousy" within the alliance.[24] The duke reluctantly complied. Although Marlborough was soon appointed to represent his government in the Anglo-Dutch condominium being set up in Belgium, his absence at the front and the strong position which the Dutch already held within the administration greatly reduced his influence.

The determination with which the Dutch had reacted in frustrating Joseph's diplomacy in Münster and Belgium demonstrated how important their barrier was to them. It also suggested how necessary it would be to flatter Dutch aspirations for a strong barrier settlement, lest recalcitrance on the part of Joseph or Charles prompt them to sign a separate peace with France that guaranteed their demands. During the second half of 1706, both England and the emperor were well aware of this danger. At one point, the duke of Marlborough even predicted that the Dutch would fight on for no more than one year and then conclude a separate peace.[25]

Moreover, Louis XIV also realized he could exploit this rift within the Grand Alliance. He had enjoyed considerable success in the past in dissolving European coalitions by offering one or two of his enemies advantageous peace terms. Indeed, over the previous year, he had made two attempts to split the alliance, first by offering the maritime powers favorable terms, then by promising Joseph all of Italy in exchange for his defection. In both cases, his overtures had been rebuffed.[26] Nevertheless, within a matter of weeks after his defeat at Ramillies, Louis decided to take advantage of the allies' bickering over Belgium by offering attractive peace terms to the Dutch. Through his agent in Rotterdam, the Dutchman Hennequin, Louis secretly approached the Estates at the end of July and communicated his readiness to award them a favorable trade treaty with France as well as a free hand in Belgium. At the same time, he offered to divide the Spanish inheritance, with Charles receiving Castile, the Indies, Naples, and Sicily and Philip Milan, the Aragonese crownlands, Navarre, and Guipúzcoa. Finally, he agreed to recognize Anne as queen of England and Scotland.[27] Louis realized that his terms would be unacceptable to the emperor, who wanted all of Italy, if not Spain, and to the English, who were bent on breaking the French trading monopoly with Spanish America and on securing French recognition of the Protestant succession. Yet, by tailoring his proposal to fit all of the war aims of the

Dutch, he expected to detach them from the alliance or at least secure their aid in pressing England and the emperor to come to terms.

In fact, the Dutch were eager to accept Louis's offer, but were unwilling to desert their allies by concluding a separate peace. Instead, the grand pensionary, Antonie Heinsius, pressed the French for somewhat better terms for his allies, including the exchange of Milan for Naples and Sicily, hoping that such concessions might persuade the English to drop their insistence on the entire Spanish inheritance. At the same time, he communicated Louis's proposals to Marlborough in hope of winning him over to a compromise peace.[28] The Godolphin ministry stood firm, however, and when news arrived of Prince Eugene's triumph in Italy, the Dutch broke off their secret talks.[29] Within a few weeks, Louis attempted to resume negotiations by commissioning Max Emanuel to contact both the English and Dutch. Yet, the English again refused to be drawn into talks which could only widen the rift between their Habsburg and Dutch allies. In order to avoid such a conflict, Godolphin urged that representatives of the three allied powers meet to draw up a list of peace demands that could be presented to the French. In this way, any disagreements between the Estates and the emperor could be resolved in secret, thereby enabling them to present a united front to the enemy. Although they valued the leverage which separate talks gave them over their allies, the Dutch bowed once again before Godolphin's wishes.[30]

Godolphin's proposal met with a somewhat more enthusiastic reception from Joseph, who immediately dispatched Count Sinzendorf to The Hague with instructions both to confide the Habsburg *desiderata* and entrust the ensuing negotiations to the duke of Marlborough.[31] The emperor's confidence was well placed. In his discussions with Heinsius and the pensionary of Amsterdam, Willem Buys, Marlborough secured the major points contained in Sinzendorf's instructions. These included not only the demand for the entire Spanish monarchy but also the restoration of the empire's borders as defined by the Peace of Westphalia. Joseph was even partly successful in his plans for the duchy of Lorraine, which had been overrun by Louis's troops at the beginning of the war and forced to declare its neutrality. He had hoped that Leopold could be compensated for Savoy's imminent acquisition of Montferrat and also strengthened against future French aggression by the cession of the three neighboring fortresses of Metz, Toul, and Verdun. The Dutch refused to allow these demands to be written into the peace preliminaries largely because of the ill feeling generated in the United Provinces by Charles of Lorraine's recent candidacy in Münster. Yet, they did join with Marlborough in agreeing to exclude any mention of Max Emanuel and Joseph Clement from the preliminaries in order to tie their eventual restoration to the transfer of French territory to Lorraine. The dynasty suffered its only significant setback when Heinsius and Buys inserted an article in the preliminaries forbid-

ding any future union of the Spanish and Austrian Habsburg dominions under one ruler.[32] Once the preliminaries had been composed,
Heinsius and Marlborough each sent letters to Max Emanuel declaring
that their governments would not enter into future peace negotiations
without the knowledge and participation of their allies.

In terminating their secret talks with Hennequin and agreeing to the
preliminaries, the Dutch had given up at least temporarily any chance
of securing a general peace based on a partition of the Spanish
inheritance. Yet, despite these concessions, they remained confident
that simply the threat of their future defection was now sufficient to
guarantee allied compliance with their barrier demands. Here too the
Dutch had miscalculated, especially with regard to the stance of the
English government. While the emperor was determined to limit Dutch
ambitions in the Low Countries, the English were also hesitant to
allow an extensive barrier, partly because they feared that it would
alienate the archduke's Belgian subjects. Furthermore, the duke of
Marlborough was strongly inclined to side with Habsburg interests
since he still hoped to secure the Belgian governorship for himself.[33]
The Dutch had already received an indication of the English position
in early October when the London ministry rejected their request that
it approve in advance any barrier settlement which they presented to
the archduke.[34] After they had made a fruitless attempt to reach an
understanding with Sinzendorf, the Dutch relented and sent the British
a list of eight Belgian and eight French towns. To their dismay, the
Godolphin ministry rejected three of the Belgian towns on the grounds
that they were unnecessary for the maintenance of a strong barrier.[35]
Without English support, the Dutch could not hope to win an advantageous settlement from either the archduke or the emperor. They
therefore decided to postpone further negotiations for a barrier treaty.

In obliging the United Provinces to adhere to the preliminary peace
articles and to put off their extravagant barrier demands, the English
government had done a great service to Habsburg interests. Meanwhile, the Dutch were committed to the further prosecution of the war
principally on behalf of the archduke and the growing English commercial empire, without having secured any guarantee that their own
ambitions in Belgium would ever be fully satisfied. In exchange the
Habsburg brothers were obliged to sacrifice their Belgian subjects to
further Dutch imperialism until a permanent barrier agreement could
be reached. Judging from the reports of the duke of Marlborough, the
United Provinces were not long in exploiting their advantage.[36] Indeed, as early as August 1706, he had resigned his position as English
representative in the Anglo-Dutch condominium explaining that "I
shal [sic] be asham'd to have my name in a government that must end
in confusion."[37] The archduke attempted to retrieve the situation by
sending a second patent to Marlborough entrusting him with the
government of the Low Countries. Yet, the duke was once again

compelled to decline the nomination amid a hail of Dutch protests and "indecent expressions against the imperial court and the king of Spain."[38] Within two years, popular discontent with Dutch misrule would help prompt the towns of Bruges and Ghent to throw open their gates to the French. Of course, in the aftermath of Oudenarde, the temporary sacrifice of Belgium seemed to have been a small price to pay for having forestalled barrier talks—hopefully until after the conclusion of peace, when the Dutch could no longer threaten a separate peace with France. As Wratislaw stated in a letter to the archduke: "One must accept the lesser evil and content oneself with their [the Estates'] promise to devote the revenue [of Belgium] to the raising of troops and the continued prosecution of the war."[39]

Indeed, as the war entered its eighth year, the diplomatic outlook was very favorable for the house of Habsburg. The United Provinces were still a loyal, if hesitant, ally. Meanwhile, in the eternal triangle of coalition diplomacy, it was the emperor who had the decisive edge and the Dutch who were isolated and obliged to bow before their allies' wishes. Regarding both the barrier and the question of peace, Joseph felt he could afford to be patient and discriminating, confident that he need only follow England's lead in these delicate matters.[40] For the while at least, only Louis XIV stood in the way of complete victory.

The Hague Talks

In the two years after the preparation of the joint peace preliminaries, there was a minimum of diplomatic contact between France and its enemies. The Dutch did continue to meet secretly with Louis's agents, but the ministers of the Estates continued to behave like a wayward daughter who, while tempted to elope with her lover, was unwilling both to incur the wrath and forfeit the protection of her family. At the same time, the French military triumphs of 1707 and early 1708 encouraged Louis XIV to offer the Dutch peace terms which they were bound to reject.

With the defeat at Oudenarde and the fall of Lille, the king redoubled his efforts to entice the United Provinces into signing a separate peace. In mid-December secret negotiations were resumed through the Hague envoy of Holstein-Gottorp, Hermann Petkum. A few weeks later Philip V dispatched the Belgian Count Bergeyck to Holland to open separate discussions with the Dutch ministry. Both attempts failed, but they did demonstrate once again that the United Provinces were willing to accept a settlement based on a division of the Spanish succession. In his final meeting with Bergeyck on 15 January 1709, the pensionary of Gouda, Bruno Vanderdussen, indicated precisely what compromise his government was willing to accept when he failed to include Naples and Sicily in the list of Spanish possessions which it demanded on behalf of the archduke.[41] Upon learning of Bergeyck's report, Louis took note of Vanderdussen's hint, although he was as yet unwilling to agree to such terms.

As he had during his talks with Hennequin in 1706, Heinsius informed Marlborough of the secret negotiations hoping either to entice or frighten the British into considering a compromise peace. On this occasion, however, Joseph's ambassador to The Hague, Baron Heems, learned of the talks and immediately informed Vienna.[42] There was, of course, nothing that Joseph could do to stop the Dutch from treating separately. Indeed, by delivering a stern warning to The Hague, he might push them into finally betraying the coalition on the reasoning that they had already lost the good will of their Habsburg ally. Instead, the emperor continued to place his faith in England's ability to keep the Dutch loyal to the alliance. At the same time, however, he and his ministers agreed that the Estates should be induced once again to commit themselves to a comprehensive list of allied peace aims. Prince Eugene was given full powers to negotiate new preliminaries with the allies to replace those that had been drawn up two years earlier. Once formal peace talks had actually begun, a second minister would be sent to assist him.[43]

In the three weeks between 27 February and 20 March, the new Privy Conference met to draw up instructions for the negotiations.[44] Only Trautson, Prince Eugene, and the three chancellors attended the meetings regularly, while Joseph participated solely to ratify or revise their final recommendations. Prince Salm, who had become ill earlier in February, missed all but the last session. Meanwhile, Count Schönborn was excluded from all of the meetings, just as he had been from the critical December and January Conferences that had discussed peace terms for the pope.

Of foremost concern to the emperor and his ministers was the dynasty's claim to the entire monarchy of Charles II. Meeting under Eugene's direction, the Conference confirmed early in its first session that there was to be no partition of the Spanish inheritance between the archduke and Philip of Anjou. Granting Philip compensation in Italy was specifically ruled out for several reasons. It was pointed out with some justification that Bourbon control of either Sicily or Naples would expose the monarchy's Adriatic shoreline and would also facilitate future cooperation between France and Turkey. Of considerably more importance was the argument that undisputed control of Italy was needed to provide a geographic link between the two branches of the dynasty. The ministers tactfully refrained from explaining why it would be necessary to maintain ready communication between Madrid and Vienna. Nevertheless, it was obvious to everyone present. After ten years of marriage, Joseph and Amalia had still not produced a male heir, and with the passing of each month, the possibility of a succession in Vienna had become increasingly remote. As early as 1706, Count Wratislaw had reported to Barcelona that "there is no hope here of a

[male] succession," and by the beginning of 1708, Trautson was anxiously admonishing Moles that the archduke would have to provide an heir for the Austrian branch of the dynasty.[45] In response to the crisis, the court in Vienna had recently found a wife for Charles in Amalia's cousin, Elizabeth Christine of Brunswick. Yet, to resolve the succession in both Spain and Germany, Charles would have to provide two male heirs before Joseph's death. Meanwhile, should one of the Habsburg brothers die before Elizabeth had any children, the survivor would have to rule both in Madrid and Vienna. It would not be easy for Joseph to assert his claim to a country that had fought so hard for Philip of Anjou. Similarly, as Count Schönborn was quick to point out to his colleagues in Vienna, the German electors would never permit Charles to succeed his brother as Holy Roman emperor as long as he was also king of Spain.[46] Given these potential difficulties, it was essential that the dynasty deny the Bourbons a foothold in Italy from where they could frustrate a single Habsburg ruler's attempts to maintain himself on the two thrones. "Under these circumstances," wrote Wratislaw in January 1706, "if a partition should be entered into, the Italian part is absolutely necessary."[47] Despite his growing attachment to Spain, even the archduke agreed with Wratislaw's caution that Italy had to be secured first.[48]

Since the maritime powers were opposed to a resurrection of the monarchy of Charles V, the court realized that it would not be wise to explain to them the main reason for its anxiety over the possible compensation of Philip in Italy. Instead, it hoped to win over the British by pointing out that Bourbon control of Naples or Sicily would endanger the lucrative trading route to the Levant. The Conference was confident, however, that Marlborough would enforce his government's earlier pledge to secure the entire Spanish monarchy for the archduke.[49] Meanwhile, if the Dutch insisted on a partition, Eugene was directed to suggest awarding Belgium to Philip as a means of intimidating them into dropping their demand. To ensure further that the Bourbons would not attempt to seize the Spanish crown following the extinction of Charles's or Joseph's line, the Conference urged Eugene to seek repeal of that article of the 1706 peace preliminaries which had forbidden a future union of the Spanish and Austrian Habsburg dominions. If the allies refused to drop the article, the prince was empowered to suggest the insertion of a clause allowing for a temporary union of the crowns until they could be divided again between two legitimate Habsburg princes. Failing this concession, Eugene was to seek the adoption of an article requiring Louis XIV to renounce for all time his dynasty's right to Spain and its dependencies.

In its initial meeting of 27 February, the Conference also discussed the peace aims of its allies and the empire, though a final decision was not reached concerning them until well into March. At first there was considerable opposition within the ministry to some of the English demands because it was felt that the French would never accept them. Only in the final session on 20 March did Joseph overrule the majority in agreeing to press for Louis's recognition of Queen Anne and the dismantling of Dunkirk's fortifications. In view of the monarchy's utter reliance on London's good will in its relations with the Dutch, refusal to support these claims would have been foolhardy. At the same time, however, he confirmed the Conference's earlier judgment against pressing for French recognition of the Protestant succession on the grounds that it violated the legitimate rights of several Catholic dynasties. The Conference was considerably more liberal in approving The Hague's claims against France only because it was determined to frustrate Dutch aspirations in the Spanish Low Countries. Consequently, it voted to support The Hague's demand for numerous additional barrier towns in French Flanders in the hope that they would not then seek a further expansion of the fortress line in the Spanish Netherlands. Similarly, while it readily agreed to back the Dutch and English in their quest for advantageous commercial treaties with France, the Conference instructed Eugene to fight the United Provinces' attempt to retain its economic stranglehold on Belgium. In order to limit Dutch military and commercial gains in the Low Countries, the Conference cautioned that a final barrier treaty should not be discussed at the final peace conference, where France and the United Provinces could combine against the allies, but rather at a separate meeting between the representatives of the archduke and the Estates General.

Perhaps the most remarkable of the Conference's peace deliberations concerned the demands that were to be put forward on behalf of the Holy Roman Empire. It was Joseph's responsibility as emperor both to define and press Germany's territorial claims against France. Yet, just as he had favored Austrian over imperial interests during the conduct of military operations, Joseph could now be expected to give precedence to dynastic objectives during the peace talks as well. In its first session, the Conference had recommended that the empire first call for the restoration of all territories seized by France since the accession of Charles V. The emperor's ministers did not, in fact, take this demand seriously and settled on it only as a means of placating the German princes and providing a flexible bargaining position with the French. Instead, they agreed to seek a settlement on the basis of the Peace of Westphalia. This implied the restoration of certain territories lost by Lorraine since 1648 and virtually all of Alsace, including not only Strasbourg but also ten imperial cities that had been placed under French protection by the Peace of Westphalia, though formally retained by the empire. France would keep only the former Habsburg possessions in Alsace and the three bishoprics of Metz, Toul, and Verdun, all of which had been ceded in 1648.[50]

To secure further territorial gains for the empire, the Conference planned to repeat the strategy it had employed during the drafting of the 1706 preliminaries of bargaining with the fate of Max Emanuel and Joseph Clement. Once again no mention was to be made of the two banned electors in the forthcoming peace preliminaries unless further advantages could be secured for the empire in exchange for their restoration. In no event, however, was Max Emanuel to regain the Upper Palatinate or any of the other territories already ceded at his expense. In a 12 March Conference between the emperor and his ministers, it became clear that Joseph was still intent on tying the restoration of the two Wittelsbachs to a strengthening of Lorraine's frontier with France. To buttress further Germany's western defenses, it was also decided to press for the cession, or at least the demolition, of those fortresses situated in territory that had been relinquished by the empire in 1648. If, on the other hand, the maritime powers were unwilling to press for a strengthened *Reichsbarriere* against France or even for a return to the 1648 frontier, the emperor agreed with his ministers that more modest demands would have to be substituted in the peace preliminaries.

The peace formula drafted by the Conference in February and March 1709 was consistent with the military strategy it had pursued since the beginning of the reign. There was a minimum of conformity with the peace aims of its allies, especially when they threatened to jeopardize its own objectives. Meanwhile, the monarchy's interests in Italy and the dynasty's aspirations in Spain continued to be placed ahead of the welfare of the *Reich*. This is not to say that Vienna was not eager to regain for the empire what it had lost to France over the past half century. Joseph himself was genuinely concerned about the need to protect the independence of Lorraine and its smaller neighbors by strengthening Germany's western frontier. Moreover, even in the absence of Schönborn and Salm, there were still a number of men in the Conference, among them the two Austrian chancellors and the future *Obersthofmeister* Trautson, who were committed to achieving a satisfactory peace for the empire. Considering that the imperial army counted only Landau among its prizes of war and that Trier on the Mosel, Breisach, and Kehl on the Rhine right bank, much of southern Belgium, and all of Lorraine were still in Louis's hands, settlement based on the Peace of Westphalia would be very fortunate for Germany, even when balanced against the partial restoration of Max Emanuel and Joseph Clement. Furthermore, Vienna may be credited with having displayed some selflessness in demanding from France those sections of Alsace that had remained part of Germany in 1648 rather than the numerous Habsburg enclaves that had been lost in that year. Nevertheless, it must be kept in mind that, whereas the Conference considered its demand for the entire Spanish inheritance a *sine qua non* for peace, its claims on behalf of the empire were entirely flexible. Only after Habsburg interests in Italy and Spain had been secured would an inch of French territory be awarded to the empire.

The allies would have to be in a commanding bargaining position before the emperor's diplomats would be able to impose a return to the borders of 1648.

Prince Eugene was fully aware of Joseph's priorities when he departed Vienna on the morning of 13 March, still some weeks before the Conference had completed drafting his instructions. During the previous year, he had not left for the front until the beginning of June, partly because of the delay in securing the dispatch of John William's contingent, and had reached Belgium with his army barely in time to save Marlborough and the common cause from a serious reverse. On this occasion, he expected to arrive in the Low Countries long before the opening of the campaign. Nevertheless, when he entered The Hague in the opening week of April, the prince found that the French had launched yet another surprise offensive.

Originally Louis XIV had intended to open the 1709 campaign with a bold stroke against Lille. Toward this end, his generals had worked throughout the winter making preparations for the assembly of an army of 150,000 under Vendôme's successor, Marshal Villars. By the end of February, however, the king was no longer concerned with regaining the initiative in Flanders but rather with the prospects of an immediate peace. Beginning in the first week of December, all Europe had been gripped by freezing temperatures. The cold wave lasted almost without interruption until mid-March. At one point in early January, the canals of Venice froze over, as did the broad mouth of the Tagus. Even the swift flowing Rhône was almost completely covered with a sheet of ice. In fact, nowhere was the cold more intense than in France, where the vineyards froze and the livestock perished in great numbers. At the beginning of February, Louis was informed that the seed corn for the coming harvest was already dead in the ground. Meanwhile, any chance of importing grain from Africa and the Levant was greatly reduced by the British fleet, which now blockaded southern France from its new winter base at Port Mahón.[51] With his people facing a devastating famine, the king decided to seek an immediate peace. Remembering the indiscretion committed by Vanderdussen during the talks with Bergeyck, Louis elected to approach the Dutch, confident that they would agree to at least a token partition of the Spanish inheritance. In the opening week of March, the president of the Parlement of Paris, Pierre Rouillé de Marbeuf, crossed into Belgium on his way north. Following his instructions, Rouillé made no attempt to shield his identity or the objective of his mission. Instead, French agents spread throughout the United Provinces bringing word of his journey and advocating an immediate peace.[52] Bowing to popular pressure, as well as to their own inclinations, Buys and Vanderdussen began meeting with Rouillé at Moerdijk.

When Prince Eugene arrived at The Hague, the talks were already in their third week. Although he was still without instructions from

Vienna, which was just now learning of the latest Franco-Dutch talks, he acted instinctively to protect the dynasty's interests. On 7 April he visited with Heinsius informing him of the emperor's determination to secure the entire Spanish monarchy, including Naples and Sicily.[53] Since he still had no intention of deserting the alliance, Heinsius was now faced with the same choice that had confronted him in the autumn of 1706: either he must win British consent to a partition or else meekly join with his allies in rejecting the latest French overtures. Once again, it was England's position that was crucial in deciding which way the Dutch would jump. One week earlier the English General Cadogan had assured Eugene that the queen was intent on demanding the entire Spanish inheritance.[54] Nevertheless, when Marlborough arrived by boat from London on the evening of the ninth, the prince was among the first to meet him.

Fortunately for the monarchy, the Godolphin ministry had reacted angrily to the latest display of Dutch weakness. Furthermore, the Whig landslide in the recent parliamentary elections and the growing reports of famine in France had emboldened it to stand firmly by its past promises. As he met with Prince Eugene, Marlborough informed his comrade that he had been instructed to cooperate with him in securing not only the expulsion of Rouillé but also Dutch reaffirmation of the preliminaries of 1706.[55] In turn, Eugene sought to further their understanding by promising to support England's demand for the demolition of Dunkirk's defenses and by disclosing that he had been instructed by Joseph to reach an accord with him in all matters.[56] Having formed a united front, the English and Austrian generals presented their verdict to Heinsius and Buys. The Dutch ministers protested in vain their government's desire to continue the talks with Rouillé and expressed once again their willingness to yield Naples and Sicily in exchange for peace.[57] In the end, however, they were obliged to capitulate. On 21 April Rouillé was presented by the Dutch with the comprehensive list of allied demands and given the choice of accepting them or leaving for home.

Once again, the Dutch had been obliged to place their faith in the strength of the alliance rather than in the promises of Louis XIV. While Rouillé sent home for further instructions, they joined with Marlborough and Eugene in preparing for the coming campaign. Yet, for Louis XIV, the resumption of hostilities represented an unacceptable risk. Meeting the allies' peace demands now seemed preferable to presiding over the starvation of his people and the disintegration of his armies. Upon reading the terms sent him by Rouillé, the king broke into tears. They would have to be accepted. Torcy volunteered to go personally to The Hague, hopeful of reducing the allied demands, but intent upon concluding the peace for which all France now yearned. In fact, when Louis's foreign minister entered the Dutch capital on 6 May, the allies were in no mood to compromise. Sensing that famine could by itself bring the enemy to its knees, the British were busy enforcing a total blockade of food exports to France. The Dutch were at last induced to suspend their lucrative trade with France and Joseph was pressed to seal off food shipments from the empire.[58] Meanwhile, the British envoys to Denmark and Sweden were instructed to threaten to seize all ships carrying Polish grain to French ports.[59] The revelation that it was Torcy himself who carried Louis's latest peace offer merely served to persuade the allies that the once mighty king was going to Canossa.

With both Eugene and Marlborough temporarily absent from The Hague, Torcy renewed the well-worn French strategy of dealing separately with the Dutch. Yet, he quickly found that the Estates had themselves become possessed by the certainty of achieving complete victory. In a series of interviews with Heinsius, Buys, and Vanderdussen, he failed to gain the slightest reduction in the peace demands that had been handed to Rouillé two weeks earlier. Meanwhile, the grand pensionary rejected Torcy's request for an armistice, insisting sanguinely that France would first have to come to terms.[60] With the return of Eugene and Marlborough, Heinsius broke off the discussions, notifying the foreign minister that further negotiations would have to be conducted jointly with the other members of the alliance. There were, in fact, Prussian, Savoyard, and Portuguese diplomats present at The Hague, ready to represent their sovereigns' interests in the upcoming peace talks. In addition, two deputies had recently arrived from the Nördlingen Association, which had been commissioned by the Regensburg Diet to represent the empire's claims. Nevertheless, when the peace negotiations began on 20 May, the triumvirate of Eugene, Marlborough, and Heinsius, along with Buys, Vanderdussen, and the English Lord Townshend, represented the demands of the Grand Alliance. Assisted by Rouillé, the French foreign minister dealt with the coalition's terms country by country. Neither Marlborough nor Heinsius encountered any difficulty in presenting their countries' claims. When Eugene followed with the demand for the entire Spanish inheritance, Torcy again raised no objection. The French diplomats did resist, however, when the prince proceeded by demanding that all of Alsace be restored to the empire. Moreover, the deadlock worsened when Buys presented Victor Amadeus's claim to the recently captured Dauphiné fortresses of Fenestrelle and Exilles. Since France still occupied the duchy of Savoy and the Piedmontese port of Nice, Torcy insisted instead on a restitution of the *status quo ante bellum.*[61]

In fact, Torcy had been empowered by Louis to surrender both fortresses to Savoy and to yield most of Alsace as well.[62] He reasoned, however, that the triumvirate could eventually be persuaded to modify their protégés' demands, once their own claims had been met. What Torcy had failed to realize was that the allied diplomats were convinced that France was incapable of continuing the war and would therefore eventually have to accept their terms. For this reason, Prince Eugene's initial demands on behalf of the empire actually exceeded the minimum terms contained in his instructions. Even when Torcy abruptly broke off the first day's talks by asking for passes to return home, both Marlborough and Eugene remained confident that he was only bluffing.[63] Meanwhile, the prince appealed to the Nördlingen Association's two deputies to assist him in keeping Heinsius from forcing a reduction in Germany's demand for all of Alsace.[64] In fact, the Dutch were also holding firm, and when the two Frenchmen returned to the peace table on the following evening, they encountered the same terms as the previous day.

The deadlock continued. At one point, Torcy offered to yield all of Alsace on the condition that Philip of Anjou be given Naples.[65] Yet, while Eugene's instructions permitted him to settle for only part of Alsace, Spanish Italy remained nonnegotiable. With the impasse still unresolved, Torcy approached Heinsius on the evening of 22 May and announced that he was leaving for home. The grand pensionary persuaded him to stay on, but when the two sides met on the following morning, Torcy asked the allied diplomats to draw up a list of their demands for presentation to the king. They readily agreed and immediately set to the task of drafting the document.

Torcy's request represented a desperate but clever attempt to reduce the allies' demands. Since the document which they were to draw up was little more than an ultimatum, he hoped that they would moderate their terms in order to guarantee its acceptance by Louis XIV. Torcy had judged correctly. Shaken by the impasse in the negotiations, Heinsius had at last begun to advocate a reduction in the empire's territorial gains, lest they sabotage any chance of a settlement.[66] As the allied diplomats prepared to draft their final terms, the grand pensionary was determined to force Prince Eugene to retreat from his position. At this point, the prince received some timely assistance from Vienna. On the afternoon of the twenty-third, he was joined by Count Sinzendorf, whom Joseph had dispatched in reply to his urgent requests for help. The emperor had hesitated before entrusting the pliable Sinzendorf with such a crucial mission, fearful that he would not prove forceful enough during the critical peace negotiations.[67] Yet, it was the Austrian chancellor who now brought fresh wind to the flagging banner of imperial interests. During the ensuing two days, Sinzendorf fought hard for the retention of a firm *Reichsbarriere,* demanding not only Alsace but also that Lorraine be restored to its 1648 frontier and be further strengthened by the cession of Metz, Toul, and Verdun.[68] When on the evening of 25 May, the Dutch negotiators presented their colleagues with a provisional draft which failed to meet these terms, Sinzendorf and Eugene continued the debate. Nevertheless, the Dutch refused to jeopardize the chances of peace for the sake of a lethargic

Reich and a neutral duke of Lorraine. After much heated discussion, most of their proposals were accepted without revision.

The new peace preliminaries restored to the empire only that part of Alsace granted it by the Peace of Westphalia. This did not include the ten imperial towns, however, which except for Landau were now consigned to France in full sovereignty. On the other hand, Germany was permitted to keep Breisach, despite its cession to France in 1648 and its capture earlier in the war. In addition, France was obliged to dismantle its west bank fortresses of Hüningen, Fort Louis, and Neu Breisach, as well as all fortifications constructed in Alsace since 1648. Eugene and Sinzendorf still hoped to win further advantages for the empire by tying them to the restoration of Max Emanuel and Joseph Clement, for while it recognized Bavaria's territorial losses, the document omitted any mention of the two Wittelsbachs' eventual reinstatement.[69] Nevertheless, the emperor's representatives were deeply disturbed by their failure to win a strong *Reichsbarriere.*

The remaining articles conformed more closely to Vienna's expectations, although they reflected throughout the discerning hand of their Dutch authors. It was stated clearly in the preliminaries that the archduke was to receive the entire inheritance of Charles II, except for those territories to be ceded to his allies. Furthermore, the Habsburg dynasty's hold on the Spanish crown was guaranteed by Article 6, which affirmed its rights in perpetuity, while excluding France's claims for all time. With one exception the preliminaries did not specify the extent of Charles's territorial debt to Savoy, Portugal, or the United Provinces, leaving that to be determined by future negotiation. This solution offered the Habsburgs the opportunity to limit their territorial concessions since it enabled them to hold separate talks with each ally after the war was over, thereby eliminating the threat of interference from France or the other members of the coalition. The only such territory specified in the preliminaries was Spanish Guelders, which the Dutch had long claimed and which they now forced Eugene and Sinzendorf to surrender.[70] Meanwhile, the Dutch made ample provision for their barrier. While not defined for Belgium, it was to include the eight French places of Furnes, Knocke, Condé, Ypres, Menin, Tournai, Lille, and Maubeuge. To ensure that Charles awarded them a sufficient fortress line in Belgium itself, the Dutch were to retain control of the province until an agreement was reached. They also inserted a clause in the preliminaries over the vehement protests of Eugene and Sinzendorf permitting them to garrison Joseph Clement's capitals of Bonn and Liège, as well as nearby Huy, until a barrier treaty was concluded. Moreover, yet another article affirmed the right of their protégé, the landgrave of Hesse-Cassel, to garrison the strategic Rhine River fortress of Rheinfels. Several additional articles dealt with the peace aims of the other members of the coalition. Among them were each of England's earlier claims, to which was now added the demand for Newfoundland. In addition, Louis XIV was forced to recognize the Prussian crown and Hanoverian electorate, grant commercial privileges to the maritime powers and Portugal, evacuate Neuchâtel, and—despite Torcy's recent protests—cede Fenestrelle and Exilles to Savoy.

It was this long list of concessions that the allies now intended to extract from Louis XIV. Every article of the allies' treaty obligations had been met, if not exceeded, a feat that no one would have thought possible when the coalition was first formed. Yet, there was now little question in anyone's mind that the French king would accept these conditions. It remained only for him to carry them out. To ensure that Louis faithfully executed each of the peace provisions, the Dutch had inserted a number of stipulations in the preliminaries. According to these, the king was to have two months in which to withdraw his troops from Spain as well as from all other areas that he had ceded or returned to the allies. Within the same period of time, he was to procure the duke of Anjou's renunciation of the Spanish throne and departure from the peninsula. Once these conditions had been met and Charles had been installed on the Spanish throne, Article 37 of the preliminaries guaranteed that the present armistice would continue until the conclusion of a formal peace treaty. If, however, Philip refused to surrender his claims, Article 4 obligated Louis to join with the allies at the end of the two months in forcibly removing him from the peninsula.[71]

To the Dutch ministers, such stipulations were necessary to guarantee the full execution of the peace terms. They remembered Louis XIV as the man who had broken virtually every treaty he had signed in over a half-century as king of France. Unless he was compelled to join the allies in forcibly removing Philip from Spain, the Dutch feared that Louis would secretly encourage his grandson to continue the struggle. Indeed, one of their agents had reported recently that the king was preparing to send French "deserters" to Spain to help his grandson once peace had been signed.[72] Finally, the Dutch were determined not to allow France to reap the benefits of peace and recover its strength while they and their allies were compelled to carry on the war against Philip. Although they were willing to fight on in Spain without French assistance, the British and Austrian negotiators readily accepted the Dutch demands for a guarantee for they did not see it as a threat to Louis's eventual ratification of the preliminaries. They were confident that Louis would have no difficulty in convincing his grandson to renounce the Spanish throne, especially since Article 4 of the preliminaries ensured that further resistance would be futile.[73]

On the morning of 27 May, the seven allied diplomats presented their peace terms to Torcy and Rouillé. After reading through the document, the French negotiators withdrew in order to consider it in private. When they returned early that evening, it became clear that the two men were still unwilling to concede on three points: the empire's retention of Breisach, the dismantling of France's fortifications on the Rhine west bank, and the loss of Fenestrelle and Exilles. For this reason, they refused to sign the preliminaries, insisting instead that they present them to the king. Torcy also inveighed bitterly against the guarantee sought by the allies. Four days earlier, he had rejected Heinsius's demand for six cautionary towns—three additional fortified places in France along with three in Spain that presently held French garrisons—as proof of his master's good faith.[74] Now Louis was being asked instead to make a guarantee that threatened the possibility of war with his own grandson.[75] Torcy left for home in the early hours of the following morning, Rouillé staying behind to receive the king's reply. As the foreign minister's coach disappeared into the night, the allied diplomats continued to believe that Louis would accept their terms. Meanwhile, they affixed their signatures to the preliminaries, confident that Rouillé's would not be far behind.

It was 5 June when news of Louis's rejection of the preliminaries reached The Hague. Upon being notified by Rouillé, the stunned allied diplomats frantically attempted to resume negotiations, intent upon making the minor modifications which they felt would lead to a settlement. In reply, Rouillé could only answer that he was not empowered to treat further. Before leaving for France, however, he did point to five of the preliminary articles, including those pertaining to Alsace (10 and 11), Portuguese trade rights (20), the banned electors (29), and the final conditions for peace (37) as the principal causes for the king's rejection.[76] The allied negotiators attributed Louis's rejection to their demands for a guarantee specifically to Articles 4 and 37, and expressed almost unanimously the opinion that they had required too much of him. The Dutch deputy, Goslinga, volunteered that he would have concluded peace without Article 37. Although he had never favored requiring Louis to take military action against Philip, Marlborough now cited the implications of Article 4 as ample justification for the king's rejection of the preliminaries.[77] Only Prince Eugene seemed to feel that the demand for a guarantee was not at the root of the problem. Instead, in a letter to Joseph, he blamed the empire's projected gains in Alsace for Louis's decision to continue the struggle.[78] Within a week, however, he too expressed the opinion that the six cautionary towns would have provided a sufficient guarantee and that the allies should have limited themselves to that demand.[79]

In fact, Articles 4 and 37 were not to blame. Like his enemies, Louis XIV was confident that he could persuade his grandson to leave Spain without having to use force. Following council meetings on 1 and 2 June, the king and his ministers had actually decided in favor of signing the preliminaries, only to be swung over at the last moment by the grand dauphin's impassioned plea for the rights of his son Philip.[80] In the end, therefore, it had been the allies' demand for the entire Spanish inheritance which had once again frustrated all attempts at peace. Had they been willing to compensate Philip with a piece of that huge empire, Louis most certainly would have signed. As it was, he realized that the allies would never compromise: Joseph demanded Italy, the Dutch Belgium, the British Spain and the Indies. There was no recourse left but to recall Rouillé.

Of course, even with the loss of all of the Spanish monarchy, Louis still might have agreed to a settlement had he not been required to cede so much French territory as well—particularly in Alsace. To the king, Spain's dominions were still merely appendages, many of which were already beyond his power to possess. He still controlled Alsace, however, and after three-quarters of a century of French rule, it was the flesh and blood of France. Surely the allies would have accommodated the king in Alsace, as well as in the Dauphiné, had they only realized that peace depended on it. Had they done so, Torcy would have affixed his name to the preliminaries while still at The Hague, rather than bring them back to Versailles for Louis's final consideration. Instead, Eugene and Sinzendorf were so convinced of Louis's readiness to conclude peace that they fought hard and decisively for imperial interests, while their allies bowed at least in part to their wishes. For the sake of the empire, victory and peace now eluded them!

Summer Solstice

History was being made and unmade at The Hague during the spring of 1709. Yet, while Joseph eagerly awaited each report from his representatives at the peace talks, he was also preoccupied with the latest turn in the continuing intrigues at court. By naming Wratislaw to the new Privy Conference in February, he had excited the jealousy of those who had opposed the Bohemian count's gradual but inexorable emergence as the man who stood closest to him. There soon arose around the two empresses a circle of ministers and courtiers who were determined to gain admission to the new body. Among them were several former members of the old Conference system, including Gundaker Starhemberg, Schönborn, Kinsky, Martinitz, and Waldstein, as well as the Cardinal Sachsen-Zeitz, the only Hungarian notable whom Joseph could ever include among his most trusted advisors.[81]

The intrigues of the empresses and their partisans were further complicated by the impending resignation of Prince Salm. During the previous autumn, the ailing lord high steward had again sought Joseph's permission to retire to his estates. With the papal conflict at its height, the emperor had turned down his requests, insisting that he wait at least until spring and hopefully until the conclusion of a general peace.[82] By January Salm was again talking about leaving Vienna.[83] After having missed most of the critical Conferences of February and March, he had written to the archduke, citing his growing debility and confessing that he could barely read the written reports and expeditions that were placed before him.[84] At the end of April, he actually set the date for his departure, but was then persuaded to postpone it once more until the next courier had arrived from The Hague.[85] With the news of Torcy's mission, Salm decided to stay on still longer, leading the perplexed Wratislaw to write "nobody knows whether or not Salm is going to leave, and it appears as if he himself does not know."[86]

The fact remained, however, that the day of Salm's departure was creeping ever closer. As in past years, the anticipation of his retirement brought a renewed struggle for power. While Amalia and her partisans continued to press for more positions within the Conference, another faction began conspiring to seize the leadership of the ministry from Trautson following Salm's resignation. The man behind this latest intrigue was the Favorite's uncle and Joseph's representative at the Imperial Diet, Cardinal Lamberg. Though he had served capably at Regensburg, Lamberg was an individual of dubious character and integrity who, like his nephew, counted among his vices a decided weakness for alcohol, women, and above all, political intrigue. In the early years of the war, he had twice approached Max Emanuel in an effort to secure and strengthen his own position in southern Germany as prince-bishop of Passau. Although these negotiations aroused considerable anger in Vienna, he did not hesitate two years later to become an active candidate for the Bavarian military governorship, and then for the post of imperial vice-chancellor.[87] With Joseph's succession, he urged the widowed Eleonore to secure for him the post of high steward, a move that alienated not only the grief-stricken empress but Prince Salm as well.[88] Once Salm had begun to speak of resigning, Lamberg revived his candidacy. On the pretext of taking the cure at nearby Baden, he traveled to Vienna at the end of 1707 in a vain attempt to secure the support of the outgoing lord high steward.[89] Though frustrated on this occasion by Joseph's designation of Trautson as Salm's successor, the cardinal did not despair. When Salm renewed his resignation request in the following autumn, Lamberg again journeyed to Vienna, still hoping to profit by his and his nephew's long-standing friendship with the emperor. When Joseph again refused to consider him for the post, the cardinal suggested that he might succeed the late Count Öttingen as Aulic Council president.[90] Only when Joseph ordered him to return to his post at Regensburg did Lamberg finally leave court.[91] In his absence, however, Leopold von Lamberg continued to press the emperor to reverse his decision.

By the beginning of 1709, the persistent cardinal had aroused a formidable array of enemies, who now dedicated themselves to his continued exclusion from court. Wratislaw and Eugene, who had always detested and distrusted him, were joined by the threatened Trautson and by Seilern, whose enmity for the cardinal went back to a time when he had served as Lamberg's assistant at Regensburg.[92]

Meanwhile, the wide circle of Wratislaw's enemies and Salm's friends split into two camps. The two empresses, Mansfeld, and Salm himself actively opposed the cardinal for a host of reasons, not the least of which was his association with the dissolute Favorite.[93] Franz Ferdinand von Rummel, now bishop of Vienna, led the campaign to retain his former benefactor at court as a means of warding off both Lamberg and Wratislaw.[94] At the same time, however, a small group of ministers supported the Favorite's efforts to secure Cardinal Lamberg's elevation. Both Schönborn and Starhemberg worked with him, hoping to secure in return a place in the new Conference. In addition, Count Windischgrätz was sufficiently moved by his hatred for Wratislaw to back the Lambergs, despite his friend Salm's sharp rebukes and later ostracism.[95]

With both Wratislaw and Salm leading the attack against it, the Lamberg faction had little chance of succeeding. Moreover, as he had from the very start, Joseph remained indifferent to the cardinal's pretensions. Although he compensated his friend with a virtually useless position in the new Conference, he continued to withhold from both Lambergs the political power which they craved. When he learned that the cardinal would be making yet another journey to Baden in early June, the emperor reassured Wratislaw that he would make "no innovation," that the latest intrigue would prove little more than a *"comédie des partisans."*[96] In fact, after four weeks at court, the cardinal was obliged to return to his post at Regensburg empty-handed. Before leaving, he let it be known that he would not accept any future position as the emperor's first minister, "not wishing to remain at a court where everyone pursues his own interests."[97] As always, the hard-drinking cardinal preferred his grapes sour.

With Lamberg's departure, the two court factions were permitted the luxury of resuming their struggle for votes in the Privy Conference. Throughout the summer, the two empresses continued to press Joseph to admit their protégés. Among them, Schönborn was particularly insistent, supported as he was by Salm and the frequent petitions of Lothair Francis.[98] Although he was indignant at Schönborn's effrontery, the emperor began to waver before the archchancellor's repeated pleas. He declared, however, that no decision would be made on Schönborn's candidacy before Prince Salm's retirement.[99]

As it was, this was not to be long in coming. It is ironic that Count Wratislaw, who had been conspiring for four years to force the lord high steward's resignation, now found himself an idle spectator in the last moments before his adversary's fall from power. In the end it was Salm's tragic flaw—his insufferable pride—that proved his undoing. For the past few months, he had been trying to dissuade Joseph from investing the Favorite with the Bavarian landgravate of Leuchtenberg, principally because Lamberg's elevation as landgrave would give him precedence in all court ceremonial.[100] After Salm had threatened to resign if the investiture was made, Amalia approached Joseph and persuaded him to elevate the hated Lamberg only to the rank of prince. This concession appeared to mollify the lord high steward, who soon announced that he would stay on until the conclusion of peace.[101] Yet meanwhile, he secretly dispatched an agent to Regensburg with instructions to mobilize opposition to Lamberg's investiture.[102] In fact, the agent easily won over Prussia, which had designs of its own on Leuchtenberg, as well as several of the other estates, which were annoyed at not having been consulted earlier by the emperor. When Cardinal Lamberg presented Joseph's request for ratification of the Favorite's investiture, the Imperial Diet exploded in protest.[103]

Upon learning of Salm's machinations, the emperor summoned him to his quarters and angrily berated him.[104] Nursing his injured pride, the ailing lord high steward soon asked Joseph for permission to retire to his estates. On this occasion, the emperor at last consented. Too proud to give satisfaction to his enemies, Salm told the other ministers that he was leaving Vienna for the Rhenish spa of Schlangenbad and would be back in a few days. Only after his departure on 26 August did Joseph indicate that he had resigned all his offices and would not be returning.[105] In the end, it had been serious flaws in Prince Salm's character that had hastened, and in part justified, his fall from power. His domineering nature, vanity, and jealousy of others were the principal causes for the falling out with Eugene and Wratislaw, although they too deserve a share of the blame. Nevertheless, Salm's personal weaknesses should not be allowed to detract from his contribution in both foreign and domestic policy. Awed by the greatness of Prince Eugene as general, minister, and diplomat, historians have tended to regard Joseph's *Hofkriegsrat* president as virtually incapable of error. Although he was absent at the front during most of the reign, the premise of Eugene's infallibility is amply reinforced by his close alliance with the brilliant Wratislaw in all questions of state policy. Yet, if history has shown us anything, it is that personal genius does not always lead to the best, or only, solution to a problem. In fact, Prince Salm usually found himself in agreement with his two nemeses. When he did not, however, he too showed great perceptiveness. Benefit of hindsight does indeed enable us to concur with his original judgment that the Comacchio venture represented a worthwhile risk and that the transfer of Prince Eugene to Spain involved a necessary sacrifice. Salm's wisdom was recognized by Joseph, who kept him at court long after his strength had abandoned him. When he departed Vienna, he had only a year left to live.

Following Salm's resignation, the emperor moved to answer the demands of the two empresses and hopefully resolve the last of the court intrigues. On 28 August he announced that Schönborn, Waldstein, and Gundaker Starhemberg would be formally admitted to the Privy Conference. The victorious Wratislaw party was rudely shocked by the news. Count Trautson, who was to be installed as lord high steward on the following morning, unsuccessfully urged the emperor to reverse his decision.[106] Although he could excuse Starhemberg's appointment on grounds of ability and Schönborn's in view of the need to appease Lothair Francis, Wratislaw was highly critical of the admission of the inexperienced Waldstein.[107]

What both men still did not know, however, was that Joseph intended these three appointments to serve only as meaningless concessions to Lothair Francis and the two empresses; in reality he had no intention of admitting any of these men to his innermost councils. Wratislaw and his cohorts got an initial hint of Joseph's design two days later, following Baron Heems's arrival from The Hague with a report on the latest peace prospects. With Heems's appearance, Joseph informed a surprised Wratislaw that he, Seilern, and Trautson were to meet alone with the baron and secretly draft new peace priorities for the monarchy.[108] On 31 August they received a second clue as the emperor called a meeting to discuss the continuing struggle between Cardinal Grimani and the imperial General Hesse-Darmstadt, but invited only Wratislaw, Seilern, and Trautson to meet with the *Hofkriegsrat* vice-president. Only two days later did the full Conference convene to deliberate the matter, with the three new appointees present for the first time.[109]

In fact, though he had just broadened the Conference membership, Joseph was now bent on circumventing it and entrusting all real power to a much smaller circle of his most trusted and able ministers. Not only were the three new appointees to be excluded from this inner circle, but also Windischgrätz, Mansfeld, and the hapless Cardinal Lamberg. In effect, Joseph was following up the administrative reform of February with a political purge of far greater significance. In the words of one historian, the latest Conference reform represented the "last and most decisive" break between the Austrian Habsburgs's pursuit of imperial and strictly dynastic interests.[110] Given the exclusion of Schönborn and his friend Windischgrätz, along with the belated retirement of Salm, pro-German sentiment in the Conference was indeed at a low ebb. Yet, in view of the recent sacrifice of imperial interests in the papal peace treaty and the Hague preliminaries, a further setback for the empire's partisans hardly seems to have been necessary. Instead the principal significance of—and motivation behind—Joseph's action lay in his decision to rule through a triumvirate of Wratislaw, Seilern, and Trautson and, following their return from The Hague, Prince Eugene and Sinzendorf. In particular, this new formula presaged the political hegemony of Wratislaw, at least until the tentative and unambitious Trautson could gain more experience in the conduct of state affairs.

During the next few weeks, the outlines of the new Privy Conference system began taking a definite shape. The *engere Konferenz,* or inner

Conference, of Wratislaw, Seilern, and Trautson was entrusted with the initial discussion of all policy matters and would either confer directly with Joseph or report to him about the progress of their deliberations. Only after they had completed their preparations and reached a tentative decision on the subject at hand would the full Conference be convened, invariably in the presence of the emperor. As we have seen this was the procedure that was followed in March-April 1711 in planning the return of Comacchio to the pope. There were some exceptions to this rule. When discussing imperial affairs, the inner Conference would comprise Schönborn and Windischgrätz as well; when deliberating questions of military finance, it was joined by *Hofkammer* President Starhemberg, *Hofkriegsrat* Vice-President Herberstein, and Commissary General Schlick. Meanwhile, matters of a purely dynastic nature that were considered too delicate to entrust to the larger circle of ministers were never brought before the full Conference. Instead, Joseph would meet secretly with his three most trusted ministers and reach a final decision solely on their recommendations. To prevent the outer group of ministers from learning of their exclusion from these deliberations, Joseph instructed Sinzendorf to keep secret those communications that he sent to Vienna which he felt might be discussed only by the *petite Conférence* since, "if the others discover that we have hidden some measure from them, this will provoke complaints and division at court."[111] For Wratislaw and his associates, the situation was ideal. As the Bohemian chancellor himself admitted in a letter to Sinzendorf: "With Prince Salm no longer here, we only have Schönborn to fight at this court. Otherwise, we always continue with the heart of the Conference . . . and, though Seilern draws out the time with his prolixity, I must admit that he is less difficult over points I have raised."[112]

Of course, these precautions alone did not put a halt to the intrigues. The Favorite in particular persisted in plotting against the Wratislaw party, and Cardinal Lamberg made at least one more surprise visit to Vienna before the end of the year.[113] Nevertheless, the purge of August 1709 had broken the back of their court coalition. Within the next few weeks, Gundaker Starhemberg and even Count Windischgrätz made their peace with Wratislaw and his allies.[114] Having lost hope of achieving real power at court, Schönborn also began to drift away from the Lambergs.[115] In the absence of Prince Salm, the two empresses made a futile attempt to protect their dwindling flock, Eleonore at one point threatening to enter a convent unless the "intrigues" against her protégés came to a halt. Eleonore's dare came to naught, however, while Wratislaw wryly observed that "the emperor would probably take satisfaction from this . . . and take another mistress."[116] In fact, Joseph was spending increasing amounts of time with his present mistress, the youthful Countess Marianne Pálffy, to the further detriment of his relationship with the two empresses. Meanwhile, he continued to entrust the preparation of state affairs to his most intimate advisors.

With Heems's arrival in Vienna, the new inner Conference was immediately charged with the crucial task of reviewing and revising the monarchy's peace aims. In fact, the Conference had already begun reevaluating its position earlier in the summer. Upon first learning the content of the 27 May preliminaries, Joseph had expressed his satisfaction with the advantages that Eugene and Sinzendorf had secured for the monarchy.[117] From the very beginning, however, a majority of the Conference was sharply critical of the two men's performance. The Germans Schönborn, Salm, and Seilern criticized their failure to secure all of Alsace, with the vice-chancellor observing bitterly that the monarchy and the maritime powers had achieved all their demands, while the empire had been left in the cold.[118] Led by Mansfeld, several of the ministers also expressed their dismay at the gains made by the Dutch at the expense of Spain and the empire.[119]

In their reports to Vienna, Eugene and Sinzendorf had defended the concessions they had given the Dutch in Belgium, arguing that this was the price the dynasty would have to pay for attaining the entire Spanish inheritance. They had also pointed out that only French, and not Belgian, barrier towns had been specified in the preliminaries and added that losing Guelders to the Dutch was little different than losing it to Prussia.[120] Vienna's attitude, however, was influenced not by these arguments but rather by another document sent by Prince Eugene only a short time earlier. This was the latest Dutch barrier project, which had been presented to Marlborough, who had then secretly forwarded a copy to Eugene.[121] Aiming at nothing less than the total economic subjugation of Belgium, the project represented the Estates' price for continued loyalty to the Grand Alliance and the Habsburg demand for the entire Spanish inheritance. Aside from raising the number of Belgian barrier towns and concentrating them in the wealthier western half of the country, it permitted the United Provinces to occupy all Belgium in periods of international crisis and obligated Spain to pay it the handsome sum of 3.5 million florins annually for the maintenance of its garrisons. While the latest project had not been inserted in the Hague preliminaries, and had been rejected by the Godolphin ministry in favor of a more moderate counterproject, it was clear to the Conference that the Dutch intended to hold onto Belgium until they had secured the archduke's acceptance of their demands. Moreover, it was also feared that the mentioning of the barrier in the peace preliminaries, though vague and indefinite, had given the French the opportunity to act as guarantors of any agreement subsequently worked out between Charles and the United Provinces.[122]

What disturbed the ministers most, however, were the gains made by the Dutch in the rest of the empire, where Austrian, rather than Spanish Habsburg, interests were at stake. The Conference suspected that the Dutch intended to occupy Liège, Huy, and Bonn permanently instead of just until the conclusion of a formal barrier treaty. In a frantic letter to Sinzendorf, Wratislaw warned that "through Bonn, the Dutch are masters of the four Rhenish electors and, hence, of the empire."[123] Although he chose not to amplify his statement, it became clear from Wratislaw's later correspondence that the ministry feared the Dutch would win a decisive influence in the election of future ecclesiastical electors and, in the event of Joseph's death without male heirs, be in the position to prevent a Spanish Habsburg or even a Catholic from succeeding as emperor.[124]

Because of the extensive advantages promised the Dutch, Joseph seriously considered withholding his ratification of the Hague preliminaries.[125] When word of the French rejection reached Vienna, he instead instructed the Conference to recommend revisions in the original terms. Upon reconvening, the ministers readily forgot their earlier criticism of the settlement in Alsace, since everyone now realized that the terms had not been overly lenient but rather too oppressive for Louis to accept. In its report to the emperor, the Conference suggested that the terms being demanded on behalf of the empire could be reduced by allowing France to preserve all of its fortifications in Alsace, except for those at Neu Breisach.[126] Regarding the Dutch, however, the ministry was hardly in a compliant mood. It held firmly to its original judgment that the barrier be expanded only at French expense and that France be excluded from all of the upcoming territorial settlements between the dynasty and its Dutch, Savoyard, and Portuguese allies. In addition, the Conference rejected the cession of Guelders without proper compensation and urged the emperor to make common cause with Prussia in opposing Dutch designs on the territory. Moreover, the common front with Marlborough and the London government was to be preserved as the best means of frustrating the latest barrier project.[127]

Although Joseph approved these recommendations soon after their presentation, they were already obsolete when the new inner Conference began its deliberations two months later. Word had arrived from Prince Eugene at the end of August indicating that a strong peace party had emerged in the United Provinces, favoring the granting of compensation to the duke of Anjou to the launching of a "new war" against France. Together with Sinzendorf and Heems, the prince now urged that peace aims be kept moderate in order to keep the Dutch loyal.[128] What Eugene did not say, but what was now easy to see, was that the monarchy's intended resistance to the Dutch barrier demands would also have to be largely forgotten.

When Trautson, Wratislaw, and Seilern began their secret consultations with Heems on 4 September they recognized better than ever before the precarious diplomatic position in which the dynasty presently found itself. Over the past seven years, it had stood to gain most by the prosecution of the war. Its fortunes had reached a high point at the Hague talks when it had come very close to securing the entire Spanish succession, along with handsome gains for the moribund *Reich*. Now, however, the continued prosecution of the war offered no additional advantages, only further sacrifices both for the monarchy and dynasty. On the one hand, the three ministers could see that the *Erblande* were already impoverished by years of heavy taxation, yet would have to bear the burden of future campaigns that because of France's strong defensive position, now promised to be more difficult and demanding than those of the past. The war in Hungary would also have to be brought to an end. On the other hand, they now realized for the first time that a future peace settlement would entail considerable territorial sacrifices as well. At the very least, the dynasty would have to pay off its allies for their continued financial and military support. With the passing of each day, the size of this debt increased, as did the threat that one of its allies would forsake the coalition for a separate peace with France. No wonder that the ministers wrote to the emperor, "The fortunes of war lie not in our, but in foreign hands. . . . The fortunes of war lie almost solely in the power and caprice of the allies."[129] The sooner peace could be concluded, the less the dynasty would lose to its allies.

After meeting for eight consecutive days, the inner Conference drafted its recommendations. Recognizing Articles 4 and 37 of the Hague preliminaries as potential obstacles to peace, it adopted the suggestion of Marlborough and Eugene in urging that only cautionary towns be demanded of France.[130] In order to facilitate French compliance with these terms, the demand for the three Spanish places was also dropped. Instead, Louis need provide only French fortresses, preferably three along his northern frontier (Douai, Thionville, and Arras) and three along the Pyreneen border with Spain (Collaire, Mont Louis, and Bellegarde). In place of a two-month truce, the French king would be granted an armistice of indefinite duration and not be obligated to assist in Philip's expulsion from the peninsula. Even if Louis abandoned his neutrality and secretly aided his grandson, the truce with France would not expire until mid-April, in time for the opening of the next campaign.[131]

If Heems and the three ministers were generous in handling the question of security from France, they were at least reasonable in dealing with Dutch aspirations in the Low Countries. They recognized for the first time the United Provinces' claim to an expanded barrier within Belgium itself. Although the most recent barrier project was still considered far too extravagant, they now recommended that Sinzendorf reopen negotiations with the Dutch on the basis of the more moderate British proposal. The ministers also gave up hope of saving Guelders for the archduke and aimed instead at obtaining minor concessions from the Dutch. In recommending compliance with the territorial demands of their Dutch allies, they wrote: "This security is the only [advantage] they seek in this so costly war and we ourselves must provide them with it since they can secure a strong barrier nowhere else."[132] In fact, the ministers had been obliged to assume this accommodating posture by the compelling need to keep the Dutch loyal to the allied cause and to the monarchy's continuing demand for the entire Spanish succession.

Having contemplated a revision in the security clauses of the Hague preliminaries as well as certain sacrifices of the archduke's Belgian patrimony, the inner Conference now prepared to reevaluate the empire's role in the coming settlement. Joseph instructed the four men to meet with Schönborn before formally presenting their recommendations on the new demands to be placed on the empire's behalf. The participation of the imperial vice-chancellor was, of course, largely a formality since they had already discussed among themselves what further sacrifices the empire would now have to make.[133] Nevertheless, the meetings with Schönborn were not destined to be totally anticlimactic, for events in far-off Flanders were at that very moment changing the whole complexion of the war.

The Lost Victory

Even before the collapse of the Hague peace talks, the allies had been preparing themselves for another campaign. Both Eugene and Marlborough believed that one more battlefield defeat would compel Louis XIV to make peace, providing that the obnoxious security articles of the Hague preliminaries were omitted. Yet, while one more victory in the field would translate into victory at the peace table, it was also true that an allied setback or even a military stalemate could seriously compromise the coalition's bargaining position. The reason for this paradox rested with the Dutch, whose recent eagerness to press forward with the campaign reflected their impatience for peace more than it did their confidence in ultimate victory. Prince Eugene was well aware of the tenuous position of the allies when he wrote to Sinzendorf on 11 June:

> It is true [that] a victory can improve our terms even further. The change will only be slight, however, since the Dutch definitely do not desire France's total humiliation. If the military undertakings do not yield at the very outset the favorable results that one expects of them, I very much fear that the [coalition's] present steadfastness will become completely transformed and we will lose far more than we could have gained. I have often said that France's advantage is that, when it has held the upper hand, it has always extended its conquests as far as it possibly could. An unbelievable expenditure of effort and blood is necessary to reach a situation like the present. Yet all, or at least a majority, of its enemies are afraid to humiliate it completely, never realizing that it will undoubtedly recover within a few years and begin anew to molest its neighbors. I know the people with whom we have to deal and I dare repeat that we risk far more than we can gain.[134]

There was more than a measure of truth and wisdom in these words, not only in their prediction that Dutch impatience for peace would be hard to restrain, but also in the intimation that, with France already weakened, the United Provinces or some other allied power would justify a compromise peace by pointing to the apparent restoration of the balance of power. Indeed, the only interest the Dutch now had in continuing hostilities came from the front in Flanders, where each allied advance would secure another barrier fortress for them at the next peace conference.

Clearly none of the allies was being sustained by the promise of progress on other fronts. Following George Louis's dismal failure in the previous campaign, everyone had come to realize that the stalemate on the Upper Rhine would continue indefinitely. Most of the Anglo-Dutch mercenaries had been recalled from the imperial army. Although they were quick to express their dismay at the empire's poor showing in the Hague preliminaries, the German princes also continued to divert their contingents from the Rhine to Flanders in exchange for Anglo-Dutch subsidies. George Louis indicated his own profound disenchantment by staying in Hanover until the beginning of August.[135] Nor did the front in southeastern France promise any great advantages to the allies. Although Victor Amadeus had managed to capture Exilles and Fenestrelle in the preceding campaign, the Austro-Savoyard army was severely handicapped by the unfavorable Alpine terrain and the exceptionally short campaigning season. Aware of the poor prospects of achieving further successes in the Dauphiné, Victor Amadeus had also elected not to journey to the front. Meanwhile, he had already diverted his energies eastward by renewing his earlier demand for the cession of Vigevano. In Spain itself, the archduke's situation was slowly improving. Despite Phillip's insistence that he would fight to the death, Louis XIV had withdrawn his armies from the peninsula, mainly in order to reinforce Villars, but also to impress the allies with his good intentions. At the same time, reinforcements for Starhemberg's army continued to reach Barcelona from Italy. Despite these developments, however, the allied armies in both Portugal and Catalonia remained too weak to mount an offensive. Even isolated Sicily continued to hold out against the forces of the coalition, if only because the Austrian army in Naples was unable to coordinate its invasion plans with the British fleet.[136]

Given the meager military prospects elsewhere, it was apparent to both sides that, at present, a decisive allied victory could be achieved only on the fields of Flanders. On orders from Versailles, Marshal Villars discreetly avoided contact with the main enemy force. When Marlborough and Eugene invested Tournai at the end of June, he made no attempt to save the town. When following its capture they besieged Mons, Villars again kept his distance, fortifying a heavily wooded area ten miles southwest of the town. Despite the marshal's excellent defensive position, the two allied commanders decided to attack him, hoping to deliver the decisive *coup de grâce*. After a day-long battle, in which 110,000 allied soldiers were pitted against 90,000 Frenchmen, Villars's army was eventually forced to retreat. Yet, Marlborough and Eugene were obliged to pay the price for their audacity. As Villars's army withdrew from the battlefield, it left behind it 8,000 allied dead and 16,000 wounded, roughly double its own casualties. The French army had not been crushed—only the myth of allied invincibility.

The bloody battle of Malplaquet had been fought on 11 September, the day on which the inner Conference concluded its initial series of meetings with Baron Heems. Vienna did not receive word of the engagement until the nineteenth, however, and like the initial accounts reaching Versailles, London, and The Hague, it indicated only that the allied army had been victorious. Believing that France had suffered yet another humiliating defeat, the court's hopes for a settlement became more sanguinary than ever. In a letter to Sinzendorf, Wratislaw hinted that both Spain and the empire might now secure territorial advantages beyond those enumerated in the Hague preliminaries.[137] This view became more widespread when word arrived from The Hague of renewed Dutch firmness in the aftermath of Malplaquet.[138]

It was under the impact of these favorable tidings that the inner Conference was now encouraged to discard its earlier pessimism and draft more extensive demands for the empire. In two secret meetings with Trautson, Seilern, and Wratislaw, Joseph voiced once again his desire to see Lorraine compensated for its loss of Montferrat.[139] In the three ministers' deliberations with Schönborn and Heems, the emperor's wishes translated into a demand for the three bishoprics and the restitution of Lorraine's 1624 frontier with France. During its meetings with the vice-chancellor, the inner Conference also reconsidered the possibility of obtaining the whole of Alsace. In addition, the idea of annexing Dunkirk to Belgium, instead of merely securing its demilitarization, was also broached for the first time. Regarding the garrisons sought by the Dutch in Liège, Huy, Bonn, and Rheinfels, the ministers resumed the firm stance that they had taken earlier in the summer. Hopefully all mention of the four places was to be deleted from the future peace preliminaries. At the very least, however, the fortifications of Liège, Huy, and Bonn were either to be razed or garrisoned by imperial troops.[140]

It was only on 2 October that the full details of Malplaquet reached Vienna. After a fortnight of optimism and sanguinary speculation, the news came as a rude shock to everyone. Count Trautson gloomily reported a general conviction at court "that we lost as much from it [Malplaquet] as the enemy."[141] Indeed, the monarchy now definitely appeared to be caught between the prospects of a long and difficult war and those of a peace settlement dictated to it by its allies. As a result the empire's peace objectives were reduced yet again in order to appease the war-weary Dutch. In the recommendations it submitted to Joseph on the morning of 9 October, the ministry warned that the Dutch might no longer support the demands made on behalf of the empire in the Hague preliminaries. Although it reiterated the need for a strong *Reichsbarriere* and cited the noble military effort of the Nördlingen Association, the report also pointed out that the Dutch had contributed from 44 to 45 million florins annually to the allied cause, or approximately one hundred times the empire's expenditure. The Dutch, therefore, could not be ignored. Although an attempt would be made to achieve the same terms that had been won for the empire four months earlier, only Strasbourg and Breisach could now be insisted upon. The report did express the hope that the restoration of Max Emanuel would enable the empire to retrieve more land in Alsace and perhaps an enclave or two for Lorraine. Nevertheless, there remained almost no chance that such advantages could be achieved. Joseph was, as always, hopeful that more substantial gains might yet be obtained for the empire, and for Lorraine in particular. With Heems leaving for The Hague on 19 October, the emperor wrote to Sinzendorf urging him to try to strengthen the duke of Lorraine's frontier with France, pointing out that it "not only benefits him and his house but will also be especially beneficial to the repose of the Roman Empire and [Europe] in general."[142] Yet Joseph's pleas could not obscure the fact that he and his ministers had once again sacrificed the interests of the empire on the altar of Habsburg dynasticism.

Of course, Vienna's readiness to surrender the empire's claims in Alsace did not automatically ensure that the dynasty's own objectives could be safeguarded. With the pyrrhic victory at Malplaquet, the chances increased that the Dutch would force a partition of the Spanish inheritance, either by concluding a separate peace or by dragging the allies into a compromise with Louis XIV. In addition, it was already certain that the Dutch would be able to blackmail Joseph into permitting a considerable expansion of their barrier in Belgium, if not also in the possessions of Joseph Clement.

Back at The Hague, the Dutch were, in fact, picking the first fruits of the "victory" at Malplaquet by using their renewed leverage against the English. Since April they had been trying in vain to secure English acceptance of their latest barrier project. Marlborough had handled the initial talks with the Dutch. Once he had received a copy of their demands, however, he had entrusted further negotiations to Lord Townshend, rather than risk his own reputation and standing in Vienna by having to conclude such an agreement. For its part, the powerful Whig Junto was eager to conclude a barrier accord with the United Provinces, partly because it was seeking in exchange their guarantee of the Protestant succession, but also because it felt—unlike Marlborough and his Tory colleagues—that the award of a strong barrier would strengthen rather than weaken their commitment to the Grand Alliance. At first, however, there appeared to be little chance that the English would bow before the stiff Dutch terms. Although the young and inexperienced Townshend received no assistance from Marlborough, who was determined to steer clear of the negotiations, he continued to receive instructions from London directing him to base any settlement on its own, much milder, counterproject. Moreover, in order to insure Dutch loyalty to the alliance, the Godolphin ministry had also instructed Townshend to include in any agreement a clause binding the United Provinces not to conclude peace until the entire Spanish inheritance had been recovered.[143]

The talks remained deadlocked until August when the Dutch began to make some important discoveries that severely compromised England's bargaining position. First they learned that the English were secretly pressing the archduke to cede strategic Port Mahón to the British crown. A few weeks later they also received confirmation of earlier rumors that, in the dark months after Almansa, the London government had actually compelled Charles to grant it a favorable trade treaty in exchange for increased military support.[144] The English considered both concessions to be just compensation for their increasing commitment in the peninsula. Nevertheless, their actions clearly violated the Grand Alliance treaty which promised the maritime powers equal commercial advantages in the Spanish Empire. The English were now cast in the role of hypocrites whose strenuous efforts to limit Dutch gains in Belgium had been surpassed only by their own secret attempts to extract considerable concessions for themselves elsewhere in the Spanish Empire. The Godolphin ministry hastened to assuage its angered ally, first by promising it identical commercial privileges in Spanish America, then by postponing indefinitely its own attempt to annex Port Mahón. Yet these remedial measures could hardly repair the damage already inflicted on England's image as a faithful ally. In view of the recent revelations, what moral obligation did the Dutch have to England? On the morrow of Malplaquet should not the United Provinces now seek their own selfish interests? Only by meeting the Estates' barrier demands could the Godolphin ministry be sure of retaining their loyalty. When negotiations resumed between Townshend and the Dutch deputies, it took only five days to reach a final agreement.

Signed on 29 October, the treaty represented a devastating blow to Habsburg sovereignty in Belgium. Thirteen Belgian places were to be garrisoned by the Dutch, who were to enjoy full autonomy from the government in Brussels, including the right to raise one million florins in taxes annually. Additional towns might be garrisoned if war threatened from *any* direction. Seven towns in French Flanders were to be ceded to the Dutch in full sovereignty, as well as any places subsequently conquered by allied arms (see map). A separate article con-

firmed the annexation of Guelders without compensation and the
provisional occupation of Liège, Huy, and Bonn.[145] Originally intended to serve as a barrier, Belgium would now become a Dutch
fortress and marketplace.

In return for their almost total capitulation, the British managed
some advantages of their own. The Dutch were obliged to guarantee
the demilitarization of Dunkirk and to drop the channel port of
Ostend from the list of barrier fortresses, securing in exchange the
major commercial center of Dendermonde. Much more important,
they did agree to provide England with military support in repelling
any foreign attempt to overthrow the Protestant succession. Although
the English ministers were somewhat aghast at the extent of Townshend's concessions, they realized that they were in no position to
renegotiate the terms. They balked only at ratifying the separate
articles, and then only because they feared Prussia's reaction to the loss
of Guelders.[146] In fact, the real victims of the Townshend Treaty were
the Habsburg brothers. Even the earlier British demand for a Dutch
pledge not to conclude peace until the entire Spanish monarchy had
been recovered had been deleted from the final treaty. Hence, Joseph
and Charles could not even console themselves with assurances of
continued Dutch fidelity.

For the moment, the Godolphin ministry elected to keep the treaty
from Joseph and Charles. Consequently, Vienna still believed that
negotiations were in progress and that the British were keeping the
dynasty's own best interests in mind. Even Eugene and Sinzendorf
were as yet unaware that their friend Marlborough had abandoned
Townshend and Belgium to their fate. Believing that the duke was still
the chief British negotiator, Joseph had been considering new ways of
retaining his loyalty. The Belgian governorship was now out of the
question, Marlborough having only recently written Charles withdrawing his candidacy.[147] Instead, in a 14 September meeting with his
inner Conference, he had agreed to allow the duke's three daughters to
inherit the imperial principality of Mindelheim, which had been
awarded him following the victory at Blenheim, despite the strictures
of the Salic Law.[148] Wratislaw had notified Marlborough of the emper-
or's decision in a letter on 18 October. At the same time, Joseph had
addressed a second note to the duke, pleading for his assistance in
restraining Dutch ambitions in Belgium.[149] In his five years as Bohemian chancellor, Wratislaw had never been cited for his subtlety.

Just as the previously faithful Godolphin ministry had recently
deserted the Habsburgs in order to secure its own interests, so had
Marlborough abandoned them in order to protect his own career and
reputation. Nevertheless, he still continued to demonstrate the deference toward the court at Vienna which he had always considered a
necessary ingredient in his own personal diplomacy: within a fortnight
after the conclusion of the barrier accord he visited Eugene and

Sinzendorf at The Hague and secretly divulged the contents of the treaty.[150]

Upon returning from the front, Eugene joined with Trautson, Wratislaw, and Seilern in considering the Townshend Treaty. They were profoundly dismayed by the London government's almost total abandonment of its earlier counterproject, as well as of its decision not to insist upon a Dutch guarantee of the entire Spanish inheritance. Upon meeting with Joseph one week later, on 23 December, they could suggest only that Sinzendorf approach Heinsius to secure somewhat more acceptable terms. Above all else, they were still intent on deleting any mention of the garrisons in Joseph Clement's lands or at Rheinfels.[151] Of course, with the Godolphin ministry now committed to the Estates' interests, there was little chance that Sinzendorf would be able to negotiate any meaningful revisions in the Townshend Treaty. Even Prince Eugene, who had been an earlier advocate of direct negotiations with the Dutch, now confided to the archduke that subsequent talks would be quite fruitless.[152]

It was not long before the court's initial sense of shock and dismay transformed into one of bitter disillusionment. At the beginning of January, Wratislaw wrote to Charles admonishing him that the Anglo-Dutch accord should "serve as a warning how dangerous it is to allow oneself to enter into a treaty with these powers."[153] A few weeks later, the Conference submitted a written report to Joseph in which it expressed a total lack of confidence in the loyalty of its two main allies.[154] In view of the unexpected harshness of the Townshend Treaty, it is not surprising that the ministry should have taken this view. What is indeed, remarkable, is that it had taken so long for Vienna to realize that the British and Dutch were capable of such behavior in the first place. In concluding their barrier accord, the maritime powers had, after all, only been acting in their own best interest. They had not violated any of the treaties previously concluded within the alliance. What they had done was to begin seeking repayment for services already rendered to the dynasty. The Dutch had sought compensation in Belgium, the British in the Mediterranean and America. Considering the extent of the dynasty's prospective gains, the price was not unreasonable. Since Joseph and his ministers had become accustomed to expecting—and demanding—the entire Spanish monarchy, they were quite naturally shocked to discover their allies' plans. As late as August 1709, they had defiantly refused to allow any significant territorial losses to the Dutch and any concessions whatsoever to the duke of Anjou. They should have realized, however, that with the Bourbon defeat their allies would seek to supplement what little they could win from France itself by securing further advantages from the Spanish Empire.

Had peace been concluded at The Hague in the spring of 1709, Joseph would have been able to forestall many of the Dutch demands.

Not only might he have gained the entire Spanish inheritance, he would have also prevented the Dutch from blackmailing him or the British into conceding a greatly expanded barrier. Yet, in May 1709, no one in Vienna had foreseen the advantages of an early peace. Indeed, during the negotiations with Torcy, it had been the Dutch deputies who were most eager for a settlement, not Eugene or Sinzendorf. Having let this opportunity pass, Joseph had suddenly lost control of the dynasty's fortunes. Belgium had already been sacrificed. Sicily might follow. To save these territories and the rest of the Spanish inheritance, the emperor needed the assistance of his allies. Yet, as he looked about him, he saw only the faces of adversaries.

The Crumbling Alliance

As 1709 came to a close, the monarchy's best hope of recovering the entire Spanish patrimony lay in the success of the coming campaign. In particular, the court looked to Marlborough and Eugene to achieve the decisive victory that had eluded them at Malplaquet. The year 1710 offered no such triumphs, however. Indeed, as the year progressed, it soon became apparent that the emperor's attention would be devoted not so much to military preparations as to continuous, at times frantic, efforts to hold together the anti-Bourbon coalition.

The first crisis was not long in coming. Even before the start of the new campaign, developments in the east were threatening to deprive the allies of their military advantage in Flanders. With Charles XII's defeat at Poltava, Denmark and Saxony had concluded a new alliance with the tsar and reentered the Northern War. By the beginning of 1710, the Danes had landed in Scania and the Russians had invaded Poland, once again in the name of King Augustus. Although victory appeared certain for his Saxon and Danish protégés, Joseph was hardly pleased by their good fortune. In defeat, Augustus had shown himself the most docile of the empire's great princes, almost totally dependent on the emperor's favor. At the same time, the new king, Stanislaus, had been careful to maintain friendly relations with Vienna, even to the point of ignoring Prince Rákóczi's many overtures. Should Augustus again succeed to the Polish throne, he could be expected to set out on the path blazed by Max Emanuel and Frederick of Prussia; Joseph even feared that he might eventually seek the imperial crown.[155] Sweden's defeat might also lead to the further expansion of Prussia, and as the Bohemian chancellor warned Count Sinzendorf, "This court fears the aggrandizement of the king of Prussia more than [it welcomes] the weakening of the Swede."[156] Of more immediate danger to the monarchy and the alliance as a whole was the possibility that a widening of the Northern War would prompt Saxony, Denmark, Prussia, and perhaps the Brunswick princes of Hanover and Wolfenbüttel to withdraw their mercenaries from the army in

Flanders. Although all of these states were eager to continue receiving Anglo-Dutch subsidies, the threat of Swedish intervention in the empire might soon compel them to recall their forces. The Swedish General Crassow had only recently withdrawn his small army into the empire to protect it from the advancing Russians. Although he was presently quartered in Swedish Pomerania, Crassow might elect to strike against Saxony or the Danish possessions in Holstein. Worse yet, there was always the danger that he might be followed into Germany by the Russians. Indeed, there were even widespread rumors that the sultan would give Charles XII an escort of 50,000 Tartar cavalry for his trip home through the empire.[157]

Faced with this explosive situation, the emperor felt compelled to walk a tightrope between Sweden and its enemies. On the one hand, he was careful not to antagonize Charles XII, especially while that eccentric monarch had the ear of the sultan. Hence, Joseph continued to abide by the religious clauses of the Second Treaty of Altranstädt, despite growing pressure from Silesia's Catholic estates.[158] At the same time, he and his ministers agreed that the changing balance of power in the east justified a policy of benevolent neutrality toward Charles's enemies. He soon recognized Augustus as king of Poland. He also tried to discourage the Swedish king from returning home through Habsburg territory and refused altogether to grant refuge to Russian cossacks who had fought against the tsar.[159] Moreover, despite Charles's pleas, he followed the lead of England and the United Provinces in refusing to enforce the broken peace treaties of Travendal and Altranstädt (1706).

To prevent the empire from becoming a battlefield, Joseph took steps to guarantee its neutrality. In December 1709, he had asked the diet to declare the neutrality of the imperial possessions of both Sweden and its enemies. Although it debated the proposal for over three months without either passing or rejecting it, Joseph secured an Anglo-Dutch guarantee of the empire's neutrality on 31 March in a convention signed at The Hague. Two days later, the diet belatedly concurred. Prussia, Saxony, Hanover, and Denmark all joined the Hague Convention within the next few weeks. Meanwhile, the ruling council in Stockholm provisionally approved it, pending Charles's final ratification. As a last precaution, the allies opened negotiations with the council for the signing up of Crassow's troops as mercenaries in Marlborough's army.[160]

By late spring, the emperor's diplomacy seemed to have forestalled at least temporarily the threat of a new conflict and of massive withdrawals from the army in Flanders. Nevertheless, in the meantime, it had become evident that much more would have to be done to prevent several of the monarchy's allies from withdrawing voluntarily from the war against France. In the spring of 1710, some of these states were beginning to question the value of their continued adherence to the Grand Alliance. Louis XIV no longer appeared to threaten the balance of power. Moreover, for most members of the coalition, a continuation of the war did not offer much chance of advancing their own territorial ambitions. While France's remarkable defensive strength was partly responsible for this attitude, the emperor himself was also at fault for not having shown sufficient sensitivity to his allies' war aims. At present, only the Dutch appeared to be fully contented, their demands having been met by the British in the recent Townshend Treaty. It still remained for him to respond to the needs of the other members of the coalition and to shore up the cracks that now began to appear in the facade of allied unity.

By the beginning of 1710, the smoldering dispute with Victor Amadeus over the fate of Vigevano was threatening to cause a total break between Savoy and the monarchy. Throughout the previous year, the Conference had urged firmness in refusing to concede to the duke's demands. While agreeing with his ministers' judgment that Victor Amadeus's threats were merely a *Schreckschuss* aimed at frightening rather than betraying the alliance, Joseph had nonetheless feared the effect that the present controversy would have upon the maritime powers. He had therefore accepted his allies' offer to mediate the dispute and informed the Conference that he was indeed prepared to yield an equivalent for Vigevano as soon as details could be worked out with the duke.[161] At the same time, however, Joseph had resorted to the practice of using imperial legal powers to improve his negotiating position. During the summer of 1709, he approved Aulic Council judgments requiring Savoy to assume a share of Milan's public debt and pay Montferrat's imperial war levy. He also published two additional *conclusae* which asserted that the Montferrat dependency of Langhe was not legally a part of the territory ceded to Savoy in the Treaty of Turin.[162] Two months later imperial commissioners began posting proclamations throughout Langhe, calling upon its inhabitants to give their allegiance to the emperor and forbidding them to take an oath to the house of Savoy.[163]

Instead of making Victor Amadeus more pliable, Joseph's actions only enraged him.[164] Within a matter of weeks, he was in contact with French agents in Genoa, discussing the possibility of a separate peace.[165] Fearing that he would in fact desert the alliance, the maritime powers immediately rushed to the duke's aid. By the middle of January, the chief Austrian negotiator in Turin, Count Nesselrode, was reporting that the Anglo-Dutch mediators had decided in Savoy's favor on each of the disputed points.[166] Within two months, Joseph capitulated on the most essential question by promising to cede the Milanese district of Novara as an equivalent.[167]

While negotiations were continuing with Victor Amadeus and the allied mediators, the emperor was also obliged to turn his attention to the latest demands of the king of Prussia. Having failed to benefit from his earlier alliance with the emperor, Frederick had turned to the maritime powers in 1706, hoping to receive better treatment from them. After four years, he had come away empty-handed. England had failed to press the Estates to disgorge Moers and Lingen. During the Hague talks, neither ally had pushed for the recovery of the Orange estates in France. Furthermore, with the conclusion of the Townshend Treaty, England had seemingly forsaken the Prussian claim to Guelders. In the second half of 1709, Frederick had again begun to consider withdrawing from the heretofore largely unprofitable war against France and redirecting his forces against Sweden. He became a party to the new Russo-Saxon-Danish alliance and in October 1709 initiated secret talks with the French for the withdrawal of all Prussian troops from the west.[168] Yet, Frederick was still hesitant to make the final break, just as he had been four years earlier. Instead, at the beginning of 1710, he gave the allies a second chance to meet his territorial demands by threatening to withhold his forces from Italy and Belgium.[169] When this failed, he reverted to the strategem he had used in 1706 of informing Vienna that he was secretly meeting with the French. On this occasion, however, Frederick attempted to make the threat seem more genuine by leaking the information through an unofficial source. A few weeks later the Prussian General Grumbkow followed with an urgent letter to his friend Eugene, ostensibly written without Frederick's knowledge, in which he warned that disaster was imminent and urged him to visit Berlin at once.[170]

In a 15 February meeting of the inner Conference, Joseph directed Eugene to pass through Berlin on his way to the front and effect a reconciliation with the king.[171] In a 3 April interview, Eugene agreed to Frederick's demand that an annual *Hofkammer* subsidy covering recruitment costs for the Prussian corps in Italy be raised from 30,000 to 100,000 taler.[172] In return, the king promised to keep his army in the west. Once again Frederick had accepted subsidies in lieu of concrete political and territorial advantages. For the emperor, it was a small price to pay for the continued service of Prussia's 30,000 mercenaries.

Not so easily disposed of were the demands of Elector Lothair Francis of Mainz. Even before an accord had been reached with Berlin, Joseph learned to his astonishment that the archchancellor was preparing to forsake him as an ally. Like the rulers of Savoy and Prussia, Mainz was dissatisfied with Joseph's continued shunting of his interests, in this case the interests of the empire and especially of the Nördlingen Association. The meager gains secured for the empire at the Hague talks persuaded the archchancellor to look around for new friends. When the Dutch diplomat Adolf Hendrik Count Rechteren approached him three months later and proposed a permanent alliance between the association and the Estates General, Lothair Francis immediately jumped at the opportunity. With its pledge of Dutch troops and subsidies for the Rhine frontier and a strengthened *Reichs-*

barriere, Rechteren's plan for a *foedus perpetuum* stood in sharp contrast to Vienna's cavalier treatment of the association's military and territorial needs.[173]

The imperial court did not learn of the projected alliance until the beginning of March, while the archchancellor was still busily gaining the consent of the association's members. The Conference's concern centered once again on the growth of Dutch influence among the smaller, *kaisertreu* princes of the empire. At the moment, it was particularly alarmed that the Dutch might use their leverage with Lothair Francis and the association to win German support for their peace objectives, especially with regard to Sicily. Like many of the other electors, Mainz had already expressed a willingness to sacrifice Sicily rather than continue the war.[174] An alliance with the United Provinces would almost certainly assure the German princes' acquiescence to the loss of the island, especially if in exchange the Dutch agreed to secure Alsace for the empire.

To keep the loyalty of the Nördlingen Association, Joseph now had to demonstrate to Lothair Francis his willingness and ability to obtain a much larger *Reichsbarriere* from the French. Of course, Joseph himself remained sincerely interested in strengthening the empire's western frontier and especially the duchy of Lorraine. Over the last year, he had even toyed with the idea of ceding the former Habsburg possessions in Alsace to Lorraine, should these be obtained from France at the next peace conference.[175] Joseph no longer faced the problem of gaining Dutch acceptance of larger territorial advantages for the empire, since the Estates were now also eager to strengthen their bond with the association. Rather his chief concern was that the Dutch—and the French—would probably never consent to a demand for both Alsace and an undivided Spanish inheritance. At long last, it appeared as if the imperial interests might take precedence over those of the dynasty.

With new peace talks about to begin at the town of Gertruydenberg, Joseph's dilemma was a very real one. The time for a dictated peace had passed. Louis XIV was well aware that his diplomatic position had improved considerably since May 1709. Malplaquet had restored his confidence in French arms. He had also noticed the unsettling effect that the battle had had on the Dutch and English public. Moreover, despite the allies' recent efforts to defuse the Northern War, he was still hopeful that Charles XII would turn his attention westward, perhaps even involving Sweden and Turkey in a war with the Habsburg monarchy. Over the winter, he had resisted the allies' efforts to retain the Hague preliminaries as a basis for future talks, insisting instead on the negotiation of an entirely new settlement. Only after he had learned of the signing of the thirty-year Russo-Turkish truce had the king softened his position and decided to resume direct peace negotiations.[176] Still, he had no intention of accepting the hard terms presented to him a year ago. In his instructions to Marshal D'Huxelles and the Abbé Polignac, Louis demanded not only compensation for his grandson but also the discarding of Articles 4 and 37 in exchange for the surrender of four French cautionary towns and the promise of his neutrality.[177]

Given the present military situation in Spain, Louis's terms could hardly be judged immoderate. Philip still held the bulk of the peninsula and it was now clear that he had no intention of giving it up. While he could accept Philip's forced exile in Sicily or some other territory, he would not himself perform the onerous task of expelling his grandson from Spain. At present, neither the emperor nor the Estates were prepared to agree to both of Louis's conditions. Joseph was still willing to accept the king's offer of cautionary towns if, by doing so, peace could be achieved.[178] That he realized that territorial concessions might also have to be made to the French becomes clear in a subsequent letter to Prince Eugene in which he admitted that "it is no longer possible to divide up and portion out foreign kingdoms at will as in past years."[179] Alas, the emperor could still not envision any further sacrifices in the dynasty's own territorial aims, especially in Italy. The entire Spanish inheritance remained his unflinching objective. Meanwhile, the Dutch were as willing as ever to concede Sicily to Philip but were steadfastly opposed to dropping Articles 4 and 37 from the peace preliminaries. It was still inconceivable to them that France should enjoy the benefits of peace while they and their allies continued the struggle against Philip. Moreover, they remained unconvinced by Louis's claim that he had no control over his grandson and further suspected that he would secretly send aid to the peninsula once an agreement was reached. Only the British could accept both of the French demands, but they were initially unwilling to contradict the wishes of either ally. By supporting each in its objectives, they guaranteed at least the temporary resurrection of the Hague preliminaries.

Of course, there still lurked the danger that the Dutch would abandon Sicily at the first sight of French resistance. During February, Townshend and Sinzendorf had actually increased the chances of this by agreeing to let Buys and Vanderdussen meet alone with the French diplomats. They reasoned that unilateral negotiations would prove less cumbersome and present a more united front to the enemy. In fact, the Dutch had already shown signs of weakening during the winter exchanges with Versailles.[180] Responding to this threat, Townshend compelled Buys, Vanderdussen, and the grand pensionary to pledge not to enter into any agreement with the French that contradicted the Hague preliminaries.[181] Nevertheless, the British were nearly as helpless against the Dutch as their Austrian ally. The recent barrier treaty had lain bare their vulnerability. Moreover, the hawkish stance of the Godolphin regime was also being undermined at home, where rising taxes and the carnage at Malplaquet had at last begun to reduce public enthusiasm for the war.

In their initial early March meetings with D'Huxelles and Polignac at Gertruydenberg, the Dutch negotiators stood firmly by their commitments, demanding that Louis XIV surrender the entire Spanish inheritance. Joseph received the news of his ally's renewed resolution with a mixture of relief and gratitude.[182] Yet, when the French negotiators stubbornly refused to drop their demand for Sicily, apprehension grew in Vienna that Dutch resistance would eventually buckle. By the end of March, the continuing deadlock had revived past fears of a separate accord between Louis and the Estates, and moved the Conference to demand the admission of Sinzendorf and Eugene to the Gertruydenberg negotiations.[183] Meanwhile, the continuing assurances of the English brought little comfort, since it was widely suspected that the Godolphin ministry was no longer able—or willing—to restrain the Dutch.[184]

Still, Joseph remained adamant in insisting that Philip receive "nothing at all, especially nothing in Italy."[185] To preempt what he foresaw as the inevitable Dutch sacrifice of Sicily, he began to press once again for the dropping of Articles 4 and 37 from the preliminaries as the least costly way of gaining peace with France. He shared Marlborough's judgment that the allies could easily conquer Spain by themselves once they had secured French neutrality. He had already discussed the idea of a separate allied settlement with Versailles in a 7 March session of the inner Conference. Once Philip had been isolated, he proposed sending 6,000 Austrian troops to Spain, hopefully in Anglo-Dutch pay, as part of a 20,000-man allied expeditionary force.[186] By 27 March, the emperor was writing to Queen Anne and the Estates General expressing his readiness to help recover Spain once a separate peace had been worked out with Louis XIV.[187] A few days later he instructed Sinzendorf to offer the 6,000 Austrians for this purpose once his allies had agreed to drop Article 37 (and presumably Article 4) from the peace preliminaries.[188]

In his letter to the queen, Joseph had made clear his belief that peace could be attained either by accepting Louis's own security proposal or by granting compensation to Philip, but had emphasized that he would never agree to the latter course presently favored by the Dutch. In reality, he was wrong in assuming that the allies had these alternatives, for Louis XIV was determined not to give in until they had conceded on both points. The emperor did not realize his error until 4 April, when the latest dispatches from Sinzendorf indicated that Louis XIV would probably never sign a separate peace without first having obtained compensation for his grandson. Not unexpectedly, Sinzendorf's report also included a Dutch request that Philip be compensated with a part of the Spanish inheritance. Joseph acted with equal predictability in rejecting his ally's proposal. In addition, he announced to his ministers that he now favored the breaking off of further negotiations since they could no longer bring a favorable verdict for the dynasty.[189]

It was, of course, hopeless to expect that the Dutch would submit meekly to Joseph's call. They were determined to avoid the endurance test of the previous year and not permit so expendable a territory as Sicily to stand in the way of a settlement. Buys and Vanderdussen continued meeting with the French negotiators, countering Vienna's protests with their own pleas for the sacrifice of Sicily. In carrying on the talks, they also ignored the counsel of Marlborough, who was convinced that the French were not sincerely interested in peace.[190] In past years, this would have been unthinkable, but the Dutch were aware of the duke's falling stock with the Whig Junto and the queen herself. In fact, though Marlborough continued to stand by his Austrian colleagues, the Godolphin ministry had already decided to accept the Dutch demand, if such a concession could secure a settlement.[191]

On 24 April, Buys and Vanderdussen finally capitulated to the French, informing D'Huxelles and Polignac that the allies would indeed concede Sicily and possibly Sardinia to Philip. In exchange, however, the Dutch demanded that Louis XIV guarantee his grandson's abdication of the Spanish throne according to the terms set down in the Hague preliminaries. As expected, they also indicated that all of Alsace would have to be returned to the empire in exchange for the partial restoration of Max Emanuel and Joseph Clement.[192] In the past year's talks, Louis had already offered to concede Alsace in exchange for Naples. It was still not clear, however, whether he would accept responsibility for deposing Philip, now that an honorable exile had been secured for him. Nevertheless, the Dutch were determined not to compromise on this question. When Louis rejected their demand, they announced immediately that further talks would be pointless and hastened with preparations for the coming campaign. Only several weeks later, after Eugene and Marlborough had besieged the strategic fortress of Douai, did the king reconsider his decision. On 17 June D'Huxelles and Polignac again approached the Dutch. They proposed that Louis be given four months in which to secure his grandson's abdication. If these efforts proved unsuccessful, the king would then help subsidize the subsequent allied military operations in the peninsula.[193] The Dutch continued to require, however, that Louis expel Philip by himself before peace could be considered.

By insisting that France assume sole responsibility for Philip's expulsion, the Dutch had actually exceeded the letter and intent of the Hague preliminaries. Their demand aroused the greatest indignation at Versailles. "They would fain be idle spectators in a war between grandfather and grandson," remarked Torcy. The king himself declared defiantly that, if he was to be compelled to wage war, he preferred to wage it on his enemies rather than his children. Meanwhile, the latest Dutch demands were well received in Vienna. For the last two months, the court had realized that any peace settlement would undoubtedly entail the loss of part of Spanish Italy.[194] Now the Dutch themselves had helped avert this loss by pushing their own demand for security too strongly. In fact, though the peace talks dragged on for another month, their failure was already certain.

The allies departed Gertruydenberg a united front, much as they had The Hague one year earlier. Queen Anne immediately promised to resume the struggle with renewed vigor. The Estates General busied itself with military preparations, while also issuing a statement accusing Louis XIV of negotiating in bad faith.[195] The emperor was particularly pleased by the renewed resolution shown by the Dutch. Following the conclusion of the Townshend Treaty, he and his ministers had despaired of London's ability to keep them loyal to the alliance. In the end, they had remained faithful. Though they and the British had at length consented to the sacrifice of Sicily, the Dutch had by their refusal to compromise on the question of security amply demonstrated their willingness to continue the war. Never again would Joseph express any doubt of their loyalty. Indeed, it would be one of the great ironies of the Grand Alliance that the United Provinces, though they had been the first to waver, would now to be among the last to desert the monarchy.

Notwithstanding the renewed firmness of the Estates General, the increasing prospects of a military stalemate now reemerged as the greatest threat to the cohesiveness of the anti-Bourbon coalition. All along France's borders the allies could wage little more than a war of attrition. For the second straight year, no progress could be expected in the Alpine valleys of the Dauphiné. On the Upper Rhine, the imperial army continued to disintegrate. George Louis had recently resigned his command, taking home the Hanoverian troops that had accompanied him to the front in 1707.[196] Though he succeeded automatically as imperial commander-in-chief, Prince Eugene had no intention of deserting the crucial military and diplomatic front in Flanders. Instead, with Joseph's permission, he appointed the mediocre General Gronsfeld to command in his absence. At the same time, he used his supreme authority to pull still more Austrian and German contingents from the Upper Rhine.[197] The transfer of these troops to Flanders helped to maintain the allies' numerical advantage over Marshal Villars's army. Following the fall of Douai, Marlborough and Eugene went on to capture Béthune, Aire, and Saint Venant. Nevertheless, Villars continued to frustrate their hopes for a final, decisive battle by refusing to commit his army except under the most favorable circumstances.

With the front in Flanders bogged down in siege warfare, the alliance resumed its gradual slide toward dissolution. Relations with Victor Amadeus took a sharp turn for the worse in July, when the emperor announced that Novara could not be transferred to Savoy until the proper procedure had been determined by the Aulic Council. At the same time, he decided to delay confirmation of the duke's claims to Langhe, also on the pretext of awaiting a judgment by the Aulic

Council. Joseph did not notify Turin of this second postponement until well into September.[198] Yet, long before he had received word from the emperor, Victor Amadeus had already taken action of his own. During August, he had contacted the French commander in the Dauphiné, Marshal Berwick, and reopened negotiations for a separate peace.[199] Despite rumors that the duke was secretly treating with Louis XIV, Vienna still remained confident that he would not desert the coalition.[200]

During the summer of 1710, Joseph feared not for the loyalty of the United Provinces, Prussia, or Savoy, each of whose designs on Habsburg or imperial territory had always given him some measure of security. Rather it was England, heretofore his strongest support within the alliance, yet, the country over which he enjoyed the least diplomatic leverage, whose ultimate intentions now caused him the greatest anxiety. Even before the collapse of the Gertruydenberg talks, it had become apparent that Queen Anne was determined to purge her ministry. The queen's decision stemmed from her intense hatred of the Whigs and particularly of the Whig Junto that had dominated the Godolphin ministry following its party's landslide victory in the 1708 elections. As long as the Whigs had enjoyed popular support, she had sullenly coexisted with them while relying on the counsel of Godolphin and Marlborough, both moderate Tories, and her close confidante, Marlborough's wife, Sarah. Yet, by the spring of 1710, the Marlboroughs had fallen out of favor with the queen. Meanwhile, the Whigs had squandered public support on the foolhardy political trial of the Tory religious zealot, Dr. Henry Sacheverell. Up to this point, the conduct of the war had played no part in the rivalry between the Whigs and Tories. Yet, as Anne and the Tories endeavored to increase their popular backing, they decided to use the war's growing unpopularity as a weapon against the Whigs. Shortly after the collapse of the Gertruydenberg talks, the Tories abandoned the cry for "no peace without Spain," partly out of a growing conviction that such a goal was unattainable, but principally out of political expediency.

The queen made her first move on 24 June by cashiering the earl of Sunderland, Marlborough's son-in-law and a powerful member of the Whig Junto. Although she immediately sent assurances to her allies insisting that Sunderland had been dismissed for purely personal reasons and that she was still determined to continue the war, Count Gallas reported that all the talk among the queen's Tory cohorts was of an early peace.[201] In addition, the imperial ambassador indicated that Anne would soon dissolve parliament and hold new elections. If the Tories were victorious, as seemed likely, nothing would stand in the way of a speedy Anglo-French settlement. The allies could do nothing to prevent the queen from carrying out her intentions. They tried nonetheless. The Dutch ambassador, Vryberg, visited Anne on 11 July and urged her not to dissolve parliament. The queen, however, angrily reproached him for meddling in her government's internal affairs.[202] On 16 July, Joseph followed with a tactfully worded letter of his own, in which he expressed the fear that further changes within the ministry or the dissolution of parliament might have a debilitating effect on the alliance.[203] At the suggestion of the inner Conference, the letter was dispatched to Eugene and Marlborough, who carefully reviewed it before sending it on to London.[204] Notwithstanding this precaution, Gallas fared no better than Vryberg. Upon delivering the letter on 11 August, he was engaged in heated debate by the queen's new advisors. Following the encounter, he reported gloomily, "My fears are greater than my hopes."[205]

The queen was not long in answering Joseph's request. On 19 August, she dismissed Godolphin, replacing him with the Tory arch-conspirator Robert Harley. One week later Gallas reported that Anne had sent an agent to Hanover to offer George Louis the command of the British army in the Low Countries following Marlborough's eventual dismissal.[206] For the moment, the duke was permitted to continue at his post. He was, however, the sole survivor. One by one the remaining Whig ministers were forced out of office. Finally, at the end of September, the queen dissolved parliament and called for new elections. Although the outcome was never in doubt, the election campaign itself gave a good indication of the future direction of England's war policy. Tory propagandists capitalized most on the growing unpopularity of the war, blaming the Whigs and Marlborough, "the butcher of Malplaquet," for prolonging it needlessly. The past actions of the allies themselves provided excellent cannon fodder for the merciless Tory broadsides. These pointed to recently published reports of the Townshend Treaty as proof of Dutch greed and of the Whigs' willingness to prolong the war solely for the purpose of expanding their ally's barrier in Flanders. They also accused the emperor of shirking his military responsibilities and criticized the former ministry for permitting Vienna to shift an increasing financial burden onto its own shoulders. As proof, the Tories cited Godolphin's approval of a request by Gallas that the maritime powers assume the recent 70,000 taler increase in recruitment subsidies promised to the king of Prussia.[207] When the balloting was over, the Tories had won two-thirds of the seats in the House of Commons.

In the week following Godolphin's dismissal, Prince Eugene had written Gallas suggesting that it was not unlikely that the Tories were already secretly treating with the French.[208] In fact, at that very moment, Gallas's own chaplain, the French agent Gualtier, was establishing contact with the Tory earl of Jersey. In undertaking separate talks, the English were seeking not only an early peace, but also greater advantages for themselves at the expense of their Dutch and Habsburg allies. They realized, however, that until a settlement could be reached with France, it was essential that they sustain England's obligations to the coalition. Only then would they be able to retain sufficient leverage in their negotiations and, at the same time, prevent a stampede of their allies to the peace table. Consequently, during the rest of the 1710 campaign, they continued to express and outwardly demonstrate their intention to continue the struggle. When the new parliament convened in November, the Tory Commons promptly voted the customary six million pounds for the next campaign.[209] By their diplomacy, the English also showed an abiding concern for the cohesiveness of the alliance. When it was learned that Charles XII had rejected the Hague Convention and vetoed attempts to enlist Crassow's corps, the queen immediately joined her allies in forming an armed neutrality league to help defend the empire against Swedish attack. To keep Victor Amadeus from concluding a separate peace, she presented him with a gift of 100,000 pounds "over and above his Subsidy, for especial Service in prosecuting the War against France."[210] In Vienna the queen's generosity was regarded with disgust as the latest sign of London's deference to the house of Savoy.[211] In fact, it was British diplomacy that was keeping Victor Amadeus from deserting the Grand Alliance.

The policies of the new Tory regime had a somewhat therapeutic effect on Joseph's own war effort. On the one hand, the emperor was encouraged by London's continuing financial and diplomatic efforts. At the same time, however, the lingering fear of a betrayal prompted him to increase the monarchy's own military commitment. Upon the urging of Count Sinzendorf, who had just returned from his long absence at The Hague, Joseph agreed to accept the queen's request that he bolster the Austrian forces fighting in Spain.[212] By so doing, he hoped to defuse Tory resentment over his reputed lethargy in prosecuting the war. In addition, he hoped to win on the battlefield what the queen and her ministers no longer considered to be attainable or worth the sacrifice. Current reports from the peninsula seemed to give substance to these expectations. Two more troop conventions with the Godolphin ministry had raised the Austrian army in Spain to over 12,000.[213] After receiving these reinforcements, Guido Starhemberg had resumed the offensive and won two major victories against Philip at Almenara and Saragossa. By the latest accounts, he was marching on Madrid. With the war in Hungary winding to a close, still more troops might be sent to the peninsula to help secure the Spanish crown for the dynasty. For the moment, however, there remained a major limitation to the number of men that could be sent there. Over the past two years, Joseph had refused to release the maritime powers from the pledge they had given in 1703 to bear the full cost of the war in Spain. Only recently the Conference had reaffirmed this policy, and in a convention concluded between Eugene and Marlborough on 29 October, the Tory regime had been obliged to undertake the same financial responsibilities that had been outlined in each of the four troop accords concluded by the Godolphin ministry.[214] For this reason, however, the British agreed to accept only 2,000 Austrians for shipment to Spain. Although this number was subsequently raised to 2,500, the emperor realized that any substantial reinforcement of the archduke's army would have to come at his own expense. At the beginning of December, he made this decision. On the recommendation of his ministers, he announced that he would dispatch 5,000 additional troops and maintain them from his own resources.[215]

"The sea powers will not be able to say that we are doing nothing for the Spanish war," boasted Count Trautson. Indeed, after years of relative neglect, the Spanish front had at last assumed primary importance in the emperor's eyes. His assistance, however, came some months too late. The fateful news reached Vienna at the beginning of the new year. Following its recent victories, the allied army had proceeded to Madrid, occupying it on 21 September. Both Starhemberg and the archduke had actually opposed making the Bourbon capital their main objective, urging instead that the army seal off the French border. Yet, they had been overruled by their Anglo-Dutch advisors. The allies realized their error soon afterward when a new French army under Marshal Vendôme passed through the Pyrenees. On 11 November they abandoned Madrid and headed back to the coast. At the town of Brihuega, only fifty miles east of the capital, Vendôme surprised and captured the English General Stanhope's corps of 5,000 men. Starhemberg managed to save the rest of his army by repelling Vendôme's subsequent attack at Villaviciosa. Nevertheless, he was obliged to hasten his retreat deep into Catalonia.

With these ill tidings, the emperor's concern shifted suddenly from the conquest of Spain to his brother's own safety. There was now general agreement in the Conference that Charles might soon be expelled from the peninsula. Even if he could maintain his foothold in Catalonia, all hope of a renewed offensive against Castile had now disappeared.[216] In a report which it presented to the emperor at the end of February, the Conference expressed its own dismay at the continued resiliency of France:

> It is almost impossible to conceive how it can be that, after Your Imperial Majesty's and your allies' arms have conducted the present war already ten whole years, always with such fortune, glory and reputation, the French enemy and its enormous strength, having been broken and brought down to the lowest depths through so many heroic victories, still as of a few months ago is again arisen and now in the position not to receive terms from the allies but to prescribe them instead and everywhere spread its accustomed arrogance and fear.[217]

At London and The Hague, Joseph's allies were reaching the same conclusions. Never noted for their support of the war in Spain, the Dutch were now telling Sinzendorf that "there remains no other way than to win back Spain through France."[218] Across the Channel, the queen was giving Gallas her assurances that Brihuega had excited, rather than dampened, her desire to conquer Spain.[219] She was, of course, being less than candid. So long as Starhemberg's successes held open the possibility of victory in the peninsula, she and her Tory ministers had seen no reason to jettison the Hague preliminaries. In his secret negotiations with Gualtier, Jersey had offered no concrete concessions to Louis XIV. However, with the news of Starhemberg's flight to the coast, their patience came to an end. On 23 December, Jersey informed Gualtier that England was now willing to leave Philip in possession of Spain and the Indies.[220]

As the war entered its final phase, Joseph could be sure of securing only what he already possessed.

VII

Conclusion

The emperor could do nothing without his allies.
—Heinrich Wilhelm Count Wilczek

Although the talks between Jersey and Gualtier were conducted in the greatest secrecy, it was not long before word of them reached Vienna. As in the past, the disheartening news was transmitted by the duke of Marlborough, most probably from intelligence he had received from his own agents at Versailles. While they were not privy to the details of the secret talks, Joseph and his ministers could "easily anticipate what disastrous consequences these would have" on the dynasty's war aims. Arriving as it did amid reports of further setbacks in Spain, Marlborough's revelation encouraged a swell of pessimism within the Conference. In a report which it handed to the emperor on 24 February, the ministry painted the present diplomatic and military situation in the blackest hues. It spoke not only of the imminent loss of Spain but also of the continuing deterioration of the Italian and German fronts, and even predicted that Marshal Villars would soon lead a second descent on Swabia. Pointing to the recent outbreak of hostilities between Turkey and Russia, the Conference concluded by expressing the fear that the Northern War would result either in a Turko-Swedish occupation of Poland and Saxony or in the emergence of Russia as a powerful menace in the Balkans.[1]

In fact, such pessimism was unwarranted. The empire was not destined to relive the events of 1707. Aware that time was on his side, Louis XIV was intent on remaining on the defensive during the coming campaign. Not to do so would be to jeopardize the present military stalemate and the rapprochement with England. In the east, Charles XII had already decided to spend the rest of the winter at Bender. With the arrival of summer, the sultan would desert him by concluding a favorable peace settlement with the tsar. Indeed, only Spain was lost to the dynasty, and in witnessing its loss, the Conference had momentar-

215

ily overlooked the monarchy's strong position elsewhere on the continent. Even before the advent of spring, this was being further strengthened by some timely diplomacy. By April the peace embassy of
Seifullah Aga and Count Pálffy's successful negotiations were settling
the monarchy's affairs east of Vienna. In Italy relations with Savoy
were normalized during March, following Joseph's decision to concede
the investiture of Langhe. After having spent the past two summers in
his capital, Victor Amadeus now agreed to resume personal command
of the forces fighting in the Dauphiné. Together with the secret decision to ransom Comacchio to the pope, Joseph's belated announcement that Langhe would soon be surrendered to Victor Amadeus
ensured the emperor against a revival of princely opposition to his
leadership within the peninsula. Joseph also strengthened his hand
among the loyal princelings of the Nördlingen Association. Thanks
largely to the insistence of Sinzendorf, who had returned to The Hague
in October, the Dutch agreed to recall Count Rechteren from Germany
and shelve temporarily their projected alliance with the association. In
its place, Lothair Francis accepted Joseph's demand that he be admitted to any future treaty as head of the Austrian Circle. The emperor's
influence within the association was further strengthened by the death
in January of Elector John Hugo of Trier. He was succeeded by
Charles of Lorraine, Joseph's unsuccessful candidate in the 1706
election in Münster and a determined advocate of Habsburg interests
in the empire.

In the spring of 1711, the monarchy's defensive bastions in Italy,
Germany, and Hungary were all secure. That faraway Spain could not
be salvaged was already apparent. It was to be in Vienna itself,
however, that the dynasty's aspirations were dealt the most telling
blow. In the previous year, Joseph had ordered that steps be taken to
establish a *Pestfront* along the military border with Turkey—a system
of quarantine posts aimed at preventing the future spread of plague
from the Balkans into the Habsburg lands.[2] Despite these precautions,
however, a smallpox epidemic had broken out in Vienna in the closing
months of 1710.[3] By the beginning of November, it had spread to
court, with both Count Trautson and the Princess Dietrichstein coming down with the illness.[4] Yet, the greatest concern was for the
emperor himself. Unlike his younger brother, Joseph had never contracted the disease during his childhood, a fact that had caused some
anxiety among his ministers in recent years.[5] To reduce the chances of
contracting it now, he secluded himself for six weeks. At the beginning
of December, he took the further step of moving his quarters into the
southwest or so-called Spanish wing of the Hofburg. Only shortly
before Christmas did he reemerge from seclusion and begin again to
attend the councils of state.[6]

Yet, the epidemic had not run its course. In mid-March the
disease struck at court a second time.[7] On this occasion, however,
Joseph did not take further precautions. On 7 April he was himself

taken slightly ill, albeit not sufficiently either to miss the four-hour Conference on Comacchio that was held on the following morning or to postpone a subsequent afternoon jaunt into the Vienna woods. Upon his return from the hunt, he had grown perceptibly weaker but attributed his condition to the exertions of the day and the excesses of his Easter diet. It was only on the ninth, when Joseph awoke with a fever and a slight rash, and on the following day, when the marks spread rapidly throughout his body, that smallpox began to be feared.[8] By the eleventh, there was no longer any question that the emperor had at last contracted the dread disease. Yet, for a man just three months from his thirty-third birthday, there could still be hope. By the fourteenth, Joseph's fever had fallen off considerably, and he had begun to regain his strength. Trautson, himself so recently immunized, was permitted to visit his master on each of the next two days and was able to report that his condition was improving steadily. Despite these hopeful tidings, the emperor refused to permit Prince Eugene into his chambers early on the sixteenth, just prior to the latter's departure for the front, out of fear that he might also be infected.[9] A few hours after the field marshal had left Vienna, Joseph's fever rose sharply. By late evening, he was delirious. At half past ten on the following morning, 17 April 1711, Joseph I died.

As the news of the young emperor's death spread throughout the city, the Privy Conference met to make arrangements for an orderly succession. It was decided to summon Charles from Spain. At the same time, the ministers adopted Seilern's judgment that the Empress Eleonore serve in his absence as regent. The change in leadership was not without some immediate and unsettling effects. As one of her first acts, the regent postponed the restitution of Comacchio, pending Charles's return from Spain. Since the inner Conference was determined to keep Joseph's secret understanding with the pope from Eleonore, her brother John William, and the other German princes, it was helpless to forestall her action.[10] The empress was also quick to vent her long-standing indignation at the moral turpitude of Joseph and his friends. Leopold von Lamberg had escaped her wrath, having passed away only five weeks before the emperor. Joseph's last mistress was not so lucky. Marianne Pálffy was forced to return the fortune in jewels that she had received from the late emperor, forbidden to appear in the presence of Eleonore or Amalia, and eventually compelled to marry as an alternative to being expelled from court.[11] Initially the regent also sought to punish Count Pálffy for his daughter's indiscretions by recalling him from the negotiations at Szatmár. Since Pálffy, Locher, and Károlyi were presently trying to conclude a final settlement before knowledge of Joseph's death became known to the rebels, Eleonore's notification was received with the greatest consternation.[12] Following an appeal from Locher, however, the regent permitted Pálffy to complete his mission.

While Eleonore might undo her son's work in Italy and Hungary, it

was already beyond her or anyone else's power to save the situation in
Spain. It was in vain that she tried to hold England to its coalition
vows by admitting it as a party to a new perpetual alliance between
Austria, the Nördlingen Association, and the United Provinces. The
Tory government merely neglected to ratify the treaty.[13] Meanwhile,
Joseph's death brought the loss of Spain one step closer to reality by
confronting the monarchy's allies with the resurrection of the European empire of Charles V. Faced with this alternative to a Bourbon
succession in Spain, most of its allies lost their enthusiasm for the
Habsburg cause in the peninsula. Joseph's former ministers were not
blind to the situation. When in the days following his death, the
visiting Tory earl of Peterborough suggested to Wratislaw that Victor
Amadeus be given Spain and Charles be permitted to round off his
Italian possessions with Piedmont and Savoy, the Bohemian chancellor reported it to the archduke with the greatest enthusiasm.[14] Unfortunately, Peterborough's proposal, like so many of his earlier military
initiatives in Spain, came without the foreknowledge or approval of his
superiors. Nor did Charles himself entertain any illusions about the
ultimate fate of his Spanish "subjects." Even before learning of his
brother's death, he had written Wratislaw echoing Vienna's judgment
that "the allies will sustain not more than one or two campaigns and
then conclude a damaging peace" and urging that, while Spain was
surely lost, Italy had to be saved for the dynasty.[15] Indeed, when the
news of Joseph's death reached him at Barcelona, the archduke must
have pondered the cruel irony of his fate. It had been in that very city
nearly two centuries earlier that the future Emperor Charles V had
received word of the death of his grandfather, Maximilian I, and of his
succession to the Austrian Habsburg lands. In both cases, the news
implied an eventual journey to Vienna and election as Holy Roman
emperor. Furthermore, for the citizens of Barcelona both in 1519 and
1711, the significance of their ruler's succession was greeted with the
greatest misgivings; then as now, Austria was the heart of the dynasty,
not Spain. Yet, it was not the similarity but rather the disparity
between the fate of these two men that presently gave the archduke
cause for regret—and his Catalan partisans cause for panic. Whereas
Charles V had left Spain willingly, the archduke did so only with the
greatest reluctance, for he realized that there was little chance of his
ever returning.

   The ease with which the archduke was elected to succeed his brother
in October 1711 as Emperor Charles VI attested to the fact that Spain
was no longer within the dynasty's grasp. The German electors, who
would have surely opposed placing a Spanish king on the imperial
throne, unanimously supported the archduke's candidacy. Clement XI
also worked for Charles's election, partly because he was still seeking
the transfer of Comacchio and partly because he foresaw the day when
he no longer need recognize the archduke as king of Spain.[16] It was

England, however, that could most easily dismiss the chimera of a reunion of the empire of Charles V. As it joined with the Dutch in securing the archduke's election, the Harley ministry continued to press on with its secret talks with the French. To gather popular support for the eventual abandonment of Spain, the Tory press meanwhile made maximum use of the threat to the balance of power that would be posed by Charles's succession to both the Spanish and Danubian monarchies. Hence, Anne and her ministers were spared the embarrassment of disclosing that they had conceded Spain to Philip V some months prior to Joseph's death. Of course, they continued to prop up the alliance and dispense huge sums of money for the war effort, just as they had in the second half of 1710.[17] Victor Amadeus received another extraordinary gift of 100,000 pounds, and Frederick was paid his new 100,000 taler recruitment subsidy from the British exchequer.[18] Nevertheless, what was obvious to the caretaker government in Vienna could not be hidden from the other members of the Grand Alliance. Immediately after Joseph's death, John William opened secret talks with Versailles in an attempt to save the Upper Palatinate. He was followed in July by Prussia, and in the autumn by the Dutch.[19] Victor Amadeus did not undertake negotiations of his own only because he realized that the British would safeguard his interests. The replacement of Marlborough by the Tory duke of Ormonde in December 1711 marked the end of British military participation in the war. Although the Dutch resolved to carry on the struggle, their crushing defeat at Denain finally inclined them toward peace. A peace congress having convened at Utrecht in January 1712, a settlement was finally concluded fifteen months later on 11 April 1713. Signing on the same day were England, the United Provinces, Prussia, Savoy, and Portugal. Only the Habsburg monarchy and the empire remained at war.

Without the assistance of his allies, however, Charles VI was incapable of altering the judgment at Utrecht. At the Peace of Rastatt (6 March 1714), the monarchy received nothing beyond what it already held in its possession: Milan, Mantua, Finale, the Presidii, Naples, Sardinia, and most of Belgium.[20] Meanwhile, for the Holy Roman Empire, in whose name a second treaty was concluded at Baden six months later, there were no territorial gains whatsoever; rather, peace was signed on the basis of the *status quo ante bellum*. Even the banned electors, Max Emanuel and Joseph Clement, were reinstated with all their titles and possessions. In returning the Upper Palatinate to his Wittelsbach cousin, Elector John William received the sum of one million florins as compensation from the emperor.

For the Habsburg dynasty, the peace settlement with France had fallen short of its maximum war aims. Spain and the Indies had been lost to Philip V; Sicily, the last jewel in the Italian necklace, had been secured for Savoy by the British. Nevertheless, the treaties of Utrecht,

Rastatt, and Baden had abandoned nothing that was crucial to the interests of the monarchy itself. Germany and Italy continued to provide an adequate buffer with France. In fact, with the acquisition of Belgium, Naples, and Sardinia, the monarchy had assumed new responsibilities that clearly went beyond the scope of its traditional interests and commitments. Although Charles was later able to reduce the exposure of his Italian possessions by exchanging Sardinia for Sicily, the greatly expanded Habsburg empire remained, if anything, overextended and far more vulnerable to aggression on its periphery than it had been in the past.

The reason for this lay not only in the monarchy's new geographical expanse but also in the changing relationship with the rest of Europe. In the opening years of the War of the Spanish Succession, it had benefited greatly from the extensive military assistance of its allies, and particularly of England. Blenheim had been gained with British troops, Turin with British money; yet both had served Austrian interests almost exclusively. With the continuing triumphs of Joseph's reign, however, the crises of the past were forgotten and the realities of the future began to exercise an increasing influence over the allies. Both Savoy and the German princes no longer envisioned a French threat to their own security. The maritime powers ceased to speak of a French menace to the balance of power. Rather, they looked on the growing acquisitions of Emperor Joseph as well as the increasing independence of his own foreign and military policies, and began to consider more closely their own interests. In this sense, the secret Anglo-French peace talks were only the logical result of a process that had brought the Habsburg monarchy and its allies from a grave military crisis to an unprecedented succession of conquests. Joseph's own policies largely encouraged the allies to go their separate ways by failing to take their own war aims sufficiently into account. Over these six years, he devoted the monarchy's limited resources to the pursuit of specifically Austrian interests. This was the case in Hungary, and also in Italy, where the maritime powers still remembered the Treaty of Milan and Daun's expedition to Naples during the otherwise disastrous 1707 campaign. Throughout the struggle, he took his allies for granted, relying increasingly on British money and diplomacy to maintain the alliance and provide him with the support he needed in critical situations. Only with the revelation of the Townshend Treaty did Vienna at last realize that England, like the rest of its allies, was becoming more and more responsive to the consideration of its own national interests. Having failed to anticipate this trend within the coalition, Joseph took remedial action during 1710 to satiate the demands of his allies. Nevertheless, with France everywhere on the defensive and the allies already in control of Italy and the Low Countries, it was becoming increasingly difficult to justify continued vigilance in the prosecution of the war. This was especially the case in England and the United

Provinces, where the electorate was more keenly aware of domestic fiscal issues and immediate national interests than it was of the long range impact of a Bourbon succession in Spain.

Joseph's last chance to forestall disaster came at Gertruydenberg, where he attempted unsuccessfully to secure a victorious peace by the sacrifice of Articles 4 and 37. Having failed here, he had no choice but to follow the lead of his allies and hope that they would not cast him adrift while pursuing their own separate interests. As the Conference had already pointed out to him on the eve of the peace talks, there could be no alternative to the Anglo-Dutch alliance so long as France continued to threaten European peace and security.[21] Indeed, even after England's desertion and the conclusion of peace, Charles VI was left with little choice but to preserve his ties with England and the United Provinces, even though both these powers presently saw no need to strengthen or maintain the sprawling Habsburg monarchy and intended, as Max Braubach points out, to extend their favor to the continent's smaller states.[22]

Meanwhile, the Habsburg monarchy was as yet unprepared militarily to face diplomatic isolation and withstand alone the future aggressions of its neighbors. Aside from the establishment of the Vienna City Bank, which was in itself a milestone in the evolution of public credit operations, the program of fiscal and administrative reform which Joseph initiated in the *Erblande* remained incomplete. Although he had helped to streamline the bureaucracy and increase both fiscal and military revenue, the estates retained control over the levying of the *Contributio* and, hence, the final say in the raising of taxes. Like his foreign allies, the estates of the *Erblande* had provided Joseph with considerable assistance out of a shared appreciation of the threat posed by the monarchy's enemies. As with his allies, however, their generosity lasted only so long as the crisis itself. Once they perceived the moment of danger to have passed, the crown no longer enjoyed sufficient leverage to enforce its requests for their assistance. This was made evident by the gradual decrease in the size of the *Contributio* after 1706, a phenomenon that is only partly attributable to the progressive impoverishment of the *Erblande*. Yet, as a great power with new and far-flung territorial commitments, the Habsburg monarchy could not afford to base its defense on the consensus either of the *Erblande*'s estates or of its foreign allies. The crown had to gain full control over the resources of the monarchy, and of the *Erblande* in particular; only then could it utilize them whenever it sensed the need, rather than when the estates deemed it necessary. Such a coup could be accomplished only in peacetime, when the crown could give full attention to internal reform and to the inevitable resistance of the estates and their dependent bureaucracies, without having to fear for the effects of their disobedience and obstructionism on the course of a foreign war.

Herein lies the double tragedy of Joseph's death: while he was not blessed with peace, he was succeeded by his brother Charles, who had neither the vision, the energy, nor the boldness to attempt major reform; at the same time, Joseph's premature death saddled Charles with the need to secure the estates' recognition of an orderly female succession, a task which he needlessly complicated by abrogating the *Pactum Mutuae Successionis* of 1703 and disinheriting Joseph's two daughters. Internal reforms that Joseph might have completed—the abolition of the separate Fiscal and War offices; the introduction of a universal excise; the drafting of a higher, fixed quota for the *Contributio;* perhaps even a modification of the *Robot*—had to wait a half century for Maria Theresa and Joseph II, and then only after the loss of Silesia had changed dramatically the course of central European history.

Despite the problems which the Habsburg monarchy faced following the death of Joseph I, the accomplishments of his reign remain both considerable and significant. At the time of his succession, virtually the entire Spanish monarchy was still in the hands of the Bourbon powers. Hostile armies were poised on the borders of the Tyrol in the south and across the breadth of the Hungarian plain in the east. The monarchy's finances were in no position to contribute decisively to the further prosecution of the war. By 1711 this picture had changed totally. To the dismay of the pope, Austrian hegemony in Italy was already an established fact, with or without the sanction of imperial authority. The diplomatic history of the peninsula in the next two decades would bear this out. Notwithstanding the treaty of January 1709, the final judgment of the cardinals' commission, and the frequent promises of both Joseph and Charles, Clement XI was to die without securing the return of Comacchio. Only in 1724, three years after his death, was the Ferrarese town returned to papal sovereignty. Upon the succession of a Bourbon prince in Parma in 1731, both France and Spain sought an imperial patent of investiture from Charles VI, despite the ruling of the cardinals' commission in favor of papal suzerainty. Such were the realities of Habsburg hegemony in Italy.

In Hungary, Joseph had prevailed against the national coalition assembled by Prince Rákóczi and effected a reconciliation between crown and country, albeit at the price of perpetuating the kingdom's autonomy and accepting constitutional limitations on royal authority. Although this solution contrasted sharply with both the European-wide trend against corporate sovereignty and Joseph's own attempts in the *Erblande* to create a single, centralized administration, it corresponded well with the realities of Hungary's unique political position in the Habsburg monarchy. The Hungarian nation could be expected to oppose any diminution of its sovereignty and autonomy, especially so long as the crown persisted in viewing it as an essentially foreign appendage. As Joseph's shabby treatment of his royal ministers demonstrates, he was by education and outlook incapable of conceiving and initiating a well-coordinated policy of *douce violence* aimed at disarming the suspicions of the Magyar nobility. Given these limitations a political compromise was the only viable *modus vivendi*. The wisdom of the peace of Szatmár was destined to be borne out by Joseph's two immediate successors, who adhered strictly to its provisions, as well as by future kings whose attempts to subvert the country's constitution resulted in widespread disaffection, if not open revolt. Meanwhile, the achievement of a permanent peace between crown and country enabled Hungary to begin a remarkable economic and demographic recovery that would last through the end of the century.

Within Germany, Joseph's legacy was more limited and less durable, though no less significant. During his reign, he was successful in frustrating the growing territorial ambitions of the larger states—particularly those of Brandenburg-Prussia—while at the same time managing to keep them bound to the Grand Alliance. Nevertheless, the empire remained a political body too small to accommodate the growing cancer within. The relentless growth and ambitions of the lay electors made a perpetual continuation of their essentially symbiotic relationship impossible. Joseph realized this was already the case with Brandenburg-Prussia and initiated the fateful policy of opposing its further expansion. Whether Prussia could be contained, as had the Palatinate at White Mountain or Bavaria at Blenheim, remained to be determined. Nevertheless, yet another life struggle between the Habsburg emperor and one of his vassals was already inevitable.

Notwithstanding the verdict of the Silesian wars and the other setbacks which it suffered between 1733 and 1748, the monarchy was destined nonetheless to establish itself as a great continental power largely because of its triumphs during Joseph's reign. The secure frontiers that he had acquired made it possible for his successors to weather these defeats until the Theresian reforms had enabled the crown to utilize more fully the monarchy's economic resources. Despite its position in the heart of Europe, the Habsburg state continued to benefit from this security for over two centuries until the forces of nationalism and the disappearance of the last of these buffers made its dismemberment possible.

In searching for an explanation of the dramatic successes of Joseph's reign, one must first look beyond the borders of the Habsburg monarchy. It should not be forgotten that it was the dynamics of balance of power diplomacy—in this case the fear of Louis XIV and the monarchy's own obvious weakness—that was the decisive factor in the formation of the Grand Alliance. The entry of England and the United Provinces into the war made it possible for the emperor to contest the will of Charles II with some chance of success. Moreover, Victor Amadeus's decision to oppose Bourbon hegemony in Italy transformed the expulsion of the French army from the peninsula from a remote fantasy into a dramatic reality. Battle luck was also an important ingredient in the allies' success, just as the sudden drought that began with Malplaquet was instrumental in causing the collapse of the coalition.

Beyond these crucial elements, the role played by the emperor and his ministers also assumes great importance. Unlike Leopold, Joseph did not lack the initiative to make bold or difficult decisions and act upon them with dispatch. At the same time, his policies were moderated by a sense of pragmatism that generally characterized his conduct of both foreign and domestic affairs. Like most of his contemporaries, he would resist stubbornly any agreement or action that promised to sacrifice his own personal prestige or dynastic interests. Yet, in his diplomacy, the emperor was always willing to make compromises that brought him closer to his main objectives. His capitulation to Charles XII at Altranstädt and the lenient terms that he granted the pope in 1709 and the Hungarian rebels two years later illustrate this point.

The objectives themselves were well-defined by priority. More than any previous Habsburg, Joseph placed the creation of a strong, secure Danubian state ahead of all imperial, dynastic, and confessional interests. Hence, from the very beginning of the reign, Italy and Hungary remained the emperor's two principal concerns, as befitted their proximity to the heart of the monarchy. In successfully pursuing his goals on these two fronts, he was obliged to sacrifice his interests elsewhere on the continent. With the resources of the Austrian and Bavarian Circles being siphoned off into Hungary and Italy, the imperial army was never able to recover Germany's lost lands in Alsace and Lorraine. Meanwhile, nowhere were the effects of Joseph's priorities more apparent than in far-off Spain. Only after the conquest of Italy did he begin to concern himself with the purely dynastic interests which Spain represented. Even then the continuing troubles in Hungary prevented him from sending large numbers of troops to his brother's aid until the end of the reign. Perhaps more fatal yet to the archduke's cause was the critical decision of December 1708 to dispatch Guido Starhemberg to Catalonia in place of Prince Eugene. Notwithstanding Starhemberg's considerable skills, only the great Eugene could have commanded the complete obedience of Charles's allied advisors and withstood their disastrous strategy of marching directly on Madrid. Only in his peace diplomacy was Joseph able to give full support to his brother. Having already secured all of the monarchy's war aims except Sicily, he had little to lose in holding out for the whole of Spain. Indeed, at the time, there appeared no reason for the emperor to moderate these demands, especially since the awarding of compensation for Philip in part of Italy or Spain would merely have endangered the dynasty's remaining holdings in either peninsula. Notwithstanding Joseph's diplomatic initiatives at the Vatican, The Hague, and Gertruydenberg, the fact remains that his military policies predetermined the loss of Spain just as they made possible the reconquest of Italy and Hungary. In laying out his grand strategy, Joseph I sacrificed for all time the universal monarchy of Charles V—and the lifelong dream of the future Charles VI—for the new reality of a defensible Danubian empire.

In speaking of Joseph's policies, however, it is impossible to over-look the work of his ministers. It is difficult to ascertain precisely how great a share of the monarchy's foreign and domestic policy originated in the mind of the monarch, largely because no records were ever kept of individual meetings between Joseph and his ministers. There were instances in which the emperor resisted the advice of his ministers and pursued policies which were clearly of his own making. Nevertheless, in the overwhelming number of cases in which the emperor and the Conference were in general agreement, it is difficult to trace the exact origins of ideas and, hence, of policy. Given Joseph's passion for hunting and women, and the large number of preliminary Conferences that met in his absence, it is certainly safe to attribute the great bulk of the contribution to the ministers themselves.

In this light, the emperor appears more as an arbiter rather than as the dynamic force in the formulation of state policy. Although he performed this function with discretion and wisdom, Joseph's suc-cesses hinged to a much greater degree upon the ability of the ministers themselves. In this sense, he made perhaps the greatest single contribu-tion to the upward fortunes of the Habsburg monarchy during the critical years of the War of the Spanish Succession. Upon succeeding as emperor, he ferreted out the incompetents of his father's regime and replaced them with men of proven ability. He valued and supported their counsel to the exclusion of all other figures at court, whether the representatives of the estates, foreign diplomats, the two empresses, his ambitious favorite Lamberg, or his own mistresses. To be sure Joseph was not without his flaws. His moral fiber was thin at best. Poor relationships with his parents, wife, and brother indicated a certain excess of temperament and dearth of compassion. Yet, given the nature of the emperor's ties with his ministers, it is difficult to envision how his shortcomings could have adversely affected the conduct of state affairs. Indeed, even his own detachment from the intricacies of policy-making had the advantages of encouraging the exchange of different viewpoints within the Conference and of permitting policy to become the work of several authors, rather than the creation of a single mind.

Further compounding the tragedy of Joseph's death was the break-up of much of the ministry. Prince Salm, the most powerful figure at the beginning of the reign, had already left court in September 1709 and died a short time thereafter. His great adversary Count Wratislaw followed him to the grave in December 1712, barely a year after Charles's return from Spain. Joseph's last lord high steward, Trautson, was replaced by Charles's childhood tutor, Prince Liechtenstein.[23] When Baron Seilern died in 1715 at the ripe age of 69, only four of Joseph's ministers remained at court: Prince Eugene, whose absence at the front had limited his influence in political matters; Gundaker Starhemberg, who had never played a major role in foreign or military policy; Sinzendorf, perhaps the least creative of the Josephine ministers; and Schönborn, unquestionably the least powerful among them. Together with Emperor Charles's Spanish *camarilla,* these men would dominate the domestic and foreign affairs of the Habsburg monarchy over the next three decades. Only with Maria Theresa would the interregnum come to an end.

Notes

Abbreviations: *Archival Sources*

	Allgemeines Verwaltungsarchiv, Vienna
	Graf Harrach'sches Familienarchiv: 206, 211, 220, 242, 246, 271, 299, 315
	Archivo Histórico Nacional, Madrid
	Sección de Estado: 8692
FSSA	Fürstlich Salm-Salm'sches Archiv, Anholt, Germany
	III: 54, 59a–61, 78, 128, 132, 149
	Geheimes Staatsarchiv, Munich
	Kasten Blau: 45 (Nr. 12–13), 404
HHSA	Haus- Hof- und Staatsarchiv, Vienna
FK	Familienkorrespondenz
	A: 16, 18, 22, 33, 51, 54
	Sammelbände: 96
	Familienakten: 96
GK	Grosse Korrespondenz: 40, 65–67, 69–74d, 90b
LH	Lothringisches Hausarchiv: 18, 42, 151, 166
MEA	Mainz Erzkanzler Archiv
	Korrespondenz:89–92
ÖA	Österreichische Akten
	Österreich Staat: 2
	Böhmen, Schlesische Akten: 4–5
RHR	Reichshofrat
	Verfassungsakten, Reichshofrat: 5, 11, 26
RK	Reichskanzlei
	Kleinere Reichsstände: 346, 471
V	Vorträge: 6b
	Weisungen nach München: 1b
SA	Staatenabteilung
	Bavarica: 67a
	Brandenburgica: 29–30
	Rom: 85–86, 93
	Sardinien: 28, 35, 40, 44
	Schweden: 18a–18b

SK   Staatskanzlei
          Diplomatische Korrespondenz, Kleinere Betreffe: 4,
          16
          Instructionen: 7, 13
V   Vorträge: 12–16, 51
UA   Ungarische Akten: 186–93, 431d
          Houghton Library, Cambridge, Massachusetts
SCC   Stepney-Cardonnel correspondence, 1702–10
          Magyar Országos Levéltár, Budapest
          Nádor Levéltár: 3, 7
          Sinzendorf Familien-Archiv, Ernstbrunn, Austria
          3/1, 3/4

I. Introduction

Opening quote: Salm to Joseph, 28 January 1703, FSSA, III, 59b.

II. The Erblande: *Administration and Finance*

Opening quote: Salm to Wratislaw, 27 March 1705, replying to a reference by Wratislaw, HHSA, SK, Diplomatische Korrespondenz, Kleinere Betreffe 16.

1. Thomas Fellner and Heinrich Kretschmayr, *Die österreichische Zentralverwaltung* (Vienna, 1907), I, i, 156, iii, 3–4.

2. A. P. Pribram, "Die niederösterreichischen Stände und die Krone in der Zeit Kaiser Leopolds I.," *Mitteilungen des Instituts für österreichische Geschichtsforschung*, XIV (1893), 603–6; H. I. Bidermann, "Die Wiener Stadt-Bank," *Archiv für österreichische Geschichte*, XX (1859), 344, 404.

3. Otto Hintze, "Der österreichische und der preussische Beamtenstatt im 17. und 18. Jahrhundert," *Historische Zeitschrift* (1901), 409–10, 424–25; Viktor Thiel, "Die innerösterreichische Zentralverwaltung 1564–1749," *Archiv für österreichische Geschichte*, III (1930), 550; Bidermann, "Stadt-Bank," 343.

4. John P. Spielman, *Leopold I of Austria* (New Brunswick, N.J., 1977), 19, 27.

5. Dolfin 9 December 1708 report, Alfred Ritter von Arneth, *Die Relationen der Botschafter Venedigs über Österreich im achtzehnten Jahrhundert* (Vienna, 1863), 2.

6. Casimir Freschot, *Mémoires de la Cour de Vienne* (Cologne, 1705), 105.

7. Corner 16 March 1690 report, Venier 11 December 1692 report, Ruzini 19 December 1699 report, Joseph Fiedler, *Die Relationen der Botschafter Venedigs über Deutschland und Österreich im siebzehnten Jahrhundert* (Vienna, 1867), II, 277, 312, 390.

8. Ruzini 19 December 1699 report, Fiedler, *Relationen*, II, 390; Maréchal de Villars, *Mémoires du Maréchal de Villars*, I (Paris, 1884), 292, 320.

9. Venier 11 December 1692 report, Ruzini 19 December 1699 report, Fiedler, *Relationen*, II, 312, 390; Villars, 292.

10. Villars, 320; Max Braubach, *Prinz Eugen von Savoyen* (Vienna, 1963–65), I, 287.

11. Salm to Leopold, n.d., FSSA, III 60.

12. Leopold to Marco D'Aviano, 18 April 1698, Onno Klopp, *Corrispondenza epistolare tra Leopoldo I. imperatore ed il P. Marco D'Aviano capuccino* (Graz, 1888), 324.

13. Ruzini 19 December 1699 report, Fiedler, *Relationen,* II, 392; Braubach, *Prinz Eugen,* II, 427; Oswald Redlich, *Das Werden einer Grossmacht. Österreich von 1700 bis 1740,* (4th ed. (Vienna, 1962), 55.

14. Bartholdi May 1705 pro memoria (misdated 12 November 1705), Arnold Berney, *König Friedrich I. und das Haus Habsburg (1701-1707)* (Berlin, 1927), 255.

15. Pedro Voltes Bou, *Barcelona durante el gobierno del Archiduque Carlos de Austria* (Barcelona, 1963), I, 12; William Coxe, *History of the House of Austria* (London, 1847), III, 1.

16. Eduard Vehse, *Memoirs of the Court of Austria* (Philadelphia, n.d.), II, 83–85; Braubach, *Prinz Eugen,* I, 287–88.

17. *Feldzüge des Prinzen Eugen von Savoyen* (Vienna, 1867–92), III, 56; Redlich, *Weltmacht des Barock. Österreich in der Zeit Kaiser Leopolds I.* (Vienna, 1961), 398.

18. Joseph to John William, 26 February 1701, Adolf Hilsenbeck, *Johann Wilhelm, Kurfürst von der Pfalz von Ryswicker Frieden bis zum spanischen Erbfolgekrieg 1698-1701* (Munich, 1905), 35.

19. *Ibid.;* Joseph to Louis William, 28 August, 3 October 1701, Philipp Röder von Diersburg, *Kriegs-und Staatschriften des Markgrafen Ludwig Wilhelm von Baden* (Karlsruhe, 1850), I, 44, 47.

20. "Everyone believes that the emperor ought to give your majesty more responsibility." Salm to Joseph, n.d., FSSA, III 59b; Parisot to Charles of Lorraine, 22 January 1703, HHSA, LH 51.

21. Joseph to Louis William, 18 April, 19 July, Leopold to Louis William, 7 July 1703, Röder, I, 152, 180, 176.

22. "The whole blame for all our misfortune and [for the] delay of all business rests with our two presidents and so long as they remain, I see no solution. My most important task now is to persuade the emperor to dismiss them. There is good cause for hope but . . . unless it takes place soon, it will be too late." Joseph to Louis William, 18 April 1703, Röder, I, 152.

23. Salm to Joseph, 31 October 1704, HHSA, RK, Kleinere Reichsstände 471.

24. Braubach, *Prinz Eugen,* I, 365, 445–46.

25. Max Grunwald, *Samuel Oppenheimer und sein Kreis* (Vienna, 1913), 98, 141.

26. Braubach, *Prinz Eugen,* I, 366.

27. Franz Fr. von Mensi, *Die Finanzen Österreichs von 1701 bis 1740* (Vienna, 1890), 92.

28. *Ibid.,* 31, 94–100.

29. *Ibid.,* 95–100; Whitworth to Harley, 29 December 1703, Ernö Simonyi, ed., *Angol diplomatiai iratok. II. Rákóczi Ferencz korára* (Pest, 1871–1877), I, 86.

30. Mensi, 327–28, 332–33; Braubach, *Prinz Eugen,* II, 30, 399. To Prince Salm belongs the honor of being the first person to hand his private silver over to the government. Whitworth to Harley, 19 January 1704, Simonyi, I, 112.

31. Mensi, 93–94, 99–100, 166; Hugo Hantsch, *Reichsvizekanzler Friedrich Karl Graf von Schönborn (1674-1746)* (Augsburg, 1929), 69.

32. Mensi, 93, 98–100, 103. It was this desperate situation which prompted Prince Eugene to make the famous, if somewhat exaggerated comment, that "if the whole monarchy were reduced to the last extremity and were to perish unless 50,000 florins or even less could be raised immediately, I can assure your excellency that it could not be prevented from happening" to Guido Starhemberg, 3 October 1703, *Feldzüge,* V, Supplement, 126.

33. Bidermann, "Stadt-Bank," 351–53; Mensi, 180, 183–85; Fellner and Kretschmayr, I, i, 97–98.

34. Fellner and Kretschmayr, I, i, 100–101.

35. *Ibid.,* 101, 106–7, "Unvorgreifliche Gedanken über den gegenwärtigen Zustand," 10 March 1704, iii, 41; Mensi, 189ff.

36. Fellner and Kretschmayr, I, i, 102–3, 106; Mensi, 191–205.

37. Salm to Wratislaw, 13 February 1705, HHSA, SK, Diplomatische Korrespondenz, Kleinere Betreffe 16; Leopold to Harrach, 1 March 1704, Allgemeines Verwaltungsarchiv, Graf Harrach'sches Familienarchiv 211; Braubach, *Prinz Eugen,* II, 35.

38. Beschluss of 12 April 1704 Conference, *Feldzüge,* VI, 727–35; Braubach, *Prinz Eugen,* II, 43–44, 50–51.

39. Braubach, *Prinz Eugen,* II, 35.

40. Stepney to Cardonnel, 4 August 1703, Houghton Library, SCC.

41. Salm to Joseph, 31 October 1704, HHSA, RK, Kleinere Reichsstände 471; Stepney to Harley, 10, 17 December 1704, Simonyi, I, 590, 596; Braubach, *Prinz Eugen,* II, 99–100, 416.

42. Stepney to Harley, 20 December 1704, Simonyi, I, 598.

43. Stepney to Harley, 10 January 1705, *ibid.* 623; Wratislaw to Charles, 22 February 1705, *Feldzüge,* VII, 545.

44. Stepney to Harley, 14, 17, 21 January 1705, Simonyi, I, 632–38.

45. Joseph Maurer, *Cardinal Leopold Graf Kollonitsch* (Innsbruck, 1887), 397.

46. Salm to Wratislaw, 6 February 1705, HHSA, SK, Diplomatische Korrespondenz, Kleinere Betreffe 16; Joseph to Salm, 14 March 1705, FSSA, III 59b.

47. Stepney to Cardonnel, 26 November 1704, 14 February 1705, Houghton, SCC; Wratislaw to Charles, 22 February 1705, *Feldzüge,* VII, 545; Braubach, *Prinz Eugen,* II, 102–3.

48. Wratislaw to Charles, 22 February 1705, *Feldzüge,* VII, 545; protocols of 5, 6, 10, 12 February, 20, 26, 28, 30 March 1705 Conferences, HHSA, SK, V 12; Joseph to Salm, 14 March 1705, FSSA, III 59b.

49. Salm to Wratislaw, 13 February 1705, HHSA, SK, Diplomatische Korrespondenz, Kleinere Betreffe 16; Joseph to Salm, 14 March 1705, FSSA, III 59b. As Prince Salm and this narrative suggests, Professor Spielman's contention that the young court was in permanent control of the government after 1703 is contradicted by the sources. Cf. Spielman, 196–97.

50. Wratislaw to Charles, 18 April 1705, "Eigenhändige Correspondenz des Königs Karl III. von Spanien mit dem Obersten Kanzler des Königreiches Böhmen, Grafen Johann Wenzel Wratislaw," *Archiv für Kunde österreichischer Geschichtsquellen,* XVI (1856), 15.

51. Stepney to Harley, 29 April 1705, Simonyi, I, 70–71.

52. Stepney to Marlborough, 10 June 1705, Houghton, SCC; Eduard Winter, *Frühaufklärung* (East Berlin, 1966), 177.

53. Stepney to Cardonnel, 27 May 1705, Houghton, SCC; Sophie of Han-

over to Frederick I, Ernst Berner, *Aus dem Briefwechsel König Friedrichs I. von Preussen und seiner Familie* (Berlin, 1901), 59.

54. Joseph to Charles, 20 May 1705, HHSA, FK, Sammelbände 1.

55. Bartholdi pro memoria, Berney, *Friedrich I.*, 255.

56. Wratislaw to Sinzendorf, 22 May 1709, HHSA, GK 71; Gerhard Granier, *Der deutsche Reichstag während des spanischen Erbfolgekrieges (1700–1714)* (Bonn, 1954), 85; Braubach, *Geschichte und Abenteuer* (Munich, 1950), 93.

57. Dolfin 9 December 1708 report, Arneth, *Relationen,* 8.

58. Marlborough to Stepney, 11 August 1702, Sir George Murray, ed., *The Letters and Dispatches of John Churchill, First Duke of Marlborough from 1702 to 1712* (London, 1845), I, 157.

59. Gustav Turba, *Reichsgraf Seilern* (Heidelberg, 1923), 192.

60. Stepney to Harley, 3 June 1705, Simonyi, II, 109; Stepney to Cardonnel, 3 June 1705, Houghton, SCC.

61. Arneth, "Eigenhändige Correspondenz," 7; Salm to Wratislaw, 16 January 1705, HHSA, SK, Diplomatische Korrespondenz, Kleinere Betreffe 16; Stepney to Cardonnel, 14 February, to Harley, 4 March 1705, Houghton, SCC. For a fuller treatment of Joseph's Bohemian chancellor, cf. Elfriede Mezgolich, "Graf Johann Wenzel Wratislaw von Mitrowitz" (U. of Vienna dissertation, 1969).

62. Franz Mathis, "Neue Aspekte zur Plannung des süddeutschen Feldzüges von 1704," *Mitteilungen des österreichischen Staatsarchivs,* XXVII (1974).

63. Salm to Wratislaw, 13 February 1704, HHSA, SK, Diplomatische Korrespondenz, Kleinere Betreffe 16; Stepney to Cardonnel, 26 November 1704, 14 February 1705, Houghton, SCC.

64. Henry Frederick Schwarz, *The Imperial Privy Council in the Seventeenth Century* (Cambridge, Mass., 1943), 166, 172, 187; Fellner and Kretschmayr, I, i, 42, 54–57.

65. Prince Johann Josef Khevenhüller-Metsch, *Aus der Zeit Maria Theresias, 1742–1776* (Vienna, 1907), I, 69–70n; Stepney lists 34 councillors, "Conseilliers d'etat de l'Empereur Joseph," Simonyi, II, 112–13.

66. Stepney to Cardonnel, 6 June 1705, Houghton, SCC.

67. The eight were: imperial affairs (incl. Scandinavia and Poland); Hungary; France, England, and Holland; Spain (incl. Portugal); Italy; Switzerland; Turkey (incl. Russia); financial-military ("Politico-Militaria"). Stepney to Marlborough, 6 June 1705, Houghton, SCC; Fellner and Kretschmayr, I, iii, 45.

68. Braubach, "Ein rheinischer Fürst als Gegenspieler des Prinzen Eugen am Wiener Hof," *Diplomatie und geistiges Leben im 17. und 18. Jahrhundert* (Bonn, 1969), 325.

69. Salm to Joseph, 26 May 1702, 25 January 1703, plus several without date, FSSA, III, 59b; Salm to Joseph, 31 October 1704, HHSA, RK, Kleinere Reichsstände 471.

70. Salm to Joseph, 31 October 1704, HHSA, RK, Kleinere Reichsstände 471; Salm to Joseph, n.d. FSSA, III 59b, 61, to Leopold, n.d., FSSA, III 61 (all written between Blenheim and Leopold's death). Salm first mentions the possibility of resigning in a letter written to Joseph apparently before the June 1703 purge. cf. FSSA, III 59b.

71. Joseph to Salm, 7 January 1705, FSSA, III 59a, 14 March 1705, FSSA,

III 59b; Salm to Wratislaw, 13 February 1705, HHSA, SK, Diplomatische Korrespondenz, Kleinere Betreffe 16; Stepney to Harley, 2 May 1705, Simonyi, II.

72. Bartholdi pro memoria, Berney, *Friedrich I.*, 255; Braubach, *Prinz Eugen*, II, 135; "Rheinischer Fürst," 325–26; Hantsch, 381.

73. Salm 12 May 1705 memorial, FSSA, III 59b. For Prince Eugene's record as *Hofkriegsrat* president, cf. Johann Heinrich Blumenthal, "Prinz Eugene als Präsident des Hofkriegsrates (1703–1713)," *Der Donauraum*, IX (1964).

74. Salm to Leopold, n.d., FSSA, III 61.

75. Eugene to *Hofkriegsrat*, 6 August, 9 October 1705, *Feldzüge*, VII, Supp., 309, 431.

76. Braubach, "Rheinischer Fürst," 327.

77. Salm to Wratislaw, 16 January 1705, HHSA, SK, Diplomatische Korrespondenz, Kleinere Betreffe 16; Wratislaw to Charles, 4 July 1705, Arneth, "Eigenhändige Correspondenz," 17–18. Wratislaw was a member of the Hungarian and Anglo-Dutch-French Conferences.

78. Salm to Joseph, n.d., FSSA, III 59b.

79. Braubach, *Prinz Eugen*, II, 148–50.

80. Joseph to Salm, 22 August 1706, FSSA, III 59a.

81. Salm 12 May 1705 memorial, FSSA, III 59b.

82. Wratislaw to Charles, 16 December 1706, Arneth, "Eigenhändige Correspondenz," 33; DeTheillieres to Leopold of Lorraine, 20 January 1707, HHSA, LH 18.

83. HHSA, SK, V 12.

84. Wratislaw to Charles, 16 December 1706, Arneth, "Eigenhändige Correspondenz," 33.

85. "One tries to get rid of Moles and his party. . . . When Wratislaw's turn comes, I am firmly convinced that he will be supported by Prince Eugene, to whom no one can refuse anything. Moreover, it is recognized that Wratislaw has a secret understanding with the emperor . . . and that he will sustain himself in the Conferences by a depth of judgment and of impartiality which his enemies cannot attain; but these are the same reasons which multiply his enemies." DeTheillieres to Leopold of Lorraine, 20 January 1707; also cf. 29 May 1707, HHSA, LH 18.

86. Of those nineteenth-century historians who first seriously evaluated Joseph's character, Alfred von Arneth presents a fairly well-balanced view of the emperor's strengths and weaknesses, whereas Carl von Noorden delivers a most damning judgment. Cf. Arneth, *Prinz Eugen von Savoyen* (Gera, 1888), III, 198–99; Noorden, *Europäische Geschichte im achtzehnten Jahrhundert. Der spanische Erbfolgekrieg* (Düsseldorf, 1870–1882), III, 441–45.

87. Dolfin 9 December 1708 report, Arneth, *Relationen*, 4; Braubach, *Prinz Eugen*, I, 441.

88. C. E. Bonneval, *Mémoires* (London, 1737), I, 56.

89. Braubach, *Prinz Eugen*, II, 133–34. One of Joseph's hunting companions, the so-called Count Raueskoet, was imprisoned for a fortnight on orders from Eleanore. Some months later he appeared at Versailles with a plan to kidnap his former patron while he was hunting without an escort near the French lines at Landau. Louis XIV was so offended by the plan that he ordered Raueskoet expelled from France and promptly sent word to Louis William at Landau, warning him of Raueskoet's intended revenge. Chamillart to Louis William, 2 November 1704, Röder, III, 97.

90. Bartholdi 2 March 1706 report, Berney, *Friedrich I.*, 269–70, also 166; Karl Otmar Fr. von Aretin, "Kaiser Joseph I. Zwischen Kaisertradition und österreichischer Grossmachtpolitik," *Historische Zeitschrift,* CCXV (1972), 533; Dolfin 9 December 1708 report, Arneth, *Relationen,* 3; DeTheillieres reports, HHSA, LH 18; Braubach, *Geschichte und Abenteur,* 180–84, *Prinz Eugen,* II, 129–32, 427.

91. Hanns Leo Mikoletzky, *Österreich. Das Grosse 18. Jahrhundert* (Vienna, 1967), 76; Braubach, *Prinz Eugen,* II, 132–34, 427–28.

92. On their growing estrangement cf. Leopold Lamberg to Franz Joseph Lamberg, 7 January 1711, HHSA, FK, A 51; Wratislaw to Charles, 26 April 1710, HHSA, FK, A 18.

93. "I must report in the highest secrecy to Y. M. that neither the emperor's life style nor the empress' state of health make any further issue likely." Wratislaw to Charles, 26 January 1706, HHSA, FK, A 18. For the bleak prospects of a male succession, cf. Wratislaw to Charles, 9 August 1705, 16 March 1707, Arneth, "Eigenhändige Correspondenz," 20, 35; DeTheillieres to Leopold of Lorraine, 8 May 1709, HHSA, LH 18; Trautson to Charles, 15 January, 25 April 1708, HHSA, GK 70; Dolfin 9 December 1708 report, Arneth, *Retationen,* 5; Hantsch, 380.

94. Sinzendorf to Charles, 28 August, 21 November, 22 December 1708, HHSA, GK 74a; 17, 19 January 1709, HHSA, GK 74b. Joseph's refusal to support his brother's candidacy as Roman king, and hence, as his successor in the empire, indicates that he was still hoping for a son. Cf. Anna Benna, "Ein römischer Königswahlplan Karls III. von Spanien (1708–10)," *Mitteilungen des österreichischen Staatsarchivs,* XIV (1961), 15.

95. Braubach, *Prinz Eugen,* II, 207, 446.

96. Benna, "Königswahlplan," 15.

97. HHSA, SK, V 51, FK, Familienakten 96. Moreover, the existence of numerous cut-out sections among the emperor's notes suggests that sketches of an even more embarrassing nature were scrupulously deleted at one time by some unnamed official or archivist.

98. Dolfin 9 December 1708 report, Arneth, *Relationen,* 4.

99. Berney, "Die Hochzeit Josephs I.," *Mitteilungen des Instituts für österreichische Geschichtsforschung,* XLII (1927), 65.

100. HHSA, SK, V 12–16, 51, FK, Familienakten 96.

101. Bartholdi 2 March 1706 report, Berney, *Friedrich I.,* 270, 166.

102. Bartholdi's misanalyses of court policy and policy making are rather typical of the naiveté among foreign diplomats in Vienna. For example, he counted the new imperial vice chancellor, Count Schönborn, as a Prussophile, though Schönborn unquestionably worked hardest among Joseph's ministers to frustrate Prussian ambitions in Germany. Bartholdi pro memoria, Berney, *Friedrich I.,* 257.

103. Aretin, 533.

104. Braubach, *Prinz Eugen,* II, 131–32, 182, 207, III, 19.

105. Salm to Joseph, 25 January 1703, FSSA, III 59b; Salm to Wratislaw, 27 February 1705, HHSA, SK, Diplomatische Korrespondenz, Kleinere Betreffe 16; Mensi, 115.

106. Mensi, 63–65, 81n.

107. *Ibid.,* 102.

108. Stepney to Harley, 27 May 1705, Houghton, SCC; August 1705 Conference, HHSA, SK, V 12; Stepney to Harley, 7 October 1705, Simonyi, II, 219–20.

109. "Consignationen über die Verwilligungen . . . 1705–1711," HHSA, ÖA, Böhmen, Schlesische Akten 4; Mensi, 24, 26ff.

110. Mensi, 106–7, 110–11, 124.

111. *Feldzüge*, X, 8.

112. Bidermann, *Geschichte der österreichischen Gesamt-Staats-Idee, 1526–1804* (Innsbruck, 1867), II, 135–36.

113. Protocol of 25 February 1706 Conference, HHSA, SK, V 12; Mensi, 11, 16–17; Brigitte Holl, *Hofkammerpräsident Gundaker Thomas Graf Starhemberg und die österreichische Finanzpolitik der Barockzeit (1703–1715)* (Vienna, 1976), 145–46.

114. Gunther Erich Rothenberg, *The Austrian Military Border in Croatia, 1522–1747* (Urbana, Ill., 1960), 68, 80, 104; Thiel, 520–23, 596ff.; Redlich, *Grossmacht,* 22–23.

115. "Unvorgreifliche Gedanken über den gegenwärtigen Zustand," 10 March 1704, Fellner and Kretschmayr, I, iii, 41; Thiel, 574.

116. Salm 12 May 1705 memorial, FSSA, III 59b; Stepney to Cardonnel, 3 June 1705, Houghton, SCC; to Harley, 3 June 1705, Simonyi, II, 108–9.

117. Bidermann, *Gesamt-Staats-Idee,* II, 10–11; Fellner and Kretschmayr, I, i, 161, 260.

118. Eugene to Joseph, 9 July 1705, *Feldzüge,* VII, Supp., 248–49, IX, 38; protocol of 19 August 1705 Conference, HHSA, SK, V 12; Salm to St. Saphorin, 19 January, 23 March 1707, FSSA, III 128; Bidermann, *Gesamt-Staats-Idee,* II, 13, 118.

119. Bidermann, *Gesamt-Staats-Idee,* II, 14, 120–23. Negotiating teams sent to Graz and Innsbruck by the emperor at the beginning of 1707 were unable to reach a settlement with the estates. Eugene to Joseph, 9, 30 October, to *Hofkriegsrat,* 6 December 1705, *Feldzüge,* VII, Supp., 425, 461, 509, VIII, 58; protocol of 22 February 1705 Conference, HHSA, SK, V 12; Bidermann, *Gesamt-Staats-Idee,* II, 109.

120. Eugene to Innsbruck Privy Council, 30 December 1706, 23 February 1707, *Feldzüge,* VIII, Suppl, IX, Supp.

121. Oskar Regele, *Der österreichische Hofkriegsrat, 1556–1848* (Vienna, 1949), 21; Bidermann, *Gesamt-Staats-Idee,* II, 12. Only in 1743 were the separate War and Fiscal offices abolished altogether. Rothenberg, 102.

122. Khevenhüller-Metsch, 70; Mensi, 116–17, 119; Holl, 200–206.

123. Eduard Ritter von Strobl-Albeg, *Das Obersthofmarschallamt* (Innsbruck, 1908), 80; Mensi, 107–8, 155; Grunwald, 172. Joseph even levied a 400 fl. tax on those individuals whom he had dismissed from the Privy Council in June 1705. Johann Philipp Lamberg to Harrach, 21 July 1705, Allgemeines Verwaltungsarchiv, Graf Harrach'sches Familienarchiv 271.

124. Mensi, 155.

125. *Ibid.,* 103–7, 124.

126. Stepney to Harley, 14 March 1705, Houghton, SCC; Joseph to John William, 30 October 1704, Geheimes Staatsarchiv, Kasten Blau 45, Nr. 12.

127. Alfred Fischel, *Christian Julius v. Schierendorff, ein Vorläufer des liberalen Zentralismus unter Josef I. und Karl VI.* (Vienna, 1906), 157; protocol of 14 October 1705 Conference, HHSA, SK, V 12; Ludwig Bittner, *Chronologisches Verzeichnis der Österreichischen Staatsverträge* (Vienna, 1903), I, 125.

128. Stepney to Harley, 18 June 1705, Houghton, SCC; Mensi, 204–5.

129. *Ibid.,* 207; Carl Schwabe von Waisenfreund, *Versuch einer Geschichte des österreichischen Staats- Credits- und Schuldwesens* (Vienna, 1860), II, 360–61.

130. Schwabe, II, 360–61; Fellner and Kretschmayr, I, i, 106–7, 217.
131. Schwabe, II, 86; Bidermann, "Stadt-Bank," 381–82.
132. Mensi, 212, 220, 238, 254; Bidermann, "Stadt-Bank," 382ff.
133. Mensi, 105, 239, 329. For details see below p. 83.
134. *Ibid.,* 106–11, 166ff., 236, 240, 243–56.
135. *Ibid.,* 106–7, 124; "Repartition . . . " 4 December 1710, Magyar Országos Levéltár, Nádor Levéltár, 7.
136. Sinzendorf 15 March 1702 report, Arneth, "Hauptbericht des Grafen Philipp Ludwig von Sinzendorff an Kaiser Leopold I nach Beendigung seiner Mission in Frankreich," *Archiv für österreichische Geschichte,* XIII (1854), 15ff., 23ff.
137. "It is quite common for one problem to be solved only to find that new difficulties have taken its place." Salm to St. Saphorin, 21 October 1706, FSSA, III 128.
138. "Anmerkungen und Motiva zu Errichtung einer Academia sowol deren Manufacturen als höheren Wissenschaften," Fischel, 298, also 296; Mensi, 117; Bidermann, *Gesamt-Staats-Idee,* II, 19, 136–37; Pribram, *Das böhmische Commerzcollegium und seine Thätigkeit* (Prague, 1898), 23; Holl, 198–200.
139. Stepney to Boyle, 15 June 1709, Simonyi, III; Bidermann, "Stadt-Bank," 370.
140. Bertold Bretholz, *Geschichte Böhmens und Mährens* (Reichenberg, 1924), III, 59–61.
141. Fischel, 219; Holl, 148–49.
142. Gustav Korkisch, "Der Bauernaufstand auf der Mährisch Trübau-Türnauer Herrschaft 1706–1713," *Bohemia. Jahrbuch des Collegium Carolinum,* XI (1970), 168, 212–14, 234.
143. Norbert Conrad, *Die Durchführung der Altranstädter Konvention in Schlesien 1707–1709* (Vienna, 1971), 47, 202–15, 250.
144. Paul Bernard, *Jesuits and Jacobins* (Urbana, Ill., 1973), 23.

III. Germany: *Blenheim Aftermath*

Opening quote: Bartholdi 2 March 1706 report, Berney, *Friedrich I.,* 267.
1. Hubert Gillot, *Le régne de Louis XIV et l'opinion publique en Allemagne* (Nancy, 1914).
2. Hans Sedlmayr, *Johann Bernhard Fischer von Erlach* (Vienna, 1956), 28.
3. Anna Coreth, *Österreichische Geschichtsforschung in der Barockzeit (1620–1740)* (*Veröfflichungen der Kommission für neuere Geschichte Ös-terreichs,* XXXVII [1950]), 24.
4. Hans Aurenhammer, *J. B. Fischer von Erlach* (Cambridge, Mass., 1973), 49–53; Sedlmayr, 31–32.
5. Sedlmayr, 47.
6. Adam Wandruszka, *Österreich und Italien im 18. Jahrhundert* (Vienna, 1963), 114.
7. Villars, 438.
8. John William to Joseph, 26 January, 26 February 1701, Hilsenbeck, 33–35.
9. Leopold to Louis William, 23 May 1702, Louis William to Leopold, 18 July 1702, Röder, I, 67, 72; *Feldzüge,* VI, 576; Grunwald, 189.
10. Redlich, *Grossmacht,* 38.

11. Cf. Lothar Gross, "Der Kampf zwischen Reichskanzlei und österreichischer Hofkanzlei um die Führung der auswärtigen Geschäfte," *Historische Vierteljahrschrift,* XXII (1924), *Die Geschichte der Deutschen Reichshofkanzlei von 1559 bis 1806* (Vienna, 1933); Heinrich Kretschmayr, "Das Deutsche Reichsvicekanzleramt," *Archiv für österreichische Geschichte,* LXXXIV (1897); Gerhard Seeliger, *Erzkanzler und Reichskanzleien* (Innsbruck, 1889).

12. Gross, *Reichshofkanzlei,* 59–63; Hantsch, 77.

13. J. P. v. Lamberg to Harrach, 11 May 1705, Allgemeines Verwaltungsarchiv, Graf Harrach'sches Familienarchiv 271.

14. Hantsch, 78.

15. *Ibid.* 81; Gross, *Reichshofkanzlei,* 67.

16. Karl Wild, *Lothar Franz von Schönborn Bischof von Bamberg und Erzbischof von Mainz 1693–1729* (Heidelberg, 1904); Fritz Redlich, *The German Military Enterpriser,* II (*Vierteljahrschrift für Sozial-und Wirtschaftsgeschichte,* XLVIII [1965]) 17.

17. HHSA, SK, V 12; Gross, *Reichshofkanzlei,* 349; Hantsch, 81.

18. Hantsch, 81. For Schönborn's relationships at court, also cf. "Reichsvizekanzler Graf F. K. Schönborn und Hofkanzler Graf Philipp Ludwig Sinzendorf" in *Études européennes* (Paris, 1973) and Braubach, "Friedrich Karl von Schönborn und Prinz Eugen" in *Diplomatie und geistiges Leben.*

19. "Unvorgreifliche Gedanken über den gegenwärtigen Zustand," 10 March 1704, Fellner and Kretschmayr, I, iii, 41.

20. Fellner and Kretschmayr, I, iii, 43, 48.

21. Wild, 135.

22. Oswald Gschliesser, *Der Reichshofrat* (Vienna, 1942), 1–5, 15ff., 45, 48, 60; August Siemsen, *Kur-Brandenburgs Anteil an den kaiserlichen Wahl-Kapitulationen von 1689 bis 1742* (Weimar, 1909), 14–15; Schwarz, 89, 108; Fellner and Kretschmayr, I, i, 158–59, 231–32, ii, 9.

23. Öttingen correspondence, March 1705, HHSA, RHR, Verfassungsakten, Reichshofrat 11; Salm 12 May 1705 memorial, FSSA, III, 59b; Euchar Gottlieb Rinck, *Josephs des Sieghaften Röm. Kaysers Leben und Thaten* (Cologne, 1712), II, 30.

24. Rudolf Smend, *Das Reichskammergericht* (Weimar, 1911), 218–22; Granier, 110–13. The Chamber Court also seems to have been paralyzed by the princes' failure to defray its operating expenses. Roger Wines, "The Imperial Circles, Princely Diplomacy and Imperial Reform 1681–1714," *Journal of Modern History,* XXXIX (1967), 2.

25. Gschliesser, 67; Gross, *Reichshofkanzlei,* 395; Smend, 218–19; 223.

26. For a detailed treatment of the imperial military system, cf. Max Jähns, "Zur Geschichte der Kriegsverfassung des Deutschen Reichs," *Preussische Jahrbuch,* XXXIX (1877); Hans Erich Feine, "Zur Verfassungsentwicklung des Heil. Röm. Reiches seit dem Westfälischen Frieden," *Zeitschrift der Savigny-Stiftung für Rechtsgeschichte,* LII (1932); Anton Karl Mally, *Der österreichische Kreis in der Exekutionsordnung des römisch-deutschen Reiches* (Vienna, 1967).

27. Joseph to Louis William, 12 June 1704, Röder, II, 36; Braubach, *Prinz Eugen,* II, 43; Redlich, *Grossmacht,* 16.

28. Marlborough to Hedges, to Harley, 10 October 1704, Murray, I, 500–501; Emil Heuser, *Die dritte und vierte Belagerung Landaus im spanischen Erbfolgekrieg (1704 und 1713)* (Landau, 1896), 277ff.

29. Victor Loewe, *Preussens Staatsverträge aus der Regierungszeit König*

Freidrichs I. (Leipzig, 1923), 21–22; Berney, *Friedrich I.,* 158, 175, 204–8, 221–24.

30. *Feldzüge,* VI, 95; Redlich, *Grossmacht,* 28.

31. Berney, *Friedrich I.,* 88, 101, 113.

32. Marlborough to Godolphin, 28 August, 29 September, 3 October, 3 November 1704, Henry L. Snyder, ed., *The Marlborough-Godolphin Correspondence* (Oxford, 1975), I, 359, 373–75, 392; to Heinsius, 26 September, to Harley, 29 September, 17 October 1704, Murray, I, 485, 487, 507.

33. Marlborough to Godolphin, 7 November 1704, Snyder, I, 394; to Lothair Francis, to Harley, 13 November, to Stepney, 3 December 1704, Murray, I, 536, 538, 550–51; Joseph to Leopold, 1 December, referat of 13 December 1704 Conference, HHSA, SA, Brandenburgica 29; Loewe, 58.

34. Noorden, "Die preussische Politik im spanischen Erbfolgekriege," *Historische Zeitschrift,* XVIII (1867), 315; Berney, *Friedrich I.,* 126–27.

35. Braubach, *Prinz Eugen,* II, 50ff.

36. Marlborough to Wratislaw, 28 April, 1 May 1705, Murray, II, 19, 26.

37. Marlborough to Raby, 21 April, to Wratislaw, 1 May 1705, *ibid.,* II, 8, 26–27; Wratislaw to Charles, 18 April 1705, "Eigenhändige Correspondenz," 15; Berney, *Friedrich I.,* 128.

38. Joseph to Louis William, 9 May 1705, Röder, II, 108.

39. Louis William to Joseph, 30 May, 6 June 1705, *ibid.,* 110, 113.

40. Marlborough to Louis William, 29, 31 May, Louis William to Marlborough, 2, 15 June 1705, *ibid.,* 109–13, 118.

41. Marlborough to Louis William, 31 May 1705, Murray, II, 63; Berney, *Friedrich I.,* 138–39.

42. Marlborough to Wratislaw, 16, 18 June 1705, Murray, II, 111; Noorden, *Erbfolgekrieg,* II, 161–62.

43. Marlborough to Joseph, 18 June 1705, Murray, II, 109–10.

44. Villars, 347.

45. Heinsius to Marlborough, 15 July, 1705, B. Van't Hoff, ed., *The Correspondence 1701-1711 of John Churchill First Duke of Marlborough and Anthonie Heinsius Grand Pensionary of Holland* (Utrecht, 1951), 192; Marlborough to Harley, 16 July 1705, Murray, II, 169; Stepney to Cardonnel, 4 July 1705, Houghton, SCC; Kurt Arnold, *Geschichte des Niederrheinisch-Westfälischen Kreises in der Zeit des Spanischen Erbfolgekrieges (1698-1714)* (Bonn, 1937), 104.

46. Marlborough to Louis William, 19 June 1705, Murray, II, 117.

47. Marlborough to Louis William, 5 July, to Wratislaw, 1 July 1705, *ibid.,* 140–41, 146–47.

48. Frederick to Sophie, 1 August 1705, Berner, *Briefwechsel,* 68; Marlborough to Raby, 14 September 1705, Murray, II, 264; Noorden, "Preussische Politik," 321; Berney, *Friedrich I.,* 172.

49. Braubach, *Die Bedeutung der Subsidien für die Politik im spanischen Erbfolgekriege* (Bonn, 1923), 139, 146.

50. Salm to Gallas, 18 July 1705, Höfler, "Die diplomatische Correspondenz des Grafen Johann Wenzel Gallas," *Archiv für österreichische Geschichte,* XLI (1869), 305.

51. "Notes by Sunderland . . . July 1705," Snyder, I, 464.

52. Eugene to Joseph, 9, 17 July 1705, *Feldzüge,* VII, Supp., 250–51, 276.

53. Joseph to Louis William, 6 August 1705, Röder, II, 145.

54. Stepney to Harley, 18 June 1705, Houghton, SCC.

55. Sigmund Riezler, *Geschichte Baierns* (Gotha, 1913–14), VII, 492ff., 554, 601ff., VIII, 5, 11–12, 15–16; Gustav Baumann, *Der Bauernaufstand von Jahre 1705 im bayerischen Unterland.* (*Verhandlungen des historischen Vereins für Niederbayern,* LXIX–LXX [1936–37]), I, 14, 18–19, 23–24.

56. 22 July, 29 August 1705 instructions, HHSA, RK, Weisungen nach München 1b; Baumann, I, 22.

57. Karl von Wallmenich, *Der Oberländer Aufstand 1705 und die Sendlinger Schlacht* (Munich, 1906), 7–8.

58. *Ibid.,* 8; *Feldzüge,* VII, 381–82.

59. Eugene to Löwenstein, 25 August 1705, Alexander Kaufmann, "Auszüge aus der Correspondenz des Fürsten Maximilian Karl von Löwenstein mit dem Markgrafen Ludwig von Baden und dem Prinzen Eugen von Savoyen," *Archiv für österreichische Geschichte,* XXXVII (1867), 224.

60. Instructions to Löwenstein, 16 September 1705, HHSA, RK, Weisungen nach München 1b.

61. Joseph to Louis William, 2 September 1705, Röder, II, 161.

62. Joseph to Louis William, 9, 19, 26 September 1705, *ibid.,* 167ff.

63. Louis William to Joseph, 24 September 1705, *ibid.,* 171.

64. Louis William to Joseph, 5 October 1705, *ibid.,* 178.

65. Referat of 10, 20 September 1705 Conferences, HHSA, RK, V 6b.

66. Bartholdi 12 November 1705 pro memoria, 2 March 1706 relation, Berney, *Friedrich I.,* 255ff., 264.

67. *Ibid.,* 146–47, 149; protocol of 14 October 1705 Conference, HHSA, SK, V 12.

68. Berney, *Friedrich I.,* 150.

69. Wratislaw to Gallas, 9 September 1705, Höfler, "Diplomatische Correspondenz," 307; Marlborough to Wratislaw, to Sinzendorf, 24 September 1705, Murray, II, 273–74; to Heinsius, 21 September 1705, Heinsius to Marlborough, 26 September 1705, Van't Hoff, 213, 215.

70. Noorden, *Erbfolgekrieg,* II, 299–303. See below pp. 82–83.

71. Marlborough to Harley, 31 August, to Stanhope, 3 October, to Stepney, to Joseph, 7 October 1705, Murray, II, 247, 288–89, 295–96.

72. Marlborough to Schönborn, to Sinzendorf, 3 December 1705, *ibid.,* 337.

73. Ludwig Hüttl, *Max Emanuel der Blaue Kurfürst* (Munich, 1976), 429, 446–54, 465–69.

74. Instructions to Löwenstein, 22 October 1705, HHSA, RK, Weisungen nach München 1b.

75. Protocol of 18 November 1705 Conference, HHSA, SK, V 12; *Feldzüge,* VII, 390.

76. Instructions to Löwenstein, 21 November 1705, HHSA, RK, Weisungen nach München 1b; protocol of 18 November 1705 Conference, HHSA, SK, V 12.

77. Protocol of 18 November 1705 Conference, HHSA, SK, V 12.

78. Protocols of 18, 20 November 1705 Conferences, HHSA, SK, V 12; Instructions to Löwenstein, 21 November 1705, HHSA, RK, Weisungen nach München 1b.

79. Baumann, II, 12; Wallmenich, 17ff., 52, 70, 74–76, Kriechbaum to Eugene, 25 December, Löwenstein to Joseph, 26 December, to Eugene, 28 December 1705, *ibid.,* 154–55, 161.

80. Wallmenich, 14; Marlborough to Harley, 1 January 1706, Murray, II, 372–73.

81. Baumann, II, 51, 61.

82. *Ibid.*, 54–55; Riezler, VIII, 187; Wallmenich, 11.

83. Protocol of 3 February 1706 Conference, HHSA, SK, V 12; Riezler, VIII, 187, 198–200.

84. Riezler, VIII, 191, 195–96, 198–200, 424; Baumann, II, 65.

85. Protocol of 16 December 1705 Conference, HHSA, SK, V 12.

86. Franz Feldmeier, "Die Ächtung des Kurfürsten Max Emanuel von Bayern und die Übertragung der Oberpfalz mit der fünften Kur an Kurpfalz (1702–1708)," *Oberbayerisches Archiv* (1914), 164, 169, 176.

87. Georg Sante, "Die kurpfälzische Politik des Kurfürsten Johann Wilhelm vornehmlich im spanischen Erbfolgekrieg 1690–1716," *Historisches Jahrbuch,* XLIV (1924), 43–44.

88. Referat of 10, 20 September 1705 Conferences, HHSA, RK, V 6b.

89. Feldmeier, 195–200.

90. *Ibid.,* 209; Conrad, 109.

91. Noorden, *Erbfolgekrieg,* II, 302–3.

92. Erich Hassinger, "Preussen und Frankreich im Spanischen Erbfolgekriege," *Forschungen zur Brandenburgischen und Preussischen Geschichte,* LIV (1943), 58–65; Berney, *Friedrich I.,* 161.

93. Berney, *Friedrich I.,* 163–64.

94. *Ibid.,* 164; Salm to Marlborough, 28 April 1706, Murray, II, 492.

95. Berney, *Friedrich I.,* 167–68.

96. Protocol of 27 April 1706 Conference, HHSA, SK, V 12.

97. Salm to Marlborough, 28 April 1706, Murray, II, 492–93.

98. *Ibid.,* 144; Marlborough to Harley, 9 May 1706, Murray, II, 498.

99. Wratislaw to Charles, 10 July 1706, HHSA, FK, A 18.

100. Joseph to Baden, 4 July 1706, Röder, II, 266.

101. *Feldzüge,* VIII, 365.

102. In a 30 June letter to St. Saphorin, Schlick wrote: "Those who have the direction of affairs remain responsible for them. I have no other right or competence than to report [the truth]. In leaving Vienna I have said in fact that, if I did not attribute the guilt to the margrave, certain men would see that I shared the blame . . . I will certainly not misrepresent anything I hear or see against the service of the emperor, but I am not an instrument for the support of sinister cabals and would prefer to sacrifice my fortune than to have a hand in the ruining of a man of ability, honor, and reputation." Braubach, *Prinz Eugen,* II, 441.

103. Wratislaw to Charles, 31 August 1706, Arneth, "Eigenhändige Correspondenz," 26.

104. Joseph to Louis William, 28 August 1706, Röder, II, 279.

105. Marlborough to Harley, 23 September 1706, Murray, III, 146.

106. *Feldzüge,* VIII, 370.

107. Wratislaw to Charles, 31 August 1706, Arneth, "Eigenhändige Correspondenz," 26; Noorden, *Erbfolgekrieg,* II, 509.

108. Louis to William, to Marlborough, 7 September 1706, Röder, II, 288. Joseph does not appear to have convinced Heinsius, who continued to criticize the emperor's misuse of imperial contributions for the Italian and Hungarian fronts and who at one point asked Marlborough, "How can those who do so little for the empire possibly hope to pursuade others?" Heinsius to Marlborough, 17, 30 December 1706, Van't Hoff, 283, 287.

109. Protocol of 17 July 1706 Conference, HHSA, SK, V 12.

110. Louis William to Joseph, 26 July 1706, Röder, II, 275.

111. Stepney to Harley, 15 September 1706, Simonyi, III; Ragnhild M. Hatton, *Charles XII of Sweden* (London, 1968), 222; Otto Haintz, *König Karl XII. von Schweden* (Berlin, 1958), I, 163; Jaroslav Goll, "Der Vertrag von Alt-Ranstädt. Österreich und Schweden 1706–1707," *Abhandlungen der königl. böhmischen Gesellschaft der Wissenschaften,* series VI, vol. X (1881), 7.

112. Stepney to Hedges, 26 March 1704, Simonyi, I, 209.

113. Hatton, 217.

114. Ernst Carlson, *Der Vertrag zwischen Karl XII. von Schweden und Kaiser Joseph I. zu Altranstädt 1707* (Stockholm, 1907), 18.

115. *Ibid.;* Goll, 29; Hatton, 223; C. Grünhagen, *Geschichte Schlesiens* (Gotha, 1886), II, 397–98.

116. Goll, 13; In two other letters, Rákóczi actually urged Stanislaus to join with him in repelling the common Habsburg menace. Rákóczi to Stanislaus, 14, 17 September 1706, Fiedler, *Actenstücke zur Geschichte Franz Rákóczy's und seiner Verbindung mit dem Auslande,* III (*Archiv für österreichische Geschichte,* XLIV [1871]), 426–27.

117. 5 September referat of 4 September 1706 Conference, HHSA, RK, V 6b.

118. Hassinger, *Brandenburg-Preussen, Russland und Schweden 1700–1713* (Munich, 1953), 158.

119. 5 September referat of 4 September 1706 Conference, HHSA, RK, V 6b; Joseph's notes of 14 September 1706 Conference, HHSA, SK, V 51; Goll, 6, 12.

120. Gabriel Syveton, "Au camp d'Altranstädt. Besenval et Marlborough," *Revue d'histoire diplomatique,* XII (1898), 595; *Louis XIV et Charles XII au camp d'Altranstädt, 1707. La mission du Baron de Besenval* (Paris, 1900), 73–74; Goll, 9–10; Carlson, 9; Haintz, I, 165.

121. Goll, 10, 12.

122. Joseph's notes of 14 September 1706 Conference, HHSA, SK, V 51.

123. Referat of 31 January 1707 Conference, HHSA, SA, Schweden 18a.

124. Goll, 13; Hatton, 222; Haintz, I, 161.

125. 13 February referat of 10 February 1707 Conference, HHSA, SA, Schweden 18a.

126. Wratislaw to Charles, 21 February 1707, "Eigenhändige Correspondenz," 33; 20 February 1707 rescript, HHSA, SA, Schweden 18a.

127. Carlson, 8.

128. *Ibid.,* 9; Goll, 24.

129. Carlson, 9.

130. 20 January 1707, Instructions for Ricous, *Récueil des Instructions données aux ambassadeurs et ministres de France depuis les traités de Westphalie jusqu'à la revolution française,* II: *Suède,* A. Geffroy, ed. (Paris, 1885), 219–234; Syveton, "Au camp d'Altranstädt," 584–89, 600, *Louis XIV et Charles XII,* 69, 71.

131. Harley to Robinson, 12 October 1706, 8 February 1707, James F. Chance, ed., *British Diplomatic Instructions, 1689–1789* (London, 1922–26), I: *Sweden,* 30–32; Stepney to Harley, 28 August 1706, Simonyi, III, 219–20.

132. Marlborough to Godolphin, 29 April 1707 (O.S.), Snyder, II, 757–62.

133. Marlborough to Salm, to Sinzendorf, 1 May 1707, Murray, III, 348, 350.

134. Referat of 13 May 1707 Conference, HHSA, SA, Schweden 18a.

135. Joseph's notes of 14 September 1706 Conference, HHSA, SK, V 51.

136. Salm to Joseph, 15 May 1707, HHSA, SA, Schweden 18a.

137. Goll, 25.

138. Referat of 17 June 1707 Conference, HHSA, SA, Schweden 18a.

139. Goll, 25.

140. Carlson, 10.

141. *Ibid.*

142. DeTheillieres to Leopold of Lorraine, 4 March 1707, HHSA, LH 18.

143. Braubach, *Subsidien,* 85.

144. *Feldzüge,* IX, 40.

145. Protocol of 18 June 1706 Conference, HHSA, SK, V 12; Joseph's notes of 30 June 1706 Conference, HHSA, SK, V 51.

146. Hantsch, 88; Berney, *Friedrich I.,* 171.

147. Loewe, 45, 51, 62, 77; Hantsch, 63–64.

148. Hantsch, 89. Friedrich Karl admitted to his uncle that no Aulic Council judgment was necessary. *Ibid.,* 135.

. 149. Joseph's notes of 20 July 1707 Conference, HHSA, SK, V 51; Wild, 117–19.

150. Berney, *Friedrich I.,* 171; Braubach, *Subsidien,* 118–19.

151. Heinz Polster, *Der Markgraf Christian Ernst von Bayreuth-Brandenburg und seine Rolle in den Reichskriegen (1689–1707)* (Erlangen, 1935), 123–50. Winston Churchill flippantly attributes Bayreuth's selection to the emperor's preference for a Catholic. He was, in fact, a Protestant. *Marlborough: His Life and Times* (London, 1934), V, 270.

152. Marlborough to Eugene, 27 December 1706, to Gueldermalsen, 14 January 1707, Murray, III, 268, 285.

153. DeTheillieres to Leopold of Lorraine, 4 March 1707, HHSA, LH 18.

154. Wratislaw to Charles, 24 March 1707, HHSA, FK, A 18.

155. Berney, *Friedrich I.,* 182–83; Churchill, V, 272.

156. Referat of 13 May 1707 Conference, HHSA, SA, Schweden 18a; Harley to Robinson, 3/4 June 1707, Chance, I: *Sweden,* 35.

157. Referat of 17 June 1707 Conference, HHSA, SA, Schweden 18a.

158. Goll, 26.

159. Wratislaw to Charles, 6 July 1707, HHSA, FK, A 18.

160. Joseph's notes of 3, 8 July 1707 Conferences, HHSA, SK, V 51.

161. Carlson, 13.

162. Protocols of 26, 28, 30 July 1707 negotiations, Goll, 39–43.

163. Mediators to Piper/Hermelin, 1 August 1707, *ibid.,* 46.

164. Protocol of 2 August 1707 negotiation, *ibid.,* 46–47. Joseph's confirmation of Christian August was welcomed by Charles XII as settling in his favor the long-standing dispute between Sweden and Denmark over succession rights in the bishopric of Lübeck-Eutin. By a 1647 treaty, Lübeck's next six bishops were to be taken from the Holstein-Gottorp dynasty. Though Denmark had recognized this agreement, its king had violated it at the end of 1705, when he invaded the bishopric and placed his brother Charles on the throne. Persuaded by an Anglo-Dutch pension and the threat of Swedish force, Prince Charles renounced his claim in August 1706. Yet, despite English pressure, Joseph refused to release an Aulic Council judgment made in Christian August's favor out of fear that he would alienate Denmark, which had 35,000 mercenaries serving with the alliance. Instructions to Pulteney, 18 August 1706, Chance, III: *Denmark,* 23; Rinck, 105; Marlborough to Harley, 18 November 1705, to Stepney, 6 January 1706, Murray, II, 325, 384; Noorden, II, 517–18.

165. Supplementary article of 2 August 1707 protocol, Goll, 47.

166. Referat of 10 August 1707 Conference, HHSA, SA, Schweden 18b.
167. Carlson, 21–22.
168. Protocols of 4, 5 August 1707 negotiations, Goll, 48–49.
169. Conrad, 21–23; Granier, 96–97; Grünhagen, II, 396–97.
170. Salm 15 May 1707 votum, HHSA, SA, Schweden 18a.
171. Referat of 17 June 1707 Conference, HHSA, SA, Schweden 18a.
172. Joseph's notes of 17 June 1707 Conference, HHSA, SK, V 51.
173. Joseph's notes of 12 August 1707 Conference, HHSA, SK, V 51; referat of 10, 12 August 1707 Conferences, HHSA, SA, Schweden 18b.
174. *Ibid.*
175. Referat of 24 August 1707 Conference, HHSA, SA, Schweden 18b.
176. Joseph to Wratislaw, 14 August 1707, HHSA, SA, Schweden 18b; protocol of 14 August 1707 Conference, HHSA, SA, Schweden 18b.
177. Wratislaw to Joseph, 17 August 1707, HHSA, FK, A 16.
178. Wratislaw to Joseph, 20 August 1707, HHSA, FK A 16 and SA, Schweden 18b.
179. Wratislaw to Joseph, 28 August 1707, FK, A 16 and Goll, 52–53.
180. For complete terms, cf. Carlson, 34–35, 65–69.
181. For Anglo-Dutch guarantee, cf. *ibid.,* 46–49, 54–71.
182. Berney, *Friedrich I.,* 183–84; Loewe, 83; Arnold, 111.
183. Marlborough to Salm, 1 May 1707, Murray, III, 348–49.
184. Granier, 104–5.
185. Polster, 177–79, 183–84, 192.
186. Marlborough to Harley, 23 June 1707, Murray, III, 437; Arnold, 120; *Feldzüge,* IX, 52.
187. Haintz, I, 175; Klopp, *Der Fall des Hauses Stuart* (Vienna, 1885–88), XIII, 523.
188. Marlborough to Wratislaw, 15 August 1707, Murray, III, 516.
189. Carlson, 30. Conrad, 52, offers a slightly different version.
190. Bruyninx to Stepney, 15 December 1706, Simonyi, III; Syveton, *Louis XIV et Charles XII,* 118; Hassinger, *Brandenburg-Preussen,* 217.
191. Referat of 4 September 1706 Conference, HHSA, RK, V 6b; Joseph's notes of 14 September 1706 Conference, HHSA, SK, V 51; Hassinger, *Brandenburg-Preussen,* 195–96, 209–10; Loewe, 86.
192. Hassinger, *Brandenburg-Preussen,* 187–90, 194–95, 210–11; Marlborough to Frederick, 18 October 1706, Murray, III, 178.
193. Loewe, 89–90; Rinck, 265.
194. Referate of 13 February 1707 Conference, HHSA, SA, Schweden 18a; Hassinger, *Brandenburg-Preussen,* 210–11.
195. Hatton, 151.
196. Marlborough to Salm, 28 January 1707, to Sinzendorf, 7 March 1707, Murray, III, 306, 330. Queen Anne did recognize Stanislaus in March 1708. The Dutch, however, did not follow suit and neither government ever guaranteed the first Altranstädt treaty. Hatton, 227.
197. Marlborough to Wratislaw, 15 August 1707, to Robinson, 16 August 1707, Murray, III, 516–17; Goll, 30, 32–33, protocol of 5 August negotiation, 49. Indeed, the English and Dutch subsequently joined Prussia in pressing both Charles and Joseph to extend the treaty provisions to include Silesia's Calvinists. Conrad, 152–55, 160–61.
198. After having received Joseph's request for Anglo-Dutch mediation the English secretary of state, Robert Harley, wrote, "The Court of Vienna,

according to their usual custom of being behind hand, have this day made the first application for the Queen's interposition of their behalf so that they must be always in debt to the foresight of their friends more than their own ease for their preservation." to Robinson, 3/4 June 1707, Chance, I: *Sweden, 35.*

199. Marlborough to Heinsius, 5 December 1$07, Murray, III, 650.

200. *Feldzüge,* X, 17, 27, 72, 82, Supp. 62, 71–76; Granier, 107–8.

201. Émile Bourgeois, *Neuchâtel et la politique en Franche-Comté (1702–1713),* (Paris, 1887), 81, 215, 217.

202. Salm to Saint-Saphorin, 19 December 1706, 4 July 1707, FSSA, III, 128; referat of 24 February 1708 Conference, HHSA, SK, V 13.

203. Referat of 27 December 1707 Conference, HHSA, SK, V 13.

204. 25 January 1708 reply to Royal Prussian Petita, HHSA, GK 74a.

205. Hantsch, 135; Wild, 118–19; Feine, "Verfassungsentwicklung," 87; Reinhold Koser, "Brandenburg-Preussen in dem Kampf zwischen Imperialismus und reichständischer Libertät," *Historische Zeitschrift* XCVI (1906), 203.

206. Instructions to Prince Eugene, February 1708, *Feldzüge,* X, Supp. 46–47.

207. *Ibid.,* X, 88, 286, 528–29, Supp., 170, 173.

208. *Ibid.,* 45, 72, Supp., 71–76; Braubach, *Prinz Eugen,* II, 223, 451.

209. Granier, 20; Wild, 125.

210. Granier, 146; Satisfaktionsdekret, 21 July 1706, Karl Zeumer, *Quellensammlung zur Geschichte der Deutschen Reichsverfassung* (Leipzig, 1904), 404.

211. Johann Philipp Lamberg to Harrach, 19 March 1706, Allgemeines Verwaltungsarchiv, Graf Harrach'sches Familienarchiv 271. Though Augustus had converted to Catholicism in 1696 in order to win the Polish crown, he still followed a Protestant religious policy in order to retain Saxony's former leadership of the *corpus evangelicorum* in the Imperial Diet. Adolph Frantz, *Das Katholische Directorium des Corpus Evangelicorum* (Marburg, 1880), 1–5, 51.

212. Frieda von Esebeck, *Die Begründung der hannoverschen Kurwürde* (Bonn, 1935), 96; Ulrich Kühne, "Geschichte der böhmischen Kur in den Jahrhunderten nach der Goldenen Bulle," *Archiv für Urkundenforschung,* X (1928), 62–63, 70.

213. Esebeck, 96–97, 100–101; Granier, 145, 147–49. 153–56.

214. Carl Minha, "Die Deutsche Politik Kaiser Joseph I." (U. of Vienna dissertation, 1934), 52; Aretin, 542, 544.

215. Feldmeier, 204, 233–34.

216. *Ibid.,* 235–36, 238.

217. *Ibid.,* 241, 245, 254–56; Sante, 47.

218. Feldmeier, 256–57; Sante, 52.

219. Feldmeier, 258.

220. *Ibid.,* 260–61.

221. Schönborn to Lothair Francis, 28 April, 9 May 1708, Lothair Francis to Schönborn, 19 May 1708, HHSA, MEA, Korr. 89.

222. Schönborn to Lothair Francis, 16 May 1708, HHSA, MEA, Korr. 89.

223. Joseph's notes of 5 November 1707 Conference, HHSA, SK, V 51; Granier, 154; Esebeck, 95

224. Eugene to John William, 10 June 1708 *Feldzüge,* X, Supp., 108–10.

225. Eugene to John William, 14 June 1708, *ibid.,* 116–17.

226. John William to Eugene, 18 June 1708, *ibid.,* 125.

227. Schönborn to Lothair Francis, 23 June 1708, HHSA, MEA, Korr. 89.
228. Feldmeier, 268.
229. Esebeck, 100–101; Granier, 148.
230. Eugene to Joseph, 29 April, 11 June 1708, *Feldzüge*, X, Supp., 81–83, 114–15.
231. Schönborn to Lothair Francis, 27 May 1708, HHSA, MEA, Korr. 89; Esebeck, 101.
232. Granier, 165–66.
233. 30 June 1708 Reichsgutachten, Zeumer, 405; Granier, 160–63. Hanover was formally admitted to the Electoral College on 7 September. 6 September 1708 Ratifikations-Commissions-Dekret, Zeumer, 407; Granier, 166–67.
234. Eugene to Joseph, 15 June 1708, *Feldzüge*, X, Supp., 117.
235. Eugene to George Louis, 28 June 1708, Marlborough to Eugene, 24 June 1708, *ibid.*, 131–32, 141. Apparently, the elector was neither deceived nor pleased by the plan worked out by the two generals. Cf. Sinzendorf to Charles, 28 August 1708, HHSA, GK, 74a.
236. Eugene to George Louis, 21 Seitember, 14, 17 October, 11 November, to Joseph, 11, 14 November 1708, *Feldzüge*, X, Supp., 244–45, 287–88, 296, 327–30, 332.
237. Minha, 104–5.
238. Schönborn to Lothair Francis, 31 March 1711, instructions to Sinzendorf, 1 April 1711, HHSA, MEA, Korr. 89; Joseph's notes of 1 April 1711 Conference, HHSA, SK, V 51.

IV. Italy: *The Struggle for Hegemony*

Opening quote: Protocol of 3 January 1708 Conference, HHSA, SK, V 13.
1. Noorden, *Erbfolgekrieg*, I, 159; Klopp, *Der Fall*, IX, 18, 117, 284.
2. *Feldzüge*, VIII, 53, IX, 34.
3. Joseph to Louis William, 18 May 1706, Röder, II, 254.
4. Regele, 56; Braubach, *Prinz Eugen*, I, 353, 442; Joseph to John William, 30 September 1704, Geheimes Staatsarchiv, Kasten Blau 45, Nr. 12.
5. Wratislaw to Charles, 22 February 1705, *Feldzüge*, VII, 546.
6. Wratislaw to Gallas, 14, 21 March 1705, C. Höfler, "Gallas," 300–301.
7. Wratislaw to Charles, 22 February 1705, *Feldzüge*, VII, 546, Eugene to Gallas, 29 May 1705, *ibid.*, Supp., 156; Braubach, *Prinz Eugen*, II, 106.
8. Eugene to Joseph, 26 April 1705, *Feldzüge*, VII, Supp., 104.
9. Redlich, *Grossmacht*, 44–45.
10. Protocols of 19, 26, 29 August 1705 Conferences, HHSA, SK, V 12.
11. Protocol of 26 August 1705 Conference, *ibid.*; Joseph to Louis William, 2 September 1705, Röder, II, 161.
12. Sinzendorf to Charles, 13 September 1705, *Feldzüge*, VII, 540.
13. Marlborough to Stepney, 6 January 1706, Murray, II, 384.
14. Eugene to Gundaker Starhemberg, 12 September, to Joseph, 16 September, to Tarini, 17 September, to *Hofkriegsrat*, 30 October 1705, *Feldzüge*, VII, Supp., 371, 374, 381, 458; Marlborough to Stepney, 6 January 1706, Murray, II, 384.
15. Mensi, 391.

16. Marlborough to Godolphin, 17 October 1704, Snyder, I, 381; to Heinsius, 20, 28 October 1704, Van't Hoff, 143, 146.

17. Marlborough to Stanhope, 3 October, to Wratislaw, 5 October 1705, Murray, II, 288–89, 293.

18. Wratislaw to Gallas, 13 December 1705, Höfler, "Gallas," 310; Noorden, *Erbfolgekrieg,* II, 357.

19. Marlborough to Harley, to Hedges, 14 November 1705, Murray, II, 323; Hanns Leo Mikoletzky, "Die grosse Anleihe von 1706," *Mitteilungen des österreichischen Staatsarchivs,* VII (1954), 276–77.

20. Marlborough to Harley, 18 November 1705, Murray, II, 324–25; Mensi, 353–54, 391–92.

21. Marlborough to Harley, 14 November, to John William, 22 November 1705, Murray, II, 323, 329–30.

22. Marlborough to John William, Instructions to Lescheraine, 31 December 1705, to Harley, 5 January 1706, Murray, II, 368–69, 375–76.

23. Mikoletzky, "Anleihe," 276–77.

24. *Ibid.,* 284; Mensi, 393–94; Gustav Otruba, "Die Bedeutung englischer Subsidien und Antizipationen für die Finanzen Österreichs, 1701–1748," *Vierteljahrschrift für Sozial- und Wirtschaftsgeschichte,* LI (1964), 200.

25. Mensi, 393–94, Otruba, 201; Braubach, *Subsidien,* 40.

26. Bartholdi 2 March 1706 relation, Berney, *Friedrich I,* 268–69.

27. Braubach, *Prinz Eugen,* II, 145, 148.

28. *Feldzüge,* VIII, 84, 180.

29. Marlborough to Sinzendorf, 9 May, to Eugene, 25 May 1706, Murray, II, 497, 524.

30. Eugene to Joseph, 1, 9 October, 21 November 1706, *Feldzüge,* VIII, Supp., 256, 261, 311.

31. Eugene to Joseph, 22 December 1706, *ibid.,* Supp., 329–30.

32. Heinsius to Marlborough, 25 January 1707, Van't Hoff, 293.

33. Elke Jarnut-Derbolav, *Die österreichische Gesandtschaft in London (1700–1711)* (Bonn,
Marlborough to Eugene, 27 December 1706, Murray, III, 268–69.

35. Marcus Landau, *Rom, Wien, Neapel während des spanischen Erbfolgekrieges* (Leipzig, 1885), 286–88; *Feldzüge,* V, 50. .

36. Eugene to Joseph, 8 February 1707, *Feldzüge,* IX, Supp., 25.

37. Marlborough to Wratislaw, 10 January, to Eugene, 7 March 1707, Murray, III, 279–80, 326.

38. Wratislaw to Charles, 15/16, 16 December 1706, 16 March 1707, Arneth, "Eigenhändige Correspondenz," 27, 31, 34; Eugene to Joseph, 8 February 1707, *Feldzüge,* IX, Supp., 19–20.

39. Eugene to Victor Amadeus, 15 February 1707, Feldzüge, IX, Supp., 27.

40. Eugene to Joseph, 1, 9, October 1706, *Feldzüge,* VIII, Supp., 256, 261; 16 March 1707, *ibid.,* IX, Supp., 60.

41. For text, cf. *Feldzüge,* IX, 347–59.

42. Eugene to Joseph, 16 February 1707, *Feldzüge,* IX, Supp., 31.

43. Eugene to Marlborough, 22, 25 March 1707, Murray, III, 375.

44. Marlborough to Sinzendorf, 14 February, 6 June, to Wratislaw, 7 March, 6 June 1707, Murray, III, 315, 329, 389, 392; Godolphin to Marlborough, 14 September 1707, Snyder, II, 913; Heinsius to Marlborough, 15 March 1707, Van't Hoff, 307.

45. Marlborough to Harley, to Eugene, 10 May 1707, Murray, III, 357, 360; Braubach, *Prinz Eugen,* II, 191.
46. Wratislaw to Charles, 21 February 1707. Arneth, "Eigenhändige Correspondenz," 33.
47. *Feldzüge,* IX, 108, 177.
48. Godolphin to Marlborough, 15, 28 April 1707, Snyder, II, 751-52, 755-56, 872.
49. Braubach, *Prinz Eugen,* II, 198–200, 209.
50. *Feldzüge,* V, 50; Redlich, *Grossmacht,* 27; Heinrich Benedikt, *Kaiseradler über dem Apennin. Die Österreicher in Italien, 1700–1866* (Munich, 1964), 174–75.
51. Braubach, *Prinz Eugen,* II, 193.
52. Joseph to Castelbarco, 25 October 1706, *Feldzüge,* VIII, 489, Eugene to Joseph, 31 October, 10 November 1706, *ibid.,* Supp., 276, 294.
53. Eugene to Joseph, 8 February 1707, *ibid.,* IX, Supp., 17–19.
54. Harley to Stepney, 21 December, Stepney to Harley, 28 December 1706, Simonyi, III, 290, 295; Marlborough to Salm, 12 December 1706, 24 January 1707, to Sinzendorf, 6, 12 December 1706, 24 January 1707, to Wratislaw, 6, 12 December 1706, 21 January 1707, Murray, IV, 243–99 *passim;* 23 February 1707 edict, Ettore Parri, *Vittorio Amadeo II ed Eugenio di Savoia nelle Guerre della Successione spagnuola* (Milan, 1888), 235–36; Aretin, 56.
55. Eugene to Joseph, 9 March 1707, *Feldzüge,* IX, Supp., 55.
56. Villars, 202–3.
57. Hantsch, 54.
58. Turba, *Die pragmatische Sanktion* (Vienna, 1906), 18.
59. *Ibid.,* 7–10.
60. Redlich, *Grossmacht,* 24–25. In 1713, however, Charles did revise the *Pactum Mutuae Successionis* to permit his own female descendants to succeed ahead of the two daughters of his dead brother. It is this generally forgotten innovation of the Pragmatic Sanction that made inevitable a future conflict over the Austrian succession between the descendants of Joseph's two daughters and Charles's designated heir, Maria Theresa.
61. Hantsch, 45.
62. Stepney to Harley, 29 April 1705, Simonyi, II, 70.
63. August Fournier, "Zur Entstehungsgeschichte der pragmatischen Sanktion Kaiser Karl's VI," *Historische Zeitschrift,* XXXVIII (1877), 43ff.
64. Wratislaw to Charles, 16 March 1707, Arneth, "Eigenhändige Correspondenz," 39.
65. Charles to Wratislaw, 15/16 December 1706, *ibid.,* 27; Hill to Hedges, 22 July 1705, W. Blackley, *The Diplomatic Correspondence of The Right Honorable Richard Hill* (London, 1845), 582.
66. Stanhope to Godolphin, 24 November 1706, Philip Henry, Earl Stanhope, *History of the War of the Succession in Spain* (London, 1836); Stepney to Harley, 28 December 1706, Simonyi, III, 295.
67. Charles to Wratislaw, 15/16 December 1706, Arneth, "Eigenhändige Correspondenz," 27.
68. Voltes Bou, *Barcelona,* II, 172.
69. Wratislaw to Charles, 10 March 1710, Arneth, "Eigenhändige Correspondenz," 108.
70. Charles to Wratislaw, 8 November 1707, *ibid.,* 47ff.
71. Eugene to Joseph, 1 December 1706, *Feldzüge,* VIII, Supp., 316–17; Braubach, *Prinz Eugen,* II, 191.

72. Charles to Wratislaw, 17 July 1707, Arneth, "Eigenhändige Correspondenz," 43.

73. In a 26 April 1710 letter to the archduke Wratislaw states: "Your Majesty's person does not have sufficient capacity or experience to discharge the important and extensive offices of the Spanish monarchy." He goes on to tell Charles that he is liable to fill high government posts with incompetents. *Ibid.,* 113.

74. Benedikt, *Das Königreich Neapel unter Kaiser Karl VI.* (Vienna, 1927), 67.

75. Joseph's notes of 26 April 1707 Conference, HHSA, SK, V 51; Wratislaw to Charles. 16 March 1707, Arneth, "Eigenhändige Correspondenz," 34.

76. Joseph's notes of 26 April 1707 Conference, HHSA, SK, V 51.

77. Benedikt, *Neapel,* 65, 67–68.

78. Wratislaw to Charles, 2 May 1707, Arneth, "Eigenhändige Correspondenz," 40.

79. Charles to Wratislaw, 17 July 1707, *ibid.,* 43.

80. Landaa, 327–29; Benedikt, *Neapel,* 66, 68.

81. Charles to Wratislaw, 8 November 1707, 8 February 1708, Arneth, "Eigenhändige Correspondenz," 47, 60.

82. Sinzendorf to Charles, 14 June 1708, HHSA, GK 74a.

83. Charles to Wratislaw, 11 July 1708, Arneth, "Eigenhändige Correspondenz," 68.

84. Referat of 25 September 1709 Conference, HHSA, SK, V 14; Landau, 343–45, 348–49; Benedikt, *Neapel,* 93ff.

85. Sinzendorf to Charles, 17 January 1709, HHSA, GK 74b; Landau, 349; 2 September referat of 31 August/2 September 1709 Conferences, HHSA, SK, V 14.

86. Gschliesser, 13.

87. For the most recent example of this interpretation, cf. Aretin, 544–63.

88. Aretin, 549–55.

89. Granier, 122.

90. DeTheillieres to Leopold of Lorraine, 29 May 1707, HHSA, LH 18; Marlborough to Wratislaw, 6, 12 December 1707, Murray, III, 245, 250; Schönborn to Lothair Francis, 23 May 1708, HHSA, MEA, Korr. 89.

91. *Feldzüge,* VII, 54, Eugene to Gallas, 23 October, to Joseph, 23, 30, October 1705, Supp., 442, 446, 453; Fischel, 157.

92. Ingomar Bog, *Der Reichsmerkantilismus* (Stuttgart, 1959), 35; *Feldzüge,* VIII, 332–33, X, 58. By agreement with Victor Amadeus Joseph exempted Savoy from its financial obligations under the war levy. Joseph to Castelbarco, 25 October 1706, *Feldzüge,* VIII, 489–90.

93. Negotiated for 1707: Tuscany, 900,000 florins, Genoa, 300,00 florins, Lucca, 90,000 florins. Braubach, *Prinz Eugen,* II, 171; Eugene to Joseph, 23 February, 3, 27, 30 April, 29 May 1707, *Feldzüge,* IX, Supp., 35–36, 79–80, 112, 115–16, 155–56.

94. Eugene to Joseph, 3 October, 9 November 1707, *Feldzüge,* IX, Supp., 189, 213–14; protocol of 3 January 1708 Conference, HHSA, SK, V 13.

95. *Feldzüge,* VII, 6; Landau, 165, 169–70, 174–75, 182.

96. Cf. H. von Zwiedineck-Südenhörst, "Die Obedienz-Gesandtschaften der deutschen Kaiser an den römischen Hof," *Archiv für österreichischen Geschichte,* LVIII (1879).

97. Stepney to Marlborough, 30 May 1705, Houghton, SCC.

98. Benna, "Preces Primariae und Reichshofrat (1559–1806)," *Mitteilungen*

des österreichischen Staatsarchivs, V (1952), 96; Landau, 196.

99. Clement wrote to Fathers Rummel and Bischoff, Cardinals Grimani, Kollonics, Lamberg and Sachsen-Zeitz. Stepney to Cardonnel, 9, 12 September 1705, Houghton, SCC.

100. Referat of 10 September 1705 Conference, HHSA, SK, V 12; Landau, 194.

101. Eugene to Joseph, 15, 29 December 1706, *Feldzüge,* VIII, Supp., 325, 335–36.

102. Landau, 250–52.

103. *Ibid.,* 261–62.

104. Referat of 15, 19, 20 May 1707 Conferences, HHSA, SK, V 12.

105. Joseph's notes of 24 May 1707 Conference, HHSA, SK, V 51; Joseph to Martinitz, 24 May 1707, HHSA, SA, Rom 86.

106. Martinitz to Joseph, 23 June 1707, HHSA, SA, Rom 85.

107. Martinitz to Joseph, 17 September 1707, HHSA, SA, Rom 85.

108. Landau, 264–65.

109. Hans Kramer, *Habsburg und Rom in den Jahren 1708–1709* (Innsbruck, 1936), 25.

110. Landau, 276–77.

111. Braubach, *Prinz Eugen,* II, 459; Dolfin 24 March 1708 report, Marcello Giudici, *I Dispacci di Germania dell' ambasciatore veneto Daniel Dolfin 3°* (Venice, 1908), II, 203. In fact, the 637,000 florins subsequently collected in Parma were so high that Joseph ultimately approved a refund of approximately 100,000 florins. Joseph's notes of 7 November 1708 Conference, HHSA, SK, V 51; *Feldzüge,* X, 58.

112. J. Söltl, "Von dem römischen Papst. Ein Vortrag für den römischen König Joseph I.," *Historische Zeitschrift,* VI (1861), 24–40.

113. Joseph's notes of 27 December 1706 Conference, HHSA, SK, V 51; Kramer, 14.

114. Joseph to Eugene, 12 April 1707, HHSA, GK 90b.

115. Seilern to Joseph, 18 December 1707, FSSA, III 132.

116. Protocol of 26 January 1708 Conference, HHSA, SK, V 13.

117. Protocols of 2, 31 March 1708 Conferences, 31 March Conclusa, HHSA, SK, V 13.

118. Wratislaw to Charles, 2 August 1708, Arneth, "Eigenhändige Correspondenz," 70.

119. Wratislaw to Charles, 30 August 1708, HHSA, FK, A 18.

120. Lamberg 3 March 1708 memorial, HHSA, FK, A 51.

121. Sinzendorf to Charles, 21 November 1707, HHSA, GK 74a; Wratislaw to Charles, 15 January 1708, Arneth, "Eigenhändige Correspondenz," 59.

122. DeTheillieres to Leopold of Lorraine, 20 January, 29 May 1707, HHSA, LH 18.

123. Sinzendorf to Charles, 21 November 1707, HHSA, GK 74a.

124. Dolfin 9 December 1708 report, Arneth, *Relationen,* 3–4; Aretin, 533.

125. Braubach, *Prinz Eugen,* II, 447.

126. *Ibid.,* 34; *Geschichte und Abenteuer,* 200–201; HHSA, FK, A 51.

127. Wratislaw to Charles, 6 March 1708, HHSA, FK, A 18.

128. Wratislaw to Charles, 7 April 1708, HHSA, FK, A 18; Leopold Matthias Lamberg 3 March 1708 memorial, HHSA, FK 51.

129. *Ibid.*

130. Benedikt, *Der Pascha-Graf Alexander von Bonneval* (Graz, 1959), 19–20.

131. Kramer, 14–15; Landau, 365–68.

132. Protocols of 16 July, 2, 5 August 1708 Conferences, HHSA, SK, V 13; Kramer, 31.

133. Protocols of 16 July, 2 August 1708 Conferences, HHSA, SK, V 13; *Feldzüge,* X, 196.

134. Protocol of 5 August 1708 Conference, HHSA, SK, V 13; Sinzendorf to Charles, 28 August 1708, HHSA, GK 74a.

135. *Feldzüge,* X, 195–96, 200; Landau, 378.

136. Landau, 384.

137. *Feldzüge,* X, 200–202.

138. Protocol of 25 September 1708 Conference, HHSA, SK, V 13. Wratislaw had expressed this opinion as early as 16 September, in a letter to the archduke. Arneth, "Eigenhändige Correspondenz," 76.

139. Joseph to Königsegg, 26 September 1708, HHSA, GK 40.

140. Protocols of 25, 27 September 1708 Conferences, HHSA, SK, V 13.

141. Referat of 12 October 1708 Conference, HHSA, SK, V 13; Sinzendorf to Charles, 4 October 1708, HHSA, GK 74a.

142. Referat of 12 October 1708 Conference, HHSA, SK, V 13.

143. Protocol of 27 September 1708 Conference, referat of 12 October 1708 Conference, HHSA, SK, V 13.

144. Wild, 155.

145. Schönborn to Lothair Francis, 21 July 1708, HHSA, MEA, Korr, 90; referat of 12 October 1708 Conference, HHSA, SK, V 13; Sinzendorf to Charles, 17 January 1709, HHSA, GK 74a.

146. Schönborn to Lothair Francis, 16, 23 May 1708, HHSA, MEA, Korr. 89; Sinzendorf to Charles, 14 June 1708, HHSA, GK 74a; Joseph to Castelbarco, 4 July 1708, HHSA, Sa, Sardinien 40.

147. Landau, 370.

148. Protocols of 25, 27 September 1708 Conferences, HHSA, SK, V 13.

149. *Feldzüge,* X, 200–202; Kramer, 63; Landau, 405–8.

150. Marlborough to Estates General, 24 October 1708, Murray, IV, 275.

151. Marlborough to Palmes, 21 October, to Estates General, 24 October 1708, Murray, IV, 273, 275; Sinzendorf to Charles, 4 October 1708, HHSA, GK 74a; Kramer, 63–64.

152. *Feldzüge,* X, 208–9.

153. Landau, 379, 403.

154. Protocol of 1 December 1708 Conference, HHSA, SK, V 13.

155. 31 August Instructions, *Récueil,* XVII: *Rome,* G. Hanotaux, ed. (Paris, 1911), 374, 414.

156. For details on these negotiations cf. Tessé 3 October report, *Récueil,* XIX: *Florence, Modène, Gênes,* E. Driault, ed. (Paris, 1912), 69; 31 August Instructions, XVII: *Rome,* 381–82, 402, 404–5, 412.

157. *Récueil,* XVII: *Rome,* 369.

158. 31 August, 5 November Instructions, *Récueil,* XXVII: *Rome,* 399, 415–16; Kramer, 37–38.

159. *Feldzüge,* X, 214.

160. Sinzendorf to Charles, 4 October 1708, HHSA, GK 74a.

161. Carl Ringhoffer, *Die Flugschriften-Literatur zu Beginn des spanischen Erbfolgekriegs* (Leipzig, 1881), 110–17; Kramer, 110.

162. Sinzendorf to Charles, 4 October 1708, HHSA, GK 74a; Landau, 411.

163. Protocol of 1 December 1708 Conference, HHSA, SK, V 13.

164. Protocols of 1, 17, 18 December 1708 Conferences, HHSA, SK V 13,

of 2, 3 January 1709 Conferences, HHSA, SK, V 13; Hantsch, 121, 387.

165. Protocol of 17, 18 December 1708 Conferences, HHSA, SK, V 13. In addition to Seilern and Windischgrätz, Sinzendorf, Trautson, Herberstein and Gundaker Starhemberg were present.

166. 17 December Wratislaw *votum,* HHSA, SK, V 13.

167. 17 December Salm *votum,* HHSA, SK, V 13.

168. Landau, 422.

169. Protocol of 2, 3 January 1709 Conferences, HHSA, SK, V 13.

170. *Feldzüge,* X, 218.

171. Landau, 425–28.

172. HHSA, ÖA, Österreich Staat 2.

173. Protocols of 14, 15, 16 February 1709 Conferences, HHSA, SK, V 13.

174. Kramer, 100.

175. Protocol, referat of 7 November 1709 Conference, HHSA, SK, V 13.

176. Protocols of 15, 16 February 1709 Conferences, HHSA, SK, V 13.

177. Protocol of 13 April 1709 Conference, HHSA, SK, V 13.

178. Landau, 432.

179. Protocols of 22 May, 20 July 1709 Conferences, HHSA, SK, V 14.

180. Landau, 431.

181. Kramer, 98.

182. Protocol of 20 July 1709 Conference, HHSA, SK, V 14.

183. Kramer, 119.

184. Protocol of 14 October 1709 Conference, HHSA, SK, V 14.

185. Referat of 7 November, protocol of 12 November 1709 Conferences, HHSA, SK V 14; Kramer, 121.

186. Joseph's notes of 12 November 1709 Conference, HHSA, SK, V 51; Kramer 121.

187. Referat of 31 December 1709 Conference, HHSA, SK, V 14; protocols of 9 January, 24 April 1710 Conferences, HHSA, SK, V 15.

188. *Feldzüge,* XI, 36, 41. Comacchio yielded approximately 100,000 florins annually in taxes. Braubach, *Prinz Eugen,* II, 262.

189. Referat of 31 December 1709 Conference, n.d. protocol of 1709 Conference, HHSA, SK, V 14.

190. Hantsch, 113.

191. Protocol of 11 March 1710 Conference, HHSA, SK, V 15.

192. Ludwig Fr. von Paster, *History of the Popes,* transl. by D. E. Graf, (London, 1940), XXIII, 80–81.

193. Protocols of 15, 24 April, 5 May 1710 Conferences, HHSA, SK, V 15.

194. Protocol of 9 October 1710 Conference, HHSA, SK, V 15.

195. Protocol of 21 October 1710 Conference, HHSA, SK, V 15.

196. Joseph's notes of 31 October 1710 Conference, HHSA, FK, Fam. 96; protocol of 31 October 1710 Conference, HHSA, SK, V 15.

197. Joseph to Castelbarco, 31 October 1710, HHSA, SA, Sardinien 28.

198. Protocol of 7 January 1711 Conference, HHSA, SK, V 16.

199. 11 March 1711 referat, HHSA, SK, V 16.

200. They also proposed that these future acquisitions could be given to the archduke in the event that he failed to win Spain, thereby permitting the younger Habsburg line to "establish itself and expand in Italy, which in the future would become a great factor in the all important equilibrium of Europe. . . ." *Ibid.*

201. *Ibid.* At about the same time that he made this offer, Albani gave the court a second incentive to preserve relations by announcing his uncle's

willingness to permit the Milanese church to be assessed 300,000 florins during 1711. Since 1709, Joseph had refrained from levying taxes on the clergy in Milan. Protocol of 24 July 1710 Conference, HHSA, SK, V 15; protocol of 15 March 1711 Conference, HHSA, SK, V 16.

202. 11 March 1711 referat, HHSA, SK, V 16.

203. Protocol of 8 April 1711 Conference, HHSA, SK, V 16.

204. Wratislaw to Sinzendorf, 8 April 1711, HHSA, GK 71; Wratislaw to Charles, 22 April 1711, Arneth, "Eigenhändige Correspondenz," 147; protocol of 8 April 1711 Conference, HHSA, SK, V 16.

205. Joseph's notes of 8 April 1711 Conference, HHSA, FK, Fam. 96.

206. For information on the war levy in Parma from 1709 to 1711, cf. *Feldzüge,* XI, 36, 41, XII, 264, XIII, 320; protocol of 25 October 1710 Conference, HHSA, SK, V 15.

207. Wratislaw to Charles, 27 March 1708, HHSA, FK, A 18; Joseph's notes of 12 April 1708 Conference, HHSA, SK, V 51; Charles to Wratislaw, 11 July 1708, Arneth, "Eigenhändige Correspondenz," 68.

208. Protocol, referat of 20 September, protocol of 3 November 1708 Conferences, HHSA, SK, V 13; Wratislaw to Charles, 6 November 1708, HHSA, FK, A 18.

209. Sinzendorf to Charles, 28 August 1708, HHSA, GK 74a.

210. Wratislaw to Charles, 15 January 1711, Arneth, "Eigenhändige Correspondenz," 136.

211. Protocol of 9 October 1708 Conference, HHSA, SK, V 13; protocol of 16 December 1709 Conference, HHSA, SK, V 14; Trautson to Sinzendorf, 7 June 1710, HHSA, GK 70.

212. Gschliesser, 26.

213. Joseph's notes of 23 December 1709 Conference, HHSA, SK, V 51; protocol of 23 December 1709 Conference, HHSA, SK, V 14; Wratislaw to Sinzendorf, 25 December 1709, HHSA, GK 71.

214. Trautson to Sinzendorf, 26 April 1710, HHSA, GK 70.

215. Wratislaw to Sinzendorf, 23 April, 3 May 1710, HHSA, GK 71; protocols of 3, 4, 30 May, 20 June, 15 July 1710 Conferences, HHSA, SK, V 15.

216. Sinzendorf to Charles, 14 June 1708, HHSA, GK 74a.

217. Cf. below pp. 170, 195.

218. Sinzendorf to Charles, 28 August 1708, HHSA, GK 74a.

219. Wratislaw to Charles, 15 January 1709, HHSA, FK, A 18; Granier, 228.

220. Granier, 227–29. Joseph eventually compensated the duke of Guastalla with the Mantuan towns of Sabionetta and Bozzolo.

V. Hungary: *The Rákóczi Rebellion*

Opening quote: Wratislaw to Charles, 18 April 1705, Arneth, "Eigenhändige Correspondenz," 17.

1. Ignácz Acsády, *Magyarország története I. Lipót és I. József korában (1657–1711)* (Budapest, 1898), 536; Ágnes Várkonyi, "Hapsburg Absolutism and Serfdom in Hungary at the Turn of the XVIIth and XVIIIth Centuries," in *Nouvelles études historiques* (Budapest, 1965), I, 359–60, 364–69, "A Jobbágyság Osztályharca a Rákóczi-Szabadságharc idején," *Történelmi Szemle,* VII (1964), 376.

2. Theodor Mayer, *Verwaltungsreform in Ungarn nach der Türkenzeit*

(Vienna, 1911), 10–11, 16–17, 19–20, 24, 51–54, 83–84; Ignaz Aurelius Fessler, *Geschichte von Ungarn* (Leipzig, 1877), IV, 525.

3. Sándor Márki, *II. Rákóczi Ferencz,* (Budapest, 1907–1910), I, 290; Gyula Szekfü, *Magyar történet,* IV (Budapest, 1935), 278–79.

4. Tamás Esze, *II. Rákóczi Ferenc tiszántúli hadjárata* (Budapest, 1951), 83–87; P. Z. Pach, "Le problème du rassemblement des forces nationales pendant la guerre d'indépendence de François II. Rákóczi," *Acta Historica. Academiae Scientarum Hungaricae,* III (1956), 100–102; Márki, I, 290, 293; Várkonyi, "Jobbágyság," 376.

5. E. Révész, *Esquisse de l'histoire de la politique religieuse hongroise entre 1705 et 1860 (Studia Historica. Academiae Scientiarum Hungaricae,* XXVI [1960]), 5–17; Acsády, 561; Márki, I, 285, 479; Fessler, IV, 515; Bidermann, *Gesamt-Staats-Idee,* II, 53, 156.

6. Kurt Wessely, "The Development of the Hungarian Military Frontier until the middle of the eighteenth century," *Austrian History Yearbook,* IX–X (1973–1974), 57.

7. Pach, 99–102; Márki, I, 285, 293; Acsády, 533–34, 561; Esze, 9; Várkonyi, "Absolutism and Serfdom," 385, "A Dunántúl felszabadítása 1705-ben," *Századok,* LXXXVI (1952), 403–7.

8. Stepney to Marlborough, 16 April 1704, Simonyi, I, 242; Ladislas Baron Hengelmüller, *Hungary's Fight for National Existence* (London, 1913), 175. For a survey of Hungarian society and politics, cf. Henrik Marczali, *Hungary in the Eighteenth Century* (Cambridge, 1910) and Béla Király, *Hungary in the Late Eighteenth Century* (New York, 1969).

9. Árpád Markó, "Les soldats français dans la guerre d'indépendence hongroise," *Revue des études hongroises,* 1933. For Rákóczi's relations with Versailles prior to 1705, cf. Béla Köpeczi, *La France et la Hongrie au début du XVIIIe siècle* (Budapest, 1971), 35–57 and Émile Pillias, "Louis XIV et le problème hongrois," *Nouvelle revue de Hongrie,* LIV (1936).

10. Kálmán Benda, "II. Rákóczi Ferenc török politikájának elsö évei 1702–1705," *Történelmi Szemle,* V (1962), *Le projet d'alliance hungaro-suédo-prussienne de 1704 (Studia Historica. Academiae Scientiarum Hungaricae,* XXV [1960]); Gábor Kiss, "Franz Rákóczi II., Peter der Grosse und der polnische Thron," *Jahrbücher für Geschichte Osteuropas,* XIII (1965), 348–49.

11. Stepney to Hedges, 6 May, to Kaunitz, 20 May 1704, Simonyi, I, 268, 281–84; Churchill, IV, 178.

12. Albert Lefaivre, "L'Insurrection magyar sous François II Ragoczy," *Revue des questions historiques,* XXV (1901), 544; Hengelmüller, 184–85.

13. Whitworth to Hedges, 5 March 1704, Simonyi, I, 158–62; Hengelmüller, 185.

14. Hengelmüller, 182–84.

15. Fessler, V, 5. For Latin text, cf. Höfler, "Zum Ungarischen Ausgleich im Jahre 1705," *Archiv für österreichische Geschichte,* XLIII (1870), 220; Stepney to Harley, 16 May 1705, Simonyi, II, 85.

16. Stepney to Marlborough, 27 May, to ?, 27 June 1705, Houghton, SCC.

17. The Hungarian Conference comprised Salm, Öttingen, Wratislaw, Seilern, Sinzendorf, Kinsky, and Prince Eugene. Wratislaw to Gallas, 17 June 1705, Höfler, "Ungarischen Ausgleich," 303.

18. Stepney to Cardonnel, 13 June 1705, Houghton, SCC.

19. L. B. F. Lamberty, *Mémoires pour servir à l'histoire du XVIIIe siècle,* III (Paris, 1726), 607–8.

20. "Observations Secrètes . . . de Mars 1704. . . . ," Simonyi, I, 226.

21. Stepney to Harley, 20, 27 June 1705, *ibid.*, II, 138, 144–52; Jeszensky 18 June 1705 relation, Höfler, "Ungarischen Ausgleich," 303.

22. 9 July 1705 resolutio, Joseph to Goëss, 4 July 1705, HHSA, UA 188.

23. Stepney to ?, 1 July 1705, Houghton, SCC.

24. Salm to Wratislaw, 6 February 1705, HHSA, SK, Diplomatische Korrespondenz, Kleinere Betreffe 16; Wratislaw to Charles, 18 April 1705, Arneth, "Eigenhändige Correspondenz," 15; Eugene to *Hofkriegsrat*, 22 May 1705, *Feldzüge*, VII, Supp. 140.

25. Salm to Leopold, n.d., FSSA, III 61; Salm to Wratislaw, 16 January, 6, 27 February 1705, HHSA, SK, Diplomatische Korrespondenz, Kleinere Betreffe 16.

26. Salm to Joseph, 10 May 1705, HHSA, RK, Kleinere Reichsstände 471; Stepney to Harley, 13 May 1705, Simonyi, II, 82; Eugene to Joseph, 18 May 1705, *Feldzüge*, VII, 426, Supp. 126.

27. Stepney to Marlborough, 16 May 1705, Simonyi, II, 87.

28. "Journal des Ministres Plénipotentiaires . . . 21 September 1705," Simonyi, II, 439–40; Eugene to Joseph, 18 May 1705, *Feldzüge*, VII, Supp., 125–26.

29. Benda, "II. Rákóczi Ferenc török politikájának elsö évei," 210; Louis Rousseau, *Les relations diplomatiques de la France et de la Turquie au XVIIIe siècle* (Paris, 1908), I, 130–32, 136–37.

30. Stepney to Harley, 5 September 1705, Simonyi, II, 202.

31. Stepney to Harley, 6 June 1705, *ibid.*, 111; Eugene to Joseph, 18 May 1705, *Feldzüge*, VII, Supp., 125–26.

32. Joseph to Gallas, 7 June 1705, Höfler, "Ungarischen Ausgleich," 216.

33. *Ibid.*, 209; *Feldzüge*, VII, 28.

34. By Rákóczi's account 35 towns were destroyed in the July raids alone. Rákóczi to Vetes, 29 July 1705, Fiedler, *Actenstücke*, I (*Fontes Rerum Austriacarum*, IX [1855]), 282, 369.

35. Stepney to Harley, 25 July, 22, 26 August 1705, Simonyi, II, 176, 193, 195; Hengelmüller, 252.

36. Salm to Esterházy, 25 June 1705, Magyar Országos Levéltár, Nádor Levéltár 3.

37. Esze, 83–87; Pach, 103; Márki, II, 367–68.

38. Rákóczi to Louis, 8 July 1705, Fiedler, *Actenstücke*, II (*Fontes Rerum Austriacarum*, XVII [1858]), 452. Louis had increased Rákóczi's monthly subsidy from 15,000 to 75,000 florins. Chamillart to Vetes, 19 May 1705, Fiedler, *Actenstücke*, I, 281.

39. Rákóczi to Vetes, 29 Juls 1705, Fiedler, *Actenstücke*, I, 282, 284, 369, 371.

40. Márki, II, 367–71; Szekfü, 298; Hengelmüller, 261–67.

41. Pach, 106–7.

42. Köpeczi and Várkonyi, *II. Rákóczi Ferenc* (Budapest, 1955), 205–6.

43. Rouillé to Vetes, 8, 21 September, Torcy to Vetes, 30 September, 6 October 1705, Fiedler, *Actenstücke*, I, 286–88.

44. "Contrary to our expectations, our arms have not been successful and the planned objectives of our operations have proved beyond our means. Therefore, our principal pretensions will be reduced and moderated." Joseph to Wratislaw, 22 October 1705, HHSA, UA, 191.

45. "Journal des Ministres . . . 3 December 1705," Simonyi, II, 476–77.

46. Stepney to Harley, 28 November, 2, 12 December 1705, *ibid.,* 249–72, *passim.*

47. Stepney to Harley, 4 November 1705, Simonyi, II, 229.

48. "Journal des Ministres . . . 3, 9 December 1705," Sinzendorf to mediators, 2 December 1705, *ibid.,* 476–79, 553.

49. Stepney to Harley, 23 December, Dutch mediators to Stepney, 14, 24 December 1705, *ibid.* 277–307, *passim*; 14 December memorial, HHSA, UA 188.

50. Stepney to Harley, 2 December 1705, Simonyi, II, 255–56.

51. Joseph to mediators, 18 December 1705, HHSA, UA 188.

52. Fessler, V, 27–28; Hengelmüller, 273; *Feldzüge,* VII, 461.

53. "Journal des Ministres . . . 20 December 1705," Stepney to Harley, 23 December, Dutch mediators to Stepney, 24 December 1705, Simonyi, II, 297, 304–6, 484.

54. Joseph to Gallas, 23 December 1705, Höfler, "Ungarischen Ausgleich," 276.

55. Stepney to Harley, 11, 16, 20 January 1706, Simonyi, II, 342, 351, 359.

56. Referat of 25 January 1706 Conference, HHSA, UA 189; Stepney to Dutch mediators, 21 January, to Harley, 23 January, Hamel Bruynincx to Stepney, 23 January 1706, Simonyi, II, 365–76.

57. Rákóczi to Louis XIV, 30 December 1705, Fiedler, *Actenstücke,* II, 454.

58. F. Krones, "Zur Geschichte Ungarns im Zeitalter Franz Rákóczi's II." *Archiv für österreichische Geschichte,* XLII (1870), 294; Hengelmüller, 286–88.

59. Hengelmüller, 301.

60. Wratislaw to Joseph, 2, 3, 5, 6 May 1706, HHSA, UA 190.

61. Stepney to Harley, 1 May 1706, Simonyi, III, 1.

62. Salm to Wratislaw, 30 April 1706, HHSA, UA 189; Wratislaw to Salm, 29 April 1706, FSSA, III, 128. Indeed, if we are to believe Desalleurs, the princess urged her husband not to accept the offer. Cf. Hengelmüller, 310–11.

63. Rechteren to Wratislaw, 24 May, Wratislaw to Rechteren, 26 May, Stepney and Rechteren to Wratislaw, 29 May 1706, HHSA, UA 190.

64. Wratislaw, Lorraine to mediators, 13 June 1706, Simonyi, III, 68, 71.

65. Stepney to Harley, 14 June 1706, *ibid.,* 73.

66. For the complete list, cf. Fessler, V, 38–42; for the published original, cf. "Puncta Pacis . . . ," HHSA, UA 431d.

67. Wratislaw to Princess Rákóczi, 22 June 1706, HHSA, UA 190.

68. Fessler, V, 38–42; "Kurzer Abstract . . . ," n.d., HHSA, UA 190.

69. Dutch mediators to Lorraine, 30 June, Stepney to Harley, 2 July 1706, Simonyi, III, 98, 106.

70. Hengelmüller, 321.

71. Stepney to Harley, 6 July 1706, Simonyi, III, 125.

72. Joseph to Lorraine, 29 June 1706, HHSA, UA 190.

73. Joseph's notes of 30 June Conference, HHSA, V 51; Joseph to Louis William, 4, 18 July 1706, Röder, II, 266, 272.

74. Joseph's notes of 11 July Conference, HHSA, V 51; Wratislaw to mediators, Stepney to Harley, 12 July 1706, Simonyi, III, 138–39.

75. Fury to Lewis, 21 July 1706, Simonyi, III, 163; Hengelmüller, 327.

76. Stepney to Harley, 31 July, 4 September 1706. "'Tis very hard on the labouring, paying, fighting Allies, to have their good offices so rewarded." Tilson to Stepney, 6 August 1706. The announcement that Joseph had with-

drawn 4,000 men from the Upper Rhine for service in Hungary increased further the allies' criticism. As Secretary Harley wrote to Stepney on 13 August, "That while the Queen and the States were exerting themselves with success to the utmost on the behalf of the House of Austria, in Spain, in Italy, in Flanders and Brabant, and yet the Court at Vienna have not the least Complaisance for the Queen or the States, and are so far from doing anything to give assistance, that they by their conduct put greater difficulties upon the allies, so that the French really reap the benefit of our victories. . . ." Also cf. Harley to Stepney, 17 August 1706. Simonyi, III, 176, 184, 190, 206, 228.

77. Fessler, V, 38.

78. Stepney to Harley, 24 July 1706, Simonyi, III, 168. Rákóczi was fully aware of his success in manipulating the mediators. On 4 August 1706, he wrote the diplomat Groffey boasting that "I have had the great pleasure of convincing the mediators of the slight sincerity of the Vienna court. They hold it for certain that the blame lies there that it has not come to the conclusion of peace. Fiedler, *Actenstücke*, III, 21, 24.

79. Enclosure of 4 August 1706, Simonyi, III, 181.

80. Fessler, V, 43; Hengelmüller, 328.

81. Enclosure of 4 August 1706, Simonyi, III, 181–82; Hengelmüller, 330.

82. "Since I have begun to acquaint myself with the French court, I have become convinced that it will not spare us its beautiful words and money, but will never commit itself to anything tangible. Your Highness must be very careful that the singing of these sirens not bring Your Majesty and the country to ruin. Press for the conclusion of the alliance and, if it does not respond readily, it is my opinion that Your Majesty use the presently favorable opportunity to conclude peace with the Vienna court. . . ." Vetes to Rákóczi, 16 February 1706, Fiedler, *Actenstücke*, I, 42, 375; cf. also Vetes to Rákóczi, 10 May 1706, *ibid.*, 45, 378.

83. Wratislaw had the benefit of a letter written by Rákóczi to Louis XIV which had been intercepted by John William and sent to Vienna. Klopp, *Der Fall*, XII, 167.

84. Louis had justified this demand by professing a reluctance to ally with rebels against their rightful sovereign. Rákóczi to Vetes, 20 March 1706, Fiedler, *Actenstücke*, I, 289, 377; to Max Emanuel, 20 March 1706, Simonyi, II, 571–72.

85. Rákóczi to Fierville, 21 April 1706, Fiedler, *Actenstücke*, III, 405.

86. Strattmann to Joseph, 29 March 1706, HHSA, UA 191; Fessler, V, 75. "I believe that the situation will quickly lead to a formal dethronement, especially if we can reach an accord with the king of Sweden." Rákóczi to Groffey, 4 August 1706, Fiedler, *Actenstücke*, III, 421.

87. Vetes to Rákóczi, 19 October, 29 November 1706, Fiedler, *Actenstücke*, I, 46, 48, 380.

88. Vetes to Rákóczi, 19 March 1707, *ibid.*, 49, 382.

89. Rákóczi to Louis XIV, 18 December 1706, *ibid.* II, 474.

90. Strattmann to Joseph 9, 29 March, 5, 12, 26 April 1706, protocol of 9 December 1706 Conference, HHSA, UA 191; Stepney to Harley, 24 October 1706, Simonyi, III, 258.

91. Stepney to Harley, 14 August 1706, Simonyi, III, 192.

92. Hamel Bruynincx to Stepney, 22 December 1706, *ibid.*, 291.

93. Fessler, V, 54–55.

94. Bidermann, *Gesamt-Staats-Idee*, II, 155; Redlich, *Grossmacht*, 184.

95. Stepney to Harley, 11 January 1707, Simonyi, III, 301.
96. Fessler, V, 58.
97. This narration of the events at Ónod is based on Fessler, V, 59–65. Historians have been left to debate whether the violence on the floor of the Ónod Diet on 6 June 1707 was worked out beforehand by Rákóczi and his lieutenants. In his memoirs, the prince asserts that the attacks on Rakovsky and Okolicsanyi were completely spontaneous. Meanwhile, in a statement issued in 1714 entitled "Particularités secraites de la prentendue Diette d'Onod de 1707," Vetes accuses Rákóczi of having plotted the two men's death (cf. Fiedler, *Actenstücke*, I, 292–94). Since Vetes was awaiting amnesty from King Charles III at the time these charges were published, his word can also not be accepted as hard evidence. Consequently, we can rely only on our knowledge of the events of 3–9 June 1707 in speculating whether the murder of Rakovsky and Okolicsanyi was committed in the first or the second degree.
98. Fessler, V, 68.
99. *Feldzüge*, IX, 307; Joseph's notes of 3 August Conference, HHSA, V 51.
100. Meadows to Harley, 3 September 1707, Simonyi, III, 336.
101. Fessler, V, 71–72.
102. Meadows to Harley, 14 December 1707, Simonyi, III, 350.
103. Pach, 107–8, 110; Márki, I, 485–89.
104. Fessler, V, 73.
105. Manifestos of 4, 20, 25 August 1707, HHSA, UA 192; Fessler, V, 68.
106. Landau, 439; Kramer, 118. For the failure of Rákóczi's papal diplomacy, cf. Benda, "Rákóczi és a Vatikán," *Történelmi Szemle*, II (1959).
107. Joseph's notes of 23 December 1707 Conference, HHSA, V 51.
108. Meadows to Hamel Bruynincx, 14 December 1707, Simonyi, III, 353.
109. Lamberg 3 March 1708 memorial, HHSA, FK A 51; Meadows to Harley, 3, 7, 10, 14 March 1708, Simonyi, III, 365–68.
110. Lamberg 10 March 1708 memorial, HHSA, FK A 51.
111. Sinzendorf to Charles, 17 March 1708, HHSA, GK74a; Fessler, V, 80; Rinck, 428.
112. Meadows to Harley, 2 June 1708, Simonyi, III 380.
113. Meadows to Harley, 13 June 1708, *ibid.,* 382.
114. *Ibid.; Feldzüge*, X, 10–11.
115. Meadows to Harley, 14 July, 4 August 1708, Simonyi, III, 388, 392; Rinck, 425–27.
116. Sinzendorf to Charles, 31 July 1708, HHSA, GK 74d.
117. Vetes to Rákóczi, 23 June 1708, Fiedler, *Actenstücke*, I, 95.
118. Vetes to Max Emanuel, 19 July 1707, *ibid.,* 63.
119. Rákóczi to Vetes, 13 October 1707, *ibid.,* 80, 295; Fessler, V, 65–66, 78. Nor was Rákóczi's luck any better with Charles XII or Tsar Peter. He approached both princes during the course of 1707, and although the tsar actually concluded an alliance in September promising him the Polish crown and aid against Joseph, Charles XII's departure from Silesia ended any chance of future cooperation.
120. Lefaivre, 563.
121. Rákóczi to Vetes, 29 April 1708, Fiedler, *Actenstücke*, I, 95, 323.
122. Rousseau, 214; Köpeczi, 221.
123. Vetes to Rákóczi, 1 February, 1 May 1708, Fiedler, *Actenstücke*, I, 83, 92.
124. Fessler, V, 84.

125. Sinzendorf to Charles, 14 June, 31 July 1708, HHSA, GK 74a.

126. Protocol of 8 May 1708 Conference, HHSA, SK, V 13; referat of 18 June 1708 Conference, HHSA, RK 6b; Fessler, V, 85–86.

127. Joseph's notes of 24 August 1707 Conference, HHSA, SK, V 51.

128. Eugene to Hofkriegsrat, 19 September 1708, *Feldzüge,* X, Supp., 239; Fessler, V, 85–87.

129. Wratislaw to Charles, 15 January 1709, HHSA, FK, A 18; F. Krones, 316, 322; Köpeczi, 221.

130. Meadows to Harley, 1, 8, 12, 15 September 1708, Simonyi, III, 386–400.

131. Vetes to Rákóczi, 3 July 1708, Fiedler, *Actenstücke,* I, 96–97.

132. J. Perenyi, "Projets de pacification européenne de F. Rákóczi en 1708–1709," *Tudomány Egyetum. Annales. Sectio Historica,* VI (1964); Köpeczi, 203–21.

133. Rákóczi to Marlborough, 18 October 1708, Fiedler, *Actenstücke,* II, 17; Meadows to Sunderland, 3 November 1708, Simonyi, III, 408.

134. Fiedler, *Actenstücke,* II, 18–52; Fessler, V, 92–93.

135. Fessler, V, 91.

136. Meadows to Sunderland, 3 November 1708, Simonyi, III, 408; Palmes to Raby, 27 January, 4 February 1709, Fiedler, *Actenstücke,* II, 125.

137. Meadows to Harley, 5, 16, 23 January, 2 February, to Boyle, 20 February 1709, Simonyi, III, 416–22, 428.

138. Meadows to Boyle, 22 June 1709, *ibid.,* 445; Rinck, 514–16.

139. Meadows to Harley, 2 June 1708, Simonyi, III, 380.

140. Sachsen-Zeitz to Wratislaw, 10 June 1709, HHSA, GK 65; Meadows to Boyle, 20 July 1709, Simonyi, III, 448.

141. Wratislaw to Charles, 27 November 1709, HHSA, FK, A 18; Fessler, V, 97.

142. Sinzendorf to Kellers, 8 April 1709, HHSA, GK 74d; Vetes to Rákóczi, 15 August, Rákóczi to Vetes, 8 December 1709, Fiedler, *Actenstücke,* I, 141, 336. To help curtail desertion and boost enlistments, a confederate conclave meeting at Sárospatak in December 1708 belatedly promised all *kuruc* soldiers permanent release from serfdom if they served until the war's end. The resolution appears to have come too late, however. Esze, 87; Pach, 110–11; Várkonyi, "Jobbágyság," 377.

143. Eugene to Heister, 30 November 1709, *Feldzüge,* XI, Supp., 271.

144. Bidermann, *Gesamt-Staats-Idee,* II, 23.

145. Wratislaw to Sinzendorf, 14 September 1709, HHSA, GK 71; 23 January 1710 decree, HHSA, UA 192.

146. Fessler, V, 101.

147. Rákóczi to Lamberg, Hamel Bruynincx, 29 July 1709, Fiedler, *Actenstücke,* II, 66.

148. Hamel Bruynincx to Rákóczi, 2 November 1709, *ibid.,* 77; protocol of 14 October 1709 Conference, HHSA, SK, V 14.

149. Palmes to Raby, 9 August 1710, Fiedler, *Actenstücke,* II, 123.

150. Trautson to Sinzendorf, 1 March, Wratislaw to Sinzendorf, 4 March 1710, HHSA, GK 70, 71.

151. Protocol of 15, 16 February 1710 Conferences, HHSA, SK, V 15.

152. Joseph's notes of 15 February 1710 Conference, HHSA, SK, V 51; referat of 24 February 1710 Conference, HHSA, SK, V 16.

153. Wratislaw to Sinzendorf, 10 January 1711, HHSA, GK 71.

154. Wratislaw to Sinzendorf, 20 December 1710, HHSA, GK 71; protocols of 18, 19, 22 December 1710, 6, 12, 18 January, 1, 22, 23 February 1711 Conferences, referat of 22 February 1711 Conference, HHSA, SK, V 15, 16.

155. Sutton to Dartmouth, 8 December 1710, 7, 22 January 1711, Akdes Nimet Kurat, *The Despatches of Sir Robert Sutton, Ambassador to Constantinople (1710–1714)*, (London, 1953), 29, 32, 37; Marlborough to St. John, 2 January, St. John to Palmes, to Peterborough, 30 January 1711, Simonyi, III, 470, 475, 477.

156. Joseph to Pálffy, 26 September 1710, Imre Lukinich, *A szatmári béke története okirattára* (Budapest, 1925), 15; Wratislaw to Charles, 28 October 1710, HHSA, FK, A 18; Fessler, V, 107–8.

157. Wratislaw to Charles, 28 October 1710, HHSA, FK, A 18; Pálffy to Trautson, 9 January 1711, HHSA, UA 193; Joseph to Pálffy, 18 February 1711, Lukinich, 255–60.

158. Palmes to St. John, 20, 31 December 1710, 31 January 1711, bsimonyi, III, 467, 469, 480.

159. Pálffy to Trautson, 9 January 1711, Lukinich, 227–28.

160. Joseph to Pálffy, 22 December 1710, 19 January 1711, protocol of 19 January 1711 Conference, Lukinich, 217–18, 231–32.

161. Joseph to Pálffy, 19 January, protocol of 19 January 1711 Conference, Lukinich, 231–32.

162. Protocol of 10 February 1711 Conference, *ibid.,* 248–50; Wratislaw to Sinzendorf, 11 February 1711, HHSA, GK 71.

163. Protocol of 10 February 1711 Conference, Lukinich, 248–50.

164. Wratislaw to Sinzendorf, 14 February 1711, HHSA, GK 71.

165. Pálffy to Eugene, 8 February 1711, Lukinich, 246.

166. Restitution was guaranteed up to the first 10,000 florins. Protocol of 14 February 1711 Conference, Lukinich, 250–53.

167. Wratislaw to Charles, 26 October 1710, HHSA, FK, A 18.

168. Protocol of 14 February 1711 Conference, Lukinich, 250–53.

169. *Ibid.*; Wratislaw to Charles, 18 February 1711, HHSA, FK, A 18.

170. Eugene to Pálffy, 17 February 1711, Lukinich, 253–55.

171. Joseph to Pálffy, 18 February 1711, *ibid.,* 255–60.

172. Pálffy to *Hofkriegsrat*, 25 February 1711, *ibid.,* 266–68.

173. Locher to Eugene, 16 March 1711, *ibid.,* 272; Fessler, V, 116.

174. Fessler, V, 117.

175. Pálffy to Eugene, 7 April 1711, Lukinich, 288–90.

176. Fessler, V, 117–18.

177. Fessler, V, 120–21; Redlich, *Grossmacht,* 152. Which he, nonetheless, never did. Both Rákóczi and Bercsényi would spend the rest of their lives in exile.

178. Joseph to Pálffy, 18 February 1711, Lukinich, 259–60.

179. Trautson to Sinzendorf, 28 February 1711, HHSA, GK 70.

180. Protocol of 16 April 1711 Conference, HHSA, SK, V 16.

181. Acsády, 254.

182. Trautson to Sinzendorf, 19 July 1710, HHSA, GK 70.

183. Palmes 14 February 1711 report, Simonyi, III, 483.

184. *Feldzüge,* VII, 53, IX, 34; Mensi, 107.

185. Nonetheless, during 1709 Joseph directed his ambassador in London not to criticize the passage of new laws persecuting Ireland's Roman Catholics. Jarnut-Derbolav, 268–69.

186. Palmes 18 March 1711 report, Simonyi, III, 488.
187. St. John to Peterborough, 18 May 1711 (O.S.), H. H. Fieldhouse, "St. John and Savoy in the War of the Spanish Succession," *English Historical Review,* L (1935), 289.

VI. The Spanish Inheritance: *Alliance Diplomacy*

Opening quote: Trautson to Sinzendorf, 8 April 1711, HHSA, GK 70.
1. Joseph's notes of 17 July 1707 Conference, HHSA, SK 51.
2. Referat of 7 January 1707 Conference, HHSA, SK, V 13; Marlborough to Galway, 28 September 1707, Murray, III, 599; instructions to Prince Eugene, n.d., Eugene to Joseph, 17 April 1708, *Feldzüge,* IX, Supp., 47, X, Supp., 67.
3. 14 April 1708 convention, *Feldzüge,* X, Supp., 68–69.
4. Wratislaw to Charles, 15 January 1708, Arneth, "Eigenhändige Correspondenz," 56.
5. Joseph's notes of 12 December 1707, 7 February 1708 Conferences, HHSA, SK, V 51.
6. Joseph to Eugene, 11 July 1708, HHSA, GK 90b.
7. Wratislaw to Charles, 26 January 1706, Arneth, "Eigenhändige Correspondenz," 21; 26 April 1708, HHSA, FK, A 18.
8. Charles to Starhemberg, 3 October 1708, Archivo Histórico Nacional, Sección de Estado 8692.
9. Klopp, *Der Fall,* XIII, 88–98; Braubach, *Subsdien,* 96; Voltes Bou, *El Archiduque Carlos de Austria. Rey de los Catalanes* (Barcelona, 1953), 186, 190; Pribram, *Österreichische Staatsverträge. England I: 1516–1748* (Innsbruck, 1907), 249–50.
10. For the war in Spain, cf. David Francis, *The First Peninsular War 1702–1713* (New York, 1975).
11. Voltes Bou, *Barcelona,* I, 141–42, 147–48, 171–74, II, 170; Braubach, *Subsidien,* 37, 185; Churchill, V, 67–68.
12. Pieter Geyl, *The Netherlands in the Seventeenth Century, II: 1648–1715* (London, 1964), 312; *Feldzüge,* X, 48–49.
13. Marlborough to Godolphin, 30 August 1706, Snyder, II, 653–54.
14. Arnold, 132, 138.
15. Granier, 128–29; Wolfgang Peters, "Die Franche-Comté, Neuchâtel und die oranische Sukzession in den Plänen der preussischen Politik während des spanischen Erbfolgekrieges," *Forschungen zur Brandenburgischen und Preussischen Geschichte,* XXVIII (1915), 85ff; Arnold, 137.
16. Braubach, "Holland und die geistlichen Staaten im Nordwesten des Reichs während des spanischen Erbfolgekrieges," *Diplomatie und Geistiges Leben,* 191.
17. Leonard Ennen, *Der spanische Erbfolgekrieg und der Churfürst Joseph Clemens von Cöln* (Jena, 1851), 107–8; Arnold, 132.
18. Berney, *Friedrich I.,* 29, 116.
19. Cf. H. O. Lang, *Die Vereinigten Niederlande und die Fürstbischofs- und Coadjutorwahlen in Münster im 18. Jahrhundert* (*Münsterische Beiträge zur Geschichtsforschung,* III [1933]).

20. Braubach, "Holland und die geistlichen Staaten," 190.

21. Roderick Geikie and Isabel A. Montgomery, *The Dutch Barrier, 1705–1719* (Cambridge, 1930), 6; Churchill, II, 251–52.

22. Estates General to Joseph, August 1706, G. G. Vreede, *Correspondance diplomatique et militaire du Duc de Marlborough du Grand-Pensionnaire Heinsius et du Trésorier-Général des Provinces-Unies Jacques Hop* (Amsterdam, 1850), 73.

23. Geikie and Montgomery, 15–16.

24. Heinsius to Marlborough, 30 June 1706, 3 July 1706, Vreede, 227–28.

25. Marlborough to Godolphin, 26 September 1706, Snyder, II, 680.

26. Heinsius to Marlborough, 19 February 1706, Vreede, 3; *Feldzüge*, VIII, 3–4; "Mémoire du roi pour le sieur d'Alègre . . . 6 October 1705," *Récueil*, XXII: *Hollande*, L. André and E. Bourgeois, eds. (Paris, 1923), 131–51.

27. Heinsius to Marlborough, 27 July, 3 August 1706, Vreede, 61, 70.

28. *Ibid.*; Geikie and Montgomery, 61.

29. Chamillart to Hennequin, 3 October 1706, D'Avaux to Hennequin, 4, 8 October 1706, Vreede, 138–42, 148.

30. Buys to Godolphin, 15 October 1706, *ibid.*, 160–61.

31. Geikie and Montgomery, 70–73.

32. Protocol of 15 July 1707 Conference, Sinzendorf January 1707 report, HHSA, SK, V 12; Aretin, 538–43; Arneth, *Prinz Eugen*, II, 52. Further articles guaranteed the erection of a strong barrier in the Low Countries, which was to include eight towns presently under French sovereignty, advantageous commercial treaties for England and the United Provinces, and satisfaction for the claims of Prussia, Savoy, and Portugal. The preliminaries also specified the English demands for Louis's recognition of Queen Anne and the Protestant succession, the expulsion of the Stuart pretender from France, and the dismantling of the fortified French channel port of Dunkirk.

33. Marlborough to Charles, 16 July 1706, Murray, II, 701.

34. Halifax to Heinsius, 19 October 1706, Vreede, 165; Marlborough to Halifax, 21 October 1706, Murray, III, 184.

35. Geikie and Montgomery, 75–76, 87–88.

36. Marlborough to Murray, 19 October, to Harley, 21 October, to Stepney, 6 December 1706, Murray, III, 179, 183, 244.

37. Marlborough to Heinsius, August 1706, Vreede, 89.

38. Marlborough to Gueldermalsen, Stepney, Slingelandt, Heinsius, 27 December 1706, Murray, III, 269–72; Geikie and Montgomery, 84.

39. Wratislaw to Charles, 31 August 1706, Arneth, "Eigenhändige Correspondenz," 26.

40. Joseph's notes of 23 December 1707 Conference, HHSA, SK, V 51.

41. Werner Reese, *Das Ringen um Frieden und Sicherheit* (Munich, 1933), 68–69.

42. *Ibid.*, 95.

43. Protocol of 21 February 1709 Conference, HHSA, SK, V 13.

44. The following information cited from protocols of 27 February, 13, 20 March, referat of 12 March 1709 Conferences, HHSA, V 13, also published in *Feldzüge*, XI, 287–99.

45. Wratislaw to Charles, 30 November 1706, HHSA, FK, A 18; Trautson to Moles, 15 January, 25 April 1708, HHSA, GK 70.

46. Sinzendorf to Charles, 28 August, 21 November, 22 December 1708, HHSA, GK 74a.

47. Wratislaw to Charles, 26 January 1706, HHSA, FK, A 18.
48. Charles to Wratislaw, 15/16 December 1706, Arneth, "Eigenhändige Correspondenz," 72ff.
49. Protocol of 19 February 1709 Conference, HHSA, V 13.
50. The Conference did not intend to insist upon the restoration of the Franche-Comté, which had been lost only in 1678.
51. Churchill, VI, 53.
52. Geikie and Montgomery, 106–7.
53. Eugene to Joseph, 12 April 1709, *Feldzüge*, Supp., XI, 54–55.
54. Eugene to Joseph, 1 April 1709, *ibid.*, 43.
55. Reese, 134.
56. Eugene to Joseph, 12 April 1709, *Feldzüge*, XI, Supp., 56–57.
57. Marlborough to Boyle, 12, 16 April 1709, Murray, IV, 475, 479.
58. Eugene to Joseph, 14 April 1709, *Feldzüge*, XI, Supp., 60.
59. Boyle to Pulteney, 12 April 1709, Chance, III: *Denmark,* 25–26.
60. Reese, 203–06; Torcy to Louis, 7, 8, 9, 12, 14, 16 May, to Beauvilliers, 7, 14 May 1709, A. Petitot, ed., *Mémoires du Marquis de Torcy* (Paris, 1828), 212–58.
61. Torcy to Louis, 22 May 1709, Petitot, 269–70; Arneth, *Prinz Eugen,* II, 65.
62. Reese, 201; Petitot, 261.
63. Churchill, VI, 71.
64. Braubach, *Prinz Eugen,* II, 291.
65. Reese, 219.
66. *Ibid.,* 210; Braubach, *Prinz Eugen,* II, 291.
67. Braubach, *Prinz Eugen,* II, 282.
68. Aretin, 572.
69. In fact, Joseph had only recently decided to seek Joseph Clement's resignation from his numerous ecclesiastical offices and replace him with a more loyal churchman such as Cardinal Sachsen-Zeitz. Referat of 18/20 April 1709 Conferences, HHSA, RK, V 6b. Also, cf. protocol of 14 September 1709 Conference, HHSA, SK, V 14, and Sachsen-Zeitz to Joseph, 12 November 1709, HHSA, UA 192.
70. The Treaty of Münster had awarded Guelders to the United Provinces pending the transfer to Spain of an equivalent territory. Such an equivalent had never been provided by the Dutch, who now pointed to the archduke's ample booty as sufficient compensation. Geikie and Montgomery, 375–76.
71. For complete text cf. *Feldzüge*, XII, 561–66 or Petitot, 304–26.
72. Reese, 219.
73. *Ibid.,* 235.
74. Klopp, *Der Fall,* XIII, 235; Noorden, *Erbfolgekrieg,* III, 513.
75. Braubach, *Prinz Eugen,* II, 292–93.
76. Reese, 267.
77. Geikie and Montgomery, 131; Churchill, VI, 84–86.
78. Eugene to Joseph, 6 June 1709, *Feldzüge*, XI, Supp., 113.
79. Marlborough to Townshend, 13 June 1709, Murray, IV, 505.
80. Reese, 263; Churchill, VI, 81–82. In both his subsequent correspondence with Philip and appeals to the French public, Louis sought to justify his rejection of the preliminaries by arguing that they would have required him to make war on his own grandson while depriving France of the peace it so badly needed. John B. Wolf, *Louis XIV* (New York, 1968), 563–64.

81. Wratislaw to Charles, 27 March 1709, Arneth "Eigenhändige Correspondenz," 86.

82. Joseph to Salm, n.d. (late August 1708), FSSA, III 59b; Sinzendorf to Charles, 28 August 1708, HHSA, GK 74a.

83. Wratislaw to Charles, 15 January 1709, Arneth, "Eigenhändige Correspondenz," 82.

84. Braubach, *Prinz Eugen*, II, 274.

85. Wratislaw to Charles, 24 April 1709, Arneth, "Eigenhändige Correspondenz," 89; DeTheillieres to Duke Leopold, 29 April 1709, HHSA, LH 18.

86. Wratislaw to Charles, 8 May 1709, HHSA, FK, A 18.

87. Eugene to Leopold, 3 November 1704, *Feldzüge*, VI, Supp., 226–27; Cardinal Lamberg to Harrach, 4 February 1705, Allgemeines Verwaltungsarchiv, Graf Harrach'sches Familienarchiv 271. For Lamberg's career, cf. Franz Niedermayer, *Johann Philipp von Lamberg, Fürstbischof von Passau, 1651-1712* (Passau, 1938).

88. Eleonore to Charles, 20 May 1705, HHSA, FK, Sammelbände 1.

89. Sinzendorf to Charles, 21 November 1707, HHSA, GK 74a.

90. Sinzendorf to Charles, 21 November 1708, HHSA, GK 74a; Trautson to Moles, 23 December 1708, HHSA, GK 70.

91. Wratislaw to Charles, 15 January 1709, Arneth, "Eigenhändige Correspondenz," 82.

92. *Ibid.*; Granier, 9.

93. Bartholdi pro memoria, Berney, *Frederich I.*, 255; Sinzendorf to Charles, 22 December 1708, HHSA, GK 74a; DeTheillieres to Duke Leopold, 11 May 1709, HHSA, LH 18.

94. DeTheillieres to Duke Leopold, 29 April 1709, HHSA, LH 18.

95. Wratislaw to Sinzendorf, 11 May 1709, HHSA, GK 71.

96. Wratislaw to Sinzendorf, 11, 15 May 1709, HHSA, GK 71.

97. DeTheillieres to Duke Leopold, 20 June 1709, HHSA, LH 18.

98. Leopold von Lamberg to Franz Joseph von Lamberg, 10 August 1709, HHSA, FK 51; Wratislaw to Sinzendorf, 14, 28 August 1709, HHSA, GK 71.

99. Wratislaw to Sinzendorf, 14, 28 August 1709, HHSA, GK 71.

100. Salm memoria, n.d., FSSA, III 60.

101. DeTheillieres to Duke Leopold, 11 May, 20 June 1709, HHSA, LH 18.

102. Wratislaw to Sinzendorf, 14 August 1709, HHSA, GK 71.

103. Leopold von Lamberg to Franz Joseph von Lamberg, 18 August 1708, 6 April 1709, HHSA, FK 51; Granier, 132–33.

104. Braubach, *Prinz Eugen*, II, 319.

105. Wratislaw to Sinzendorf, 20, 24, 28 August 1709, HHSA, GK 71.

106. Trautson to Sinzendorf, 21 September 1709, HHSA, GK 70.

107. Wratislaw to Sinzendorf, 28 August 1709, HHSA, GK 71.

108. Wratislaw to Sinzendorf, 31 August 1709, HHSA, GK 71.

109. Protocols of 31 August, 2 September 1709 Conferences, HHSA, SK, V 14.

110. Kretschmayr, "Reichsvicekanzleramt," 436.

111. Wratislaw to Sinzendorf, 28 September 1709, HHSA, GK 71. Sinzendorf was later instructed to mark all such dispatches *secretum* in order to remind Trautson, to whom all reports were forwarded, not to let them circulate freely. Wratislaw to Sinzendorf, 12 March 1710, HHSA, GK 71.

112. Wratislaw to Sinzendorf, 7 September 1709, HHSA, GK 71.

113. Leopold von Lamberg to Franz Joseph von Lamberg, 16 November, 4 December 1709, HHSA, FK 51.

114. Wratislaw to Charles, 29 October 1709, HHSA, FK, A 18; Leopold von Lamberg to Franz Joseph von Lamberg, 16 November 1709, HHSA, FK 51.

115. Leopold von Lamberg to Franz Joseph von Lamberg, 4 December 1709, 9 January 1710, HHSA, FK 51.

116. Wratislaw to Charles, 26 April 1710, HHSA, FK, A 18.

117. Trautson to Sinzendorf, 8 June 1709, HHSA, GK 70.

118. Schönborn to Lothair Francis, 8 June 1709, HHSA, MEA, Korr. 90; Braubach, *Prinz Eugen,* II, 294–95.

119. Braubach, *Prinz Eugen,* II, 295.

120. Geikie and Montgomery, 127–28.

121. *Ibid.,* 117–18, 127; Eugene to Joseph, 6 May 1709, *Feldzüge,* XI, Supp.

122. Wratislaw to Sinzendorf, 15 June 1709, HHSA, GK 71.

123. *Ibid.*

124. Wratislaw to Sinzendorf, 18 October 1709, 2 February, 4 March 1710, HHSA, GK 71.

125. Wratislaw to Sinzendorf, 15 June 1709, HHSA, GK 71.

126. 5 July 1709 referat, protocol of 5 July 1709 Conference, HHSA, SK, V 14.

127. *Ibid.*

128. Eugene to Joseph, 11 August 1709, *Feldzüge,* XI, Supp., 215.

129. Referat of 4–11 September 1709 Conferences, HHSA, SK, V 14.

130. Eugene to Joseph, 17 June 1709, *Feldzüge,* XI, Supp., 129–30.

131. Referat of 4–11 September 1709 Conferences, HHSA, SK, V 14.

132. *Ibid.*

133. Wratislaw to Sinzendorf, 14 September 1709, HHSA, GK 71.

134. Arneth, *Prinz Eugen,* II, 68.

135. Braubach, *Subsidien,* 163–64; "Um die 'Reichsbarriere' am Ober-rhein," *Diplomatie und geistiges Leben,* 247–51; *Feldzüge,* XI, 133, 148–50.

136. *Feldzüge,* XI, 191–96; Jarnut-Derbolav, 369, 371.

137. Wratislaw to Sinzendorf, 21 September 1709, HHSA, GK 71.

138. Trautson to Sinzendorf, 24 September 1709, HHSA, GK 70.

139. Protocols of 25, 26 September 1709 Conferences, HHSA, SK, V 14; Joseph's notes of 26 September 1709 Conference, HHSA, SK, V 51; Trautson to Sinzendorf, 28 September 1709, HHSA, GK 70.

140. 9 October 1709 referat, HHSA, SK, V 14.

141. Trautson to Sinzendorf, 2 October 1709, HHSA, GK 70.

142. Joseph to Sinzendorf, 18 October 1709, HHSA, SK, V 14.

143. Geikie and Montgomery, 121–24.

144. *Ibid.,* 151–53; Douglas Coombs, *The Conduct of the Dutch* (The Hague, 1958), 207; Wratislaw to Charles, 15 January 1708, HHSA, FK, A 18.

145. Geikie and Montgomery, 156–58, for complete text 377–86.

146. *Ibid.,* 161–64.

147. Charles to Wratislaw, 30 June 1709, Arneth, "Eigenhändige Corre-spondenz," 93.

148. Protocol of 14 September 1709 Conference, HHSA, SK, V 14.

150. In this and subsequent encounters with the two Austrians, Marlbor-ough stressed that he had been excluded from the talks and had had no knowledge of their progress. Of course, his exclusion had been totally volun-tary. Marlborough to Sinzendorf, 13 December 1709, 3 January 1710, Murray, IV, 666, 673; 23 December 1709 referat, HHSA, SK, V 14; Geikie and Montgomery, 176–77.

151. 23 December 1709 referat, HHSA, SK, V 14; Wratislaw to Sinzendorf, 28 December 1709, HHSA, GK 71; protocol of 15 December 1709 Conference, HHSA, SK, V 14.

152. Eugene to Charles, 13 January 1710, *Feldzüge,* XII, Supp., 10–11.

153. Wratislaw to Charles, 8 January 1710, Arneth, "Eigenhändige Correspondenz," 99.

154. February 1710 referat, HHSA, SK, V 15.

155. Joseph to Eugene, 3 November 1708, HHSA, GK 90b.

156. Wratislaw to Sinzendorf, 6 November 1709, HHSA, GK 71.

157. Joseph to Eugene, 9 August 1710, HHSA, GK 90b; protocol of 4 August 1710 Conference, HHSA, SK, V 15.

158. 21 February 1710 rescript, HHSA, ÖA, Böhmen, Schlesische Akten 5.

159. Wratislaw to Sinzendorf, 11 December 1709, 4 March, 26 July 1710, HHSA, GK 71; protocol of 25 September 1709 Conference, HHSA, SK, V 14.

160. Protocol of 16 April 1710 Conference, HHSA, SK, V 15; *Feldzüge,* XII, 105–6.

161. Protocols of 14, 22 May, 28 November 1709 Conferences, HHSA, SK, V 14.

162. Protocols of 22, 29 July, 1 August 1709 Conferences, HHSA, SK, V 14.

163. Marlborough and Townshend to Sunderland, 5 November 1709, Murray, IV, 645.

164. Wratislaw to Sinzendorf, 2 November 1709, HHSA, GK 71.

165. Voltes Bou, *Barcelona,* II, 163.

166. Nesselrode to Wratislaw, 15 January 1710, HHSA, GK 69.

167. Schönborn to Lothair Francis, 29 March 1710, HHSA, MEA, Korr. 91.

168. *Récueil,* XVI: *Prusse,* A. Waddington, ed. (Paris, 1901), 269ff; Loewe, 107.

169. Protocol of 20 February 1710 Conference, HHSA, SK, V 15.

170. Eugene to Heinsius, 19 January 1710, *Feldzüge,* XII, 44–45, Supp., 14–15.

171. Protocol of 15 February 1710 Conference, SK, V 15.

172. Eugene to Joseph, 4 April, Smettau 12 April 1710 memorial, *Feldzüge,* XII, Supp., 34–36.

173. Arnold, 130; Wines, 22–23.

174. Aretin, 582.

175. 9 October referat of 17, 19, 22, 27 September, 1 October 1709 Conferences, HHSA, SK, V 14. In a subsequent instruction to Sinzendorf, Joseph reiterated his conviction that the duke of Lorraine "be put in such a position that with his lands, he will serve as an outpost and barrier against France . . . is needed by the [Holy] Roman empire and the common good." 1 April 1710, HHSA, SK, V 15.

176. Marlborough to Sunderland, 8 November, to Sinzendorf, 29 November 1709, to Heinsius, 20 January 1710, Murray, IV, 647, 659, 682; Rousseau, 273–75.

177. *Récueil,* XXII: *Hollande,* 232–67.

178. Joseph's notes of 30 January 1710 Conference, HHSA, SK, V 51; protocol of 30 January 1710 Conference, HHSA, SK, V 15.

179. Joseph to Eugene, 5 April 1710, HHSA, GK 90b.

180. Boyle to Townshend, 10 January 1710, L. G. Wickham Legg, *British Diplomatic Instructions 1689–1789, II: France, 1689–1721* (London, 1925), 17–18.

181. Boyle to Marlborough and Townshend, 28 February 1710, *ibid.,* 20.
182. Joseph's notes of 24 March 1710 Conference, HHSA, SK, V 15.
183. Trautson to Sinzendorf, 19, 26 March 1710, HHSA, GK 70; Joseph to Eugene, 5 April 1710, HHSA, GK 90b.
184. Trautson to Sinzendorf, 22 March 1710, HHSA, GK 70.
185. Joseph's notes of, protocol of 24 March 1710 Conference, HHSA, SK, V 15.
186. Joseph's notes of 7 March Conference, V 51; protocol of 7 March Conference, HHSA, SK, V 15; Trautson to Moles, 9 March postscript of 7 March letter, 9 March 1710, HHSA, GK 70.
187. Joseph to Anne, Estates General, Sinzendorf, Gallas, 27 March 1710, *Feldzüge,* XII, 567–74.
188. Wratislaw to Sinzendorf, 6 April 1710, HHSA, GK 71.
189. Joseph's notes of 4 April 1710 Conference, HHSA, SK, V 51.
190. Marlborough to Albemarle, 26 March, to Boyle, 12 April, 19 June 1710, Murray, IV, 703, 718, V, 53.
191. Boyle to Marlborough and Townshend, 7 March 1710, Legg, 20–21.
192. Petitot, 400–401.
193. *Ibid.,* 410–11.
194. Eugene to Joseph, 27 April, 4 June, 23 July, to Sinzendorf, 2 June 1710, *Feldzüge,* XII, Supp., 46, 99–102, 206–7.
195. Petitot, 424–26.
196. Braubach, *Subsidien,* 84.
197. Eugene to Joseph, 14 April, 7, 11 May, to Sinzendorf, 27 April, 7 May, to Gronsfeld, 11 June 1710, *Feldzüge,* Supp., 39–40, 43, 62–63, 65–66, 70–71, 117.
198. Protocols of 13, 16 July, 6 September 1710 Conferences, HHSA, SK V 15.
199. Berwick to Torcy, 5 September 1710, *Récueil,* XIV: *Savoie-Sardaigne,* Horric de Beaucaire, ed. (Paris, 1898), 270–71. For the ensuing talks, cf. *ibid.,* 27–81 and Berwick, *Memoirs of the Marshal Duke of Berwick* (London, 1779), II, 103–14.
200. Eugene to Joseph, 14 September, to Daun, 17 September 1710, *Feldzüge,* XII, Supp., 341, 350.
201. Klopp, *Der Fall,* XIII, 437–50.
202. Coombs, 224.
203. Joseph to Anne, 16 July 1710, *Feldzüge,* XII, 578.
204. Protocol of 13 July 1710 Conference, HHSA, SK, V 15; Eugene to Joseph, 3 August 1710, *Feldzüge,* XII, Supp., 236.
205. Klopp, *Der Fall,* XIII, 472; Jarnut-Derbolav, 425–29.
206. *Feldzüge,* XII, 30.
207. Francis Hare, *The Allies and the Late Ministry* (London, 1711), 73. For more on English public opinion, cf. Horst Kospach, "Englische Stimmen über Österreich and Prinz Eugen während des spanischen Erbfolgerieges," *Mitteilungen des Instituts für österreichische Geschichtsforschung,* LXXIII (1965).
208. Eugene to Gallas, 28 August 1710, *Feldzüge,* XII, Supp., 302–3.
209. Churchill, VI, 370.
210. Braubach, *Subsidien,* 178.
211. Joseph's notes of 14 October 1710 Conference, HHSA, FK, Familien-akten 96; protocols of 14, 17 October 1710 Conferences, HHSA, SK, V 15.
212. Sinzendorf to Estella, 8 September, to Charles, 10 September 1710,

266 Notes

HHSA, GK 74c; protocol of 14 October 1710 Conference, HHSA, SK, V 15.
213. Braubach, *Subsidien,* 96.
214. Protocol of 14 October 1710 Conference, HHSA, SK, V 15; 29 October 1710 Convention, *Feldzüge,* XII, 626.
215. Trautson to Sinzendorf, 13 December 1710, HHSA, GK 70.
216. Referat of 22/23 February 1711 Conferences, HHSA, SK, V 16; Joseph's notes of 23 February 1711 Conference, HHSA, SK, V 51.
217. Referat of 22/23 February 1711 Conferences, HHSA, SK, V 16.
218. Sinzendorf to Joseph, 4 January 1711, Sinzendorf Familienarchiv, 3/4.
219. Voltes Bou, *Barcelona,* II, 230.
220. Gualtier to Torcy, 7 October, 23 December 1710, G. M. Trevelyan, "The 'Jersey' Period of the Negotiations Leading to the Peace of Utrecht," *English Historical Review,* XLIX (1934), 102–3.

VII. Conclusion

Opening quote: Protocol of 16 February 1711 Conference, HHSA, SK, V 16. Wilczek was imperial ambassador to Moscow.
1. "If the tsar should be victorious [and] march into Turkish territory on this side of the Danube . . . toward Constantinople, this also would from a political standpoint be not much less unfortunate." 24 February referat of 22/23 February 1711 Conference, HHSA, SK, V 16.
2. Erich Zöllner, *Geschichte Österreichs* (Munich, 1966), 276.
3. Helmut Wyklicky, "Die Beschreibung und Beurteilung einer Blatternerkrankung im Jahre 1711," *Wiener Klinische Wochenschrift,* LIX (1957), 972–73.
4. Trautson to Sinzendorf, 5, 22 November 1710, HHSA, GK 70.
5. Wratislaw to Charles, 15 January 1708, Arneth, "Eigenhändige Correspondenz," 57.
6. Trautson to Sinzendorf, 6 December 1710, HHSA, GK 70.
7. Trautson to Sinzendorf, 18 March 1711, GK 70.
8. Wyklicky, 973.
9. Trautson to Sinzendorf, 15 April 1711, HHSA, GK 70; Braubach, *Prinz Eugen,* III, 17.
10. Wratislaw to Charles, 22 April 1711 Arneth, "Eigenhändige Correspondenz," 147.
11. Wratislaw to Charles, 22 April 1711, Lukinich, 326–27.
12. Pálffy to *Hofkriegsrat,* 22 April 1711, *ibid.,* 325.
13. Wines, 25.
14. Wratislaw to Charles, 22 April 1711, Arneth, "Eigenhändige Correspondenz," 144.
15. Charles to Wratislaw, 25 April 1711, *ibid.,* 152.
16. Redlich, *Grossmacht,* 79–80.
17. Fieldhouse, 279–80, 287–90.
18. Braubach, *Subsidien,* 178; Hare, 63, 73.
19. Braubach, "Geheime Friedensverhandlungen am Niederrhein 1711/1712," *Diplomatie und geistiges Leben,* 271ff.
20. The monarchy's one consolation came in Belgium, where the Tories repudiated the Townshend Treaty, principally out of jealousy over Dutch commercial advantages, and obliged the Estates General to agree to a much less extensive barrier (treaty of 30 January 1713).

21. That the Conference would have otherwise considered a French alliance is demonstrated in a February 1710 report written in the aftermath of the Townshend Treaty, in which the ministers report, "One would wish that . . . the Bourbon dynasty would be so disposed that the august archhouse could enter into a genuine, sincere and binding friendship with it. Through the same alliance of these two houses would the [Roman Catholic] religion and public security be best served and the archhouse would [not] out of necessity have to engage itself with non-Catholics to the great detriment of itself and its religion, as the present experience with England and Holland demonstrates. However, due to the ambition of the French crown, this [alliance] cannot be hoped for." HHSA, SK, V 15.

22. *Versailles und Wien von Ludwig XIV. bis Kaunitz* (Bonn, 1952), 67–68, 83.

23. He would return to his former post in 1722, however, to live out the last three years of his life.

Index